Neoliberalism and Globalization in Africa

Neoliberalism and Globalization in Africa

Contestations from the Embattled Continent

Edited by Joseph Mensah

NEOLIBERALISM AND GLOBALIZATION IN AFRICA
Copyright © Joseph Mensah, 2008.

First published in 2008 by PALGRAVE MACMILLAN® in the United States—a division of St. Martin's Press LLC, 175 Fifth Avenue, New York, NY 10010.

Where this book is distributed in the UK, Europe and the rest of the world, this is by Palgrave Macmillan, a division of Macmillan Publishers Limited, registered in England, company number 785998, of Houndmills, Basingstoke, Hampshire RG21 6XS.

Palgrave Macmillan is the global academic imprint of the above companies and has companies and representatives throughout the world.

Palgrave® and Macmillan® are registered trademarks in the United States, the United Kingdom, Europe and other countries.

ISBN-13: 978-0-230-60781-1
ISBN-10: 0-230-60781-0

Library of Congress Cataloging-in-Publication Data is available from the Library of Congress.

A catalogue record of the book is available from the British Library.

Design by Scribe Inc.

First edition: December 2008

10 9 8 7 6 5 4 3 2 1

Printed in the United States of America.

This book is dedicated to the cherished memories of the late Ed Osei Kwadwo Prempeh of Carleton University in Ottawa, whose untimely passing occurred on March 3, 2007, and now speaks to us posthumously through his chapter in this volume.

CONTENTS

Acknowledgments

I would like to thank all nine contributors of this volume, not only for their highly audacious scholarship, but also for their diligence in meeting all the deadlines for this project. It is certainly a great honor and privilege to work with such top-notch scholars of African development. I would also like to thank the following people, groups, and institutions for their support and assistance in bringing this book project to fruition: Judith Blau, editor of *Societies Without Borders* (SWB) and Brill Academic Publishers for their permission to use Eunice Sahle's paper on NEPAD for this volume; the international refereed journal *Studies in Political Economy* (SPE) and its editorial board for their visionary prescience that led to the four original papers for this volume (the original versions of these four papers appeared in *SPE* Vol. 77, Spring 2006); and the Ghana Institute of Management and Public Administration (GIMPA) for giving me a sabbatical placement, during which time this project was finalized.

I also reserve special thanks and appreciation to my mom (Mrs. Gladys Gyan) and dad (Mr. M.Y. Mensah); my siblings Daniel, Charles, and Victoria Mensah; and my dear friends in Ghana, including Mr. Oti Bronya Moses and family, Mr. Kwame Frempah-Yeboah and family, Dr. Roger Oppong-Koranteng, Ms. Cecilia Afosah of El Shaddai Ministries, Ms. Mavis Boateng of Accra, Ms. Sylvia Adu-Boahen of GIMPA, and Dr. Agyemang Badu, deputy rector of GIMPA. For moral support and technical and editorial assistance, I would like to thank Luba Ostashevsky, Colleen Lawrie, etc. of Palgrave Macmillan Publishing; Rosemi Mederos of Scribe, the copyeditor; and my students and colleagues at York University in Toronto. My deepest gratitude goes to my wife, Janet Mensah, and our two daughters, Nicole and Cassandra, for their unconditional love, which has enriched my life and facilitated my intellectual development over the years.

NEOLIBERALISM AND GLOBALIZATION IN AFRICA

Joseph Mensah

The dramatic transformative impacts of contemporary globalization, and all of its associated baggage on the lives of people worldwide, can hardly escape even the most cursory observer. The outcomes of the ensuing changes are neither smooth nor unilinear; rather, they are dialectical, dynamic, multifaceted, uneven, and sometimes chaotic, pointing in several different directions at once, and occurring at varying speeds and timescales in different parts of the world. And, as one might expect, the past, present, and foreseeable impacts of this transformation have elicited controversial responses that at once grab the analytical attention of both opponents (e.g., Klein 2000; Chomsky 2001; Hoogvelt 2001; Stiglitz 2003; Harvey 2007) and supporters (e.g., Sachs 2005; Norberg 2003; Wolf 2004) alike. At the heart of these controversies lies the ideology of neoliberalism, which seeks to further expand global capital accumulation through free trade, financial deregulation, privatization, and other tenets of the so-called Washington Consensus, spearheaded by the World Bank, International Monetary Fund (IMF), World Trade Organization (WTO), and kindred organizations (Harvey 2007; De Rivero 2001).

Notwithstanding the vociferous, if not acrimonious, debate surrounding neoliberal globalization, there is one thing about which there seems to be little doubt, if any—that is, the sheer scale of deprivation that marks the lives of many in the long-embattled continent of Africa, in particular (Castells 2000; McNally 2002; UNDP 2006; Bond 2006). In fact, even those who look favorably upon globalization—and its attendant capital accumulation—seem to have some reservations about its neoliberal articulation, especially as it pertains to Africa (Sachs 2005). Grant and Agnew (1996, 720) noted more than a decade ago that "from World Bank advisors to neo-Marxists and some dependency theorists there is a growing current of opinion that views Africa as in the process of 'falling out' of the world economy." Unfortunately, the African situation has not improved much since then.

Available data suggest that, over the past few years, there have been significant improvements in the living conditions of people across the world, with Africans—or, more specifically, sub-Saharan Africans—being the notable exception. For instance, the *2006 Human development report* notes that "since the mid-1970s almost all regions have been progressively increasing their HDI [Human Development Index] score . . . the major exception is Sub-Saharan Africa." In fact, a whopping twenty-eight of the thirty-one low human development countries of the world are found in sub-Saharan Africa. Moreover, while the life expectancy of the developing countries of the world, as a group, is catching up with that of the developed countries, the situation in sub-Saharan Africa is markedly different. Here, life expectancy is retrogressing, with the region as whole recording lower life expectancy than it was some thirty years ago (UNDP 2006). With the scourge of HIV/AIDS ravaging the southern and eastern segments of the continent, catastrophic reversals in life expectancies are not uncommon in such countries as Botswana, Swaziland, Zambia, and Lesotho.

The unprecedented growth in material wealth across the world in recent years (UNDP 2006), which some (e.g., Wolf 2004) might attribute to neoliberal globalization, seems to bypass the African continent. Africa witnessed a growth in per capita income of 34 percent between 1960 and 1980; the comparable figure for the two decades between 1980 and 2000 is -23 percent (McNally 2002, 46). Also, estimates by Castells (2000) show that the combined export earnings of all sub-Saharan African countries in 1980 stood at US$50 billion. By the early 1990s, it dropped to US$36 billion in current U.S. dollars, a figure that is "less than half of [tiny] Hong Kong's exports in that same period" (ibid., 83, mine in bracket). In fact, the *2006 Human development report* also notes that "Sub-Sahara Africa is the only region that has witnessed an increase both in the incidence of poverty and in the absolute number of poor. Some 300 million people there—almost half of the region's population—live on less than $1 a day" (UNDP 2006, 268–69).

The situation in the political front has not been any better, with the disintegration of central governments and killings in countries such as Liberia, Sierra Leone, Somalia, Zaire, Sudan, Chad, Rwanda, and more recently, Kenya, still vivid in our memories, thanks to the speedup in television and news broadcasting in our shrinking world. The extent of pillage, corruption, violence, and sheer destruction wrought upon Africans by the nation-state, especially during the 1980s and 1990s, has prompted commentators to use various unflattering phrases and neologisms in describing politics, as practiced on the continent: Castells' (2000) "predatory state" and "the political economy of begging"; Frimpong-Ansah's (1991) "vampire state"; and Bayart's (1989) "politics of the belly" are worthy of note here.

Unsurprisingly, different commentators have offered different diagnoses for the problems of Africa. Some blame tribalism (Kaplan 1994); others attribute the situation mainly to corruption and government mismanagement (Castells 2000); others see it as a result of intense government involvement in the African economy (Devarajan et al., 2001; World Bank, 1994); and still others put the blame squarely on neocolonialism, looting, and neoliberal globalization (Amin 1989, Bond 2006). To eschew the risk of placing a fine artificial order to a truly disordered and diverse range of theoretical positions, one can broadly liken the ensuing debate to a *continuum*, in which those blaming neoliberal globalization for most of Africa's woes are positioned at one end, and those singing the praises of that same political economic ideology at the other extreme, with many others sandwiched somewhere in-between.

Advocates of neoliberal globalization contend that African countries would do better if they integrate, or properly insert their economies, into the world economy through free trade, liberalization, privatization, and deregulation—i.e., the Washington Consensus (De Rivero 2001). The basic thrust of the neoliberal globalization argument hinges on the purported benefits of international trade couched in the infamous theory of comparative advantage. The dominant narrative posits that free trade engenders efficient allocation of resources, with all participating nations gaining in the long run from higher output and lower prices. Advanced nations may be the initial beneficiaries of this process, but the gains of free trade, it is argued, would eventually *trickle down* to even Africa. To those who espouse this view, Africa's problems are first and foremost attributable to excessive government involvement in the economy—by way of protectionism and acute restrictions on free trade—which undermines peoples' ability to meaningfully participate in the world economy. A corollary of this intense state involvement, in their view, is the proliferation of corruption, mismanagement, political cronyism, and nepotism, and their attendant ethno-tribal fetishism and tensions, which often spill over to full blown civil war in many parts of the continent. This perspective on Africa's development gained considerable currency, following the publication of the Berg Report in 1981[1]; in fact, many analysts were of the view that only the liberalization-laced strategies, or Structural Adjustment Programs (SAPs) of the IMF and World Bank, could reverse the economic misfortunes of Africa (Grant and Agnew 1996, 730). Not surprisingly, by the mid-1990s, most African economies were under SAPs, in one way or another (Mensah 2006, 5).

At the other extreme of the continuum are the opponents of neoliberalism and globalization, who contend that only through active government involvement in the economy, and effective delinking of Africa from globalization, can real development occur on the continent. Spearheaded by the likes of Samir Amin in the now famous dependency theory, this perspective contends that it is the continued dependence of Africa on the West—and the systemic exploitation by the latter through unfair terms of trade, predatory lending practices, capital market and exchange rate manipulations, and neocolonialism—that undercuts Africa's development efforts. Together with their supporters outside the continent, opponents of neoliberal globalization have mounted intense campaigns against international institutions such as the World Bank, IMF, and the WTO, which they see as setting the global agenda for the proliferation of neoliberalism and globalization. Through books such as *No logo*, by the Canadian journalist Naomi Klein (2000), and *Biopiracy*, by the Indian ecofeminist Vandana Shiva (1997), large multinational corporations have also met their match in the ensuing avalanche of highly critical commentaries. Over the years, the neoliberalism-cum-globalization opposition camp has splintered and changed into a wide range of movements in different parts of Africa and the world, with different groups directing their attacks on different parts of the equally changing target of neoliberal globalization. As we shall soon see, there are those who direct their attacks on the privatization of water; others focus on the environment and biodiversity; others are concerned with "Third World" debt and unfair trade; still others champion labor rights, immigrants' rights, indigenous peoples' rights, and many other rights, both human and nonhuman. With massive public demonstrations in Madrid (October 1994), Seattle (November 1999), Genoa (July 2001), and so on, the hypocrisies of the "First World" in general—and of the "unholy trinity" of the World Bank, IMF, and WTO (Peet 2003), in particular—in world trade, foreign aid, and debt relief have been laid bare for all progressive and conscientious observers to see.

As with many debates in the social sciences, it is at the point where the two extreme positions interpenetrate that one is most likely to find the underlying causes of Africa socioeconomic malaise. Arguably, Africa's problems are neither totally attributable to internal nor external factors—assuming one is even capable of drawing a clear endogenous-exogenous distinction. Similarly, they are not entirely due to globalization or neoliberalism; neither are they completely attributable to the protectionist policies of African governments. The crux of the matter is far more dialectical than what any dogmatic binary categorization can sustain, as we shall soon see from the chapters in this volume.

CONTESTATION FROM THE EMBATTLED CONTINENT

This book examines Africa's involvement in contemporary neoliberal globalization, drawing particular attention to the social, economic, political, and cultural costs of the grossly unbalanced structure of global wealth and power between Africa and the *Rest*. What are the subtle and not so subtle impacts of neoliberal globalization on Africa and its people? Are the Western-sponsored policy prescriptions (e.g., Post/Washington Consensus, New Partnership for Africa's Development (NEPAD), the Heavily Indebted Poor Countries (HIPCs) debt relief initiative, and the Millennium Development Goals (MDGs), and so on—really genuine attempts to redress Africa's economic malaise, or mere disguises for yet another round of accumulation by dispossession? To what extent does the neoliberal push for unbridled free trade affect the chances of African nations to industrialize? Is neoliberal globalization conducive for, or counterproductive to, Africa's tourism industry?

What are the cultural dimensions of Africa's encounter with contemporary globalization? What are the gender ramifications, if any, of the market-based capital accumulation underway in many parts of Africa? How is Africa positioned in relation to the flows and circulations enacted by the ongoing time-space compression? And how have Africans resisted neoliberal globalization over the years? These are some of the issues addressed in the book. The book dwells primarily on political-economic analysis to offer prescient theoretical and empirical insights into the controversies on the intersections between Africa's development and neoliberal globalization, at both the continental and national scales.

As the subtitle suggests, the narratives in the book pay special attention to contestations—both discursively and in practice. This emphasis rests on our deep-rooted conviction that the issues examined in the book are patently contentious, hence the deliberate attempt to even steer clear of a definitive account of what constitutes neoliberalism or globalization in this introductory phase. If nothing at all, the mere mention of terms such as capitalism, (post)-Washington Consensus, neoliberalism, time-space compression, cyber-sexuality, accumulation by dispossession, and such names as Robert Mugabe, is now enough to elicit hairsplitting debate among competing analysts.

The book is decidedly multidisciplinary. Its contributors include scholars from various social science disciplines, including political science, sociology, anthropology, geography, economics, cultural studies, and development studies. Also, it bears noting, even if parenthetically, that most of the contributors have lived or worked, or continue to live, in Africa, and thus have the cultural competence to grasp the intricacies of the African situation. Needless to declare, the book seeks to promote a nuanced understanding of the controversial issues surrounding Africa's involvement in contemporary globalization. With this book, students, policy makers, development practitioners, and scholars will understand how globalization, and its neoliberal policy prescriptions, continues to deepen the wealth and global power imbalance between Africa and the *Rest*. And, with our emphasis on contestation, readers are bound to appreciate the tactics and maneuvers deployed by the various social resistance movements in Africa to interrogate and confront this inequity.

The birth of the book is hardly random—it came out of a discernable gap in the existing literature on neoliberalism and globalization, spotted by the editorial board of *Studies in Political Economy (SPE)*—an international refereed journal of political science based at Carleton University in Ottawa, Canada. Alarmed by the acute lack of a strong political economy-based discourse on Africa's involvement in neoliberal globalization, the editorial board called for papers for a special edition on the topic. The four papers that made the final editorial selection for the special issue—including papers written by E. N. Sahle, W. J. Tettey, J. Mensah, and the late Ed Osei Kwadwo Prempeh (*SPE* 77 [Spring 2006]: 3–104)—constitute the springboard for the book. The critical acclaim accorded this special issue prompted calls from some authors and members of the editorial board to upgrade and turn the papers into a book. With the full backing of *SPE*, we (the late Ed. Prempeh and Joseph Mensah) contacted well-known scholars in the field for additional papers for the book, bringing the total number of substantive papers to twelve.

While a wide range of topics (e.g., tourism, industrialization, "African culture," land redistribution, cybersexual activities, Internet fraud, NEPAD, budget campaign, uneven development, etc.) are covered in the book, they are all unified by one approach—namely, political economic analysis—deployed on one overarching theme: neoliberal globalization in Africa. Given the diverse scholarly background of the authors, it is only natural that the book takes a multidisciplinary perspective on political economy. In addition to its broad theoretical and empirical analysis at the level of the continent, the book presents some country case studies on relevant topics, yet another obvious attraction of the book. The untimely death of Ed Osei Kwadwo Prempeh in the course of this book project took a heavy emotional toll on most of the contributors, as Ed was known in one way or another to almost all the authors of the volume. At the same time, Ed's passing fortified our collective determination to bring the project to a successful conclusion in tribute to his memory. For convenience of analysis, the book is divided into two major parts on the basis of the spatial scope of the individual papers involved—i.e., be it continental or national in coverage.

PART I: POLEMICS ON THE EMBATTLED CONTINENT

With etymological ties to the Greek word *polemikos*, which means "hostile" or "warlike," "polemics" is commonly used to hint of an aggressive refutation of a position that is widely held to be beyond reproach. Polemics are inherently controversial and combative, seeking to "shake up"—as in a related Greek word, *pelemizein*—an orthodoxy. At the risk of sounding sensational, with words such as "contestations," "embattled," and now "polemics," one is bound to expect attempts to deconstruct, or at the very least problematize, some of the prevailing diagnoses and policy prescriptions on Africa's development, especially as they pertain to the continent's involvement in neoliberal globalization. For instance, with the chapters assembled here, one would learn that, contrary to the common view in public and development circles, more money flows from Africa to the West/*Rest* than the other way around in a year; that the prevailing mantra about time-space compression and a shrinking world with unbridled capital and labor mobility is hardly sustainable in the context of Africa(ns); that when we read of *unrestrained* human mobility in a global village, it hardly relates to the African labor, seeking better life in Europe or America; that contrary to what the ideology of neoliberalism espouses, Structural Adjustment Programs, in particular, and the market, in general, are hardly gender neutral; that the rest of the world has borrowed, and continues to borrow, immensely from African culture, perhaps just as much as Africans borrow from the *Rest*; that, when it comes to so-called free trade, the West hardly practices what it preaches to Africa; that notwithstanding the neoliberal rhetoric of a global village or a homogenizing world, there continues to be a deepening economic inequity between Africa and the *Rest*; and that, contrary to the *TINA* slogan,[2] there are, indeed, feasible alternatives to neoliberalism in Africa. Needless to say, considerable overlaps exist among the various chapters in Part I, given the interweaving character of the issues implicated. Also, as a collective, the chapters in Part I set the tone for the case studies presented in Part II.

Chapter 2—written by the world-renowned political economist Patrick Bond—deals with the unequal trade and investment relationships that exist between Africa and the Western world, and shows how this phenomenon has intensified under contemporary neoliberal globalization. "Accumulation by dispossession" in Africa, Bond aptly notes, dates back to many centuries to the point at which value transfers began via appropriations of slave labor, antiquities, precious metals, and raw materials—all of which were eventually crystallized by the colonial and neocolonial relationships that ensued. With reliable empirical data and cogent, sophisticated theorizations, the chapter demonstrates that accumulation by dispossession in Africa was never resolved by the 1950s–1990s independence struggles, as similar forms of wealth extractions through imperialist relations persist across the continents; and, indeed, as some of the same kinds of primitive looting tactics are still evident. In a decidedly polemical fashion, Bond argues that the world is witnessing a political-economic passage on a global scale: from economic stagnation, amplified uneven development, and financial volatility to worsening primitive accumulation ("looting") and socioeconomic conflict. Not only that, the reforms proposed at the global level by elite bodies, in his view, are ineffectual, and actions taken by elites in the name of conflict resolution often undermine peace and development because they reinforce the very dynamic of external looting. As in several of Bond's previous writings, he suggests that if these reforms continue to fail, it is to popular struggles that we should turn, especially in Africa, where oppression is most extreme and global and local elites have the least credibility. According to Bond, the solution to the "looting of Africa," as he bluntly puts it throughout the chapter, is to be found in the self-activity of progressive Africans themselves, in their campaigns and declarations, their struggles—sometimes victorious, but still mainly frustrated—and their hunger for an Africa that can finally throw off the shackles of an exploitative world economy and a power elite who treat the continent without any respect.

Written by the editor of the volume, Joseph Mensah, Chapter 3 uses a dialectical mode of reasoning to provide a critical discussion of the debate about the cultural effects of globalization on Africa. Mensah supplements the general tendencies among analysts to examine only economic and political effects of neoliberal globalization on Africa, with an analysis that shows the heterogeneous cultural effects of the growing integration of African polities and spaces in global circuits of commodities and ideas. He takes both globalization and culture as inherently dialectical phenomena (and concepts) and demonstrates how global processes have creatively intermingled with varied African practices through "glocalization," albeit in a very uneven manner.

The common belief that African knowledge, epistemology, and ontology are patently unscientific, essentially descriptive, with no enduring taxonomies, analytical rigor, high-level philosophical abstraction is severely challenged in this chapter, with insights from the works of renowned African philosophers such as Kwame Anthony Appiah and Kwame Gyekeye. The relations of power, resistance, and contestations implicated in the cultural mixing between Africa and the *Rest* are also given considerable attention, both in terms of discourse and praxis.

In Chapter 4, the late Ed Osei Kwadwo Prempeh addresses ways to understand Africa's location within the contemporary world system and to assess the varied resistance movements on the continent. Situating himself in the literature examining counterhegemonic social movements that arise out of struggles concerning the political and economic effects of current forms of primitive accumulation, Prempeh provides important insights into the "deglobalization" and anticapitalism movements and contestations in Africa. By introducing some of the key movements for social justice in the face of processes of dispossession and appropriation, he gives much needed attention to the forms of social agency emerging within Africa that are struggling to challenge the pervasive forces and promoters of neoliberal globalization on the continent. Prempeh cautions us to be vigilant about the undemocratic tendencies of many of the emerging NGOs and civil society organizations across Africa. The dominant roles played by international NGOs on the African soil, with little or no leadership directives from, or involvement of, progressive grassroots individuals and organizations are particularly worrying to Prempeh. Lurking behind Prempeh's narrative is an intriguing paradox: neoliberal globalization weakens and, at the same time, strengthens social resistance movements. The impetus for a radical counterhegemonic alternative, in his view, emanates primarily from the destruction proclivities of neoliberal globalization.

In Chapter 5, Eunice N. Sahle uses feminist political economy analysis to show the gendered foundations of state structures and markets in Africa, and highlights the deteriorating economic situations of African women, as neoliberal reforms in the form of Structural Adjustment Programs continue to be implemented across the continent. Sahle astutely traces the gendered nature of colonial state accumulation processes that marginalized African women from access to resources and public decision-making forums. She also illuminates the deepening of these gender inequalities during the 1960s and 1970s, whence many newly independent African governments continued the colonial model of state-led economic accumulation strategies, despite the often visible role African women played during the struggle for independence. To highlight how the World Bank and IMF-sponsored neoliberal prescriptions of the 1980s and beyond have had gender-blind, but not gender-neutral, consequences, Sahle examines relevant examples involving reforms in the agricultural sector, privatization of state-owned enterprises, and the refashioning of social sector policies to show how African women have been more adversely affected by Washington consensus polices than men. More importantly, the responses of African women to the austere economic circumstances they find themselves under neoliberal Structural Adjustment Programs are highlighted. And, as readers will see, these responses have not only been in the form of legitimate social resistance movements—there is some evidence to suggest that women in Africa are increasingly straying into criminal activities, such as armed robbery and drug trafficking.

In "Globalization, Indigenization, and Tourism in Sub-Saharan Africa" (Chapter 6), Francis Adu-Febiri notes that despite its substantial tourism resources, sub-Saharan Africa still captures only a miniscule portion of the world tourism business. While the bulk of the exiting literature attributes this state of affairs to factors that are endogenous to Africa, such as the paucity of tourism infrastructure, substandard tourism services, and political instability, Adu-Febiri situates much of his explication in factors that are exogenous to Africa, with a particular emphasis on the adverse effects of neoliberal globalization. He argues that the political economy of contemporary globalization is such that regions that absorb much of the world's tourism market, and attendant revenues, have to rely, invariably, on the mass tourism that dwells mostly on the dynamic of external political and socioeconomic forces couched in globalization. The basic argument espoused by Adu-Febiri in this chapter posits that standardization and the increased homogenization engendered by globalization render mass tourism in sub-Sahara Africa less competitive internationally, not to mention its exploitative impact on local African communities. With this irony in mind, Adu-Febiri proceeds to argue that unless the political economy of globalization changes, sub-Saharan Africa is unlikely to be a major player in the world tourism industry, at least not in the near future, in his view.

With homage to Nietzsche's *Unfashionable observations* in his subtitle, Joseph Mensah demonstrates in Chapter 7 that the prevailing mantra of a global village with unrestrained movement of capital and labor is not empirically sustainable in the context of Africa. Mensah uses David Harvey's (1990) notion of "time-space compression," Manuel Castells' (2000) "space of flows" and "timeless time," and Doreen Massey's (1999) "power geometries," to show the extent to which Africa, in general, and sub-Saharan Africa, in particular, seems to be "falling out" of the network society. And given the preponderance of phrases such "electronic cottage," "global village," "shrinking world," and so on, in the overflowing literature on globalization, Mensah is keenly aware that any assertion to the contrary—or any hint to the effect that "not every one's world is getting smaller"—becomes *unfashionable*. Dwelling primarily on spatial theorizations of political economy, Mensah argues that Africa is simultaneously marginalized, exploited, and sometimes used as a basing point for capital switched from elsewhere to enhance capital accumulation and to initiate yet new cycles of exploitation and underdevelopment on the continent. Also, Mensah writes about the exorbitant cost wrought upon Africa and its people in phone rates, Internet charges, air travel costs, and so on, as a result of the acute lack of time-space compression technologies across the continent. The structural power imbalances and sociospatial differentiations embedded in globalization, and their attendant discursive practices, are also highlighted in this chapter.

In Chapter 8—the final piece of Part I—Sahle, through a critical overview of the constitutive element of the New Partnership for Africa's Development (NEPAD), shows the possibilities, limitations, and contradictions of African states' responses to the economic and political dimension of neoliberal globalization. She provides useful insights into the ways that African ruling elites' thinking on NEPAD dovetails well with the contemporary development agenda of their global counterparts. The underlying premise of the chapter is that the NEPAD initiative facilitates the (re)production of the transnational elite-driven development discourse that has deepened the existing inequality between the global north and the global south in general. Thus, in the view of Sahle, the NEPAD initiative, as it stands now, amounts to nothing than the recycling of hegemonic neoliberal development, and therefore offers not a new start for Africa, but the intensification of neoliberal policy prescription on the continent.

PART II: COUNTRY CASE STUDIES

The five substantive chapters that constitute Part II deal with fairly similar issues as those covered in Part I, except the discussions here are contextualized in specific countries. If nothing at all, they are all couched in the contestations surrounding neoliberalism, globalization, and Africa's development. Opening this discussion is Wisdom J. Tettey's thought provoking piece on "Globalization, Cybersexuality among Ghanaian Youth, and the Moral Panic" in Chapter 9. Here, Tettey shows how globalization and the accompanying electronic mediated communication innovations have created a transnational space of Internet-related sex and sexuality that—when placed in a country with shrinking economic possibilities because of neoliberal regimes imposed since the early 1980s—has facilitated sexual consumption through racial, gendered, and national self-imaginations, reproducing patterns of domination and inequality within Ghana and the larger global system. The chapter offers a probing lens into the allures and dangers to Ghanaian youth of Internet-based sexual liaisons and other forms of sex work during a period of deepening economic crisis and rise in sex tourism. Drawing primarily on political economic analysis, Tettey explores the gendered, racialized, and accumulation effects of the intertwining of global forces, technological advances, and national socioeconomic processes. He argues that the cutbacks in social services under neoliberal adjustment programs are partly responsible for the proliferation of cybersexual activities among the youth in Ghana. In his view, this trend is part of the survival maneuvers deployed by the youth in the new socioeconomic realities of neoliberal globalization.

In Chapter 10, Julius Kiiza examines the functionality of economic mercantilism or economic nationalism as an instrument of late industrialization by profiling the international trade histories of various countries, with a special emphasis on how those of Taiwan and Uganda compare. The main questions posed by Kiiza are: Does economic mercantilism make sense for late industrializers? And why are some countries, such as Taiwan, more effective than others, like Uganda, in attaining late industrialization? To answer these questions, Kiiza conceptualizes economic mercantilism from the perspective of Jacob Viner's (1948) seminal claim that the pursuit of *power and plenty*—that is, political power and economic might—is a legitimate objective of mercantilism. Convinced that the use of state power to babysit infant industries into competitive adulthood was a cardinal objective of the mercantilism practice of countries such as France, Britain, Japan, and the United States, Kiiza explores the challenges and prospects of applying a similar developmentalist measure in Africa. He chides WTO rules and other such policies, advanced by the capitalist North, on grounds that they promote the nationalistic economic interests of advanced capitalist nations, while, at the same time, undermining the efforts of latecomer industrializers such as Uganda. More pointedly, the industrialization outcomes of Taiwan (representing successful use of economic mercantilism) and Uganda (representing premature global market integration) are compared. Kiiza concludes his piece with the provocative assertion that globalization is, indeed, *"a distinctive form of economic nationalism—that of the dominant industrial economies."*

As noted earlier on, the mere mention of Mugabe's name is enough to ignite caustic debates, entailing theoretical hammer blows. In Chapter 11, Blair Rutherford discusses the land redistribution in Zimbabwe, and invariably has no choice but to invoke the "M" word. As Rutherford rightly notes, the effects of Mugabe's land redistribution, and the associated contestations, have taken on iconic status in mass-mediated international discourses as they are intimately caught up in narratives of globalization and neoliberalism. The dominant versions of these narratives are based on the assumption that African nations are reified victims or agents in relation to transnational economic, political, or cultural flows. Proponents of these processes point to the economic crises in Zimbabwe that accompanied the start, in 2000, of what its government calls the "fast-track land redistribution exercise" of forcibly taking land from largely white Zimbabweans and giving it to black Zimbabweans as evidence of what occurs when nations decide to go against the putative rational logic of globalization and neoliberalism: Zimbabweans as victims of their government's defiance of this transnational system. In contrast, President Mugabe and his supporters have characterized their land redistribution and other actions as a fight against Western forms of globalization and for national and pan-African sovereignty: Zimbabweans as overcoming their previous victim status of this system and becoming autonomous agents in and of themselves. Starting from James Ferguson's recent analysis of globalization and neoliberalism narratives and African social realities, Rutherford explores how both characterizations neglect the particular forms of transnational connections shaping the cultural politics of land in Zimbabwe. Rutherford rethinks these dominant narratives of globalization and neoliberalism not only by attending to these connections, but also by situating them in particular social projects while problematizing some of their reifications, and pointing toward alternative ways of understanding transnational influences of African political economies and their cultural politics.

Carolyn Bassett examines South Africa's People's Budget Campaign in Chapter 12. She sees the campaign as a Janus-faced response to neoliberalism that has both challenged some of the latter's core precepts and integrated others. The analysis pursued in the chapter shows that the People's Budget Campaign has used the annual national budget of South Africa to claim a public space to assess the priorities of the government as expressed through its fiscal policy. Drawing upon a series of interviews with key actors in the campaign, Bassett shows how the South African government—in its efforts to work within the neoliberal stricture of a balanced budget—has reinforced the economic and social powers of particular interest groups within the society. With the aid of examples from similar grassroots budget campaigns in Africa and elsewhere in the developing world, Bassett shrewdly theorizes the movement as a contradictory response to neoliberalism that has unmistakably been shaped by its discourses, but seeks to use these same discourses as a starting point for an extensive social critique of both the context and methodology of neoliberal policy formulation. The chapter closes with an assessment of the campaign's success in terms of transforming South Africa's state policy and enhancing economic and political knowledge of its active participants.

In Chapter 13, the final substantive chapter of Part II (and, thus, of the book), Wisdom J. Tettey again examines how globalization plays out in cyberspace, but this time within the context of Internet fraud among the youth in Ghana. As in Chapter 9, Tettey situates the proliferation of Internet fraud in the nation's political economy, and shows how the social services and employment constrictions wrought by neoliberal Structural Adjustment Programs (SAPs) interlace with Internet fraud. Through the use of "global ethnography," Tettey was able to document how the Internet frauds perpetrated by the Ghanaian youth, and their associated impacts, extend extraterritorially beyond Ghana. With neologism and terms such as "phishing," "medicine men," and "419," we get to know the complexities and undercurrents of this crimenogenic enterprise deployed by the youth in Ghana (and elsewhere in the world) to survive/resist neoliberal globalization—albeit in a framework of highly contorted moral ethos. Some of the perpetrators do not even see their activities as criminal: after all, in their view, it is VISA—a multinational corporate giant, and not the ordinary customer, which takes the hit; after all, it is only the greedy that get sucked into the vortex of their fraudulent solicitation letters; after all, it is only a way of rectifying the inequities of contemporary globalization; after all, it is just a payback for all the crimes perpetrated by Americans and Europeans through (neo)colonialism and imperialist domination—such as some the twisted moral logic under which many of them operate. Ironically, it is the same globalization that engenders the economic peripheralization of the Ghanaian youth that helps them to extend the reach and scope of their criminal activities through heightened electronic mediation and time-space compression innovations. And, of course, the police and law enforcement agencies, the world over, are found wanting, scrambling to catch up with the fast pace with which the ingenious maneuvers of the Internet fraudster move and change over space and time. The volume concludes with a brief synthesis of all the chapters, by Joseph Mensah and Roger Oppong-Koranteng, in search of a way forward for Africa.

References

Amin, Samir. 1989. *Maldevelopment*. London: Zed Books.

Bayart, Jean-François. 1989. *L'état en Afrique: la politique du ventre*. Paris: Librairie Artheme Fayard. English translation by London: Longman, 1993.

Bond, Patrick. 2006. *Looting Africa: The economics of exploitation*. London: Zed Books.

Castells, Manuel. 2000. *The information age: Economy, society, and culture*. Vol. 3 of *End of millennium*. Oxford: Blackwell.

Chomsky, Noam. 2001. Free trade and free market: Pretense and practice. In *The culture of globalization, ed.* Fredric Jameson and Masao Miyoshi. Durham and London: Duke University Press, 356–70.

De Rivero, Oswaldo. 2001. *The myths of development*. Dhaka: University Press.

Devarajan, S., D. R. Dollar, and T. Holmgren. 2001. Overview. In *Aid and reform in Africa, ed.* S. Devarajan, D. R. Dollar, and T. Holmgren, 1–41. Washington, DC: World Bank.

Frimpong-Ansah, Jonathan H. 1991. *The vampire state in Africa: The political economy of decline in Ghana*. London: James Curley.

Harvey, David. 1990. *The condition of postmodernity*. Cambridge, MA and Oxford, UK: Blackwell.

———. 2007. *A brief history of neoliberalism*. Oxford: Oxford University Press.

Hoogvelt, Ankie. 2001. *Globalization and the postcolonial world: The new political economy of development*. Baltimore: John Hopkins University Press.

Kaplan, R. D. 1994. The Coming Anarchy. *The Atlantic Monthly* 273 (2): 44–76.

Klein, Naomi. 2000. *No logo: Taking aim at the brand bullies*. Toronto: Vintage Canada.

Massey, Doreen. 1999. Power-geometry and a progressive sense of place. In *Mapping the futures: local cultures, global change*. ed. Jon Bird et al. London and New York: Routledge.

McNally, David. 2002. *Another world is possible: Globalization and anti-capitalism*. Winnipeg: Arbeiter Ring.

Norberg, Johan. 2003. *In defense of global capitalism*. Washington, DC: Cato Institute.

Peet, Richard. 2003. *Unholy trinity: The IMF, World Bank, and WTO*. London and New York: Zed Books.

Sachs, Jeffrey. 2005. *The end of poverty*. New York: Penguin.

Shiva, Vandana. 1997. *Biopiracy: The plunder of nature and knowledge*. Boston, MA: South End Press.

Stiglitz, Joseph. 2003. *Globalization and its discontent*. New York and London: W. W. Norton.

UNDP, 2006. *Human development report, 2006*. New York: UNDP.

Wolf, Martin. 2004. *Why globalization works*. New Haven: Yale University Press.

World Bank, 1994. *Adjustment in Africa*. Oxford: Oxford University Press.

NOTES

1. Published in 1981, The Berg report entitled *Accelerated development in sub-Saharan Africa: An agenda for action* was commissioned by the World Bank under the leadership of Elliot Berg, a development economist.
2. Commonly attributed to Margaret Thatcher, this is the slogan to the effect that "there is no alternative" to neoliberalism.

PART I

POLEMICS FROM THE EMBATTLED CONTINENT

CHAPTER 1

ACCUMULATION BY DISPOSSESSION IN AFRICA

FALSE DIAGNOSES AND DANGEROUS PRESCRIPTIONS*

Patrick Bond

INTRODUCTION: CRISIS AND IMPERIALISM

Consider all the attention Africa has received in recent years to "make poverty history," to provide relief from crushing debt loads, to double aid, and to establish a "development round" of trade. And yet, at best, only piecemeal critiques of imperial power emerged amid the cacophony of all-white rock concerts and political grandstanding. By 2007, one of the G8 group of nations' court jesters, Bob Geldof, finally became so frustrated that he called those attending the Heiligendamm summit "creeps," and their work, a "total farce" (Blair 2007). Geldof had earlier summed up the achievements of the G8's 2005 meeting at the Gleneagles Summit as "On aid, 10 out of 10. On debt, eight out of 10," a ridiculous formulation (Hodkinson 2005). The Geldof campaign "achieved next to nothing" because its "design allowed it to accept inappropriate markers for success that were never real proxies for justice, empowerment or accountability. And also because its demands were never in fact audacious enough" (Hertz 2005). Non-governmental organization (NGO) strategists of peacebuilding and

*A version of this chapter appeared in the *Journal of Peacebuilding and Development* in 2008.

development suffered from horizons limited by the early and mid-2000s—years of growing "humanitarian imperialism" hubris on the part of Northern elites (Bond *et al.* 2005). Former Prime Minister Tony Blair's advisor, Robert Cooper, publicly advocated "force, pre-emptive attack, deception . . . a new kind of imperialism" (Cooper 2002, 16–17).

But at its roots, this is not really so new. As was the case a century earlier, tendencies to *stagnation* have characterized the world economy over the past forty years. The average rate of growth of GDP fell from 3.6 percent during the 1960s, to 2.1 percent during the 1970s, to 1.3 percent during the 1980s, to 1.1 percent during the 1990s, and to 1 percent during the beginning of the 2000s (Harvey 2005). Since capitalism's laws of motion rely on the imperative of growth via processes *internal to the market*, this trajectory can be considered a "crisis"—in which crisis is defined not as a "breakdown" *per se*, but a state in which the normal reproduction of a system is no longer functioning, and requires processes *external* to that system to rectify its problems (Cox 1987).

As David Harvey (1999) has pointed out, during the twentieth century, especially after the Great Depression, the capitalist crisis-displacement toolbox added two new geographic and temporal displacement mechanisms. In the first, the problems are moved around as one or another group of territorially organized capitalists either push away the devaluation of their capital stocks, or resist it, resulting in more extreme uneven spatial development and intensified exploitation of weaker geographical sites. In the second, the problems are put off, insofar as a rising credit system allows today's problems to be mitigated through borrowing against the hope of tomorrow's economic growth.

In both cases, crisis-displacement strategy becomes increasingly ineffectual, especially when financial system upheavals adversely affect confidence in debt instruments (Mensah, in Chapter 7 of this volume, also draws on David Harvey's "spatial fix" to make a fairly similar point). At that point, wrote Rosa Luxemburg (1968, 347) drawing upon an earlier manifestation of the same problem, we witness "the deep and fundamental antagonism between the capacity to consume and the capacity to produce in a capitalist society, a conflict resulting from the very accumulation of capital which periodically bursts out in crises and spurs capital on to a continual extension of the market." The system then turns to more extreme forms of exploitation that occur beyond purely market production and exchange: what Harvey (2003) calls "accumulation by dispossession."

This article sets out why such a formulation is useful for analyzing peace/conflict and development problems in Africa in a context of worsening inequalities structured into global and regional economic relations.

UNEVEN AND COMBINED DEVELOPMENT

The phrase "uneven and combined development" can be invoked here, for it suggests that growth (accumulation) and decline (underdevelopment via superexploitation) happen in a systematic manner, but not one which follows either the modernization path—directly along a line of underdevelopment, "take-off," and development—or permanent dependency. Instead, accumulation at one pole and poverty at another happen systematically according to processes that we must carefully analyze and document, but that can change, depending upon political processes. In past eras, severely repressive social systems (slavery, colonialism, and apartheid) emerged to channel labor from precapitalist settings to resource-extraction zones, as Walter Rodney (1972), among others, showed. Today, as James Ferguson (2005, 381) observes, "capital 'hops' over 'unusable Africa,' alighting only in mineral-rich enclaves that are starkly disconnected from their national societies. The result is not the formation of standardised national grids, but the emergence of huge areas of the continent that are effectively 'off the grid.'"

The apparent "disconnection," as Ferguson (1990) showed in Lesotho, is misleading because one may get the impression, at first blush (as do the World Bank and aid agencies), that poverty comes from *lack* of exposure to markets. In fact, it is the migrant labor market that decisively contributes to sustained underdevelopment in a context, often of political repression. In the process, Ferguson (2006, 41–42) notes, there emerges "a frightening sort of political-economic model for regions that combine mineral wealth with political intractability," from African oil zones to occupied Iraq. The model includes protection of capital by private military companies and protection of the "Big Man," "not by his own national army but, instead, by hired guns" (Ferguson 2006, 41)—in exactly the way that the U.S. rulers of Iraq, Paul Bremer and John Negroponte, used mercenary firms for personal bodyguards. The bottom line is enhanced profit for international capital and despotism for the citizenry.

Others assume that the continent is not *sufficiently* subject to the laws of the market. Jeffrey Sachs (2005, 189–209) acknowledges the problem of looting: "Little surpasses the Western world in the cruelty and depredations that it has long imposed on Africa." But he presumes that the critique of corrupt dictators is a "political story line" of the "right" instead of giving credence to progressive, organic African anticorruption campaigning. From there, Sachs proceeds to rehearse well-known accounts of malaria, AIDS, landlocked countries, and other forms of geographically determinist analysis, and then reconciles these explanations with garden variety policy advice: adopting good governance plus "implementing traditional market reforms, especially regarding export promotion."

How does combined development create systemic conflict? Luxemburg, in 1913, showed, in the following summary, how violence "is the immediate consequence of the clash between capitalism and the organisations of a natural economy which would restrict accumulation": "Capital is faced with difficulties because vast tracts of the globe's surface are in the possession of social organisations that have no desire for commodity exchange. . . . Force is the only solution open to capital; the accumulation of capital, seen as an historical process, employs force as a permanent weapon, not only at its genesis, but further on down to the present day. From the point of view of the primitive societies involved, it is a matter of life or death; for them there can be no other attitude than opposition and fight to the finish: complete exhaustion and extinction." The next section shows how Africa's relationship with traditional markets is still having adverse consequences.

LOOTING AFRICA

Is force "the only solution open to capital" in Africa? The standard routes by which wealth flows from Africa to the North are permanent, but inadequate: exploitative debt and finance, capital flight, unfair trade, and distorted investment. Although the resource drain from Africa dates back many centuries, beginning with unfair terms of trade and then mediated through slavery, colonialism, and neocolonialism, neoliberal policies are today the most direct causes of inequality and poverty. They tend to amplify uneven and combined development, especially preexisting gender, race, and regional disparities, as we have seen above. Although the argument has to be situated in each national setting, there are *prima facie* relationships between deepening economic exploitation, neoliberal policies, and social disintegration, a "shock doctrine," in the words of Naomi Klein (2007), that can be traced, in turn, to the global scale.

Africa has seen a vast share of its resources—more than US$20 billion in 1997 alone—drained out by its own citizens (IMF 2005a, 126). James Boyce and Léonce Ndikumana (2000) estimate that over a quarter of a century, US$285 billion was drained from a core group of sub-Saharan African countries whose foreign debt was US$178 billion in 1996. Other net outflows of finance occur through debt repayment. In absolute terms, Third World debt rose from US$580 billion in 1980 to US$2.4 trillion in 2002, and much of it is now simply unpayable, a factor recognized by the G7 finance ministers in June 2005 when they agreed to a partial write-off of US$40 billion of debt owed by the eighteen poorest countries. The debt relief was conditioned by standard neoliberal policy requirements, and represented an outlay of merely US$1.5 billion each year for the wealthy countries, in comparison to their military spending in excess of US$700 billion a year. In 2002, there was a net outflow of US$340 billion in servicing this debt. Overall, during the 1980s and '90s, Africa repaid US$255 billion, or 4.2 times the original 1980 debt. As a percentage of GDP, the 2005 multilateral debt owed to the IMF and World Bank exceeded 100 percent in Sao Tome & Principe, Guinea-Bissau, Burundi, the Democratic Republic of Congo (DRC), The Gambia, Malawi, Sierra Leone, and Madagascar, several of which are mired in conflict. The few African countries without huge Bretton Woods debt repayment obligations were South Africa, Botswana, Equatorial Guinea, Namibia, Mauritius, and Swaziland.

According to Eric Toussaint (2004, 3, 384), debt inherited from dictators could be defined as legally "odious" in at least sixteen African countries, such as Nigeria under Abacha ($30 billion), apartheid South Africa (US$22 billion), or Mobuto's Zaire (US$13 billion). Such debts could therefore be eligible for cancellation, since citizens were victimized both in the original accumulation (and use of monies against the society) and in subsequent demands that it be repaid. These amounts easily exceed half of Africa's outstanding debt. As Toussaint (2004, 3) remarks, "since 1980, over 50 Marshall plans (over US$4.6 trillion) have been sent by the peoples of the periphery to their creditors in the centre."

The absolute value of loans made to dictatorial regimes might disguise sites where the debt ratios are particularly onerous. By the early 2000s, the debt remained unpayable for at least twenty-one African countries, at a level of more than 300 percent of export earnings. For countries like Sudan, Burundi, Sierra Leone, and Guinea-Bissau, it was fifteen times greater than annual export earnings. It is no coincidence that these countries have been steeped in conflict.

The Highly Indebted Poor Countries initiative failed to change the debt servicing ratios noticeably, as even World Bank officials conceded (Bond 2006b, 78–80). The small debt relief concessions—including the June 2005 G7 finance ministers' offer—came at the expense of tighter neoliberal conditionality. The largest slice of debt relief that year, for Nigeria, required a vast down payment. According to the leader of Nigeria's Jubilee network, Rev. David Ugolor: "The Paris Club cannot expect Nigeria, freed from over 30 years of military rule, to muster US$12.4 billion to pay off interest and penalties incurred by the military" (Jubilee USA 2005).

Trade liberalization has also exacted a heavy toll on sub-Saharan Africa—US$272 billion over the past twenty years, according to Christian Aid (2005) and Kraev (2005). Dependence on primary commodities, worsening terms of trade, northern subsidies, and long-term falling prices for most exports together grip African producers in a price trap as they increase production levels but generate decreasing revenues (Burnett and Manji 2007). Across Africa, four products, at most, make up three-quarters of export revenues. Natural resources accounted for nearly 80 percent of African exports in 2000, compared to 31 percent for all developing countries and 16 percent for the advanced capitalist economies. Meanwhile, agricultural subsidies to Northern farmers (mainly corporate producers) have risen steeply—by 15 percent between the late 1980s and 2004, according to the United Nations Development Programme (2005, 94), to US$360 billion per year—which has greatly intensified North-South trade inequalities. Developing countries lose US$35 billion annually as a result of industrialized countries' protectionist tariffs, $24 billion of this as a result of the Multifibre Agreement that protects especially U.S. producers.

Nonfinancial investment flows are driven less by policy—although liberalization has also been important—and more by accumulation opportunities. During the 1970s, according to the Commission on Africa, roughly one-third of foreign direct investment (FDI) to the "Third World" went to Africa; by the 1990s, this had declined to 5 percent. Thereafter, what seems like significantly rising FDI in the late 1990s and 2001 can be accounted for by the relocation of South African companies' financial headquarters to London, and by resurgent oil investments in Angola and military-ruled Nigeria. Tax fraud, transfer pricing, and other multinational corporate techniques also reduce Africa's income. In 1994, for example, an estimated 14 percent of the total value of exported oil went unaccounted for (Cockroft 2001, 4).

A final example of the processes by which the North drains the South comes from African minerals and petroleum, a major factor in violent conflict across the continent. The World Bank (hereafter, "the Bank") addressed the issue of natural capital depletion in a 2005 document, *Where is the wealth of nations?* The Bank methodology for correcting bias in GDP wealth accounting is not nearly as expansive as it should be, but at least it recognizes that extractive investments may not contribute to net GDP growth if resource depletion and pollution are factored in. The Bank's "first-cut" method subtracts factors such as fixed capital depreciation, depletion of natural resources, and pollution from the existing rate of savings, but adds savings investments in education (defined as annual expenditure). The result, in most African countries dependent upon primary products, is a net negative savings/GNI rate. For every percentage point increase in a country's extractive resource dependency, that country's potential GDP falls by 9 percent (as against the real GDP recorded), according to the Bank (2005, 54) in what is probably a conservative estimate. In sum, even the Bank now admits that exploitation of Africa's natural resources leaves the continent poorer.

The African countries most affected—i.e., with high resource dependence and low capital accumulation—include Nigeria, Zambia, Mauritania, Gabon, Congo, Algeria, and South Africa, as well as four countries emerging from intense conflict—Angola, the DRC, Liberia, and Sierra Leone—where data are not available. The Bank (2005, 55) compares the potential for capital accumulation and the actual measure of capital accumulation, and finds: "In many cases the differences are huge. Nigeria, a major oil exporter, could have had a year 2000 stock of produced capital five times higher than the actual stock. Moreover, if these investments had taken place, oil would play a much smaller role in the Nigerian economy today, with likely beneficial impacts on policies affecting other sectors of the economy." Using Bank data, Gabon's people lost US$2,241 each in absolute terms in 2000, as oil companies depleted the country's tangible wealth. Other large absolute per capita losses were US$727 in the Republic of the Congo, US$210 in Nigeria, $152 in Cameroon, US$147 in Mauritania, and R100 in Côte d'Ivoire in 2000, although Angola, the DRC, Liberia, and Sierra Leone would also probably be on list of countries whose people lost more than US$100 in tangible national wealth (World Bank 2005, 66). In net terms, even fairly prosperous countries—like Mauritius, which lost US$3,183 per person, and Botswana, which lost US$2,111 per person—witness dramatic declines in income/wealth statistics using the Bank's indicator compared to per capita GDP.

In sum, the role of extractive FDI in countries rich in oil and other resources should take into account the net negative impact on national wealth, including natural capital. The Bank's new accounting of genuine savings is a helpful innovation in the broader task of measuring looting, in part so as to establish grounds for reparations cases in a future, hopefully more just, multilateral climate.

One is left with a sense that the world economy is amplifying features of uneven and combined development that are not accidental, but are structured into economic interrelationships within the advanced capitalist world, and between the North and South. Managing large-scale resource extraction requires strong geopolitical and military capacity, and given the failure of many Pentagon missions in Africa, most notably in Somalia in 1993, local strongmen are required. For example, in Central and East Africa, according to Ian Taylor (2003, 49): "Pro-American leaders in Asmara, Addis Ababa, Kampala and Kigali seemed to be constructing a new bloc of regimes friendly to Washington's interests, linking up with South Africa as a group of states that America could do business with." A conservative estimate of three million dead in Central African wars follows logically from the victims' proximity to coltan and other mineral riches. From the late 1990s, the Uganda/Rwanda alliance was contested by a bloc composed of Laurent Kabila's DRC, Zimbabwe, Angola, and Namibia. Only with Kabila's 2001 assassination, and Pretoria's management of elite peace deals in the DRC and Burundi, has the conflict ebbed, however briefly, into a fragile peace combining neoliberalism and renewed opportunities for minerals extraction, although thousands continue to die in localized conflicts in the northeastern DRC.

Bridging sub-Saharan Africa and North Africa is another resource-rich subregion of crucial importance to U.S. imperialism. Libya is being brought into the fold of weapons certification and control, and already, U.S. troops have been deployed for small-scale interventions in Mali, Chad, and Mauritania. A site of future extraction lies between northern Nigeria and southern Algeria, where the U.S. multinationals Halliburton and Bechtel have contracted gas pipeline options. The major petroleum prize remains the Gulf of Guinea. With Africa closer than the Persian Gulf to Louisiana's oil processing plants, the world's shortage of supertankers is eased by direct sourcing from West Africa's offshore oil fields.

But the African terrain over which capital hops in search of extractive enclaves remains pockmarked by military and civil conflict, in many cases due to the way global corporations and powerful imperial states establish cozy relationships with warlord regimes. The continent's civil wars and adverse climatic conditions (droughts and floods) are increasingly identified with structural political-economic power relations of the sort examined above, ranging from post-cold war geopolitical fragility to global warming. New conflicts are in the offing because the scramble for Africa's resources has been joined from the Far East. The rapid rise of Chinese investment in Africa appears not as an anti-imperialist bulwark, but rather intra-imperial competition that will exacerbate the looting process (Marks and Manji 2007).

In spite of establishing a new Africa Command in February 2007, in order—as George W. Bush put it—to "strengthen our security cooperation with Africa and create new opportunities to bolster the capabilities of our partners," the Pentagon cannot police Africa properly. Already by 2002, Washington had established the African Contingency Operations Training Assistance program, which, according to Horace Campbell (2007, 21), provides "offensive military weaponry, including rifles, machine guns, and mortars" under the guise of "regional peacekeeping."

Although local proxies—especially South Africa—will be required to carry out sub-imperial functions (Bond 2006a, 2006b), former U.S. Assistant Secretary of State Walter Kansteiner made a frank declaration of imperial interests: "As the political and security conditions of the Persian Gulf deteriorate, the availability and appeal of reliable, alternative sources of oil for the American market grows. African oil is emerging as a clear direction U.S. policy could take to provide a secure source of energy" (Campbell 2007, 46). What do African elites get out of this, by way of a national payoff? After all, nonmilitary overseas development aid to Africa dropped 40 percent during the 1990s. Contributions from almost all developed countries fall well below the agreed United Nations target of 0.7 percent of GDP, with 0.12 percent of U.S. GDP and 0.23 percent of Japanese GDP as extreme examples. The 2003 total official aid of US$69 billion is reduced to just US$27 billion in "real" aid to poor people because of a variety of "phantom" aid mechanisms, according a study by ActionAid (2005, 1). "Untied" aid rose from US$2.3 billion in 1999 to US$4.3 billion in 2003, but declined as a proportion of total "aid." There is enough aid to ensure African elites are tied into the imperial orbit, with many African countries relying on aid as the basis for a large proportion of state expenditures.

One related legitimating strategy—which, unfortunately, far too many development and peace activists have endorsed—is the United Nations Millennium Development Goals. According to feminist economist Peggy Antrobus (2003), they suffer from "inadequate targets and indicators; their restriction to indicators that are quantifiable, when much of what is most important—such as women's equality and empowerment—is not easily quantifiable; their omission of important goals and targets, such as violence against women and sexual and reproductive rights . . . their silence on the context and institutional environment in which they are to be met." For a stronger sense of a political economy that can resist the uneven development and primitive accumulation responsible for so much conflict in Africa, African social movements are promoting more promising ways forward.

IMPLICATIONS FOR AFRICAN SOCIAL MOVEMENT STRATEGY

If the analysis stops at the level of symptoms (institutions and policies) of that power, it is not surprising that advocacy campaigns—such as Make Poverty History—turn to "the international community" to fix itself. But repeated failures of global governance reform initiatives within the existing power structure should instead generate strategies that break from such institutions (Bond 2007). We should instead more closely follow the way Hugo Chavez is trying to *delink* Latin America from the Bretton Woods institutions (through his commitment to socialism and offers of petro-financing resources) as a means of contesting their roles as central pivots of imperialism—not just malevolent institutions that need reforming.

If such a course is followed, reliance on elite deal-making in conflict situations would be less harmful. Months after Tony Blair had established the Commission for Africa, three key regimes anointed by Blair as modernizing, liberalizing states—Tanzania, Kenya, and Ethiopia—were racked by violence (Cawthorne 2005). By early 2006, Ethiopia's President Meles Zenawi had hammered his opposition with a massacre, mass arrests, and beatings, and finally, aid was put on hold to Addis Ababa, just as World Bank credit was withdrawn from Kibaki's corruption-riddled regime in Nairobi. Then, with Western consent, Congo-Brazzaville President Denis Sassou-Nguesso was chosen as the 2006 head of the African Union, notwithstanding his two ascents to power (in 1979 and 1997) through coups, between which he shifted ideology from Marxist posturing to "an unashamedly market view of economics" (Cornish 2006). A few months earlier in New York, Sassou-Nguesso demonstrated how such a shift can improve one's personal comfort, by running up a US$300,000 hotel bill during a brief UN summit. "The main purpose of the president's visit was to deliver a 15-minute speech to the General Assembly's 60th anniversary summit. He was also entertained by an American oil firm" (Allen-Mills 2006).

Within the elite global and African circuits, as Jean-Jacques Cornish (2007) recently noted, conflict resolution is at best fragile: "Things have gone distinctly pear-shaped in South Africa's two most prized mediation subjects— the Democratic Republic of Congo and Burundi. Governments put in place in both these countries as a result of South African-brokered peace processes last week saw a repeat of bodies in the streets and floods of refugees, reminiscent of their days of civil war."[1] With respect to the DRC, according to revolutionary scholar Wamba dia Wamba: "When a [transition process] takes off on a wrong footing, unless a real readjustment takes place on the way, the end cannot be good. . . . Some feel like South Africa has actively put us in the situation we are in. They had a lot of leverage to make sure that certain structural problems were anticipated and solutions proposed. They seem to have fallen into the Western logic of thinking that mediocrity is a lesser evil for Congolese if it stops the war" (Majavu 2004). The "wrong footing" amounts, simply, to self-interest, even where the highly touted South African role in Africa becomes rife with sub-imperial contradictions. In 2002, Pretoria lent US$75 million to the regime of Joseph Kabila to repay the IMF for arrears on Mobutu-era loans. According to the South African Cabinet (2002): "This will help clear the DRC's overdue obligations with the IMF and allow that country to draw resources under the IMF Poverty Reduction and Growth Facility." In the same statement, the Cabinet recorded its payment to the World Bank of $8 million for replenishment of its African loan fund, to "benefit our private sector, which would be eligible to bid for contracts financed from these resources." The same year, the United Nations

Security Council (2002) accused a dozen South African companies of looting the DRC during late 1990s turmoil that left an estimated three million citizens dead. Indeed, within eighteen months, Mbeki was negotiating multibillion dollar deals through the World Bank for South African corporate access to the DRC. In June 2005, AngloGold Ashanti was caught by Human Rights Watch (2005) giving "meaningful financial and logistical support which in turn resulted in political benefits" to brutal warlords in the Nationalist and Integrationist Front in the Eastern DRC.

Also in 2005, a diplomatic crisis erupted in the three-year-old Côte d'Ivoire conflict. According to *Business Day*, "South Africa told the UN Security Council on August 31 [2005] that its mediation efforts had removed the obstacles to implementing the latest peace accord ending the civil war in Côte d'Ivoire. It was now up to the government and rebel leaders to carry out their part of the deal." But like Mbeki's ineffectual mediation in neighboring Zimbabwe, the harsh reality emerged within days when a "highly tense meeting" of the African Union's Peace and Security Council found that Mbeki's mediation role had only "reinforced the divide" between President Laurent Gbagbo and rebel forces, thanks to Pretoria's "biased" (pro-Gbagbo) report and its delegation's endorsement of Gbagbo's antidemocratic actions in prior weeks (Kaninda 2005). These disasters led *Business Day* (2005) to ask:

> Why then, if there is little chance of success, does SA get involved? One reason might be what one could euphemistically call SA's economic diplomacy. Congo and Côte d'Ivoire are rich in mineral resources and peace there would open up new markets for South African companies. In Congo, for instance, the likes of telecoms company Vodacom took the risk of investing during that country's most troubled period. So far, the dividends have been significant. . . . It is no wonder then that Pretoria has invested so much time and resources in peace efforts in Congo. The same applies to Côte d'Ivoire. If peace and stability is restored in Congo and Côte d'Ivoire, there can be no doubt the economic and financial benefits for SA would be considerable.

Connecting the dots between imperialist relationships—entailing both accumulation processes and local compradors—is not difficult. What does seem to be beyond the grasp of many in the NGOs, research institutes, and peace industry is the kind of critique that anticipates the negative outcomes of elite deal-making. Progressive social movements are launching these critiques, and suggesting useful ways forward that address the international political economy behind Africa's looting.

Elite driven conflict resolution will not bring sustainable peace to the African continent. Similarly, elite reform proposals, ranging from Millennium Development Goals to multilateral restructuring and other forms of "global governance" (Bond 2007), will not reverse the outflow of African wealth or serve the deeper agenda of African development, which is to meet the reasonable needs of all its citizens. Social movement campaigns mostly fail, but the key examples of victory suggest principles of "decommodification" and "deglobalization of capital" that we should take seriously.

The idea of "deglobalization" has been articulated by Walden Bello, Samir Amin, John Maynard Keynes, and others. It would entail disempowering the major global institutions and replacing their functions with local and regional institutions. Instead of using hard currency loans for, say, education (whose import content is near zero), local deficit spending would be preferable, saving countries from the foreign debt trap.

Specific campaigns aimed at reversing resource flows are emerging from grassroots struggles and progressive social movements. They are targeting issues such as:

- Decommodification movements to establish basic needs as human rights rather than as privatized commodities that must be paid for;
- Campaigns to deglobalize capital, such as defunding the World Bank and securing the right to produce generic (not patented) antiretroviral medicines for people with AIDS;
- Demands for civil society oversight of national budgets; and
- Activism to ensure equitable redistribution of resources in ways that benefit low-income households, grassroots communities, and shop-floor workers.

Were there even a single genuinely Left government in Africa (Zimbabwe does not qualify due to its brutality against poor/working people by a corrupt elite), a variety of national policies could be applied to reverse socioeconomic collapse:

- Systematic default on foreign debt repayments;
- Strategies to enforce domestic reinvestment of pensions and other funds;
- Reintroduction of currency exchange controls and prohibition of tax-haven transfers;
- Refusal of tied and phantom aid, along with naming and shaming fraudulent "aid";
- Import-substitution development strategies;
- Refusal of foreign investments that prove unfavorable when realistic projections factor in costs such as natural resource depletion, transfer pricing, and profit/dividend outflows; and
- Reversal of macroeconomic policies that increase inequality.

Reversing the trends toward socioeconomic collapse in the absence of government policy in this direction requires bottom-up social movements to intensify their work, and it is crucial, in the short run, to recognize anticapitalist efforts to bridge intra-African, global-local, and Northern-African divides. They include the mid-2007 general strikes by revitalized labor movements in Swaziland, South Africa, and Nigeria; campaigning for reparations and the closure of the World Bank and IMF by Jubilee Africa; AIDS treatment advocates breaking the hold of pharmaceutical corporations on monopoly antiretroviral patents; activists fighting Monsanto's drive to introduce genetically modified crops in several African countries; blood-diamonds victims from Sierra Leone and Angola generating a partly successful global deal at Kimberley; the Kalahari Basarwa-San community raising publicity against forced removals, as the Botswana government clears the way for De Beers and World Bank investments; Lesotho peasants objecting to displacement during construction of the continent's largest dam system (intended to solely benefit Johannesburg); a growing network questioning Liberia's long exploitation by Firestone Rubber; Chadian and Cameroonian activists pressuring the World Bank not to continue funding their repression and environmental degradation; the OilWatch network of civil society activists that link Nigerian Delta communities and many others in the Gulf of Guinea and elsewhere; and Ghanaian, South African, and Dutch activists opposing water privatization.

When at its strongest, the South African chapter of the global Jubilee movement addressed political-economic exploitation, sociopolitical conflict and foreign debt, for example, in picketing eight international banks in Johannesburg in September 2005 (Jubilee SA 2005). The Washington-based Mobilization for Global Justice and a coalition of Swiss activist organizations joined Jubilee protesters in solidarity demonstrations. Citibank was a particular target, for as the UN's Special Committee against Apartheid had observed in 1979, "Citigroup has loaned nearly one-fifth of the US$5 billion plus which has gone to bolster apartheid" and, in subsequent years, made yet more loans for segregated housing and for the rollover of apartheid debt during the 1985 financial crisis. In Berne, Credit Suisse and UBS were the subjects of protest because from the early 1980s, they replaced U.S. and British banks as the main apartheid financiers. By late 2007, the case for reparations against these banks and corporations was so strong that the U.S. Appeals Court overturned a lower court rejection of an Alien Tort Claims Act lawsuit for $400 billion filed by Jubilee SA and the Khulumani victims' support group, allowing the case to proceed potentially as far as the U.S. Supreme Court, as well as in activist initiatives against the target banks and corporations.

There are no shortages of such opportunities, for African movements regularly voice anger against international capital. David Seddon and Leo Zeilig identify a "first wave" of popular struggles and "IMF riots" from the mid-1970s through 1980s that might be seen as a "precursor to the contemporary phenomenon of the "anti-globalization movement"; others are more skeptical, seeing them as merely localized expressions of anger and outrage" (Seddon and Zeilig 2005, 16–22). The second wave of popular protest during the 1990s, say the authors, was "more explicitly political with more far-reaching aims and objectives," involving eighty-six major protest movements in thirty countries evident in 1991 alone, and three dozen dictatorial regimes swept out of power from 1990–94 "by a combination of street demonstrations, mass strikes, and other forms of protest."

In no cases, however, did the three dozen dictatorial regimes give way to genuine democracies and prosecution of those responsible for long periods of enforced looting. It is here that much greater international solidarity deserves our attention. The most formidable single case of this since the antiapartheid movement itself may have been the Treatment Action Campaign's international effort to end the pharmaceutical patent monopoly on lifesaving antiretroviral medicines during the early 2000s. Given that AIDS has so much potential for generating social conflict in micro and macro settings, such cases deserve continual revisiting and revitalization, with the aim of linking issues and movements in a manner capable of responding to vast challenged represented by uneven development, primitive accumulation, and social conflict.

In sum, to become a more effective force in fighting for eco-social justice and not only peace (for one without the other is impossible), social movements need to transcend the often purely political analysis offered in the shallower (or even neoliberal) versions of development and peace studies. A far-reaching critique of capitalist social relations is crucial so as to prevent the kinds of renewed socioeconomic conflict that emerges between elites in "post-conflict" situations.

For Africa, suffering from such intense, unrelenting looting, perhaps theories such as uneven and combined development can assist with more accurate diagnoses, and potentially guide us to a broader politics of genuine, durable conflict resolution.

REFERENCES

Action Aid. 2005. *Real aid*. London: Action Aid.

Allen-Mills, T. 2006. Congo leader's £169,000 hotel bill. *Sunday Times (London)*, February 12.

Antrobus, P. 2003. Presentation to working group on the MDGs and gender equality. UNDP Caribbean Regional Millennium Development Goals Conference, Barbados.

Bakker, I., and S. Gill. 2003. Ontology, method, and hypotheses. In *Power, production and social reproduction*, ed. I. Bakker and S. Gill. Basingstoke: Palgrave Macmillan.

Blair, D. 2007. Geldof and Bono Blast G8 for Betraying Africa. *Telegraph (London)*, June 9.

Bond, P. 1999. Uneven Development. In *Encyclopaedia of political economy*, ed. P. O'Hara. London: Routledge.

———. 2006a. *Looting Africa: The economics of exploitation*. London: Zed Books; Pietermaritzburg: University of KwaZulu-Natal Press.

———. 2006b. *Talk left walk right: South Africa's frustrated global reforms*. Pietermaritzburg: University of KwaZulu-Natal Press.

——— 2007. The perils of elite pacting. *Critical currents* 1. Uppsala: Dag Hammarskjold Foundation.

Bond, P., D. Brutus, and V. Setshedi. When wearing white is not chic, and collaboration not cool. *Foreign policy in focus*, June 17, 2005.

Bond, P., and A. Desai. Forthcoming. *Uneven and combined South Africa*. London: Zed Books.

Boyce, J., and L. Ndikumana. 2000. Is Africa a net creditor? New estimates of capital flight from severely indebted sub-Saharan African countries, 1970–96. Occasional Paper, University of Massachusetts/Amherst Political Economy Research Institute, Boston and Amherst.

Burnett, P., and F. Manji, eds. 2007. *From the slave trade to "free" trade: How trade undermines democracy and justice in Africa*. Oxford: Fahamu.

Business Day (Johannesburg). 2005. Putting out fires. December 23.

Campbell, H. 2007. U.S. Africa command: A challenge to peace and security? Presentation to Kenyan Debt and Development Network, Nairobi.

Cawthorne, A. 2005. Once favoured E. African leaders lustre fades. Reuters (London), November 13.

Christian Aid. 2005. The economics of failure: The real cost of "free" trade for poor countries. London.

Cockcroft, L. 2001. Corruption as a threat to corporate behaviour and the rule of law, Transparency International UK, London.

Cooper, R. 2002. The post-modern state. In *Re-ordering the world: The long-term implications of September 11, ed. M. Leonard*. London: The Foreign Policy Centre.

Cornish, J. 2006. AU delays tough decisions. *Mail & Guardian* (Johannesburg), January 27.

———. 2007. South Africa's peace initiatives falling apart. *Mail & Guardian* (Johannesburg), September 10.

Cox, R. 1987. *Power, production, and world order*. London: Macmillan.

Ferguson, J. 1990. *The anti-politics machine*. Cambridge: Cambridge University Press.

———. 2005. Seeing like an oil company: Space, security, and global capital in neoliberal Africa. *American Anthropologist* 107:3.

Harvey, D. 1999. *The limits to capital*. London: Verso.

———. 2003. *The new imperialism*. Oxford: Oxford University Press.

Hertz, N. 2005. We Achieved Next to Nothing. *New Statesman* (London), December 12.

Hodkinson, S. 2005. Oh no, they didn't! Bono and Geldof: "We Saved Africa!" *Counterpunch*, October 27. http://www.counterpunch.org/hodkinson10272005.html.

Human Rights Watch. 2005. DR Congo: Golf fuels massive human rights atrocities. *Human Rights News*, June 2. http://www.hrw.org/english/docs/2005/06/02/congo11041.htm.

IMF (International Monetary Fund). 2005a. *Global financial stability report*. Washington.

———. 2005b. *Regional economic outlook: Sub-Saharan Africa*. Washington.

Isango, E. 2007. Fighting erupts in eastern DRC. South African Press Association (Pretoria), September 8.

Jacoby, T. 2005. Cultural determinism, western hegemony, and the efficacy of defective states. *Review of African Political Economy* 32 (104–5): 215–33.

Jubilee South Africa. 2005. Strike against corporate greed! Pamphlet (Johannesburg), September 23.

Jubilee USA. 2005. Nigerian threat to repudiate helps force Paris club to deliver debt cancellation, news release, October 20.

Kaninda, J. 2005. AU relieves South Africa of Côte d'Ivoire peace process. *Business Day* (Johannesburg), September 20.

Kaplan, R. 1994. The coming anarchy. *Atlantic Monthly* http://www.Theatlantic .com/ideastour/archive/kaplan.mhtml.

Klein, N. 2007. *The shock doctrine.* London: Penguin.

Kraev, E. 2005. Estimating demand side effects of trade liberalization on GDP of developing countries. Christian Aid, London.

Luxemburg, R. 1968. *The accumulation of capital.* New York: Monthly Review Press.

Madlala, B. 2005. Frustration boils over in protests: Community angered at snail pace service delivery. *Daily News* (Durban), October 14.

Majavu, M. 2004. Interview with Ernest Wamba dia Wamba, June 22. http://www .zmag.org.

Marks, S., and F. Manji, eds. 2007. *African perspectives on China in Africa.* Oxford: Fahamu.

Mohan, G., and T. Zack-Williams. 2005. Oiling the wheels of imperialism. *Review of African Political Economy* 104–5.

Rodney, W. 1972. *How Europe underdeveloped Africa.* Dar es Salaam: Tanzania Publishing House; London: Bogle L'Ouverture Publications.

Sachs, J. 2005. *The end of poverty.* London: Penguin.

Seddon, D., and L. Zeilig. 2005. Class and protest in Africa: New waves. *Review of African Political Economy* 103.

South African Cabinet. 2002. Statement on cabinet meeting, Government Communications and Information Service, Pretoria, June 26.

Taylor, I. 2003. Conflict in central Africa: Clandestine networks and regional/global configurations. *Review of African Political Economy* 95.

Toussaint, E. 2004. Transfers from the periphery to the centre, from labour to capital, unpublished paper, Committee for the Abolition of the Third World Debt, Brussels.

Trotsky, L. 1977. *The history of the Russian revolution.* London: Pluto.

Tsikata, D., and J. Kerr. 2002. *Demanding dignity: Women confronting economic reforms in Africa.* Ottawa and Accra: North-South Institute and Third World Network-Africa.

UNDP (United Nations Development Programme). 2005. *Human development report 2005: International cooperation at a crossroads,* New York.

United Nations. 2002. Final report, panel of experts on the illegal exploitation of natural resources and other forms of wealth of the democratic republic of the Congo, New York.

World Bank. 2005. *Where is the wealth of nations? Measuring capital for the 21st century,* conference edition, Washington.

NOTE

1. See also Isango 2007.

CHAPTER 2

CULTURAL DIMENSIONS OF GLOBALIZATION IN AFRICA

A DIALECTICAL INTERPENETRATION OF THE LOCAL AND THE GLOBAL*

Joseph Mensah

PRELIMINARY OBSERVATIONS

Since the 1980s, there has been a proliferation of academic discourse on globalization emanating from virtually all visages of the social sciences and humanities, with disciplines such as sociology, economics, political science, geography, and cultural studies taking the lead in this intellectual project (Held *et al.* 1999; Waters 1995). Perhaps the most astonishing feature of the sprawling literature is neither the enormous size, nor the diversity of disciplinary perspectives from which analysts have approached the subject, but rather the perfunctory attention given to Africa to date. As the South African economic historian David Moore (2001, 909) laments: "Globalization literature . . . is devoted largely to the advanced capitalist portion of the global economy where all the indices of production integration, shrinking distance, and the advance of the informationalisation mode of production' are on the increase. Where attention is devoted to the 'Third World,' it concentrates on

*This chapter was partly supported by a grant from the Social Sciences and Humanities Research Council (SSHRC) of Canada, for which I am grateful. The chapter first appeared in *Studies in Political Economy* 77 (Spring 2006): 57–83.

the rise and fall . . . of the newly industrialised countries of Asia. *Africa seems off the map*" (emphasis added). The few studies on Africa have come from three main points of departure. First, there are those who are convinced that Africa has little, if anything, to contribute to globalization because the continent, in their view, is made up of nothing more than dysfunctional, "non-viable economies" (de Rivero, 2001) infused with insurmountable corruption and ethnotribal conflicts. This is how *The Economist* casts this stereotype of Africa in a May 2000 cover story entitled "Africa, the hopeless continent": "[African societies are] especially susceptible to . . . brutality, despotism and corruption . . . for reason buried deep in their cultures" (15). Clearly, amidst this unflattering image is the belief that a pure, homogenous African culture, capable of causing the continent's predicaments, does exist—a position that will be contested in subsequent paragraphs.

The second point of departure posits that globalization has undermined democracy and the Westphalian nation-state in Africa with its neoliberal economic ideology propagated under the aegis of the International Monetary Fund (IMF), the World Bank, and other champions of the Washington Consensus. In the words of Thandika Mkandawire, "the state is today the most demonized institution in Africa [presumably as a result of globalization]." The third point, closely related to the second, sees globalization as a new form of decolonization. Those who espouse this view insist that globalization has fostered the exploitation of African economies, thereby widening the income gap between Africa and the *Rest* (of the world). As Bhola (2002) puts it, "[globalization] has in fact expanded worldwide profit-making opportunities that border on predatory behaviour." Several influential economists and public intellectuals—e.g., Stiglitz (2003), Chomsky (2002), Harvey (2007), Bond (2006), Soros (2000)—have expressed similar concerns about the impact globalization has had on developing economies.

The preceding points of departure see Africa's connection with globalization primarily from the perspective of political economy, with little attention paid to the cultural ramifications of the issues involved in this relationship. This analytical lapse has prompted calls from several scholars to integrate culture into the study of globalization and development (Tucker 1997, 1999; Appadurai 1996). For the most part, advocates of this cultural turn have invoked postmodern, poststructural, and postcolonial theorizations. And, given the characteristic antipositivist stance of these discursive practices, it is hardly surprising that dialectics is steadily gaining popularity in the analysis of globalization.

This chapter seeks to contribute to the literature by zeroing in on the cultural dimensions of Africa's encounter with globalization. The intent here is neither to draw a hard-and-fast line between political economy and culture, nor to downplay the important role of the former in the study of globalization, but to broaden our understanding by placing culture front and center in the ensuing discussion. This chapter uses dialectical thinking to integrate globalization with culture in the context of Africa and to discuss the following questions: What are the globalization-induced cultural connections between Africa and the rest of the world? Can we really say that there is a pure, unadulterated African culture that is being destabilized by globalization? To what extent is globalization leading to the formation of a global culture, with Africa in the midst? What relations of power and resistance are implicated in the cultural mixing underway in Africa? It is reasoned that the prevailing economic and homogenizing approaches to globalization contribute to Africa's already intense marginalization. Consequently, by introducing culture into the debate, this chapter seeks to highlight Africa's continued cultural and political-economic effects on the globe through regional innovation, socioeconomic and cultural resistance, and the creative appropriation of some external elements.[1]

A number of related themes and assumptions underlie the arguments presented in the paragraphs that follow: first, drawing upon the work of Appadurai (1996), the title of this chapter is cast as "cultural dimensions" of globalization to stress the conception of culture not so much as a noun, an object, or a superorganic entity, but as an adjective, a socially constructed, contextually sensitive phenomenon that highlights the differences in values, imaginaries, and shared social meanings of groups of people. Second, following the likes of sociologist Robertson (1995) and Tucker (1997), it is argued that the tendency to regard the global and the local as binary opposites is not theoretically sustainable. Thirdly, globalization and culture are treated as dialectical phenomena in their own right—in the sense that each is internally heterogeneous and contradictory, emanates from many different sources, exhibits a variety of forms, and resists easy synthesis and categorization.

NATURE OF DIALECTICS

The term "dialectics" was originally used to refer to the style of argumentation deployed by Socrates in many of Plato's dialogues.[2] With this style, Socrates would interrogate his followers on various philosophical issues and concepts, such as "piety" in the *Euthyphro*, "immortality of the soul" in *Phaedo*, "virtue" in the *Meno*, and "knowledge" in *Theaetetus*. Characteristically, Socrates, through the pen of Plato, would expose the inconsistencies in the answers provided by his followers without necessarily providing an adequate answer of his own. In *Theaetetus*, Socrates likens his approach to that of a midwife who is past childbearing herself, but helps others to deliver babies. With this analogy, Socrates was delivering not babies, but knowledge and thoughts.[3]

Dialectics had a distinctive, albeit related, connotation during the late eighteenth and early nineteenth centuries through the works of German philosophers, including Kant, Hegel, and Fichte. Andrew Edgar traces the common characterization of dialectics—an augmentation that begins with a thesis against which is set an antithesis before reaching a final synthesis—to Fichte (Edgar 1999, 113–15; Robinson 1998). While Hegel's dialectics, like Fichte's, usually comes in three stages, it is more subtle, complex, and historical. The first, or "universal," stage of Hegelian dialectics is one of "naïve self-certainty": a stage in which only a single, complacent, secure entity exists in a world of "pure subjectivity or universality" (Edgar 1999, 113–14). In fact, Edgar (1999) equates what occurs at this first stage to the mindset of a newborn baby who knows nothing of the world other than its own existence, or to the naivety of the creatures of the Garden of Eden "who were well-fed and cared for, but ignorant of themselves and their potential" (113–14). The point to stress is that, in the first stage of Hegelian dialectics, people are ignorant because of the lack of differentiation. The second, the "particular" stage, is where humanity (or the child) encounters the external world that invariably yields friction, resistance, and contestation, leading to the creation of the "Other." Thus, the universal breaks up, or particularizes, into subject and object, and the pure subjectivity or universality of the subject (or the child) comes into contact with the "Other," or the object. The encounter between the subject and the object, though conflictual and contradictory, is still a fruitful source of progress and discovery, not only of the self but also of human and natural history as a whole. In the third and final stage—dubbed the "individual" stage—the subject comes to see itself in the object, leading to a return to the universality of the first stage, but this time with a better understanding of the self—a better insight of the complex unity of the subject and the object.

Marx used essentially the same dialectical model in his account of the development of human history through a series of epochs. According to Marx, history began when humans broke out of the "naïve universality" of the tribal society or primitive communism, characterized by a unity that excluded differences, into a second stage of a class society (Edgar 1999, 114). This class society involves both unity and differences—it is here that humans make history, but not under conditions of their own choosing because of class conflicts and exploitation at this stage of human development (Lichtman 1970, 231). The final stage in Marx's dialectics entails communism. The idea that, through dialectics, we can pinpoint the end of history, or somehow derive absolute truths about how human society evolves, has drawn attacks from critics, such as Adorno (1973) and Lyotard (1984).

Dwelling primarily on Marx's exposition, the renowned geographer Harvey (1996) has formulated what he calls the principles of dialectics, including the following six key propositions:

1. That change and instability are characteristic, if not inherent, features of all things or systems and all aspects of systems;
2. Dialectical thinking gives priority to the understanding of processes, flows, fluxes, and relations, rather than to things, elements, and structures;
3. Parts and wholes are mutually constitutive of each other in dialectics; thus, parts are in wholes and vice versa;
4. Things or elements are always assumed to be internally heterogeneous in dialectical thinking;

5. Things many researchers treat as irreducible, and, therefore, unproblematic, are seen in dialectics to be internally contradictory by virtue of the processes which constitute them[4]; and
6. "Subjects" are interchangeable with "objects" and "causes" with "effects" in dialectics.

With the above insight, one can draw some immediate conclusions about the nature of dialectics: first, dialectics is highly skeptical of binary opposites, as things are seen to be mutually constitutive of each other. Second, dialectics espouses the primacy of process, change, and relations as opposed to structures and their elements. Third, there is nothing like unproblematic phenomenon in dialectics because things are conceptualized as being internally heterogeneous and internally contradictory. Finally, contradictions are a source of growth and discovery in dialectics (Harvey 1996 and 1995). The next sections examine the concepts of globalization and culture, and highlight their respective dialectical qualities.

GLOBALIZATION AS A DIALECTICAL PHENOMENON

As with many trendy concepts in the social sciences, the definition of globalization remains notoriously difficult to pin down in the available literature. For instance, whereas political scientist Robert Gilpin sees it as an economic phenomenon entailing the "interdependence of national economies in trade, finance, and macroeconomic policy," management scholar Stempher Kobrin insists that the process has more to do with increased technological innovation and information flows than foreign trade and investment per se (Gilpin 1987, 389; Kobrin 1997, 147–48). For his part, David Harvey sees globalization as a "time-space compression" (1990), while Roland Robertson (1992, 8) goes further to conceptualize it as "both the compression of the world and the intensification of consciousness of the world as a whole." More recently, the University of Pennsylvania sociologist Mauro Guillén (2001) defined globalization as "a process leading to greater interdependence and mutual awareness (reflexivity) among economic, political, and social units in the world, and among actors in general." Given that globalization affects the socioeconomic, spatiotemporal, and many other spheres of our lives simultaneously, it is hardly surprising that it has attracted such a wide range of interpretations, some of which are mutually reinforcing, while others are competing, if not outright contradictory.

Globalization is defined here as a multifaceted, dialectical process involving complex interconnections between socioeconomic groups, individuals, and institutions worldwide; the ultimate effects of which vary both within and between nations. While the proposed definition is not much different from those cited above, the emphasis on dialectics certainly puts it in a different light. At the same time, it bears stressing that the theorization of globalization in dialectical terms is not entirely new—more than a decade ago,

Anthony Giddens (1991, 21–22) wrote: "Globalization has to be understood as a dialectical phenomenon, in which events at one pole of a distanciated relation often produce divergent or even contrary occurrences at another." What justification is there to envisage globalization as a dialectical process? We just learned that in dialectics, "parts" and "wholes" are mutually constitutive of each other, "cause" and "effect" are often interchangeable, and things that are commonly deemed unproblematic and irreducible become internally heterogeneous and internally contradictory—how does globalization fit all of these?

Several themes from a number of studies can be deployed to demonstrate the dialectical character of globalization. For instance, the works of Tucker (1997), Robertson (1995), and many others have shown that few local events, conflicts, and interests, if any, are immune to global forces and international networks of power, commerce, and information flows. And who can forget the rich examples offered in this regard by Eric Wolf (1997) in *Europe and the people without history*: "New York suffers from the Hong Kong flu; the grapevines of Europe are destroyed by the American plant lice . . . shutdown of oil wells of Persian Gulf halts generating plants in Ohio . . . and American tropes intervene on the rim of Asia." Furthermore, we learn from the work of Bhola (2002) that "globalization is both new and old"; from Guillén (2001), that globalization is creating both convergence and divergence; from economist Raymond Vernon (1998) and historian Paul Kennedy (1993), that globalization undermines the power of nation states, and from others, including Robert Gilpin (2000) and Robert Cox (1987), that it strengthens the power of nation states. Not only that: the works of Appadrui (1996) and Jan Nederveen Pieterse (1995) have amply demonstrated that globalization is implicated in the interpenetration of indigenous and modern cultures. Also, the work of geographers Paul Knox and Sallie Marston (2001, 16–17) suggests that the more globalization intensifies, "the more valuable regional and ethnic identities become. This situation certainly chimes with Hegelian dialectics in which the encounter between the self (or the local) and the external (the global) creates friction, resistance, "Othering," and awareness of difference, which eventually lead to a better understanding of the self, or the Hegelian self-consciousness. Evidently, globalization is an internally heterogeneous phenomenon infused with several ironies, paradoxes, contradictions, and possibilities for interchange between "causes" and "effects."

Before turning our analytical gaze to "culture" in the next section, it is important to stress that, even though the concept or the theorization of globalization is reflexively connected to the phenomenon of globalization (or the referent of globalization), the two are hardly synonymous. However, because both the phenomenon and its theorization are often problematized, as done in this chapter, there is the tendency to reduce one to the other, but that is certainly not the intention here. Arguably, it is only by separating these two entities (i.e., the concept and its referent) that we can hope to avoid making misleading inferences in our attempt to grasp their dialectical interconnections.

Exploring Culture and its
Dialectical Character

Raymond Williams, the influential Welsh cultural critic, once described culture as "one of the most complicated words in the English language" (1976, 76). Perhaps nowhere is this complexity more evident than in the words of the American cultural geographer Don Mitchell (2001, 13):

> We speak frequently about English culture, or Chinese culture. . . . Or when we don't understand something, like the civil wars in the former Yugoslavia, we often say, 'Well, that's just their culture. . . .' But then we also refer to art, to symphonies, to plays as 'culture'—or perhaps 'high culture.' And as soon as we do that, we want to also talk about 'popular culture'. . . . If there is pop culture, then there also seems to be something called 'counter-culture,' 'indigenous culture,' 'youth culture,' 'black culture,' 'gay culture,' 'working-class culture,' 'Western culture,' 'corporate culture,' a 'culture of poverty,' and 'folk culture.'

While some analysts, including the preeminent cultural geographer Carl O. Sauer, treat culture as a superorganic entity capable of "causing" changes in the landscape, others see it either as "a learned behavior" (Spencer and Thomas 1973, 6), "a way of seeing or interpreting the world" (Cosgrove and Daniels 1988; Jackson 1989), or "a total way of life," or what the French geographer Paul Vidal de la Blache called *genre de vie* (Norton 2000, 13). Still, many others, including Don Mitchell (2001) and the Australian cultural analyst Chris Barker (2003) argue that culture does not exist as an entity, but is rather a construct for the purpose of analysis. Conceived this way, the meaning of culture is bound to change as analysts seek to do different things with it. How, then, is culture used in this chapter?

Drawing upon the works of Barker (2003), Said (1993), and the anthropologist William Roseberry (1989), this chapter sees culture as a dialectical, contextual, socially constructed, and contested concept connoting how people make sense of the world, and the way they attach values and meanings to the material and nonmaterial world based on their own experience and socioeconomic and political setting. Clearly this definition refuses to separate culture from political economy—it acknowledges the interpenetration of the meaningful, the symbolic, and the material in all things, and implicitly recognizes the multilayered relations of power, domination, contestation, and resistance that culture invariably engenders. This interconnection between culture and political economy has given prominence to such themes as cultural politics, cultural war, cultural imperialism, cultural capital, and the culture industry in contemporary discourse. At the same time, the present definition shies away from reductionism and offers culture "its own specific meanings, rules and practices which are not reducible to, or explainable solely in terms of, another category or level of social formation [be it social, economic, political, or political economy]" (Barker 2003, 8). In a similar vein, Said (1993, xii) noted that culture means "all those practices . . . that have relative autonomy from the economic, social and political realms." Even though culture is not seen as a superorganic entity in the sense of physical tangibility, it is deemed no less material in the philosophical sense.

Like globalization, culture is a nested, heterogeneous phenomenon characterized by change and instability. Indeed, the notion of a pure, stable, or static culture is theoretically unsustainable, especially in this era of globalization. As Said (1993, xxix) aptly points out, "all cultures are involved in one another; none is single and pure, all are hybrid, heterogeneous, extraordinarily undifferentiated and unmonolithic." Similarly, Miller (1997, 105) writes that culture "is more like an octopus, a rather badly integrated creature what passes for a brain keeps it together, more or less, in one ungainly whole." For the most part, culture derives from both the inside and the outside, and is therefore not geographically bounded. What is commonly considered intrinsic culture used to be extrinsic—and, perhaps, vice versa.

Thus, cultural flows are better conceptualized not as neat sets of linear determinations, but as "a series of overlapping, complex, and chaotic conditions" (Barker 2003, 171), or, to borrow the now popular terms of Appadurai (1996, chap. 2), as dialectical and disjunctive flows of "ethnoscapes, technoscapes, finanscapes, mediascapes, and ideoscapes." Moreover, while cultural determinists tend to treat culture as a "cause," others, notably Don Mitchell in cultural geography, see it as an "effect"—a classic case in dialectics where "cause" and "effect" are conceivably interchangeable. Also, the common encounters between local and external cultures, and their attendant identity and multicultural conflicts, are understandable in the light of Hegelian dialectics, where the meeting of the two entities breeds contestation, friction, creative destruction, and internal contradictions, all of which are sources of change, growth, and improved self-consciousness. As with globalization, it is important to acknowledge that while the concept of culture and its referent are dialectically entangled, the two are hardly synonymous. Thus, inasmuch as we can problematize both entities, as done in this chapter, we still need to consider them separate without losing sight of their Janus-like reflexivity. The following section examines how globalization has intensified the interpenetration of local and global cultures in the context of Africa, and explores some of the relations of power and resistance implicated in the process.

"GLOCALIZATION" IN AFRICA: THE INTERPENETRATION OF LOCAL AND GLOBAL CULTURES

The criticism that globalization is not only widening the income gap between Africa and the *Rest*, but also undermining the power of the nation-state in Africa has been expressed by many analysts, as we saw earlier on. At the cultural front, the main concern relates to an alleged globalization-induced obliteration of local cultural values across Africa. The fear is that globalization is moving the world toward cultural homogenization (Sklair 1991, 75–81). Proponents of the cultural homogenization thesis, including Sklair (1991) and Schiller (1976), base their arguments on a presumed cultural imperialism spearheaded by the United States. This assumption is commonly captured by neologisms such as "McWorld, "McDonaldization" (Barber 1996), and "baseball-cap-ization" (Moore 2002, 278–89). However, some scholars (e.g., Chris Barker) doubt whether "cultural imperialism" is the correct term here, to the extent that Africans, like other peoples of the developing world, actually adopt these Western values, music, and TV shows without any discernable coercion or imposition. But then, would it not be problematic to expect a blatant coercion when false consciousness is at play?[5] While it is virtually impossible to ignore the growing influence of Western (or American) cultural values across Africa, it could be argued that the cultural traffic between the West and Africa is hardly unidirectional.

Another underlying assumption of the homogenization thesis is what Samuel Huntington calls the single alternative fallacy—the argument that with the collapse of Soviet communism has come the end of history and the triumph of Western liberal democracy and Western values throughout the world. As Huntington points out, this argument overlooks the fact that many other forms of authoritarianism, nationalism, and market communism are still alive and well, not to mention the prevalence of religious alternatives that lie outside the world of secular ideologies. "It is sheer hubris," writes Huntington (2002, 20), "to think that because Soviet communism has collapsed, the West has won the world for all time and that Muslims, Chinese, Indians, [Africans] and many others are going to rush to embrace Western liberalism as the only alternative." While some scholars (e.g., Hall 2002) see Westernization as virtually identical to modernization, Huntington argues that the two are different. According to Huntington, while many societies, such as Saudi Arabia, Singapore, Japan, and many across Africa are prepared to accept modernization by adopting its key tenets—i.e., industrialization, increasingly levels of literacy, urbanization, education, and social mobilization—the same cannot be said of Westernization, which entails, among other things, Catholicism and Protestantism, the separation of spiritual and temporal authority, the rule of law, individualism, and representative bodies (Huntington 2002, 21–25). The prevalence of traditional religion, land tenure, and chieftaincy systems, and so on across Africa, for instance—despite centuries of Western cultural and intellectual subversion on the continent—points to Africans' reluctance to accept Westernization *in toto*.

The homogenization thesis also rests on the belief that cultural differences can still be theorized as dichotomies or binary opposites: Western versus non-Western or European versus African cultures. Within this framework, Western cultures are routinely said to be characterized by individualism, competition, and a separation between humans and nature (Dumont 1985; Kirkpatrick and White 1985), while "African cultures" (and, indeed, those of other developing areas) are assumed to emphasize communalism, interdependence, and a close relationship with nature (Norton 2000; Markus and Kitayama 1991).

Undoubtedly, communalism is a well-known social ethic among Africans. However, it would be a mistake to resort to any uniqueness thesis here, as communalism was common even among European aristocratic societies— something many espousers of the communal conception of African person-hood and self (e.g., John Mbiti and Placide Tempels) tend to forget. In *Bantu Philosophy*, for instance, Tempels (1959, 108) notes that: "For the Bantu, man never appears in fact as an isolated individual, as an independent entity. Every man, every individual, forms a link in a chain of vital forces . . . joined from above to the ascending line of his ancestry and sustaining below the line of his descendants." Interestingly, as Steven Lukes has adroitly revealed, Toc-queville talked of European aristocratic society, contrapuntally to American democracy, in virtually the same terms: "[In contrast to aristocratic society, in which men were] linked closely to something beyond themselves . . . Democ-racy (in America) not only makes each man forget his forefathers, but it con-ceals from him his descendants and separates him from his contemporaries."[6] A similar sentiment could be derived from Ferdinand Tönnies's masterpiece *Gemeinschaft* and *Gesellschaft* (1887) in which he likens social life in a small community (or *gemeinschaft)* to a "living organism" where people have an essential unity of purpose, work together for the common good, and are united by ties of family, whereas life in a large city (*gesellschaft*) is charac-terized by disunity, individualism, and selfishness. Clearly, communalism is not unique to Africans, even though it is usually attributed to them. One is inclined to think, as did the Ghanaian philosopher Kwasi Wiredu (1995), that this attribution is a just one, as long as the contrast between communal-ism and individualism is not overdrawn, and provided this attribution is not stretched to assert an inherent lack of human agency and critical self-reflec-tion among Africans because of any purported communalistic mindset.

A corollary of the above cultural dichotomy is the common belief that African knowledge is unscientific and inferior because it allegedly empha-sizes the collective nature of thought. Its ontology is said to be based on a mixture of magic and supernaturalism, its epistemology is seen as culturally coded, and its content is believed to be essentially descriptive, with no endur-ing taxonomies and analytical rigor (Behera and Pietim 1999). In fact, some analysts even doubt whether high-level philosophical abstraction, as against ethnophilosophy,[7] could ever be attributed to African traditional thought. As the Ghanaian philosopher Kwame Gyekye (1995, 11–12) observes: "There are some who would withhold the term 'philosophy' from African traditional thought and would reserve that term for the philosophical work being writ-ten by African philosophers today. There are others who, on the basis of . . . their conviction that literacy is not a necessary condition for philosophiz-ing, would apply 'philosophy' to African traditional thought." However, any objective reading of the works of African philosophers, such as Odhiambo (1995), Appiah (1992), and Kaphagawani (1995), on traditional African thought will dispel this erroneous supposition. The work of Atieno Odhia-mbo, for example, shows that the early British administrators and missionar-ies working among the Jo Luo people of Kenya in the late nineteenth and early twentieth centuries found a community with an established knowledge system (*reiko*), involving not only metaphysics (*Jok*) and epistemology (*piny*), but also a well-grounded development perspective (dongruok). Similarly, as a counterpoint to the supposed communalistic mindset of traditional Africans, Rosalind Shaw has demonstrated how the Temne of Sierra Leone used their common idiom of secrecy—*tok af, lef af* (meaning, talk half, leave half)—to engage in reflexive and critical monitoring of their individual actions and interactions with others. According to Shaw, by relying on this idiom, Tamne women were able to defend and protect themselves by always keeping some secrets from others, as a precaution against the practices of socioeconomic predation during the era of slavery.

Quite expectedly, Western knowledge, on the other hand, is often portrayed uncritically as being superior, logical, scientific, and hierarchical with a well-organized network of taxonomies and academic disciplines. Western knowledge is generally deemed systematic in its accumulation; its validation, until quite recently, was purportedly ascertained through a value-neutral collection and analysis of empirical data, and its theories and metanarratives were claimed to have universal applicability and validity until the recent postmodern intellectual insurgency spearheaded by radicals like Foucault, Derrida, and Lyotard. As Eric Wolf points out, such assertions of Western cultural superiority are based on the expedient assumption that the West has its own genealogy in which ancient Greece begat Rome, Rome begat Christian Europe, Christian Europe begat Renaissance, the Renaissance Enlightenment and so on, with no ties to the non-West (Wolf, 1997). Such a "mythmaking scheme," to borrow the words of Eric Wolf (1997, 5), disregards the influence of non-Western cultures on the West; it self-servingly overlooks the fact that until the fourteenth century, the West was the recipient of cultural influence from non-Western sources, especially China, India, and Africa, in what Nederveen Pieterse (1995, 45–68) calls the South-North cultural osmosis.

Moreover, as Vincent Tucker points out, by ignoring its genealogical ties with the non-West, the West has managed to label societies that deviate from its own standards as "traditional" or "primitive," notwithstanding the objective fact that they are contemporaneous with those who label them as such (Tucker 1997, 8). And as Wolf rightly points out, this genealogy "turns history into a moral success story, a race in time in which each runner of the race passes on the torch of liberty to the next relay. . . . [T]his turns into a story of how the winners prove that they are virtuous and good by winning" (Wolf 1997, 5). Beneath it all is the unfortunate presumption that Africa, in particular, has very little, if anything, to contribute to the cultural development of the West. Like all myths, there is some analytical value in cultural dichotomies—hence their enduring popularity. However, once we conceive culture in dialectical terms, it is virtually impossible to adhere to any such dichotomies. While one can still talk loosely or metaphorically about an African culture (as done in this chapter), it is argued that there is no such thing as an "essential" African culture, which can be set as a binary opposite to Western culture. The notion of a "pure African culture" is insensitive to the long-standing cultural interchange between societies, an interchange that has been intensified by contemporary globalization and crystallized by such analytical concepts as cultural hybridization and indigenization. In the final analysis, the cultural convergence argument presumes that African societies are like palimpsest upon which Westerners, especially Americans, can just (re) write their cultural ideas without any modification or human agency on the part of Africans. However, as Appadurai (1996, 32) has pointed out: "What these arguments fail to consider is that at least as rapidly as forces from various metropolises are brought into new societies they tend to become indigenized in one or another way: this is true of music and housing styles as much as it is true of science and terrorism, spectacle and constitutions."

Perhaps no one has articulated the prevalence of cultural hybridity and indigenization more shrewdly than Eric Wolf and Jan Nederveen Pieterse; the latter talks of how these processes create such multiple identities as having "Thai boxing by Moroccan girls, Asian rap, Irish bagels, Chinese tacos . . . or Mexican school girls dressed in Greek togas dancing in the style of Isidora Duncan" (Nederveen Pieterse 1995, 45–68). And in the words of Wolf (1997, x), "human societies and cultures would not be properly understood until we learn to visualize them in their mutual interrelationships and interdependence in space and time." The recognition that local cultural practices, interests, and problems have international, even global, ramifications, and vice versa, is increasingly captured by the composite term "glocalization," coined by Roland Robertson in 1995.[8] As an analytical tool, glocalization undermines the tendency to treat local issues as though they are mutually exclusive from global trends. It points to the cultural interpenetration that occurs when powerful "top-down" globalizing forces encounter "bottom-up processes of localization" (Tehranian and Tehranian 1997, 148). Economists have long deployed glocalization in micromarketing—the deliberate tailoring of multinational goods and services (such as those of MTV, CNN, and McDonalds) to suit the taste of local consumers.

Cultural Hybridity and Indigenization: The Specific Case of Africa

What are some of the cultural practices and imaginaries that Africans have borrowed from the outside world and indigenized, and vice versa? Notwithstanding the disparities in economic and political power between Africa and the *Rest*, there is much evidence that two-way borrowing and indigenization have long been the norm, not the exception, in the cultural encounter between the two entities. Cultural hybridity and indigenization are discernable in a wide range of African sociocultural spheres, including dance and music, sports and entertainment, dress and fashion, visual art and literature, and science and technology, to mention just a few. For instance, the celebrated cultural mélange between Africans, the Rastafarian movement in Jamaica, and African Americans has transformed hair dreadlocks and braids, traditionally worn by African fetish priests and women, into a global fashion phenomenon (some versions of which are even Westernized with artificial hair extensions now being worn by both Blacks and non-Blacks, men and women, in many different parts of the world). Similar indigenization is implicated in the increasing presence of African soccer players in the European soccer scene. Soccer, a staple of contemporary African sports, exported to the continent by Europeans in the colonial era and subsequently indigenized with Africans' brand of speed and dribbling maneuvers, is presently producing more African expatriate players in Europe than any other sports.

The growing popularity of African music—notably, Congolese Soukous, Ghana's *Highlife*, Nigeria's *Juju*, East Africa's *Taarab*, and South Africa's *Kwela*—and African musicians—for example, South Africa's Mariam Makeba and Hugh Maskela; Nigeria's Fela Anikulapo and Sunny Ade; Ghana's Dada Lumba; and Zimbabwe's Thomas Mapfumo—not only among African diasporic communities in the West but also among Westerners who follow world music, is a testament to the heightened cultural mixing underway. This kind of hybridity in music has occasionally led to well-received collaborations between African artists and their Western counterparts, such as those between Paul Simon, Peter Gabriel, and David Byrne and African musicians in the 1980s. Perhaps no African music epitomizes cultural mixing more than the East African *Taarab*, whose origins go back to the long history of intercultural exchange between the Swahili-speaking people of the Indian Ocean coast of Africa and the Arabic-speaking world. It features not only African instruments and Indian *tabla* drums, but also Western electric guitar, electric keyboard, violin, and accordion. Furthermore, it is now not uncommon to find Africans listening to the music of local artists on CDs or watching locally produced drama on DVDs in nearly all major African cities, from Lagos through Accra to Abidjan; from Nairobi through Harare to Johannesburg; and from Cairo through Algiers to Casablanca.[9] In fact, the proliferation of North American-style radio and TV talk show *a-la-Opera* across Africa is not much different: even though the format and technology involved can be traced to the West, the issues discussed are of local relevance. Evidently, the Western mass media are not the "opium of the African mass,"[10] they provoke human agency in the form of cultural selectivity, adaptations, and sometimes, resistance across the continent.

More substantively, the fact that Western fine art masters, including Pablo Picasso, Henri Matisse, and Jacques Lipchitz, were heavily influenced by African art is well-documented by art historians and cultural critics like Edward Said (1993) and Lori Verderame.[11] Picasso's groundbreaking *Les Demoiselles d'Avignon* (1907–9), which initiated Cubism in fine art, derives much of its inspiration from the ceremonial mask of the Dogon tribe of Mali. In his treatise *Notes of a Painter*, Matisse writes that his arbitrary use of bold colors stirred emotions that are not different from those associated with the ritualistic African art from which he had long drawn inspiration. It would take more than a single journal article to provide a broad overview of the wealth of thematic insights gained through cultural exchange between Africans and the outside world in the area of literary studies and literature over the years. The unique perspectives offered by African speech patterns and cultural interpretations in the works of such notables as Amos Tutola, Chinua Achebe, and Wole Soyinka of Nigeria; Peter Abrahams, Solomon Plaatze, John Maxwell Coetzee, Neville Alexander, and Thomas Mofolo of South Africa; Ngugi wa Thiong'o of Kenya; Nuruddin Farah of Somalia; and George Awoonor-Williams and Kwasi Brew of Ghana are now recognized by literary critics worldwide. Many of these critics—especially in the United States with the proliferation of African American studies since the 1960s—are now quick to add African writers' series to their curricula.

It is important to stress that the encounter between African and non-African cultures has not been one of a simple interpenetration and interrelationship; rather, it has been filled with contradictions, and their attendant potential for progress and self-consciousness, in the true spirit of Marx's (and, indeed, Hegel's) dialectics. Perhaps nowhere are these contradictions more evident than in literary studies and literature, where the encounter with Africa has compelled scholars to grapple with the very notion of "African literature," while the texts themselves are usually written in non-African languages (mostly in English and French). As Miller (1993, 221) observes: "In its etymology, the Latin word for letter, 'literature,' implies writing, and in literary studies it is taken for granted that the object in question will be written." This is largely true for Africa as well, with one important difference: the long shadow cast by oral traditions. It is impossible to consider Africa "literature" in any broad sense without taking orality into account. Scholars, especially in the West, are faced with the difficulty of adjusting to what appears to be a classic oxymoron: "oral literature." Miller writes that some have even resorted to the neologism "orature" to get around this bottleneck (1993, 221). Undoubtedly, such dialectical tensions have historically pushed disciplinary boundaries toward critical reflexivity and eventually toward the Hegelian self-consciousness. Several collections in the well-received monograph *Africa and the Disciplines* (Bates, Mudimbe, and O'Barr 1993) show that such dialectical tensions, and their attendant opportunities for critical reflexivity and intellectual advancement, are common in social science and humanity disciplines. In the case of anthropology, for instance, Sally Moore demonstrates that if a discipline could be said to ever have a taproot, then research in Africa could be the one for anthropology. And with the ongoing cultural turn, and the growing influence of anthropology in the social sciences and humanities, one could, by a simple extrapolation, recognize the subtle contributions of research in Africa to the Western academy (Moore 1993). Richard Sklar's contribution to the above monograph shows that political scientists studying in Africa pioneered research in such diverse area as "ethnic conflict" and "the revolutionary potential of the peasantry" (1993, 83–110). Not only that, Africanists contributed immensely to the dependency theory and the politics of modernization, and according to Sklar, the concept of neocolonialism was first featured in the writings of Kwame Nkrumah. As Sklar further notes, research in Africa is uniquely positioned to investigate the role of "dual authority," or the coexistence of modern states with traditional political systems such as chieftaincy. One might also add, even anecdotally, that in political thought, it was the admixture of Marxism and Africa communalism, in particular, that culminated in such well-known African ideologies as Julius Nyerere's *ujamaa* in Tanzania, Kenneth Kaunda's *humanism* in Zambia, Didier Ratsiraka's *fokonolona* in Malagasy, and Qadhafi's *jamariya* in Libya. While the *jamariya*, like the others, derived many of its insights from Marxism, Qadhafi ended up setting it contrapuntally not only to liberal democracy and capitalism, but also to Marxism (to some extent) in his infamous *Green Book*, with which he advocated for nonalignment among countries of the developing world.

The dialectical mixing of African and non-African scholarship goes beyond the humanities and social sciences. Through provocative books such as *Blacks in Sciences; Stolen Legacy; Africa Counts; The Pyramids; World's Greatest Men of Color;* and *Destruction of Black Civilization*, Africanists have painstakingly excavated the roots of modern science and mathematics, highlighting the contributions of Africans and people of African descent to these disciplines as a counterpoint to the Eurocentric orthodoxy that traces the origins of nearly all science and mathematics to Europe and, to some limited extent, Asia, with Africa relegated to the background, as usual (see van Sertima 1983; Fakhry 1975; Rogers 1973; Williams 1974).

Relations of Power and Resistance

While the concepts of hybridity, glocalization, and indignation may be better signifiers of the cultural connections between Africa and the *Rest* than cultural imperialism, we still need to heed Ong (1999) and Barker's (2003, 175) call to explore the unequal power implicated in such relationships. The point here is not complicated, for as Ong puts it: "When an approach to cultural globalization seeks merely to sketch out universalizing trends rather than deal with actually existing structures of power as situated cultural process, the analysis cries out for a sense of political economy and situated ethnography" (1999, 11). Even though the nexus between Africa and the *Rest* is generally two-way, when one looks hard enough, one would realize, as did Nederveen Pieterse, that "relations of power and hegemony are inscribed and reproduced within [the ongoing cultural] hybridity" (1995, 57). Globalization has long been an uneven process, not only in the geographic sense that some regions of the world have become increasingly interlinked in terms of material and cultural flows, while others, such as Africa, have become marginalized, but also in the political economic sense that the attendant socioeconomic and cultural mélange of globalization encompasses unequal power, domination, and resistance.

Unquestionably, the effects of Africa's contribution to the West in areas such as dress and fashion, sports, fine art, music, science, and technology pale in comparison to the long-standing effects of European missionary activities, colonialism, slavery, science, and technology on Africa. Most Africans are unequal participants in contemporary globalization, not only because of present power inequities, but also because of the material and epistemic violence wrought by the Western imperialism of the past. Perhaps nowhere is this power inequity more entrenched, yet overlooked, in academic discourse, than in the area of international migration and the much touted time-space compression engendered by modern transportation and communication technology. Without probing into their political economy, we are left with the misleading impression in the prevailing discourse that perhaps everyone can take advantage of these phenomena. Yet, with regards to time-space compression technologies and other physical infrastructure, the gap between Africa and the *Rest* continues to grow, creating opportunities for transnational airlines, telephone, internet, and money transfer companies, among many others, to take undue advantage of Africans at home and abroad. The power disparities accrued to holders of Western, as opposed to African, passports in international travel and tourism today, and the massive brain drain from Africa to the West, are now well known. At the same time, as the work of Ong (1999) shows, the ability of racial minority immigrants (such as Africans and Chinese) to convert their intellectual and economic capital into social prestige in the West has generally been inhibited by the racially laced moral order of many Western societies.

Globalization is a game in which the dice are clearly loaded against Africans. Still, Africans have not been the "passive doormats" of globalization over the years. There are several examples of cultural intransigence and intellectual insurgency on the parts of Africans (or, more generally, people of African descent) ever since their encounter with Western colonialism, imperialism, and now, globalization. The audacious scholarship of the likes of Frantz Fanon on colonialism and racism; Walter Rodney on European imperialism and exploitation; Kwame Nkrumah on Neocolonialism; Amílcar Cabral on liberation struggle; the Egyptian-born Marxist scholar Samir Amin on "Eurocentrism," and more recently, on what he calls the "Liberal Virus" spread primarily through Americanization; A. M. Babu on the international division of labor, espoused by Western economic theories, which compels African economies to specialize in primary commodities; and the influential Nigerian political economist Bade Onimode and social scientist Claude Ake in their hard-hitting condemnation of Western social science as a "Bourgeois Social Science" and "Imperialist Social Science," respectively, are examples of how Africans are talking back (Fanon 1963; Rodney 1974; Nkrumah 1966; Amin 1989, 2004; Onimode 1988; Ake 1982). For example, Onimode (1988, 25) contends that "*the paradigms, theories and policy prescriptions* of bourgeois social science (i.e., Western social science) in Africa are basically socially irrelevant to the African and the Third World situation." To him, Marxist social science is the only reasonable alternative; in his view, notwithstanding its shortcoming, it corresponds more to the objective social reality in Africa (*ibid.*, 40–41).

In a similar vein, Atieno Odhiambo (1995, 247) recounts the story of Samuel Ayany, the Kenya educator and public intellectual who subverted the British imperial history he taught to Kenyan students in the 1950s, not only by teaching parts of it in *Dholuo*, but also by spending much of his time teaching against colonialism itself. The work of Esteva and Prakash (1997) also points to how people across Africa (and Latin America and Asia) are increasingly challenging the purported universality of human rights, as espoused by the West. The recent criticisms by Achille Mbembe (2001) and AbdouMaliq Simone (2004) over the prevalent cynical prejudice about Africans and African cities, respectively, and by Mahmood Mamdani (1996) on the common tendency to examine African history by way of analogy to European history, instead of studying it as a process in its own right or as a legitimate unit of analysis, are just a few examples of the new additions to the enduring tradition of critical scholarship from Africa(ns). Perhaps Edward Said was not exaggerating when he said that "in general there is an oppositional quality to the consciousness of many Third World scholars and intellectuals," considering the proliferation of what Foucault might call "subjugated knowledge" in nearly all fields once dominated by Western traditions. In the final analysis, though, this resistance is not surprising, for "no matter how apparently complete the dominance of an ideology or social system, there are always going to be parts of the social experience that it does not cover and control. From these parts very frequently comes opposition, both conscious and dialectical" (Said 1993, 240). And who among us would deny that hegemonic practices tend to sow their own counterhegemonic seeds? For more on contemporary social resistance movements in Africa, consult Chapter 4 of this volume, written by the late Ed. O. Prempeh.

CONCLUSION

The conjoint analysis of culture and globalization is hardly novel—what is new here is the specific focus on Africa, using dialectical reasoning. The analysis pursued clearly indicates that both culture and globalization are multifaceted, dialectical phenomena imbued with change, flux, and instability. At the very least, the arguments presented suggest that cultural discourse has just as much to contribute to our understanding of globalization in Africa as does political economic analysis, despite the perfunctory attention given to the former in much of the existing literature. With the aid of the three related concepts of hybridization, indigenization, and glocalization, this chapter has shown that any assertion of an ongoing globalization-induced erosion of African culture is problematic. Notwithstanding the obvious economic and political power disparity between Africa and the *Rest*, the cultural encounter between the two entities has been a two-way street—indeed, that has always been the case. At the same time, there is no denying that relations of power and resistance have always been implicated in the ensuing cultural mixing. In consonance with the dialectical reasoning adopted, categorical assertions were, for the most part, eschewed with the aid of necessary caveats. For instance, the opposition mounted against the occurrence of "cultural homogenization" in favor of "cultural heteroginization" was qualified by a candid admission of the fact that some level of the former is taking place. Similarly, while some have argued that there is no such thing as culture, the arguments presented here suggest that there is culture, but not in a pure, unadulterated form. The avoidance of categorical statements is certainly not a tactical ploy to play both sides of the respective debates. Rather, it pays homage to, and reinforces the value of, dialectical reasoning, which, among other things, dissolves binary opposites and entertains internal contradictions. In addition, the slightest acquaintance with dialectics would suggest that the only dogma in its mode of thinking is that nothing is dogmatic.

REFERENCES

Abraham, W. E. 1962. *The mind of Africa.* Chicago: University of Chicago Press.

Adorno, T. W. 1973. *Negative dialectics.* London: Routledge & Kegan Paul.

Appadurai, Arjun. 1996. *Modernity at large: Cultural dimensions of globalization.* London and Minneapolis: University of Minnesota Press.

Appiah, Kwame Anthony. 1992. *In my father's house: Africa in the philosophy of culture.* Oxford and New York: Oxford University Press.

Chilcote, Ronald H. 1991. *Amílcar Cabral's revolutionary theory and practice.* Boulder and London: Lynne Rienner.

Amin, Samir. 1989. *Eurocentrism.* New York: Monthly Review Press.

———. 2004. *The liberal virus.* New York: Monthly Review Press.

Ake, Claude. 1982. *Social science as imperialism: The theory of political development.* Ibadan: Ibadan University Press.

Atieno Odhiambo, E. S. 1992. From warriors to Jonanga: The struggle over nakedness by the Luo of Kenya. In *Sokomoki: Popular culture in East African, ed.* W. Graebner, 11–22. Amsterdam and Atlanta: Rodopi.

———. 1995. Luo perspectives on knowledge and development. In *African Philosophy as cultural inquiry,* ed. Ivan Karp and D. A. Masolo, 244–58. Bloomington and Indianapolis: Indiana University Press.

Babu, Salma, and Amrit Wilson, eds. 2002. *Babu: The future that works, selected writings of A. M. Babu.* Trenton, NJ: Africa World.

Barber, Benjamin. 1996. *Jihad vs. McWorld.* New York: Ballantine Books.

Barker, Chris. 2003. *Cultural studies: Theory and practice.* London and Thousand Oaks, CA: Sage Publications.

Bates, Robert H., V. Y. Mudimbe, and Jean O'Barr, eds. 1993. *Africa and the disciplines: The contributions of research in Africa to the social sciences and humanities.* Chicago and London: The University of Chicago Press.

Behera, Deepak, and Erasmus Pietim. 1999. Sustainable development of indigenous populations: Challenges ahead. *South Africa Journal of Ethnology* 22 (1): 1–7.

Bhola, H. S. 2002. Reclaiming old heritage for proclaiming future history: The knowledge-for-development debate in African contexts. *Africa Today* 49, no. 3 (Fall): 3–21.

Bond, P. 2006. *Looting Africa: The economics of exploitation.* London: Zed Books.

Chomsky, Noam. 2002. *Understanding power.* New York: The New Press.

Cornford, Francis M. 1957. *Plato's theory of knowledge.* New York: The Liberal Arts Press.

Cosgrove, D., and S. Daniels, eds. 1988. *Iconography of landscape: Essays on the symbolic representation, design, and use of past environments.* Cambridge: Cambridge University Press.

Cox, Robert W. 1987. *Production, power, and world order: Social forces in the making of history*. New York: Columbia University Press.

Dumont, L. 1985. A modified view of our origins: The Christian beginnings of modern individualism. In *The category of the person, ed.* M. Carrithers, S. Collins, and S. Lukes, 93–122. Cambridge, UK: Cambridge University Press.

Edgar, Andrew. 1999. Dialectics. In *Cultural theory: The key concepts*, ed. Andrew Edgar and Peter Sedgwick, 113–15. London: Routledge.

Esteva, Gustavo, and Madhu Suri Prakash. 1997. From global thinking to local thinking. In *The post-development reader*, ed. Majid Rahnema, 277–89. London and New Jersey: Zed Books.

Fagan, G. H. 1999. Cultural politics and (post) development paradigm. In *Critical development theory*, ed. Ronaldo Munck and Denis O'Hearn, 178–95. London and New York: Zed Books.

Fakhry, Ahmed. 1975. *The pyramids*. Chicago: University of Chicago Press.

Fanon, Frantz. 1963. *The wretched of the earth*. New York: Grove.

Giddens, Anthony. 1991. *Modernity and self-identity*. Cambridge, MA: Polity.

———. 2000. *Runaway world: How globalization is reshaping our lives*. New York: Routledge.

Gilpin, Robert. 1987. *The political economy of international relations*. Princeton, NJ: Princeton University Press.

———. 2000. *The challenge of global capitalism*. Princeton, NJ: Princeton University Press.

Guillén, Mauro F. 2001. Is globalization civilizing, destructive or feeble: A critique of five key debates in the social science literature. *Annual Review of Sociology* 27:235–60.

Gyekye, Kwame. 1995. African philosophy. In *The Cambridge dictionary of philosophy*, ed. Robert Audi, 11–12. Cambridge, UK: Cambridge University Press.

Hall, Stuart. 1992. Cultural studies and its theoretical legacies. In *Cultural studies*, ed. Lawrence Grossberg, Cary Nelson, and Paula Treichler, 277–94. New York: Routledge.

———. 2002. The west and the rest: Discourse and power. In *Development: A cultural studies Reader*, ed. Susanne Schech and Jane Haggis, 56–64. Oxford: Blackwell.

Harvey, David. 1990. *The condition of postmodernity*. Cambridge, MA and Oxford, UK.

———. 1995. A geographer's guide to dialectical thinking. In *Diffusing geography: Essays for Peter Haggett*, ed. A. D. Cliff, P. R. Gould, A. G. Hoare, and N. J. Thrift, 3–21. Cambridge, MA: Blackwell.

———. 1996. *Justice, nature & the geography of difference*. Cambridge, MA: Blackwell.

———. 2007. *A brief history of neoliberalism*. Oxford: Oxford University Press.

Held, D., A. McGrew, D. Goldblatt, and J. Perrato.1999. *Global transformations*. Stanford, CA: Stanford University Press.

Huntington, Samuel P. 2002. A universal civilization? Modernization and westernization. In *Development: A cultural studies reader*, ed. Susanne Schech and Jane Haggis, 19–31. Oxford: Blackwell.

Jackson, Peter. 1989. *Maps of meaning: An introduction to cultural geography*. London: Unwin Hyman.

Kaphagawani, D. N. 1995. Some African conception of persons: A critique. In *African philosophy as cultural inquiry*, ed. Ivan Karp and D. A. Masolo, 66–79. Bloomington and Indianapolis: Indiana University Press.

Karp, Ivan, and D. A. Masolo. 1995. Introduction. In *African philosophy as cultural inquiry*, ed. Ivan Karp and D. A. Masolo, 4. Indianapolis: Indiana University Press.

Kennedy, Paul. 1993. *Preparing for the twenty-first century*. New York: Random House.

Kirkpatrick, J., and G. M. White. 1985. Exploring ethnopsychologies. In *Person, self, and experience: Exploring pacific ethnopsychologies*, ed. G. M. White and J. Kirkpatrick, 3–32. Berkeley: University of California Press.

Knox, Paul, and Sallie A. Marston. 2001. *Human geography: Places and regions in global context*. Upper Saddle River, NJ: Prentice Hall.

Kobrin, Stempher. 1997. The architecture of globalization: State sovereignty in a networked global economy. In *Government, globalization, and international business*, ed. J. H. Dunning, 147–48. New York: Oxford University Press.

Lichtman, Richard. 1970. *An outline of Marxism*. Toronto: Forum House Publishing Company.

Lukes, Steven. 1973. *Individualism*. Oxford: Basil Blackwell.

Lyotard, Jean-Francois.1984. *The postmodern condition: A report on knowledge*. Minneapolis: University of Minnesota Press.

Mamdani, Mahmood. 1996. *Citizen and subject*. Princeton, NJ: Princeton University Press.

Markus, H. R., and S. Kitayama. 1991. Culture and self: Implications for cognition, emotion, and motivation. *Psychological Review* 98:224–53.

Mbembe, Achille, 2001. *On the postcolony*. Berkeley, Los Angeles, London: University of California Press, 2001.

Miller, Christopher L. 1993. The challenge of intercultural literary. In *Africa and the disciplines: The contributions of research in Africa to the social sciences and humanities*, ed. Robert Bate, V. Y. Mudimbe, and Jean O'Barr, 221–76. Chicago and London: University of Chicago Press.

Miller. J. G. 1997. Theoretical issues in cultural psychology. In *Handbook of cross-cultural psychology*, ed. J. W. Berry, Y. H. Poortinga, and J. Pandey, 105. Boston: Allyn & Bacon.

Mitchell, Don. 2001. *Cultural geography: A critical introduction*. Oxford, UK: Blackwell.

Moore, David. 2001. Neoliberal globalization and the triple crisis of modernisation in Africa: Zimbabwe, the Democratic Republic of the Congo, and South Africa. *Third World Quarterly* 22:909–29.

Moore, Nancy. 2004. The myth of unadulterated culture meets the threat of imported media. *Media, Culture & Society* 24:278–89.

Moore, Sally Falk. 1993. Changing perspective on a changing Africa: The work of anthropology. In *Africa and the disciplines: The contribution of research in Africa to the social sciences and humanities*, eds. Robert H. Bates, V.Y. Mudimbe, and Jean O'Barr, 3–57. Chicago: University of Chicago Press.

Munck, Ronaldo and Denis O'Hearn, eds. 1999. *Critical development theory*. London and New York: Zed Books.

Nederveen Pieterse, Jan 1995. The cultural turn in development: Questions of power. *The European Journal of Development Research* 7 (1): 176–96.

———. 1995. Globalization as hybridization. In *Global modernities*, ed. M. Featherstone, S. Lash, and R. Robertson, 45–68. London: Sage.

———. Critical holism and the Tao of development. In *Critical development theory*, ed. Ronaldo Munck and Denis O'Hearn, 63–88. London: Zed Books.

Nkrumah, Kwame. 1966. *Neo-colonialism: The last state of imperialism*. New York: International Publishers.

Norton, William. 2000. *Cultural geography: Themes, concepts, analyses*. Don Mills, Ontario: Oxford University Press.

Ollman, B. 1990. Putting dialectics to work: The process of abstraction in Marx's method. *Rethinking Marxism* 3 (1): 49.

Ong, Aihwa. 1999. *Flexible citizenship: The cultural logic of transnationality*. Durham, NC: Duke University Press.

Onimode, Bade. 1988. *A political economy of the African crisis*. London & New Jersey: Zed Books.

Robertson, Roland. 1992. *Globalization: Social theory and global culture*. London: Sage.

———. 1995. Globalization: Time-space and homogeneity-heterogeneity. In *Global modernities*, ed. M. Featherstone, S. Lash, and R. Robertson, 25–44. London: Sage.

Robinson, Guy. 1998. *Methods and techniques in human geography*. New York: John Wiley.

Rodney, Walter. 1974. *How Europe underdeveloped Africa*. Washington, DC: Howard University Press.

Rogers, Joel A. 1973. *World's greatest men of color I & II*. New York: MacMillan.

Roseberry, William. 1989. *Anthropologies and histories: Essays in culture, history, and political economy*. New Brunswick and London: Rutgers University Press.

Said, Edward. 1993. *Culture and imperialism*. London: Vintage.

Schiller, H. 1976. *Communication and cultural domination*. New York: M. E. Sharpe.

Shaw, Rosalind. 1995. "Tok af, lef af": A political economic of Temne techniques of secrecy and self. In *African philosophy as cultural inquiry*, ed. Ivan Karp and D.A. Masolo, 25–49. Indianapolis: Indiana University Press.

Simone, AddouMaliq. 2004. *For the city yet to come: Changing African life in four cities*. Durham and London: Duke University Press.

Sklair, L. 1991. *Sociology of the global system*. New York: Harvester Wheatsheaf.

Sklar, Richard. 1993. The African frontier for political science. In *Africa and the Disciplines*, ed. Robert H. Bates, V.Y. Mudimbe, and Jean O'Barr, 83–110. Chicago: University of Chicago Press.

Soros, George. 2000. *The crisis of global capitalism revisited*. New York: Public Affairs Press.

Spencer, J. E., and W. L. Thomas, Jr. 1973. *Introducing cultural geography*. New York: Wiley.

Stiglitz, Joseph. 2003. *Globalization and its discontent*. London and New York: W.W. Norton.

Tehranian, M., and K. T. Tehranian. 1997. Taming modernity: Towards a new paradigm. In *International communication and globalization*, ed. Ali Mohammadi, 148. London: Sage.

Tempels, Placide. 1959. *Bantu philosophy*. Paris: Présence Africaine.

The Economist. Africa, the Hopeless Continent. May 13–19, 2000: p. 15.

Tucker, Vincent. 1997. *Cultural perspectives on development*. London: Frank Cass, 1997.

———. 1999. Myth of development: A critique of a Eurocentric discourse. In *Critical Development Theory*, ed. Ronaldo Munck and Denis O'Hearn, 1–26, London and New York: Zed Books.

van Sertima, Ivan, ed. 1983. *Blacks in science: Ancient and modern*. New Brunswick, NJ: Transaction Books.

Verderame, Lori. 2005. African art and Picasso. http://www.drloriv.com/lectures/arican.asp.

Vernon, Raymond. 1971. *Sovereignty at bay: The multinational spread of U.S. enterprise*. New York: Basic Books.

———. 1998. *The hurricane's eye: The troubled prospects of multinational enterprise*. Cambridge, MA: Harvard University Press.

Waters, M. 1995. *Globalization*. New York: Routledge.

Williams, Chancellor. 1974. *Destruction of black civilization*. Chicago: Third World.

Williams, Raymond. 1976. *Keywords: A vocabulary of culture and society*. Glasgow: Fontana.

Wolf, Eric. 1997. *Europe and the people without history*. Berkeley: University of California Press.

Wiredu, Kwasi. 1995. Our problem of knowledge: Brief reflections on knowledge and development in Africa. In *African philosophy as cultural inquiry*, ed. Ivan Karp and D. A. Masolo, 181–86. Bloomington and Indianapolis: Indiana University Press.

NOTES

1. This is one of many constructive insights offered by Udo Krautwurst to an earlier version of this chapter, for which I am very grateful.

2. Examples of such Socratic dialogues are *Euthyphro, Crito, Phaedo, Protagoras, Meno, and Philebus*.

3. Interestingly, Socrates' own mother Phaenarete was a midwife. See Francis M. Cornford (1957) *Plato's theory of knowledge*.

4. Ollman (1990, 49) defines contradictions in dialectics as a union of two or more internally related processes that are simultaneously supporting and undermining one another.

5. Unless, of course, one disagrees that some form of false consciousness is occurring in this case.

6. Quoted in Lukes (1973, 13).

7. Ivan Karp and D. A. Masolo define ethnophilosophy as the "study of collective forms of culture as manifestations of African philosophical systems" in their introduction to *African philosophy as cultural inquiry* (1995, 4).

8. See Roland Robertson's *Globalization: Social theory and global culture* (1995).

9. The same can be said of Africans in the Diaspora.

10. The phrase, as used here, is borrowed from Arjun Appadurai's *Modernity at large* (7), who obviously derived it from Karl Marx.

11. See Lori Verderame, African Art and Picasso, http://www.drloriv.com/lectures/african.asp.

CHAPTER 3

THE ANTICAPITALISM MOVEMENT AND AFRICAN RESISTANCE TO NEOLIBERAL GLOBALIZATION*

Edward Osei Kwadwo Prempeh

INTRODUCTION

As contemporary neoliberal globalization has intensified and consolidated since the 1980s, its hegemonic and exploitative nature has provoked new waves and modalities of contestation and resistance. The contested and politicized nature of neoliberal globalization, which Arturo Escobar (2004, 207) aptly refers to as "a new US-based form of imperial globality, an economic-military-ideological order that subordinates regions, peoples, and economies world-wide," has drawn attention to the challenge of resisting the global dominance of this process. The key political tension exists between the forces of globalization and the forces of resistance, and at the heart of this is a paradox: globalization both weakens and simultaneously reinvigorates the forces of contestation and resistance. Put another way, imperial globality is provoking the emergence of new grassroots-based social movements, which are engaged in counterhegemonic struggles that represent both a challenge and alternative to this new form of colonialism, especially specific African popular struggles and manifestations of the deglobalization of capital orientation. Indeed, the proliferation of these social movements and civil society groups,

---

*This is a posthumous publication by Ed, whose sad, untimely passing occurred in 2007 (in the middle of this book project). If you have any questions about this chapter, kindly direct them to the editor at jmensah@yorku.ca.

beginning in the mid-1980s and continuing to the present, has posed serious challenges to the hegemonic discourse and project of neoliberalism.

This can be seen in the resistance of the "movement of movements" engaged in the deglobalization struggle that seeks to present a broader challenge to the hegemonic impulses of capitalism at the World Social Forum (WSF) and the African Social Forum (ASF), key sites for the rejection of the neoliberal policies of privatization, deregulation, and commodification. This chapter attempts to provide a detailed account of how spaces are being opened up within emerging social movements in order to contest this imperial globality; in particular, the chapter looks at movements emerging out of different cultures. Both the WSF and the ASF respond to the neoliberal position that there is no alternative to neoliberalism, by suggesting in bold, assertive terms that, indeed, "Another World Is Possible, Another Africa Is Possible." It is argued that the uneven and unequal nature of capitalist globalization has intensified both the need for, and the strength of, the convergence of new social movements rebelling against the system of imperial globality. The ASF is an example of specific African knowledge arising from activist practice with roots in an African culture of resistance that was on display during the anticolonial struggle. It has significance for explaining and coming to terms with radical African progressive social movements in contestation and resistance to corporate globalization.

The first section of this chapter provides a brief survey of some of the more progressive views on understanding resistance to the neoliberal project. This survey sets the stage for the following section, which aims to outline a more radical and progressive anticapitalist alternative to neoliberal globalization. This section has two main objectives. The first is to provide a detailed analysis of the political project of the global "movement of movements." The second is to outline ways in which African civil society groups have mobilized to resist globalization.

UNDERSTANDING RESISTANCE
TO IMPERIAL GLOBALITY

The consequences of globalization—arguably one of the most wide-ranging and unsettling systemic trends in contemporary history—remain quite open and will be considerably influenced by the sorts of knowledge constructed about, and fed into, the process. To date, orthodox (and especially liberal) discourses have held an upper hand, but ample opportunities remain to salvage notions of globalization for critical theory and associated politics of emancipation (Scholte 1996, 44).

As Eleonore Kofman and Gillian Youngs (1996, 1) aptly point out, "globalization relates as much to a way of thinking about the world as it does to a description of the dynamics of political and economic relations within it. Globalization has opened up new imperatives for investigating power linkages between thought and action, knowledge and being, structure and process." The crux of the matter is globalization's tendency to disempower and exclude marginalized groups and societies. Such exclusion and disempowerment serves as the basis for a politics of resistance whose main objective is to open up space for political mobilization in opposition to the globalizing logic of the market and finance. The general insight that provides a foundation for this section is that the increasing intensity and extent of globalization has generated a counterhegemonic critique.

Indeed, Scholte's above-noted quote about the consequences of globalization highlights the growing body of critical work that seeks to establish an alternative, more critical discourse to challenge the hegemony of the prevailing neoliberal globalization discourse. Thus, Scholte (1996, 51) makes the bold claim that "critical knowledge has as its primary conscious purpose to identify disempowerment and promote politics of emancipation." The alternative critical discourse is said to expose the limits of the dominant discourse and its hegemonic power tendencies and effects. In so doing, this counterhegemonic discourse shakes the dominant discourse from its claimed timeless pedestal.

While delving into the counterhegemonic discourse, it is commonplace to examine the underlying critique of globalization that has laid the groundwork for such a discourse. There are many underlying reasons for this new oppositional politics. Central to this is the unequal and uneven nature of globalization. The political project of the countermovement is thus a struggle that seeks to transform the principles underlying globalization and radically reconfigure its foundations. This new political project has two main characteristics. First, it is an attempt at counterhegemonic mobilization and organizing in response to the hegemonic discourse of globalization. Second, the counterhegemonic discourse and literature seeks to articulate a different vision of globalization by uncovering the countervailing political dynamics to the process of globalization. How can we come to terms with the contestation and resistance to the neoliberal project?

While much scholarly attention has focused on the homogenizing thrust of the current phase of capitalist globalization in the economic, political, social, cultural, and ideological landscapes through time-space compression, global commodity cultures, or a borderless world, critics have drawn attention to the increasing marginalization of subaltern groups and the establishment of new networks of social movements—movements that are engaged in a "new politics" of contestation with the new "empire" over the exercise of power. This critical view makes important contributions to understandings of the frameworks for resisting neoliberal globalization. According to David Harvey, contemporary capitalism, as it has unfolded in the neoliberal project, is distinguished by its tendency toward expanded reproduction and the process of "accumulation through dispossession"—accumulation by dispossession is the hallmark and defining element of the dominant form of primitive accumulation. According to Harvey (2003, 184–85): "Accumulation by dispossession re-emerged from the shadowy position it had held prior to 1970 to become a major feature within the capitalist logic. . . . On the one hand, the release of low-cost assets [through privatization] provided vast fields for the absorption of surplus capitals. On the other, it provided a means to visit the costs of devaluation or surplus capitals upon the weakest and most vulnerable territories and populations." Here, contemporary capitalism is marked by the persistence of primitive accumulation as a strategy for overcoming crises of overaccumulation. Harvey borrows from Marx's views on primitive accumulation which, according to Marx, incorporates a whole range of processes: "These include the commodification of land and the forceful expulsion of peasant populations; the conversion of various forms of property rights (common, collective, state, etc.) into exclusive private property rights; the suppression of rights to the commons; the commodification of labour power and the suppression of alternative (indigenous) forms of production and consumption; colonial, neocolonial, and imperial appropriation of assets (including natural resources); the monetization of exchange and taxation, particularly of land; the slave trade; usury; the national debt, and ultimately the credit system as radical means of primitive accumulation" (Harvey 2003, 145). The strength of Harvey's intervention lies in his emphasis on the processes of accumulation by dispossession provoking the rise of new diverse social and political counterhegemonic struggles. The call to analyze and come to terms with these struggles in response to privatization, deregulation, and commodification, is summed up by Harvey (2003, 180) this way: "With the core of the problem so clearly recognized, it should be possible to build outwards into a broader politics of creative destruction mobilized against the dominant regime of neoliberal imperialism foisted upon the world by the hegemonic capitalist powers." In a similar vein, Castells seizes on the contradictions and disjunctures of contemporary globalization by highlighting the counterhegemonic processes of political activism that challenge the hegemony and disempowering effects of the neoliberal discourse and practice. For Castells (1997, 69): "People all over the world resent the loss of control over their lives, over their environment, over their jobs, and, ultimately, over the fate of the Earth. Thus, following an old law of social evolution, resistance confronts domination, empowerment reacts against powerlessness, and alternative projects challenge the logic embedded in the new global order, increasingly sensed as disorder by people around the planet." The next section provides a brief overview of the possibilities of the evolving anticapitalist, anti-imperialist, and deglobalization movements that have challenged the neoliberal project around the world. This sets up the following section to examine some of these struggles that have emerged in Africa.

THE DEGLOBALIZATION MOVEMENT AND ALTERNATIVE VISIONS

Since the late 1990s, new social movements in both the North and South, encompassing environmentalists, workers groups, anti-sweatshop activists, human rights movements, and so forth, have come together to form coalitions to resist globalization. Employing tactics such as strikes, protests, and uprisings as part of a new wave of radicalism, this new "movement of movements" for global justice and solidarity has collectively, through a struggle of resistance, articulated alternatives to the neoliberal project envisioned in the so-called Washington Consensus. These new social movements share a commitment to a common counterhegemonic discourse and project made possible by the antidemocratic nature of the globalization of capitalism.

The bankruptcy and nonsustainability of the neoliberal hegemonic order has created the need for an alternative counterhegemonic discourse, and has helped connect dispersed groups and movements in their struggle against corporate globalization. The events at Seattle in 1999 signaled the beginning of a new phase of rebellion against neoliberal globalization. Social movements, such as the Alliance for Global Justice, Center for Economic and Policy Research, "50 Years Is Enough," the Nader group Essential Action, and Jobs with Justice, among others, have mobilized globally against neoliberal globalization. The important role of these social movements—contesting the agenda of economic liberalization and the market and financial power of neoliberalism—is reflected in this nuanced and powerful account by Cecelia Lynch (1998, 158–59): "The type of normative/discursive contestation of contemporary social, economic, and political practices advanced by the antiglobalization movement at base provides an example of what social movements are able to do most effectively in world politics, that is, delegitimize particular discourse and paths of action in order to legitimize alternatives." The "movement of movements" against neoliberal globalization is therefore a struggle epitomized by political engagement and activism, inspired to reinvigorate the process of envisioning an alternative to neoliberal globalization. The crux of the political project is to challenge global capitalism and its inherently exploitative nature, and to seek to establish the conditions for a new and radical counterhegemonic vision of deglobalization.

The counterpoint to capitalist globalization is a new front of anticapitalist struggle deconstructing what some in the progressive movement refer to as "the empire." The objective of the anticapitalist movement is not to reform, but to shut down international financial institutions and provide a distinctly anticapitalist alternative by reconstructing and realigning power relations to the benefit of grassroots and progressive democratic political movements. Implicit in this is rebellion against the neoliberal globalization project and its distinctly capitalist manifestations. The resiliency of this movement is aptly noted in this poignant declaration by Fisher and Ponniah (2003, 2): "In a world of rapid globalization, where large corporations grow more powerful in their pursuit of economic expansion and profits, there are growing networks of concerned activists who are not dazzled by the promised land of globalization. They are alert instead to the dangers globalization presents to justice, cultural autonomy and the environment. These networks find themselves pitted against well-financed and well-staffed institutions, multilateral development banks, governments and transnational corporations. With limited resources but great tenaciousness, they work to make visible the damage and dangers wrought by rampant and unexamined economic expansion." It is in this light that one should view the actions at the Mobilization for Global

Justice campaign and the World Social Forum. The Mobilization for Global Justice campaign in Washington, DC (April 16–17, 2000) was very effective in bringing international attention to the campaign against the International Financial Institutions (IFIs) and the World Trade Organization (WTO). Adopting a far more militant and radical platform, the broad coalition of Third World and Northern activists' successful grassroots campaign drew attention to the Southern agenda in a way best captured in this statement by Bond (2003, 194):

> The Mobilization drew the eco-socio-economic concerns of the Global South far deeper into the fabric of the US movement than ever before. . . . Granted the protest failed to obstruct the IMF/World Bank meetings. . . . No matter, the combination of thorough preparation and the large size of the turnout in Washington helped raise public awareness about the IMF/World Bank to unprecedented levels; brought sympathetic activists from different constituencies into successful coalition; taught organizers a great deal about Washington logistics (and how they can be gummed up next time); showed South allies the extent of solidarity possibilities, encouraging them to intensify their own local critiques of the IMF/World Bank; and also facilitated a long-overdue split amongst development NGOs (a group of 22 conservative organizations sent a bizarre self-discrediting endorsement note to the IMF and the World Bank).

The power of the deglobalization movement and its oppositional agenda to envision another world is celebrated in the World Social Forum. As the political and ideological nemesis of the neoliberal ideology, the WSF initiated in Porto Alegre, Brazil, has provided an annual forum since 2001 for deglobalization activists to espouse an alternative ideological counterpoint. It has, above all, provided a foundation for a new form of social solidarity beyond the market. As Hardt and Negri (2003) noted: "Porto Alegre embodies and personifies the progressive movement against neoliberal globalization and the struggle to deconstruct the processes, structures, and institutions of global capitalism. For Michael Hardt and Antonio Negri, the WSF represents a "new democratic cosmopolitanism, a new anti-capitalist transnationalism, a new intellectual nomadism, a great movement of the multitude." Global civil society has mobilized to challenge neoliberal globalization and its hegemonic discourse of domination and economic totalitarianism. In its stead, the deglobalization movement has built a counterhegemonic discourse on a foundation of social and economic justice, ecological sustainability, and human rights. While emphasis has been placed on the global nature of these voices of protest and resistance, efforts to open up citizen spaces and mobilize at the local and national levels have been at the heart of the process of building alternatives. Indeed, one of the major strengths of the deglobalization movement is its embrace of, and respect for, difference. The vision is one that allows movements to maintain their difference.

If the movement to resist neoliberal globalization is to be a genuinely representative one and not a discourse initiated and dominated by the North, then it is essential to capture the grassroots struggles and resistance of African social movements, civil society organizations, and trade unions. How have African resistances and struggles against neoliberal globalization manifested themselves? How have African progressive forces, operating within the anticapitalist struggle, responded to "accumulation by dispossession" (Harvey, 2003), which is the defining hallmark of the continent's incorporation into the capitalist system? To these questions we now turn in the next section. Meanwhile, note the idea that Africa's connections with the world capitalist system have so far been disastrous is echoed by Patrick Bond in this volume.

AFRICAN RESISTANCE TO
NEOLIBERAL GLOBALIZATION

Attempts at deglobalization through protest and resistance in response to the uneven development of global capitalism did not just burst onto the world stage at Seattle in 1999. Anticapitalist resistance has been common in Africa since the liberation struggle that culminated in political independence began in the late 1950s. African social movements and the working class have been mobilizing to challenge state power, develop new strategies, and reject colonial rule and its resultant imperialist exploitation and capitalism. Central to this activism is a culture of resistance that merges subsistence struggle with the language, strategies, and tactics of the global movement, but with a distinctly locally based action drawn from African traditions of resistance. While a new wave of resistance to contemporary neoliberal policies is evident, it draws from the traditions and strategies of resistance of the liberation struggle in Africa. As Patrick Bond (2004, 198) notes, the effect of imperialism's exploitation of Africa in the colonial period engendered a progressive, radical tradition that included "vibrant nationalist liberation insurgencies, political parties that claimed one or another variants of socialism, mass movement (sometimes peasant-based, sometimes emerging from degraded urban ghettoes), and powerful unions. Religious protesters, women's groups, students and youths also played catalytic roles that changed history in given locales."

In contemporary times, the progressive force's critiques of neoliberalism and imperialism remain strong. The contradictions of capitalism and the continued accumulation by dispossession and appropriation that are endemic features of corporate globalization and neoliberal policies have generated new sites of conflict and resistance by African anticapitalists on the Left, through their new social movements. This could be traced back to the so-called IMF riots against the neoliberal emphasis on austerity, privatization, deregulation, and trade liberalization in the early 1980s. From this perspective, mass consciousness against neoliberal globalization in Africa began to take shape in the early 1980s. Since 2000, the movement has broadened beyond a patchwork of diverse struggles into a coordinated framework with a strong progressive grassroots base.

Some of the most sustained anticapitalist campaigns and struggles in response to accumulation by dispossession and appropriation in Africa have been waged through the African Social Forum, which has brought together progressive NGOs and social movements from all parts of the continent. The first ASF (January 5–9, 2002) brought representatives of more than two hundred African social movements from forty-five countries to Bamako, Mali, to exchange ideas, experiences, and strategies in order to generate an African alternative to neoliberal globalization, and to challenge the dominant economic policies encapsulated in the so-called Washington Consensus, as a prelude to the WSF in Porto Alegre in late January 2002. That initial gathering has since been followed up by African Social Forums in Johannesburg (August 2002), Addis Ababa, Ethiopia (January 2003), and Lusaka, Zambia (December 2004). Under the theme "Another Africa Is Possible," participants at the Bamako Forum (hereafter, "the Forum") engaged in analysis and proposed alternatives to the prevailing neoliberal world order. The objective of the Forum has been to engage, enrich, and strengthen African civil society and social movements and consolidate the world social movement. The 2002 Bamako Declaration's position on Africa's increasing deprivation through accumulation by dispossession and appropriation was as unambiguous as it was straightforward:

> A strong consensus emerged at the Bamako Forum that the values, practices, structures and institutions of the currently dominant neoliberal order are inimical to and incompatible with the realization of Africa's dignity, values and aspirations. The Forum rejected neoliberal globalization and further integration of Africa into an unjust system as the basis for its growth and development. In this context, there was a strong consensus [about] initiatives such as NEPAD [New Partnership for African Development] that are inspired by the IMF-WB strategies of Structural Adjustment Programmes, trade liberalization that continues to subject Africa to an unequal exchange, and strictures on governance borrowed from the practices of Western countries and not rooted in the culture and history of the peoples of Africa. The Forum further noted that the global architecture on financial and capital movements is seriously flawed and has led to repeated crises of the kind that happened in East Asia and more recently in Argentina. Africa too is exposed to the fragility of the system of global governance of the financial market. The Forum demands of its political leaders that they do not further inflict on Africa the unjust system of the Bretton Woods institutions in the name of financing Africa's development. Africa should, first and foremost, demand that its outstanding debts are cancelled forthwith. Africa has not only paid the financial debts many times over already, but it is the countries of the West that owe Africa debts arising from slavery and colonialism (Alternative Information and Development Center [AIDC] 2002, 1–2).

The Addis Ababa Consensus (issued on January 9, 2003), following the Second African Social Forum (ASF) held in Addis Ababa, Ethiopia (on January 5–9, 2003), reaffirmed the following as the philosophical and moral basis of the movement:

We conclude that only a dynamic civil society organized in strong and active social movements can and must challenge the neoliberal political economy of globalization. The Consensus was that we need to build a new African state and society where public institutions and policies will guarantee cultural, economic, political and social rights for all citizens. The ASF challenges national, regional and global institutions that continue to undermine our efforts to build a democratic society based on gender equality and social and economic justice. In that perspective, the African Social Forum commits itself to developing, promoting and popularizing, in a participatory manner, an alternative development paradigm based on fundamental principles of democracy, human rights, gender equality and social justice. (African Social Forum [ASF] 2003)

The ASF has provided an enabling space and environment for African social movements to voice their opinions and concerns, examine the stakes, and articulate their visions and alternatives. The defining characteristic of the ASF is the creation of open and diverse spaces for the generation of grassroots, progressive ideas, and practices for challenging, deconstructing, and ultimately displacing contemporary neoliberalism. In particular, the Forum has established a link between the debt problem and neoliberal globalization, and has mobilized African social movements around a broad agenda to address the fundamental roots and causes of the debt problem. The focus of their struggles not only has been the IMF, the World Bank, the World Trade Organization, and the G8 for debt cancellation, but also their own governments for sustaining and reproducing the debt crisis. By linking the struggle and campaign against debt with the neoliberal policies of participants' governments, the ASF has brought, into sharp focus, the need for a broad-based campaign to unite popular progressive movements on the continent. It is a testament to the growing relevance of the ASF and its commitment to provide space for alternative visions of Africa that the Forum held in Lusaka, Zambia (December 10–14, 2004) attracted approximately 650 social movement activists representing trade unions, churches, women, environmentalists, and progressive NGOs.

Taking a cue from the ASF and its position on debt, the radical African Jubilee South (AJS), a social movement with an activist base, has, for years, campaigned for the cancellation of Africa's debt, not just the Highly Indebted Poor Country (HIPC) initiative for a write-off of unserviceable debt. Jubilee South challenges the IMF, World Bank, and Northern governments' framework of Third World debt on the grounds that it fails to address the historical, social, and ecological debts of the North to the South—debts accumulated from years of slavery, colonization, and neocolonization—and from the more contemporary relationships of domination, inequality, and aggression. The movement's December 2000 conference in Senegal, "Dakar 2000: From Resistance to Alternatives," was a major watershed in this campaign because civil society, social movements, trade unions, and NGOs from Africa were united not only in their critique of the African debt crisis and structural adjustment programs in general, but also in their articulation of strategies of resistance to neoliberal globalization and alternative visions. It is worth noting the following aspects of the conference resolution: "Third World debt is illegitimate and must be cancelled without conditions; structural adjustment programmes of the IMF and the World Bank, under whatever name, including the new Poverty Reduction Strategy Papers, must be rejected; that no conditionalities should be placed on the debt cancellation process by Northern governments or creditors; and that we must more consciously take account of the ecological impacts of the debt" (quoted in Fisher 2001, 208–9).

The Forum has served as a space where African social movements can grow to be vanguards of social, political, and economic justice and to outline alternatives through resistance strategies. Symptomatic of this role has been the vociferous resistance of African social movements to the 2002 New Partnership for African Development (NEPAD) and the Blair Commission for Africa Report entitled "Our Common Interest," released on March 11, 2005. African social movements have argued that the underdevelopment of Africa is the result of a process of exploitation by Western imperialism and the plundering of resources by Western multinational capital. Both Patrick Bond and Joseph Mensah talk similarly of the systemic character of Africa's underdevelopment in Chapters 2 and 7 of this volume, respectively. Working from this perspective, these movements point out that NEPAD embraced the principles of neoliberalism and the process of neoliberal globalization as the cure for Africa's development. They have criticized NEPAD as an elite-driven, top-down program developed by African elites in alliance with Western corporate forces and institutional instruments of globalization. A communiqué issued after a meeting of social movements, trade unions, faith-based organizations, youth and women's organizations, progressive NGOs, and other populist civil society organizations in Africa in Port Shepstone, South Africa (July 4–8, 2002) noted that NEPAD: "Ignores the way the state has, itself, been undermined as a social provider and vehicle for development, particularly under the World Bank's tutelage; ignores the way that the structurally adjusted African state has, in turn, been undermining institutions and processes of democracy in Africa; does not reflect the historic struggles in Africa for participatory forms of democracy and decentralization of power; promises of democracy and good governance are largely intended to satisfy foreign donors and to give guarantees to foreign investment" (Alternative Information and Development Center [AIDC] 2002).

Rejecting NEPAD as a development path for the continent and stressing that "Africa was not for sale," the social movements concluded that: "We do not accept the NEPAD plan, as a process and in its content. We are committed to joint efforts for Africa's development and emancipation, and we call upon all African people's organizations and movements to continue their longstanding efforts to produce sustainable, just and viable alternatives that will benefit all the people of Africa" (ibid., 5).

There was also a clarion call encouraging progressive forces in Africa to campaign against NEPAD and raise awareness about the danger it poses for the continent and its people. Soweto political activist Trevor Ngwane has drawn attention to the problematic underlying assumptions of NEPAD and called for a rejection of the plan. Encouraging African social movements to initiate a campaign of "education and denunciation against NEPAD," Ngwane reminds us that civil society was not consulted when the plan was put together, and that "the document uses euphemisms and camouflage language such as 'a globalizing world,' 'exclusion,' 'globalisation' and such like; it avoids the critical language which points to the real cause of Africa's problems such as 'imperialism,' 'neocolonialism' and 'capitalism'" (Ngwane, 2002). This analysis, like the one offered by Eunice Sahle in Chapter 8 of this volume, focuses on the contradictions of neoliberal logic and the uneven and exploitative nature of the existing international economic system into which Africa has been integrated and which NEPAD deepens. For Ngwane:

> The relationship between Africa and Western Europe has been one between colonizer and colonized, exploiter and exploited. While the exact terms of this predatory relationship have evolved over time, it seems foolhardy for Mbeki and company to ask for partnership with people who still benefit from Africa's wealth at the expense of the African people. Imperialism is the problem, a partnership with it cannot be a solution. He who sups with the devil must have a long spoon. NEPAD calls for closer relations with the rich countries, it wants Africa to be "integrated" more into the global economic system. But economic development theorists such as Andre Gunder Frank and Samir Amin have long shown how integration leads to growing poverty and underdevelopment because the structure of insertion is designed to benefit the rich; they get richer and the poor get poorer (ibid., 3).

Most recently, the Blair Commission for Africa report, "Our Common Interest," called for further action on debt relief. The so-called Marshall Plan for Africa places a great deal of emphasis on deep debt relief as the cornerstone of a poverty reduction strategy. The centerpiece of that plan was the June 11, 2005 agreement by seven G8 finance ministers for a US$50–55 billion debt write-off, later endorsed at the G8 meeting in Gleneagles, Scotland (July 6–8, 2005). There was a lot of enthusiastic support for these measures, including media headlines such as "Debtor Nations Freed of Burdens" (*Los Angeles Times*, June 12, 2005); "Victory for Millions" (*Observer*, June 12, 2005), and "Blair, Bono Win One for Africa" (*Christian Science Monitor*, June 13, 2005). The *Los Angeles Times* enthused that the deal "fulfilled a decades-old dream of anti-poverty activists" (*Los Angeles Times*, June 12, 2005) and Gordon Brown, Chancellor of the Exchequer of the United Kingdom, proudly hinted that "it is the intention of world leaders to forge a new and better relationship—a new deal—between the rich and poor countries of the world and I believe that the advances we have made can be built upon. . . . This is not the time for timidity, but a time for boldness, and not a time for settling for second best, but aiming high" (*Los Angeles Times* 2005).

In response to the lavish claims and hype surrounding the announcement, African social movements were pained to emphasize that this version of the so-called Marshall Plan for Africa did not address the root causes of Africa's underdevelopment. African Jubilee South pointed out that the debt forgiveness scheme "involves the implementation of stringent free market reforms such as health and education budget cuts, financial and trade liberalization, privatization and other reforms that ensure elimination of impediments to private investment, both domestic and foreign" (African Jubilee South 2005). Indeed, the US$50 billion-to-US$55 billion debt cancellation pales in light of Africa's estimated total external debt of $300 billion, and the fact that the conditions for eligibility for debt write-off require adopting the very neoliberal policies at the root of the malaise means debt relief is premised on imposing the same harmful policies on African countries. In an ironic twist, therefore, the G8's antipoverty plan will ensure the continued exploitation of Africa. The G8 plan does not change the fundamental relationship between Africa and the Western world, which is one of unequal exploitation.

The Southern African People's Solidarity Network, in reaction to the G8 plan, reminds us that "the so-called debt cancellations . . . will lead to further accumulation of debts [because] these countries still have to toe the line and respond to demands to open up their economies for more exploitation, capital flight and other related imbalances that come with further liberalization" (African Jubilee South 2005). On June 14, 2005, the AJS stated in stark terms that:

> The costs of structural adjustment programs and creditor-imposed conditionality far outweigh the amount of debt to be cancelled. Are we to cheer when these additional promises can go the same route of other G8 pledges, that is, unfulfilled? Should we applaud when the 18 countries affected represent a tiny fraction of the world's poor? Are we to praise the G8 when these debts are not being serviced in any case (because of the countries' inability to pay), and when they would have been repudiated a long time ago as illegitimate debts if our governments had real political and economic independence. The illegitimacy of the debt resides in that they were incurred by dictatorships of various kinds, were used in consolidating and furthering their undemocratic regimes against the interests of their people and in implementing policies that have put millions of lives at risk (African Jubilee South 2005, 5).

For well-known Tanzanian professor Issa Shivji, the only alternative is to fight against the neoliberal ideology and imperialist policies that have impoverished Africa. Expressing his pessimism about the G8 initiative, Shivji draws attention to the need for an alternative nationalist, pan-Africanist vision: "And this vision has to be in opposition to the domination of imperialism, read globalization, just as the nationalist vision in the last century was in opposition to colonialism. More than ever before, we need Nkrumahs and Fanons who saw in African unity and in the unity of the oppressed people and exploited classes a counter-force, which would be the harbinger of an alternative vision and an alternative path of development."[1] The power and potential of the ASF as a new political form of counterhegemonic force against the new imperialism rests on four features: first, it provides a forum for studying and educating the African masses about the devastating impact of neoliberalism and alternatives to it; second, it provides for mass mobilization and struggles in contestation to neoliberalism and in defense of African economic, social, political, and cultural interests; third, it provides a new site for African social movements to champion alternative notions and visions of democracy that are not tied to the market economy, and to articulate new notions of power that facilitate and transform; and, fourth, it provides an avenue for redefining Africa through a discourse of dissent based on an African culture of resistance that disrupts and decenters the dominant discourse. The ASF offers space to social movements opposed to neoliberalism so they can foster networks to challenge the new global coloniality and articulate emergent alternatives to empire. In the face of accumulation by dispossession and appropriation, the Forum represents a site for a new praxis of emancipatory, democratic politics. Such examples of popular resistance to the Washington Consensus and neoliberal globalization in Africa capture the essence of African civil society, social movements, and working class challenges to neoliberal policies. They are also a reflection of, and testament to, the way that grassroots mobilization and organizing can strive to end the neoliberal experiment and establish sustainable alternatives as articulated by the anticapitalist movement.

CONCLUSION

Indeed, it can be argued that the hegemony of neoliberal globalization is being attacked by a coalition of progressive social movements articulating a radical counterhegemonic vision. The impetus for the radical alternative of deglobalization is the destructive capacities of corporate-driven globalization. This chapter has made the case for engaging with the counterhegemonic strategies and tactics of the deglobalization movement and the deglobalization battles being waged by African activists; these battles are not about mediation, but rather the explicit rejection and rollback of neoliberal globalization.

The deglobalization movement's arguments, globally and in Africa, are impressive. The terms of their engagement and contestation of neoliberal globalization are extraordinarily contemporary ones. Their emphasis on deglobalization through solidarity, that is, globalization of people, is at once consistent with the global civil society contestation, yet unique and distinctly African. However, to take a provocative stand, the radical claims and critiques coming from the deglobalization movement should not be confused with their general acceptability as a force of grassroots empowerment and change. The deglobalization account is itself contestable; the representativeness and accountability of the movement are still subject to debate. Furthermore, given the critical importance of civil society to the deglobalization movement, we would do well to heed Rita Abrahamsen's (2000, 55) cautionary note about overstating African civil society's democratic credentials: "Representation of civil society as inherently democratic is too romantic and optimistic."

Indeed, one prominent criticism of the ASF in Lusaka, Zambia in 2004 was that the speakers did not represent broadly based, progressive grassroots organizations and that the plenaries were dominated by the same speakers, mostly from well organized and financed national movements and NGOs. Trade unions and environmental and women's groups engaged in resistance to privatization, the negative environmental consequences of multinational mining corporations, and violence against women in the host country did not feature prominently on panels. This raises the question of how the ASF can hope to become truly representative of local campaigns against debt, trade, land sales, privatization of basic services, environmental degradation, and other manifestations of global capitalism on the continent. As Larmer (2005, 4) cautions:

> The ASF was affected by the same ambiguities and contradictions that run through the global social justice movement as a whole, but which are particularly marked in sub-Saharan Africa. One such issue is the dominant role of international NGOs in terms of the agenda of the ASF, and its organization and funding. Many participants, for example from Malawi, were able to attend the Forum only because of NGO funding. The financial dependency of southern civil society organizations on northern NGOs, whose raison d'etre remains critical engagement with the policy and practice of the international financial organizations, continues to influence the positions they adopt.

Nonetheless, it is important to recognize that space is being forged in Africa and elsewhere to promote radical, progressive alternatives through popular struggles of resistance through the deglobalization movement.

References

Abrahamsen, Rita. 2000. *Disciplining democracy: Development discourse and good governance in Africa.* London and New York: Zed Books.

African Jubilee South 2005 Africa needs justice not charity. http://www.wordpress.org/Africa/2107.cfm.

African Social Forum 2003. Addis Ababa Concensus, Another Africa is possible. http://www.sarpn.org.za/documents/d0000167/P163_ASF_consensus_pdf.

Alternative Information and Development Centre (AIDC). 2002. Africa Social Forum, Bamako, Mali, the Bamako declaration. http://www.aidc.org.za, 1–2.

Alternative Information and Development Center (AIDC) 2002. African Civil Society Declaration on NEPAD. http://www.aidc.org.za/?q=node/view/174.

Blair, Bono win one for Africa. *Christian Science Monitor* 97 (139): 8

Bond, Patrick. 2003. *Against global apartheid: South Africa meets the World Bank, IMF, and international finance.* London and New York: Zed Books.

———. 2004. Facing global apartheid. In *The politics of empire: Globalisation in crisis*, ed. Alan Freeman and Boris Kagarlitsky, 198 (London and Ann Arbor, MI: Pluto), in association with Transnational Institute.

Castells, M. 1997. *The power of identity*. Oxford: Blackwell.

Escobar, Arturo. 2004. Beyond the Third World: Imperial globality and anti-globalisation social movements. *Third World Quarterly* 24 (1): 207.

Fisher, John. 2001. Africa. In *Anti-capitalism: A guide to the movement*, ed. Emma Bircham and John Charlton, 208–9. London: Bookmarks.

Fisher, W., and T. Ponniah. 2003. *Another world is possible: Popular alternatives to globalization at the World Social Forum*. New York: Zed Books.

Hardt, Michael, and Antonio Negri. 2003. Foreword. In *Another world is possible: Popular alternatives to globalization at the World Social Forum*, ed. W. Fisher and T. Ponniah, xvi. New York: Zed Books.

Harvey, David. 2003. *The new imperialism*. Oxford and New York: Oxford University Press.

Kofman, Eleanore, and Gillian Youngs. 1996. *Globalization: Theory and practice*. London: Pinter.

Larmer, Miles. 2005. *Africa social forum 2004—Whose forum, which Africa?* Johannesburg, South Africa: Alternative Information and Development Centre.

Los Angeles Times, June 12, 2005. Debtro nations freed of burden. http://articles.latimes.com/2005/jun/12/world/fg-debt12.

Luxemburg, Rosa. 1951. *The accumulation of capital*. New York: Monthly Review.

Lynch, Cecilia. 1998. Social movements and the problem of globalization. *Alternatives* 23:158–59.

Ngwane, Trevor. 2002. Should African social movements be part of the New partnership for Africa's development (NEPAD)? A speech given to the African Social Forum's seminar at the World Social Forum, Porto Alegre, Brazil.

Observer (London) June 12, 2005. Victory for millions, p. 1

Scholte, Jan A. 1996. Beyond the buzzword: Towards a critical theory of globalization. *Globalization: Theory and practice*, ed. Eleanore Kofman and Gillian Youngs, 44. London: Pinter.

NOTE

1. See the Pambazuka News Weekly Forum for Social Justice in Africa, Aid with One Hand; Guns with the Other: Q & A with Issa Shivji on the G8 (July 7, 2005), 2.

CHAPTER 4

GENDER, STATES, AND MARKETS IN AFRICA

Eunice N. Sahle

The last two decades have witnessed attempts to reform the economic and political characteristics of African states along the lines of the neoliberal development paradigm. In the economic arena, most states have instituted development policies aimed at significantly reducing the role of the state. On the political front, an attempt has been made to introduce good governance practices, of which an important aspect has been the demise of one-party authoritarian political structures and the establishment of multiparty political structures. In neoliberal terms, these reforms are intended to rejuvenate Africa's stunted economic and political development and thus facilitate the continent's transition to modern market-based capitalist societies.

This chapter examines neoliberal restructuring with specific reference to reforms geared to the promotion of a market-based capital accumulation process in social formations in Africa. The chapter contends that contrary to the neoliberal theory, which informs contemporary reconfiguration of the role of the state in the economic arena in Africa and elsewhere, state structures and markets are not gender neutral. The analysis demonstrates how both the patriarchal ideology that has marked the evolution of African states has contributed to the marginalization of the majority of African women, and highlights how the promotion of market-led accumulation strategies by the transnational lending community and the governing institutions of this community, leading among them, the World Bank, is deepening this process. The chapter has three sections. The first section discusses the dominant approaches to the central concerns of this chapter and highlights the analytical power of a critical feminist political economy perspective. Section two demonstrates the gendered foundations of African states through an examination of core aspects of the state-led accumulation process in the colonial and pre-neoliberal restructuring periods. The last section analyses the key features of neoliberal market-based reforms and shows their gendered nature.

GENDER AND THE STATE VS. MARKET DEBATE: DOMINANT THEORETICAL PERSPECTIVES

The ascendancy of the global neoliberal political, cultural, and economic project has generated a significant debate on the role of the state and market in capital accumulation processes. Given space limitations, it is impossible to extensively discuss the interesting strands of all the theoretical approaches characterizing that debate; consequently, this discussion is limited to the dominant perspectives of neoliberalism, neo-Weberian, political economy and feminist political economy.

The economic dimension of the neoliberal development paradigm has its roots in the evolution of classical economic thought.[1] In its current rebirth, this approach deems the states themselves, in Africa and elsewhere, as being the main barriers to economic growth. In the neoliberal view, the role of African states in postcolonial economic development has been so extensive that it has led to the inefficient allocation of resources and hampered the entrepreneurial spirit (World Bank 1994, 17–34). Thus, for scholars working within this paradigm, the reduction of the role of the state and the promotion of the market logic with all its attendant features—for instance, the monopoly of private capital and privatization of public goods—is the key to overcoming Africa's economic stagnation.

The neo-Weberian perspective, commonly known as neopatrimonialism, has its intellectual roots in the writings of Max Weber on social, economic, and political change. According to this perspective, neopatrimonial practices have their roots in traditional African political and economic systems in which leaders (patrons) extended social and economic benefits to their local people (clients) and in return gained—in addition to extensive power—obedience, admiration, and loyalty. Most works situated in this perspective emphasize the neopatrimonial foundation of African states, which has created avenues for irrational economic practices, the concentration of power in personalized state structures, and other practices that have led to the emergence of states that are not developmental in character.[2] For studies situated within this perspective, the establishment and deepening of market initiatives will facilitate the emergence of state structures committed to eliminating economic waste through rent-seeking activities, and a technocratic bureaucratic cadre committed to promoting a rational economic and political development path.

The contributions of the political economy perspective to the debate have been an attempt to broaden the analytical terrain, given what scholars working within this approach deem to be major limitations of the preceding approaches. Central to the political economy approach is an examination of the logic and rise of a global capitalist system characterized by power asymmetry and the marginalization of countries at the periphery of this system, especially those in Africa.[3] Along these lines, Samir Amin argues that, rather than merely highlighting the "failure" or "success" of economic processes—which tends to be characteristic of mainstream studies—scholars need to explain, why owners of capital and institutions governing the expansion of global capitalism have, at times, facilitated this process and at other times constrained it (Amin 1997,14–17; Amin 1998, 13–26). Scholars using this approach also contend that the role of the state and the market in capital accumulation processes cannot be understood fully if the global and national dialectic is neglected in analytical frameworks, which tends to be the case in most studies of this phenomenon situated within the neoliberal and neo-Weberian perspective. Using such an approach, for instance, would dismantle the hegemonic explanation of contemporary African economic crises that views them as emerging solely from within national borders and having nothing to do with the local and global political, economic, and intellectual shifts (Sahle 2008). Critical political economists also call for a broader conceptualization of states and markets to incorporate the historical, political, ideological, and economic foundations that shape their role in the capital accumulation process (Mkandawire and Soludo 1999, 87–138, Sahle 2008).

While the above-noted dominant theoretical approaches offer insights to the central concerns of this chapter, their profound silence on the gendered nature of state and market-led capital accumulation strategies limits their analytical power in the study of neoliberal economic restructuring in Africa. Even the political economy approach, which addresses major gaps in the mainstream literature, has, as Joanne Cook and Jennifer Roberts argue, made gender power relations "invisible . . . with women, and things feminine, defined only in relation to the masculine norm (Cook and Roberts 2000, 3)." This chapter, then, situates itself within the critical feminist political economy tradition, which, like the political economy approach, links national and global developments in the study of the core elements of the neoliberal project. Specifically it builds its analysis on decades of critical feminist political economy scholarship that incorporates gender as an analytical category, along with cultural, historical, ideological, and structural factors in the examination of institutional, political, and economic processes, and highlights the link between social reproduction and economic production.[4]

Using this approach as an entry point, this chapter not only demonstrates the gendered nature of preexisting states, but also unmasks the gender bias in policies and concepts, which are central to the neoliberal project in Africa, such as efficiency and market initiatives and state failure. For example, the so-called market incentives in the agrarian sector, as will be demonstrated later, are gendered, and thus there is nothing neutral about them. So, contrary to the dominant perspectives, markets in any sector have to be understood as socially constructed institutions[5] whose evolution leads to a reconfiguration of societal structures, including gender power relations. In essence, neoliberal promotion of a market-led capital accumulation pattern has, in Africa as elsewhere, affected women and men differently. Yet, as Janine Brodie has argued, while neoliberalism "recommends a fundamental reordering of the mode of regulation and a new definition of the public good, [it] is silent about the gendered underpinnings of this shift" (Brodie 1994, 48).

Rise of Gendered States

Critical feminist scholars have highlighted the gendered character of states through analysis of, for instance, political participation and democratization.[6] An examination of the pattern of capital accumulation processes offers another site for an exploration of this phenomenon. This section, then, briefly demonstrates the gendered foundations of African states by examining how the patriarchal ideological foundation of African states and the evolution of the core elements of these states' accumulation strategies prior to neoliberal restructuring contributed to the marginalization of the majority of African women.

The gendered foundations of contemporary African states have their origins in European imperial projects of the nineteenth century. Colonial economic structures in the main involved the introduction of capitalist agricultural production in countries such as Zimbabwe, Senegal, Kenya, Ivory Coast, Malawi, and many others, and the extraction of the continent's mineral wealth, which saw various European interests competing for pieces of what King Leopold of Belgium referred to as "this magnificent African cake."[7] For King Leopold, Congo Free State became his highly prized piece of Africa's magnificent cake thanks to its abundance of natural resources, specifically, rubber and minerals.

The evolution of the above-cited features of colonial states' economic strategies was marked by gender bias and laid the foundation for the economic marginalization of most African women. In the agrarian sector, this process began with the land commodification process, where the colonial state deemed African men as heads of households and the rightful owners of land; consequently, men became title deed holders once Africans were allowed to own land.[8] While not all African men benefited from colonial land alienation policies—this process, like other historical developments, was mediated by cultural practices such as age, lineage, and the embryonic colonial class structure—they were nevertheless able to accumulate wealth since, as owners of land, they could access capital that could facilitate their entry to other sectors of the economy, or use their wealth for leisure activities (Gordon 2001, 277). Such a strong base for creating wealth was not available to African women, except indirectly for those who were related to men with access to the colonial political and economic machinery.

The land alienation policy was not the only element of the colonial economic structures that demonstrated the gendered foundations of African states. The introduction of cash crops affected women and men differently. Colonial officials, with the help of men from African traditional ruling structures, constructed men as farmers and the social actors who, given their masculine "essence," would be open to the modernization of the agricultural sector. Thus, men were given the role of controlling and dispensing new technology and seeds, and also access to training in modern agricultural methods (Lovett 1989, 37–38). In the eyes of colonial authorities, African women were backward, childish, and irrational, and thus could not contribute to the emerging modern agricultural sector. Colonial states' racist attitude toward African women, coupled with their patriarchal ideological framework—whose hallmark was deeply held Victorian ideas about the role of women in political, social, and economic processes—contributed greatly to the marginalization of African women in the agrarian sector. Yet, it was African women who worked in both the cash crop and the food production subsectors, as men left their villages to work in, for instance, the European plantations in Malawi, the White Highlands in Kenya, the mines of Southern Africa, or the emerging urban centers.

The gendered pattern of accumulation strategies also marked the emergence of the mining sector, which was the constitutive feature of colonial accumulation strategies in mineral rich colonies, such as contemporary South Africa, Zambia, and the Democratic Republic of Congo. In these countries, African men were forced to leave their homes to meet the economic demands generated by the colonial political economy, such as the introduction of hut and head taxes and the deepening of monetized economic activities (Ake 1981, 32–35). The establishment of mining centers was a gendered process from the outset because colonial recruiting policies prohibited African men from bringing their families to the mining towns. From the colonial states' standpoint and mining interests, it was important to extract as much labor as possible from African men—mandatory, state-sanctioned separation from their families, in addition to forced labor practices, facilitated this process.[9] Further, the policy of restricting the movement of African women to the mining towns also served the rural economic interests of the colonial state, African chiefs, and men. In the development of colonial agrarian sector, it ensured steady and cheap labor from African women in the rural areas. For the chiefs, this colonial policy ensured that they maintained their control and access to wealth from cultural practices such as bride wealth; for African men, it protected their land rights (Gordon 1989, 29–30).

The development of the mining sector had a major impact on gender and power relations in African societies. As in the newly established cash crop sector, African men could use their wages to buy properties, such as land, to pursue leisure activities, or enter emerging sectors of the colonial economy as they become open to Africans. African women did not have such options and thus ended up creating alternative economic avenues for themselves in precarious and unstable informal economic activities, such as beer brewing and the commercial sex trade. Further, the rise of the mining sector led to the establishment of a labor migration system, a development that had a profound impact on the evolution of African families because it disrupted family structures in a manner very similar to that in political economies underpinned by slavery, such as in the United States and the Caribbean. In addition, it increased the workload of African women since it changed the precolonial patriarchal, yet complementary, division of labor between women and men (Kandawire 1989, 198). This process, in addition to other colonial wage labor policies and industrialization strategies, also laid the foundation for the rise of a gendered employment pattern that limited women's access to wage employment. As Marjorie Mbilinyi demonstrates, in colonial Tanzania, a country that was once a major source of migrant labor, women and men accounted for 3 percent and 19 percent of wage earners, respectively, in 1948. Further, women whose labor, under colonial rule, was categorized as "child labor" were paid significantly less, with wages 30 percent less than those of men (Mbilinyi 1989, 220).

While the dismantling of European imperialism opened up political and economic spaces for Africans, the gendered character of colonial states' accumulation strategies did not fundamentally change in the postcolonial era. While African women contributed greatly to the anticolonial struggle, their participation in the public arena, both politically and economically, was put on the back burner as ruling elites redefined gender roles in their efforts to protect male interests. For instance, in contrast to their public roles in the anticolonial struggles, women were suddenly constructed as apolitical beings and relegated to roles that were suited to their so-called innate nature: decent and God-fearing wives and mothers, tireless farm laborers, and the mothers of the newly independent nations. These are the same women who had, in the case of Zambia, for example, contributed greatly in the nationalist struggle by "felling . . . trees to block roads making them impassable to the enemy . . . staging half-naked demonstrations, [and] taking part in civil disobedience" and mobilization campaigns and political education (Munachonga 1989, 134).

In the economic arena, the social construction of women as inferior, apolitical beings, and the gender bias embedded in various state-led accumulation strategies, resulted in deepening the marginalization of the majority of African women. For instance, during this era of state-led capitalism, a number of African states instituted various capital indigenization programs in an effort to create and expand local capitalist classes. This process mainly benefited men drawn from the dominant classes and state-appointed ethnic notables at the expense of the majority of women and men from the lower social classes. In the case of postcolonial Zambia, for example, women, who are the mainstay of agricultural production, were denied access to modern agricultural methods such as the "Train and Visit System" agricultural training program sponsored by the World Bank (Munachonga 1989, 131).

Thus, Africa's postcolonial state-led economic "boom" of the 1960s and early 1970s was a gendered process. This does not mean African women were hapless "victims" and that they were not agents of their own history, or that they did not engage the state or seek ways to improve their economic positions. But this does stress the dialectical relationship between political agency and power structures because no social or political struggles, including those of African women, occur in a power vacuum. For instance, women who were members of women's organizations closely linked to the ruling parties had better access to the state apparatus, while women from subordinate classes were generally marginalized or had their strategic demands contained during the pre-market-based reforms era.[10] Even when African women carved economic spaces for their survival, the gendered foundations of African states led to containment of the expansion and strengthening of these spaces because they were considered a challenge to the local patriarchal state ideological framework that constructed women's and men's roles differently. In Ghana, for example, the military dictatorship of Rawlings promoted a discourse that blamed the country's historically important women market traders for the country's economic crisis, and in its high noon in the late 1970s, members of its security apparatus "bulldozed Makola No.1 Market and reduced it to a pile of rubble," an act viewed by the soldiers involved as a great male disciplinary measure that would "teach Ghanaian women to stop being wicked."[11]

By the late 1970s, when the state-led capital accumulation strategy began to unravel due to internal and external political, intellectual, and economic developments, a clearly gendered accumulation pattern constituted the foundations of these states. Yet, as these states embarked on a neoliberal accumulation strategy, promoters of this development paradigm and practice neglected to take cognizance of the gendered nature of these states. It is important to note that the omission of gender issues in the era of state-led capitalism occurred not only at the level of state accumulation patterns, but also in dominant theories of development, such as modernization theory and development practices of global development institutions like the World Bank, whose development projects were presented as gender neutral.[12]

Gender and the Promotion of Market-led Accumulation

The promotion of market-led capital accumulation strategy in the global South has its origins in the onset of the global economic crisis of the late 1970s. At the global level, the post-1945 boom was facing deep fractures for a myriad of reasons, the central ones being the two oil crises of the 1970s, structural changes in economic production, and the breakdown of the Bretton Woods economic framework, especially its financial arrangement that had afforded nation-states the ability to control movement of capital.[13] In Africa, this crisis manifested itself in the inability of governments to service their debt, declining private and public investment, declining exports, and balance-of-payment problems (Sahn 1994, 3–9).

As the crisis deepened, African countries responded by embarking on economic reforms based on neoliberal economic thought, which, due to global shifts in intellectual, economic, and political arenas, had slowly become the global hegemonic economic paradigm. On the intellectual terrain, the 1970s also saw shifts in intellectual economic thought and practice. The latter was marked by the withering away of the Keynesian economic framework that had governed post-World War II economic ideas, the rise of neoliberal ideas drawn from thinkers such as Friedrich Hayek and Milton Friedman, and, in the subfield of development economics, the arrival of what John Toye has termed the "counter-revolution," embodied in the work of Deepak Lal and Ian Little, among others (Toye 1993). Fundamentally, this neoliberal revolution called for the curtailment of the role of the state in economic affairs, privatization of the public sector, promotion of the entrepreneurial spirit, liberalization of financial markets, and promotion of international free trade. Powerful as these ideas were, however, their ascendancy to hegemonic status occurred due to the earlier-mentioned unraveling of the post-World War II capitalist boom and the rise of conservative governments in the key industrialized countries—Margaret Thatcher in Great Britain, Ronald Reagan in the United States, and Helmut Kohl in Germany—whose political projects embraced the core ideas of neoliberalism.

In the context of Africa's development, this neoliberal "counter-revolution" in thought explained the continent's economic crisis and stagnation as being a result of the state's extensive role in economic affairs, especially through the expansion of publicly owned enterprises in the postcolonial period (World Bank 1981, 37). Other contributing factors were trade protection measures, such as high tariffs and licensing procedures, and overvalued currencies. In addition, agricultural policies, especially the practice of paying small-scale producers limited returns for their products, and the decline of agricultural exports in the 1970s, were seen as contributing to economic stagnation and crisis. The expenditure patterns followed by postcolonial governments—in providing subsidies in agriculture and in social sectors such as education and health, and the expansion of the civil service—were also considered to be factors.

The preceding brief outline of the central tenets of neoliberal economic policies indicates a gender-blind approach to economic processes that characterize neoliberal globalization in Africa and elsewhere. The silence on the gendered nature of economic processes becomes even more evident, as this section of the chapter demonstrates, when one examines the core reforms geared to the emergence of a capital accumulation strategy subsumed to the logic of market-led capital accumulation processes: agrarian reforms, privatization, social sector spending, and civil service reforms, which is what we turn to in the next section.

Agricultural Reforms

Given the structural reality of the dominance of agrarian production in most African economies, agricultural reform has been a central focus of neoliberal reforms in the promotion of market-led pattern of capital accumulation. As a detailed analysis of all these targeted agricultural reforms is beyond the scope of this chapter, the discussion will be limited to an examination of the much-touted reforms in the small-scale agricultural subsector. One of the core reforms in that subsector has addressed a well-studied phenomenon: the asymmetric nature of agrarian produce earnings that marked colonial and postcolonial state agricultural practices.[14] For these states, farmers in the large-scale subsector earned the equivalent of international prices in local currency for their agrarian produce, while state-owned agricultural enterprises paid small-scale farmers low prices.[15] Thus, with the onset of economic crisis and a shift in development discourse, reforms in state agricultural practices have become a focal point of neoliberal reforms. In the small-scale subsector, reforms have included, but are not limited to, the introduction of market incentives to facilitate increased agricultural output—because a core argument of neoliberalism is that declines in agricultural exports in the 1970s greatly contributed to the economic crisis (World Bank 1981, 31)—and to increase earnings for farmers in this sector. With respect to the latter, small-scale producers are no longer mandated to sell their agricultural surplus to state-owned enterprises, but can sell to private traders who, it is assumed, given their commitment to efficiency and profit making, will pay them higher prices.

Securing individual land ownership for small-scale farmers is another reform advocated under neoliberal structuring of the agrarian sector. According to the World Bank, this development is important at the household and national levels because it would lead to increases in agricultural production, thus enabling farmers and African countries to accrue more earnings from exports. According to the World Bank's land reform agenda, small-scale farmers enjoying individual land ownership are more productive than those in large-scale farming operations since the former do not incur high labor costs—they rely solely on what the World Bank calls "non-contractor labor" provided by members of households (Manji 2003, 102). Another argument put forward by the World Bank is that, armed with titled deeds, small-scale farmers can borrow capital from the emerging rural credit markets and transform land from a "dead asset" to an economic resource that they can use "to invest, accumulate wealth, and transfer . . . between generations" and, in the process, gain what the World Bank terms as "major equity benefits" (Manji 2003, 100).

Given the historical marginalization of a large segment of small-scale farmers, the call for reforms is a welcome development. However, neoliberal advocates fail to consider the cultural, political, and economic contexts that frame these reforms. Specifically, years after Ester Boserup's seminal intervention, the new development paradigm has neglected to analyze the gendered nature of agricultural production in both small- and large-scale sectors (Boserup 1970). In this era of neoliberal restructuring, small-scale producers are perceived as self-maximizing rational individuals who, unmediated by gender power relations, will take advantage of market incentives in their onward march to economic progress. Fundamental issues, such as the fact that gender power dynamics would influence women's access to, and the nature of, their interaction with private traders, are also unproblematized in this era underpinned by a development discourse promoting a dehistorized market-led accumulation strategy.

Other factors, such as the male bias that characterizes most land tenure systems in Africa, matrilineal and patrilineal specificity notwithstanding, and how this continues to limit women's agrarian production and economic well-being, are left untouched. As discussed earlier, since the early days of the land commodification process, it is African men who have benefited from this development due to the patriarchal ideological foundations of local states and societies. Consequently, the current phase of that process, rather than facilitating the ability of women to achieve the so-called "major equity benefits" only deepens their marginalization at various levels. For instance, it has been argued here, it is women who have historically constituted the backbone of agricultural production in Africa. Consequently, it is these social actors who, as Manji has argued, will end up servicing and paying the debts their husbands and other male relatives accumulate as they enter rural credit markets using their land as collateral (Manji 2003, 105).

Further, the assumed increase in agricultural productivity in the small-scale sector due to market-based land tenure is premised, as stated earlier, on the gender-blind notion of noncontractible labor. But as this chapter and other studies have argued, gender power relations shape agricultural labor processes, and given that it is women who predominantly provide unwaged labor in the agricultural sector, it is they who will contribute to whatever increases occur in this sector (Manji 2003, 105). Of course, the presentation of terms such as noncontractible labor in a gender-blind manner emerges from the failure of mainstream scholars to problematize terms such as "the family," "household," and "labor markets." These concepts do not exist, evolve, or translate in cultural, political, and economic vacuums. The notion of household, for example, which is a core concept in hegemonic economic discourses, such as the current agrarian reforms being promoted in Africa, is a gendered term (Elson 1998). A central assumption of policies such as the World Bank's contemporary land reform in Africa is that members of the household work collaboratively for the welfare of the unit, guided by "a benevolent dictator" and altruism, rather than by the rational "self-ish behaviour expected in the marketplace" (Waylen 2000, 20). Such a conceptualization of households is very limited because it fails to problematize the power politics that govern family relationships.

Using an approach that foregrounds tensions and hierarchies in household processes, Amartya Sen has argued that households should not be articulated as power-neutral places, but rather as sites embedded in power dynamics characterized by "cooperative conflict": a social practice that involves a "bargaining process" whose outcome is shaped by an individual's "gender, lifecycle and class" positioning in a household (Sen 1990 and Waylen 2000, 20).[16] Thus, a person's role in the economic sphere in any household or community is influenced by gender ideologies and other power dynamics. Such an approach to labor and household processes sheds more light on our understanding of the gendered nature of the much cherished ideology and practice of "hard work" among the Gikuyu community in Kenya. While everyone in this community is supposed to embrace the ideology of hard work and a disciplined work ethnic epitomized by the culturally held myth that "work has never killed anyone," this ideology is disseminated differently to men and women and affects them differently. Throughout their formative years, young girls of all social classes hear, "women, especially mothers, never get sick," and marrying a women who is lazy or from a lazy lineage is a disgrace.[17] These cultural gender power dynamics have historically resulted in heavy workloads for Gikuyu women, especially those involved in agrarian production, a process that will only deepen with the promotion of notions such as the World Bank's doctrine of noncontractible labor. Further, rural class dynamics in the Gikuyu community will also shape that process since women from the *ahoi*[18] marginalized class will have little room to maneuver when compared to their counterparts whose husbands own land.

In addition, the question of how neoliberal restructuring in other sectors, such as social spending (to be discussed later), would affect women's involvement in agriculture has been left out of the neoliberal agrarian reform agenda, which fails to take account of the interconnectedness of all economic production. Last, but not least, the overall decline of agricultural earnings in Africa and the other regions on the periphery of the world capitalist system, due to the asymmetrical nature of the global trading structure and the resulting impact on small-scale production, is depoliticized and framed within the ahistorical and technical discourse of comparative advantage and free market incentives.

Privatization

The privatization of government-owned public enterprises is another policy reform aimed at reducing the role of the state and thus facilitating the transition to market-led capitalism. The postcolonial pattern of accumulation in most of Africa saw the expansion of colonial public enterprises as a core component of the state-led capitalist institutional architecture. This trend was not relegated to the continent alone, but rather was a development model embraced by other countries in the so-called Third World that was informed by theories of late-modernizing societies, the rise of welfare states in the West after the 1930s economic crisis, and the contradictions generated by colonialism.

For newly independent African states, public enterprises encompassed all key sectors of their economic structures. In the financial sector, state-owned banks and insurance firms become the norm in diverse political/ideological landscapes such as President Julius Nyerere's Tanzania and President Jomo Kenyatta's Kenya. Agrarian production and marketing parastatals, such as the Agricultural Development and Marketing Corporation in Malawi (ADMARC), governed the extraction of agricultural surplus, albeit differently, for the estate and small-scale agricultural subsectors (Sahle 2008). The Industrial and Commercial Development Corporation and Malawi Development Corporation were responsible for the evolution of industrial and commercial development in Kenya and Malawi, respectively (Himbara 1994 and Kaluwa 1992).[19]

Due to historical and international political and economic conditions, the varied forms of state-led capitalism led to steady economic growth in the first decade or so of the first wave of transition to independence on the

African continent. For example, in countries such as Côte d'Ivoire, which had a strong local capitalist class and an influx of French capital, and in former colonial settler economies such as Kenya with Kenyatta's pro-Western alliance stance, economic growth was significant compared with that in other African countries. Even countries such as Malawi, considered a "colonial slum," also experienced rapid economic growth between 1964 and 1972, due to favorable international markets for agricultural commodities and Kamuzu Banda's stand against communists (Ghai and Radwan 1983, 73–74).

As Africa's postcolonial states entered a period of fiscal crisis, their reliance on public enterprises as engines of state-led capitalism came under heavy criticism, especially by scholars working within the new development paradigm of neoliberalism and the transnational lending community, including leading institutions such as the World Bank and the International Monetary Fund. According to supporters of neoliberal economic reforms, public enterprises were largely responsible for the continent's limited development and economic crisis since they were inefficient, created rent-seeking opportunities, and stifled the entrepreneurial spirit. It is in this respect, then, that neoliberal discourse presented parastatal reform along market lines as a central element in Africa's recovery from its economic quagmire. These reforms included the sale of publicly owned enterprises and a commitment to the creation of "an incentive system conducive to efficient performance" (World Bank 1981, 38). Liquidating public enterprises would supposedly not only reduce the role of the state in economic affairs, but also lead to the emergence of an independent capitalist class committed to an ethos of efficiency, comparative advantage, competition, and a free market system.

Over the last twenty years, African states have established bodies to facilitate public enterprise reforms. While absent in the mainstream literature on privatization, gender power relations within specific African countries have shaped the evolution of the privatization process. The gender-blind and ahistorical nature of the neoliberal theory that informs privatization discourse has resulted in the neglect of the gendering that marks privatization. This discourse assumes that women and men have equal access to capital and thus will participate equally in the buying of state-owned enterprises. To be sure, social class, ethnicity, religion, and other social categories mediate the ability of both women and men to participate in the accumulation process. However, in the case of African societies, historical developments have continually marginalized large numbers of women. Thus, one can make a general statement about this reality without falling into the homogenizing tendency that Chandra Mohanty's seminal work addresses.[20]

In terms of privatization programs, primary data from Malawi indicate that of the number of public enterprises sold, none were bought by a woman or a group of women. Essentially, what these figures show is the reproduction of class power: it is men drawn from the dominant class—from the upper echelons of the ruling parties, the nascent bourgeoisie, and the bureaucracy—that have benefited from Malawi's privatization process (Sahle 2008). Foreign owners of capital have also been major actors in privatization processes in various African countries. In Senegal, for instance, Yassine Fall demonstrates how the state, with the support of the World Bank, has deepened foreign capital involvement in key economic sectors through the privatization program. Even after challenges from groups in civil society against the privatization of the state-owned energy provider SENELEC, the Senegalese state went ahead and sold the company to Hydraulique Quebec (Fall 2001, 69). Further, in the telecommunications sector, the state has guaranteed the new owner, SONATEL, a seven-year monopoly in this arena, and the French RATP and SDE firms have benefited from the purchasing of former public enterprises in the transportation and water provision sectors, respectively (Fall 2001, 69).

Social Sector Spending

The reduction of social sector expenditure is another central tenet of the neoliberal capital accumulation framework. Like the privatization of publicly owned enterprises, these reforms are based on the premise that the nature of postcolonial state expenditure in sectors such as health and education was inefficient and led to the wasting of resources. Central to the rolling back of the state's involvement in the economic arena, African states have had to accept severe reductions in health spending (Turshen 1994, 79).[21] Historically, state expenditure on health has been very low in most of Africa, with the household, specifically women, carrying the burden of health care for their family members(Turshen 1994, 81).[22]

A core tenet of heath sector reforms has been the introduction of user fees a process that has had serious effects on women and children. In the Zaria region of Nigeria, the introduction of user fees led to an increase of 56 percent in maternal death and a 46 percent drop in hospital deliveries (Nanda 2002, 129). The assumption underpinning the introduction of user fees is that women and other members of marginalized social forces can avoid meeting their health costs, but as Nanda argues, this position assumes women have similar social and economic resources as men. A study on market-based health reforms in Uganda demonstrated that it is men who control access to earnings from the cash crop sector, although it is women who not only work in this sector but also take care of sick relatives (Nanda 2002, 131). In another study in Zaire about the introduction of user fees, "a rapid increase in the price of health care sharply decreased the demand for curative services, prenatal visits and clinics for children under 5 years of age (Turshen 1994, 82)." Consequently, as Elson has argued, what neoliberal economists saw as increased efficiency with the reduction of hospital costs has amounted to "simply a transfer of the costs from the hospital to the home . . . which in practice means women" (Elson 1995, 177–78). This has serious implications for women's well-being because, as women stated in a study of health sector reforms in Zambia, "they could not afford to be ill because of the time it would take away from their work"; in Ghana, "doctors reported that women were presenting much more complex, chronic and terminal ailments because they delayed seeking medical treatment" (Elson 1995, 177; Brown and Kerr 1997, 74; Porter and Judd 1999, 191–92).

The health crisis facing most African women with the evolution of neo-liberal reforms is compounded by austerity reforms in other sectors. In Mozambique, steady increase in food prices with the removal of government subsidies has led to a "widespread deterioration in the nutritional status of children and pregnant and lactating mothers in both rural and urban areas. . . . Mothers are unable to buy enough food of the right type to feed the whole family, and in many cases priority in feeding is given to adult males" (Elson 1989, 68 and Turshen 1994, 80).

While the World Bank has modified its health sector reform policies and now calls on African states to provide a clinical package that includes "perinatal and delivery care, family services, management of the sick child, [and] tuberculosis," which is linked to the HIV virus, this modification is still very limited and does not address the health needs of women beyond their role as mothers (Turshen 1994, 89). Moreover, this shift should be put in the overall context of the World Bank's approach to women's health in Africa, which is mainly geared to ensure that local states enact measures to control population growth. Further, the majority of women live in rural areas with limited opportunities for alternative economic activities in the era of state restructuring; thus, an already poor health infrastructure, coupled with neo-liberal health reforms, reduce their ability to take care of their own and their family's health (Turshen 1994, 77, 91).

Overall, reduction in social sector spending has affected women and men differently. For example, the removal of government subsidies for education has led to increased educational costs—a development that has contributed to the reproduction of the historical gender bias in education opportunities for the majority of African girls[23]—in Chad, 29.4 percent of girls and 49.6 percent of boys attend school (Tsikata, Kerr, Blacklock, and Laforce 2000, 238). Over two decades of reforms have led to a public outcry, leading some states in their attempts to gain popular support, especially in the days leading up to the holding of general elections, to promise to introduce free education—albeit not with a gender analysis.[24] Beyond reforms in education and health, the so-called rationalization of the civil service through policies such as public sector retrenchment has led to the loss of jobs in sectors that have generally been employment domains for the majority of women, such as nursing, teaching, clerical work, and low-end managerial positions. In the African context, this has led to an increased workload for women, a social trend that a Tanzanian woman characterized as "the big slavery, work with 'no boundaries' that is endless" (Mbilinyi 1989, 241). To be sure, variables neglected by neoliberal advocates, such as class, and cultural practices (such as the earlier-mentioned work ethic of the Gikuyu community in Kenya) have also compounded this trend.

Responses by African Women

Contemporary African women, like their counterparts in earlier historical periods, have, of course, responded to these new realities not only by challenging the neoliberal development model, evidenced by their strong involvement in the popular social movements of the early 1990s and the growing anti-globalization forum, but also by seeking whatever economic avenues they can find to sustain their social and economic needs. For example, these women have become the dominant workers in export-free zones as global firms establish offshore production sites in various regions of the global South. While offering women wage employment, the offshore production zones are driven by the search for cheap, flexible, and abundant labor; hence, contrary to their claims of contributing to women's empowerment, they have ensured that women are trapped in the vicious cycle of poverty due to the nature of work in these zones. The core characteristics of this kind of work are low pay, insecure wage contracts, and exploitative working conditions marked by extensive surveillance and long working hours. The social and economic well-being of women working in offshore production sites in the global South are further undermined, as Saskia Sassen has argued, because the traditional route for struggling for better wages and working conditions—through labor unions' bargaining with capital—is not open to them due to the antilabor practices, new production regimes, the reorganization of labor with the decline of the traditional economic sectors, and immigration patterns in the current phase of globalization (Sassen 1998, 111–31).[25]

As employment opportunities for women who are engaged in some form of wage-labor are scarce, African women are in constant search of additional means of meeting the economic demands and needs of their families. This social phenomenon, commonly referred to as "hassling," is especially common for women in Africa's declining middle classes, and even in segments of the upper-middle classes.[26] Nevertheless, the "hassling" trend is not limited to women in these classes—women in rural areas have also had to deal with the impact of state restructuring. In the rural areas, women have become involved in the precarious world of agricultural piecework for households that can still afford to hire workers. Piecework agricultural wages are traditionally very low and gendered: "Women receive only one-third of male wages and, unlike men, they typically choose to be paid in kind" (Geisler and Hansen 1994, 103).

Women are also increasingly engaged in activities that have historically been linked to men, such as drug trafficking and armed robbery (Taiwo 1997, 87). Further, there has been an increase in, and social remapping of, street work during this period of neoliberal restructuring. In Nigeria, a study by Sade Taiwo of commercial sex work in various cities indicates that the women engaged in this work are increasingly drawn from the educated strata, from high school to university graduates, who, while aware of the psychological violence and other problems generated by this line of work, see it as the only alternative in the current historical moment (Taiwo 1997, 88). Suffice to conclude that in the midst of economic crisis and austere economic policies, women in Africa then have to find ways to meet the economic needs of their immediate families and, in the context of the HIV/AIDS crisis, care for sick relatives. Indeed, Wisdom J. Tettey makes a similar observation, regarding the link between neoliberal policies and the proliferation crime, in his two chapters on Ghanaian youth and the Internet in this volume. In Africa, as elsewhere, women have become, to use Janine Brodie's phrase, the "shock-absorbers" of "neo-liberal restructuring" (Brodie 1994, 50). This "caring sector" is not viewed as contributing to a country's economic activities in official economic analysis. Yet, according to the United Nations Development Program: "If women's work was monetized it would add up to US$11 trillion a year, a huge contribution to the world economy" (Kerr 1999, 194).

Gender, States, and Markets: Concluding Notes

The neoliberal development theory and practice has been the hegemonic development paradigm for more than two decades now. This chapter has demonstrated the gendered nature of state- and market-led capital accumulation strategies. Thus, while the neoliberal paradigm presents capital accumulation processes and core policies and concepts (such as such as privatization, civil service retrenchment, and self-regulating markets) as gender neutral, a critical feminist political approach of this phenomenon (such as the one utilized here) demonstrates the gendered foundation of neoliberal discourses and practices. In addition to unmasking the gender bias in the neoliberal economic project, this analysis has attempted to highlight how the historical, cultural conditions and the gendered foundations of African states place structural limits on women's political agency.

REFERENCES

Ake, C. 1981. *A political economy of Africa*. Harlow: Longman.

Alvarez, S. 1990. *Engendering democracy in Brazil*. Princeton: Princeton University Press.

Amin, S. 1997. *Capitalism in the age of globalization: The management of contemporary society*. London: Zed Books.

Bangura, Y. 1992. Authoritarian rule and democracy in Africa: A theoretical discourse. In *When democracy makes sense*, ed. Lars Rudebeck, 69–104. Uppsala, Sweden: Uppsala University.

Bayart, Jean-Francois. 1993. *The state in Africa: The politics of the belly*. London: Longman.

Bond, P. 2000. *Elite transition: From apartheid to neoliberalism in South Africa*. London: Pluto.

Boserup, E. 1970. *Woman's role in economic development*. New York: St. Martin's.

Bratton, M., and Nicolas van de Walle. 1997. *Democratic experiments in Africa regime transitions in comparative perspective*. Cambridge: Cambridge University Press.

Brodie, J. 1994. Shifting the boundaries: Gender and the politics of restructuring. In *The strategic silence: Gender and economic policy*, ed. Isabella Bakker, 46–60. London: Zed Books.

Brown, R. L., and Joanna Kerr, eds. 1997. *The gender dimensions of economic reforms in Ghana, Mali, and Zambia*. Ottawa: North-South Institute.

Cook, J., and Jennifer Roberts. 2000. Towards a gendered political economy. In *Towards a gendered political economy*, ed. Joanne Cook, Jennifer Roberts, and Georgina Waylen, 3–13. London: Macmillan.

Cornia, G. A., and J. deJong.1992. Policies for the revitalisation of human resources development. In *Africa's recovery in the 1990s: From stagnation and adjustment to human development*, ed. G. A. Cornia, R. va der Hoeven, and T. Mkandawire, 246–71. New York: St. Martin's.

Cox, R. 1987. *Production, power, and world order*. New York: Columbia University Press.

Craske, M. 1998. Remasculinisation and the neoliberal state in Latin America. In *Gender, politics, and the state*, ed. Vicky Randall and Georgina Waylen, 100–120. London: Routledge.

Elson, D. 1989. The impact of structural adjustment on women: Concepts and issues. In *The IMF, the World Bank and the African debt*, vol. 2, ed. B. Onimode, 56–74. London: Zed Books.

———. 1995.Male bias in macro-economics: The case of structural adjustment. In *Male bias in the development process*, ed. Diane Elson. 164–90, Manchester: Manchester University Press.

———. 1998. Talking to the boys: Gender and economic growth models. In *Feminist visions of development: Gender, analysis and policy*, ed. Cecile Jackson and Ruth Pearson, 155–70. London and New York: Routledge.

Fall, Y.2001. Gender and social implications of globalization: An African Perspective. In *Gender, globalization, and democratization*, ed. Rita Mae Kelly, Jane H. Bayes, Mary Hawkesworth, and Brigitte Young, 49–74. Boston: Rowman & Littlefield.

Fatton, R. 1989. Gender, class and state in Africa. In *Women and the state in Africa*, ed. Jane L. Parpart and Kathleen Staudt, 47–66. Boulder and London: Lynne Rienner.

Geisler, G., and K. Tranberg Hansen. 1994. Structural adjustment and gender relations in Zambia. In *Women in the age of economic transformation*, ed. Nahid Aslanbeigui, Steven Pressman, and Gale Summerfield, 95–112. London: Routledge.

Ghai, D., and Samir Radwan. 1983. *Agrarian policies and rural poverty in Africa*. Geneva: International Labour Organisation.

Gill, S. 1988. *The global political economy: perspectives, problems, and policies*. Baltimore: John Hopkins University Press.

———. 1997. *Globalization, democratization, and multilateralism*. London: Macmillan.

Gordon, A. A. 2001. Women and development. In *Understanding contemporary Africa*, ed. April A. Gordon and Donald L. Gordon, 271–97. Boulder and London: Lynne Rienner.

Helleiner, E. 1994. *States and the reemergence of global finance: From Bretton Woods to the 1990s*. Ithaca: Cornell University Press.

Himbara, D. 1994. *Kenyan capitalists, the state, and development*. Nairobi: East African Educational Publishers.

Hyden, G. 1992. Governance and the study of politics. In *Governance and politics in Africa*, ed. Goran Hyden and Michael Bratton, 1–26. Boulder: Lynne Rienner.

Hyden, G., and Michael Bratton. 1992. *Governance and politics in Africa*. Boulder: Lynne Rienner.

Ihonvbere, J. 1989. *The political economy of crisis and underdevelopment in Africa: Selected works of Claude Ake*. Lagos: JAD Publishers.

Kaluwa, B. 1992. Malawi industry: Policies, performance, and problems. In *Malawi at the crossroads: The postcolonial political economy*, ed. Guy Mhone. Harare: SAPES.

Kandawire, J. A. K.1989. Women and development in Central Africa. In *Women and development in Africa*, ed. Jane L. Parpart, 195–207. Lahham: University Press of America.

Kerr, J. 1999. Responding to globalization: Can feminists transform development? In *Feminists doing development: A practical critique*, ed. Marilyn Porter and Ellen Judd, 190–205. London: Zed Books.

Leys, C. 2001. *Market-driven politics*. London: Verso.

Lovett, M. 1987. Gender relations, class formation, and the colonial state in Africa. In *Women and the state in Africa*, ed. Jane L. Parpart and Katheleen A. Staudt, 23–46. Boulder and London: Lynne Rienner.

Manji, A. 2003. Capital, labour and land relations in Africa: A gender analysis of the World Bank's Policy Research Report on Land Institutions and Land Policy. *Third World Quarterly* 24 (1): 97–114.

Mbilinyi, M. 1989. Women as peasant and casual labor and the development crisis in Tanzania. In *Women and development in Africa*, ed. Jane L. Parpart, 209–56. Lahham: University Press of America.

Mkandawire, T., and Charles C. Soluto. 1999. *Our continent, our future*. Trenton: Africa World Press.

Mohanty, T. C. 2003. *Feminism without borders: Decolonizing theory, practising solidarity*. Durham, NC: Duke University Press.

Molyneux, M. 1985. Mobilization without emancipation: women's interests, the state, and revolution in Nicaragua. *Feminist Studies* 11 (2): 227–54.

Munachonga, M. L. 1987. Women and the state: Zambia's development policies and their impact on women. In *Women and the state in Africa*, ed. Jane L. Parpart and Kathleen A. Staudt, 130–42. Boulder and London: Lynne Rienner.

Nanda, P. 2002. Gender dimensions of user fees: Implications for women's utilization of health care. *Reproductive Health Matters* 10 (20).

Neocosmos, M. 1993. *The agrarian question in southern Africa and "accumulation from below."* Uppsala: The Scandinavian Institute of African Studies.

Nzomo, M. and Kathleen Staudt. 1994. Man-made political machinery in Kenya: What political space for women? In *Women and politics world wide*, ed. B. J. Nelson and N. Chowdhury, 416–35. New Haven, CT: Yale University Press.

Pankhurst D., and Jenny Pearce 1996. Feminist perspectives on democratization in the south: engendering or adding women in? In *Women and politics in the Third World*, ed. Haleh Afshar, 40–47. London and New York: Routledge.

Polanyi, K. 1957. *The great transformation: The political and economic origins of our time*. Boston: Beacon.

Porter M., and Ellen Judd. 1999. *Feminists doing development: A practical critique*. London: Zed Books.

Robertson, C. 1984. *Sharing the same bowl: A socioeconomic history of women and class in Accra, Ghana*. Bloomington: Indiana University.

Sahle, N. E. 1998. Women and political participation in Kenya: Evaluating the inter-play of gender, ethnicity, class and state. In *Multiparty democracy and political change*: *Constraints to democratization, ed.* John Mukum Mbaku, and Julius O. Ihonvbere, 171–93. Aldershot, UK: Ashgate.

———. 2008 (forthcoming). *World Orders, Development and Transformation*. Hound-mills, UK: Palgrave Macmillan.

Sahn, E. D. 1994. Economic crisis and policy reform in Africa: An introduction. In *Adjusting to policy failure in African economies*, ed. David E. Sahn. Ithaca, NY: Cor-nell University Press.

Scott, V. C. 1995. *Gender and development rethinking modernization and dependency theory*. Boulder: Lynne Rienner.

Selolwane, O. 2000.Civil Society, Citizenship and women's rights in Botswana. In *International perspectives on gender and democratization*, ed. Shirin M. Rai, 83–99. New York: St. Martin's.

Sen, A. 1990. Gender and co-operative conflicts. In *Persistent inequalities*: *Women and world development, ed.* I. Tinker, 123–49. Oxford: Oxford University Press.

Sassen, S. 1998. *Globalization and its discontents*. New York: The New Press.

Strange, S. 1986. *Casino capitalism*. Oxford: Basil Blackwell.

Taiwo, S. 1997. Macroeconomic impact of economic adjustment on women. In *Women and Economic Reforms in Nigeria*, ed. Kassy Garba, Bola Akanji, and Ifeoma Isiugo-Abanihe, 83–98. Ibadan: Women's Research and Documentation Centre, University of Ibadan.

Taylor V. 2000. *Marketisation of governance*: *Critical feminist perspectives from the south*. Cape Town: SADEP.

Toye, J. 1994. *Dilemmas of development*. Oxford: Blackwell.

Tsikata, D., and Joanna Kerr, eds. 2000. *Demanding dignity*: *Women confronting eco-nomic reforms in Africa*. Ottawa: The North-South Institute.

Turshen, M. 1994. Impact of economic reforms on women's health and health care in sub-Saharan Africa. In *Women in the age of economic transformation*, ed. Nahid Aslan-beigui, Steven Pressman, and Gale Summerfield, 77–94. London: Routledge.

Waylen, G. 2000. Gendered political economy and feminist analysis. In *Towards a gen-dered political economy, ed.* Joanne Cook, Jennifer Roberts, and Georgina Waylen, 14–38. London: Macmillan.

World Bank. 1981. *Accelerated development in sub-Saharan Africa*: *An agenda for action*.

———. 1994. *Adjustment in Africa*. Oxford: Oxford University Press.

NOTES

1. Neoliberal state restructuring is not limited just to the economic structure of African states, but extends also to their political organization, which is viewed as lacking good governance structures—a situation that has manifested itself in high levels of corruption and abuse of human rights. Political reforms under neoliberal restructuring have concentrated on the promotion of good governance struc-tures and the establishment of multiparty democratic states (Hyden 1992, 2–3).

2. For extensive discussion on this, see Jean-Francois Bayart, *The state in Africa: The politics of the belly* (London: Longman, 1993); and Michael Bratton and Nicolas van de Walle, *Democratic experiments in Africa regime transitions in comparative perspective*. Cambridge: University Press, 1997).

3. For seminal arguments along these lines, see Julius Ihonvbere, *The political economy of crisis and underdevelopment in Africa: Selected works of Claude Ake* (Lagos: JAD Publishers, 1989); Samir Amin, *Capitalism in the age of globalization* (London & New Jersey: Zed Books, 1997); Patrick Bond, *Elite transition: From apartheid to neoliberalism in South Africa* (London: Pluto Press, 2000); Thandika Mkandawire and Charles C. Soluto, *Our continent our future* (Trenton: Africa World Press, 1–99); and Claude Ake, *A political economy of Africa* (Harlow: Longman, 1981).

4. Some examples: Viviene Taylor, *Marketisation of governance: Critical feminist perspectives from the south* (Cape Town: SADEP, 2000); Sonia Alvarez, *Engendering democracy in Brazil* (Princeton: Princeton University Press, 1990); Marilyn Porter and Ellen Judd, *Feminists doing development: A practical critique* (London: Zed Books, 1999); and Joanne Cook and Jennifer Roberts, op. cit.,

5. See Karl Polanyi, *The great transformation: The political and economic origins of our time* (Boston: Beacon Press, 1957) for a detailed discussion.

6. See for instance, Doon Pankhurst and Jenny Pearce, Feminist perspectives on democratization in the South: engendering or adding women in? In *Women and politics in the Third World*, ed. Haleh Afshar (London and New York: Routledge, 1996); Maria Nzomo, "Man-made political machinery in Kenya: What Political Space for Women?," in *Women and Politics World Wide*, ed. B.J. Nelson and Chowdhury (Yale University, 1994); Mikki Craske, "Remasculinisation and the neoliberal state in Latin America," in *Gender, politics and the state*, ed. Vicky Randall and Georgina Waylen (London: Routledge, 1998); Eunice Njeri Sahle, "Women and political participation in Kenya: Evaluating the interplay of gender, ethnicity, class and state," in John Mukum Mbaku and Julius O. Ihonvbere, *Multiparty Democracy and Political Change: Constraints to Democratization* (Aldershot, UK: Ashgate, 1998); and Onalena Selolwane, "Civil society, citizenship and women's Rights in Botswana," in *International Perspectives on Gender and Democratisation*, ed. Shirin M. Rai (New York: St. Martin's Press, 2000).

7. During the 1884 Berlin Conference that resulted in various European powers laying claim to various parts of Africa, King Leopold stated that he wanted to have a piece of this magnificent African cake. Quoted in the film, *This magnificent African cake*, Basil Davidson, African Film Series, vol. 3

8. For an examination of colonial state agricultural policies see, Ester Boserup, *Woman's Role in Economic Development* (New York: St. Martin's, 1970).

9. It is important to note that the gendered labor migrant system and forced labor practices were not limited to the mineral rich colonies but also to agrarian based colonies such as Ivory Coast, Senegal Malawi, Tanzania, Kenya, and many others.

10. For a discussion of the concept of women's strategic needs, see Maxine Molyneux, "Mobilization without emancipation: women's interests, the state, and revolution in Nicaragua," *Feminist Studies* 1 (2): 2–27.

11. See Clare Robertson, *Sharing the Same Bowl: A Socioeconomic History of Women and Class in Accra, Ghana* (Bloomington: Indiana University, 1984).

12. For an in-depth discussion of the gendered nature of dominant theories of development, see Catherine V. Scott, *Gender and Development Rethinking Modernization and Dependency Theory* (Boulder: Lynne Rienner, 1995).

13. There is an enormous body of literature on these themes, thus a limited sample will suffice: Eric Helleiner, *States and the Reemergence of Global Finance: From Bretton Woods to the 1990s* (Ithaca: Cornell University Press, 1994); Samir Amin,

Capitalism in the Age of Globalization: the Management of Contemporary Society, op. cit.; Robert Cox, *Production, Power, and World Order* (New York: Columbia University Press, 1987); Colin Leys, *Market-driven Politics* (London: Verso, 2001); Susan Strange, *Casino Capitalism* (Oxford: Basil Blackwell, 1986); Stephen Gill, *The Global Political Economy: perspectives, problems and policies* (Baltimore: John Hopkins University Press, 1988), and *Globalization, Democratization and Multilateralism* (London: Macmillan, 1997).

14. Michael Neocosmos, *The Agrarian Question in Southern Africa and "Accumulation from Below"* (Uppsala: The Scandinavian Institute of African Studies, 1993); and Dharam Ghai and Samir Radwan, *Agrarian Policies and Rural Poverty in Africa* (Geneva: International Labour Organisation, 1983).

15. Other benefits enjoyed by large-scale farmers included easy access to loans, production of high-earning export crops, and agricultural extension services.

16. For an extended discussion of the notion of cooperative conflicts, see Amartya Sen, "Gender and Co-operative Conflicts," in I. Tinker, ed., *Persistent Inequalities: Women and World Development* (Oxford: Oxford University Press, 1990); and Georgina Waylen, "Gendered Political Economy and Feminist Analysis," in *Towards a Gendered Political Economy*, ed. Joanne Cook, Jennifer Roberts and Georgina Waylen, p. 20.

17. References to Gikuyu metaphors drawn from some aspects of author's cultural memory. For an elaboration of the manifestations patriarchal practices by the colonial and postcolonial states and in Gikuyu and Luo communities, see Wambui Waiyaki Otieno's fascinating biography, *Mau Mau's Daughter: A Life History* (London and Boulder: Lynne Rienner, 1998).

18. Gikuyu term for the landless.

19. For details on Kenya's industrial sector, see David Himbara, *Kenyan Capitalists, the State, and Development* (Nairobi: East African Educational Publishers, 1994); and for Malawi, see Ben Kaluwa, "Malawi Industry: Policies, Performance and Problems," in *Malawi at the Crossroads: The Postcolonial Political Economy*, ed. Guy Mhone (Harare: SAPES, 1992).

20. See Chandra T. Mohanty, *Feminism Without Borders: Decolonizing Theory, Practising Solidarity* (Durham, NC: Duke University Press, 2003) for a critique of the tendency to homogenize African women and other women in the global South.

21. For figures on declining health spending, see Meredeth Turshen, "Impact of economic reforms on women's health and health care in sub-Saharan Africa," in *Women in the Age of Economic Transformation*, ed. Nahid Aslanbeigui, Steven Pressman and Gale Summerfield (London: Routledge, 1994), 7–9.

22. For detailed discussion, see G. A. Cornia and J. deJong, "Policies for the revitalisation of human resources development," in *Africa's Recovery in the 1990s: From Stagnation and Adjustment to Human Development*, ed. G. A. Cornia, R. va der Hoeven and T. Mkandawire (New York: St. Martin's, 1992), 2–68, quoted in Meredith Turshen, op. cited., 81.

23. For a powerful visual presentation of this phenomenon, see the documentary film *These Girls are Missing*, which chronicles the obstacles and struggles that young girls from a variety of regions in Africa face in attempts to gain an education.

24. Malawi and Kenya are the best examples, with Bakili Muluzi and Mwai Kibaki making the introduction of free education a central promise during their respective presidential campaigns.

25. For a seminal argument that links gender, immigration, and the reorganization of production regimes, see Saskin Sassen, *Globalization and Its Discontents* (New York: The New Press, 1998), 1–11.

26. I am indebted to friends in Malawi—Freda Chimimba and F. Msimati—and in Kenya—Irene M'kwenda.

CHAPTER 5

GLOBALIZATION, INDIGENIZATION, AND TOURISM IN SUB-SAHARAN AFRICA

Francis Adu-Febiri

INTRODUCTION

Sub-Saharan Africa tourism reflects one of the many contradictions of the subcontinent—the fact that its rich natural and sociocultural ecologies do not translate into meaningful socioeconomic development. Sub-Saharan African countries capture a disproportionately miniscule portion of the global tourism business, despite their substantial potentialities for tourism resources. To date, analysts have put little emphasis on the links between neoliberal political economy of globalization and indigenization, mediated by the legacy of colonization, in their explications of this contradiction. Instead, the focus has been *either* on factors internal *or* external to sub-Saharan Africa, without implicating the connections between these apparent disparate factors. Empirically, the globalization-indigenization dialectic and its colonial legacy interface are missing from the search for answers for sub-Saharan African tourism development. Likewise, the existing paradigms of tourism development, articulated by Jafari (1989) as the *advocacy platform, the cautionary platform, the adaptancy platform*, and the *knowledge-based platform*, are virtually silent on these dynamics.

The advocacy platform of tourism focuses mainly on internal factors—such as the paucity of tourism infrastructure, the lack of investment capital, weak business environment, the nonexistence of regional and domestic tourism, the lack of physical safety and public health facilities, and fragile tourism ministries and boards, lack of tourism promotion and marketing, substandard or low quality tourism facilities, political instability, and inadequate privatization, and so on—in accounting for the poor performance of the tourist industry. In contrast, the cautionary platform and the adaptancy platform locate the problem in the world capitalist system, or globalization, and mass tourism, respectively. Yet, the mediated political economy of neoliberal globalization compels reliance on mass or conventional tourism (as advocated by the advocacy platform) and alternative forms of tourism (as recommended by the adaptancy platform) in order to capture larger portions of the global tourism market and revenue. However, sub-Saharan Africa's attempts to develop mass tourism and externally initiated alternative forms of tourism in response to increasing neoliberal globalization have not been that successful. This is not only because of the hierarchically structured tourism industry located in the world capitalist political economy (as emphasized by the cautionary platform), or lack of understanding and adaptation of local cultures (as indicated by the knowledge-based platform), but also because of the same mediations wrought by contemporary globalization. Thus, the colonial legacy of sub-Saharan Africa interacts with the dynamics of globalization to prevent the sub-continent from promoting sustainable tourism development.

In essence, because the colonial legacy of sub-Saharan Africa serves as a conduit of globalization, the privatization and homogenization tendencies of neoliberal globalization render mass tourism in this region less competitive internationally, frustrate alternative forms of tourism as a viable alternative, and exploit local African communities. Thus, unless the colonial undertones of the political economy of neoliberal globalization change, sub-Saharan Africa is likely to continue to be the weakest player in the global tourism industry. The hope is that indigenization may contribute to this change, and thus lessen the adverse impact of globalization on tourism development in sub-Saharan Africa.

Tourism development in contemporary sub-Saharan Africa is not an indigenous enterprise. It is part of the colonial, unequal power relations reproduced by neoliberal globalization. This unequal relationship underlies Africa's tourism development challenges, a factor neglected by the advocacy platform of tourism spearheaded by the World Bank. For example, the 2001 World Bank Working Paper Series, *Tourism in Africa*, put together by Iain Christie and Doreen Crompton, never mentioned the colonial legacy in the discussion of the constraints of tourism development. Similarly, existing critiques of the advocacy platform to tourism development in Africa do not identify colonial legacy as an issue (Maluga 1973; Esh and Rosenblum 1975; Jommo 1987; Backmann 1988). It is important to look into sub-Saharan Africa's disappointing tourism development as it relates to the legacy of colonization, as this relational dynamics is a major contributor to sub-Saharan Africa's lack of socioeconomic and political power to transform its tourism industry. Indigenization of tourism provides some hope because it has the potential to empower the local, neutralize the colonial legacy, and effectively adapt the global into the local.

Indigenization is the reconstruction and reactivation of the indigene. It involves the use of indigenous philosophies, epistemologies, pedagogies, cosmologies, knowledge, skills, and cultures to interrogate neoliberal globalization and to enrich the lifeworlds of indigenous and nonindigenous peoples. With regard to sub-Saharan African tourism, indigenization entails using indigenous frameworks to change the political economy of tourism in ways that enable sub-Saharan African countries acquire economic, political, and technological power to meaningfully connect to global tourism and make tourism sustainable for the benefit of the region. This chapter uses the dialectics of globalization and indigenization to examine sub-Saharan Africa's tourism resources and its current and potential share of the global tourism business, and to offer strategies for the improvement of mass tourism in the region.

TOURISM OUT OF THE GLOBALIZATION BOX: THE GLOBALIZATION-INDIGENIZATION DIALECTIC

Sub-Sahara Africa tourism has been conceptualized and produced in the crucibles of neoliberal globalization. Constructing tourism in this way provides only a partial picture of the industry in sub-Saharan Africa. To grasp its full view, sub-Saharan Africa tourism must be placed at the interface of globalization and indigenization, where it rightly belongs. At this interface is a condition that has hitherto been unsustainable for sub-Saharan Africa, because this region did not achieve substantive sovereignty before the establishment of neoliberal globalization in the 1970s. The lifeworlds of this interface are dominated and conditioned by sub-Saharan Africa's colonial legacy. The cautionary platform's examination of tourism, paralleled in Robertson's (1992) and Giddens' (1990) conception of the dialectic between the local and the global as unequal power relations, hints on, but never analyzes, this unsustainable interface. Applying Robertson's and Giddens' global-local dialectic to leisure, Rojek (1995, 93) intimates that "with regard to leisure relations, it is evident that the tendency to generate global culture has been obstructed, both by the unintended effects of processes of globalization and by organized resistance." This notion, although, points to counterhegemonic spaces in the global, it is reflective of the conventional perspective of dialectic that posits that within the strains toward integration in the social world are forces of opposition and potential conflict that generate automatic positive change at the local or grassroots level (Marx 1967 [1867]; Coser 1956; Dahrendorf 1958).

This conventional perspective of dialectics, however, fails to capture the essence of the globalization-indigenization dialectical interface with regard to tourism development in sub-Saharan Africa, since it fails to show that the organized resistance to exploitative tourism is not usually local, and the local that resists is not necessarily indigenous. There is hardly any locally organized resistance to the neoliberal globalization-driven tourism in sub-Saharan Africa. Although the indigenous cosmologies serve as constraints

toward opposition to, and potential conflict with, globalization's construction of indigenous natural and cultural ecologies as tourism resources, they
hardly formulate any organized active resistance. They rather ignore tourism
and continue to connect to the ecologies emotionally, morally, spiritually, and
subsistently. The locals would organize active resistance only if the forces of
globalization coerce them to abrogate these connections. The indigene lives
harmoniously with tourism development so far as it is integrated and adapted
to the indigenous. In effect, the globalization-indigenization dialectic may
not always be conflictual and change-producing, it could also be integrative,
adaptive, and change-resistant.

The exploitative and coercive conditions at the interface of the globalization-indigenization dialectic, against the backdrop of colonization, contribute
to political instability, increased crime, civil wars, lack of capital, maladmin-
istration, widespread corruption, and so on, that make the interface change-
resistant rather than change-producing in sub-Saharan African countries. It
is these conditions that neoliberal tourism analysts wrongfully identify as
factors behind the poor development of tourism in these countries. What
they do not realize is that these factors and tourism underdevelopment share
the same cause—i.e., the globalization-indigenization dialect set against the
background of colonization. Colonization of sub-Saharan Africa preceded
globalization, and for that matter, the conditions the advocacy platform cites
as the causes of tourism underdevelopment are not directly related to globalization—globalization only reinforces these conditions.

We must note that in a noncolonial situation, such as what occurred prior
to the nineteenth century between West African societies, on the one hand,
and the Europeans and Arabs, on the other, the contact could rather result
in the adaptation of the global to the local. Many West African societies were
able to successfully integrate their trade with Europeans on the coast, and
Arabs in Northern Africa and the Middle East, into their indigenous commerce to enhance their local cultures, social structures, and economies. This
proto-globalization relation did not create a negative interface because there
was no colonial conduit. By extension, sub-Saharan Africa tourism could,
arguably, integrate with globalization and flourish in the absence of any
colonial legacy. Globalization is exploitative to the "poor world," primarily
because the indigenes of the "poor world" have already been displaced or
bruised by the earlier colonization process and its legacies.

TRANSFORMING THE SACRED INTO MUNDANE:
THE CASE OF SUB-SAHARAN TOURISM RESOURCES

Africa's "internationally recognized resource endowment for tourism" is
one of the major factors leading sub-Saharan African countries to consider
tourism among the means to develop their economies (Christie and Crompton 2001, iii). The resource endowment of African tourism features mainly
natural and cultural ecologies that the indigene relates to in sacred ways,
and tourism developers define as attractions. Sub-Sahara Africa has extensive

sandy palm beaches, colorful oceans, extensive tropical rain forests, numerous game parks, spectacular lakes and waterfalls, great rivers, picturesque landscapes, and sunny, warm climates. The cultural ecology is composed of integrated rituals, practices, and artifacts, such as chieftaincy and its paraphernalia, funerals, festivals, puberty and other initiation rites, clothing items, pottery, fertility dolls and other wood carvings, baskets, architecture, art, drums, blacksmithery, goldsmithery, traditional medicine, and so on.

These sacred phenomena and artifacts of indigenous Africa are what neoliberal political economy of globalization is constructing as tourism resources or attractions with cash value to place in the "free market." Without due regard to the contexts of sub-Saharan African indigenous cosmologies, these ecologies of African societies are being socially constructed as commodities by the big players in the global tourism industry for profit and consumption of international tourists. This construction process strips these critical dimensions of the African communities of their indigenous intrinsic or use value. In indigenous African cosmologies, these endowments are fundamentally spiritual, and sources of sustainable living rather than commodities for the global market. People are first and foremost connected to these natural and cultural endowments emotionally, morally, and spiritually. They are only materially significant when used for living in ways that would ensure that the nonmaterial connections are sustained. This indigenous conception of African ecologies contradicts the philosophy of neoliberal political economy that constructs Africa's physical and cultural ecologies as market resources to cater to the materialistic and hedonistic lifestyles of the West. The following report by the Ghana News Agency (2003, 1) on the Boabeng-Fiema Monkey Sanctuary in the Nkoranza District of the Brong-Ahafo Region of Ghana is an example of the sacred, nonmaterialistic connection between African indigenes and their natural endowments:

> Boabeng-Fiema Monkey Sanctuary is unique. It is the only place where two different species of monkeys, regarded as sacred—the Campbell's Mona and the Geoffroy's Columbus—live together within the same habitat in peace and in harmony with human beings. . . . There are about 500 Mona monkeys in the Sanctuary. They are brownish and omnivorous. The black and white Geoffroy's Columbus monkeys number about 200. They are vegetarians, living on leaves mainly. Boabeng-Fiema Monkey Sanctuary typifies traditional African conservation—the Ghanaian way. Here the culture of the people has been fashioned to include the acceptance of the monkeys as part of the society. The two communities (i.e., Boabeng and Fiema) came together in 1975 to pass a bye-law, prohibiting harm to the monkeys. They revere the animals with the belief that the monkeys are the children of the God of the twin-community. A visitor to the Sanctuary in the early morning would certainly hear monkeys calling loudly to one another.

At present, it is not clear how the local communities of Boabeng and Fiema are responding to this potential commodification of their sacred ecology. Could the sacredness of this monkey sanctuary be maintained in the face of increased tourism traffic to this ecological symbiosis? Could this sacredness be maintained as the ecology is transformed to a tourism resource from the outside? The local community would be interested in developing tourism with this ecology, if and when they are convinced that there could be a symbiotic relationship between the use value and cash value of this indigenous ecology.

For sub-Saharan Africa, the commodification of sacred ecologies, either for the extraction industries or for tourism, fails to strengthen the region's position in the global political economy because of the colonial legacy conduit of the globalization-indigenization dialectic. It is important to note that once the transformation of the indigenous ecologies from the sacred into the mundane succeeds, the ecologies could be preserved only when a substantial cash value is placed on these transformed ecologies. Tourism could provide this cash value. However, given the neoliberal push toward mass tourism in sub-Saharan Africa that has the tendency to destroy these ecologies, cash value is not enough to guarantee the sustenance of the natural and cultural ecologies of sub-Saharan Africa. It would take indigenized tourism to provide such a guarantee. Yet, in the global tourism industry, the strength of a country's tourism is not measured by the preservation of the ecology and empowerment of the indigenes, but rather by its market share. It is in this framework of transforming endowment to tourism resources that sub-Saharan Africa is considered the weakest player.

THE WEAKEST PLAYER IN THE GLOBAL TOURISM BUSINESS

The strength of Africa's position, as measured by the criteria of tourist arrivals and receipts, shows that although it is improving, it is the weakest player in the world tourism industry. Moreover, the improvement is occurring in tourism arrivals and not in tourism receipts. Available data show that by 1990, Africa's share of international tourism was only 2 percent in both tourist arrivals and receipts (Table 5.1).

It is important to note that the 2 percent tourist arrivals and 2 percent tourist receipts represent the share of the whole African continent. Given that major players in Africa's tourism are Morocco, Algeria, Tunisia, and Egypt,

Table 5.1 Africa's share of international tourism, 1990

Region	Tourist Arrivals	Tourist Receipts
Europe	68%	56%
North America	11%	14%
Asia & Australia	11%	13%
Latin America & Caribbean	6%	11%
Middle East	2%	4%
Africa	2%	2%
TOTAL	100%	100%

Source: Reproduced from Adu-Febiri (2003, 122).

countries that are outside sub-Saharan Africa, the latter's share in international tourism was really small. Also, "of the sub-Saharan countries, only South Africa is listed in the top forty tourism destinations worldwide, where it was 26th in 1997" (Christie and Crompton 2001, 2).

Since 1990, Africa's share of international tourist arrivals has increased to almost 4 percent, but the increase in the head count of tourists has not improved tourism receipts which still remained at 2 percent in 1997 (Christie and Compton 2001, 3). Christie and Crompton (2001, 3), however, note that in spite of its small portion of tourism arrivals, "the Africa region showed the strongest expansion in the arrivals of any world region for 1997, up to 8.1% over 1996."

It is interesting to note that the high growth rate of Africa tourism did not positively affect its tourism receipts. Another noteworthy dimension of this growth is the fact that it includes a substantial number of Africans visiting home to see friends and family. Some tourism analysts (e.g., Christie and Crompton 2001, 3) expect sub-Saharan African countries to increase their share of the world tourism market. However, these analysts are quick to caution that the expansion of sub-Sahara's share of global tourism is conditional: specifically, noting that conditions internal to Africa would determine the destiny of sub-Saharan African tourism. For instance, Christie and Crompton (2001, 3) observe that: "As essential condition, international tourism must be built upon intrinsic tourism assets that can compete internationally. Such assets may be coastal, wildlife, nature, cultural, or city-based, or selective mix of these, but they must have a distinctive quality that draws tourist to them and away from possible alternatives . . . the natural assets must be accompanied by and packaged with appropriate and competitive built assets—i.e., accommodation, tourist services, and infrastructure, as well as a safe and healthy environment for tourists. . . . This suggests that not all African countries can expect to expand their tourism sectors substantially."

The impact of factors external to the development of tourism in Africa is not featured in the preceding account. As we just noted, despite experiencing a remarkable growth rate in the 1990s, Africa's tourism receipts remained virtually the same. Internal conditions of sub-Sahara African countries are not enough to account for this situation, as the proponents of the advocacy platform would like us to believe. In responding to this bias, the cautionary and adaptancy platforms draw attention to external sources of tourism underdevelopment. However, they also overlook the external-internal nexus of tourism development, particularly the effect of colonial legacy operating at the interface of globalization and indigenization.

THE ADVOCACY PLATFORM: CULTURAL TRADITIONS OF SUB-SAHARAN AFRICA ARE THE PROBLEM

This neoliberal account of Africa's tourism postulates that factors internal to sub-Sahara Africa are to be blamed for the region's poor tourism development. Like the infamous modernization theory, this paradigm argues that internal weaknesses of the developing countries prevent them from adopting Western tourism models, particularly mass tourism. According to this platform, the success or failure of tourism in "Third World" countries depends on "whether they were Western and receptive to change or traditional and resisting change" (Jafari 1989, 21). This paradigm insists that mass tourism is the surest way to develop a viable tourism industry because profitable tourism is demand-driven, and economy of scale helps by reducing cost of producing the tourism product and thus increasing the profit margin. Mass tourism demands substantial financial investment in large scale, capital intensive tourism infrastructure, facilities, personnel, and services. The corollary of these is the replacement of traditional cultural values, beliefs, norms, and attitudes with modern ones—meaning, Western ones.

What this perspective fails to realize is that the lack of these conditions for mass tourism development is related to legacies of colonization, as they pertain to economic underdevelopment, failed states, disconnected and substandard education, corruption, and inadequate infrastructure, rather than indigenous cultures. Actually, indigenous cultures produced epistemologies, pedagogies, and cosmologies that prevented these conditions in the precolonial period. Indigenous cultures do not work against tourism—they could exist symbiotically with tourism.

Under the conditions created and sustained by the colonialism at the interface of globalization and indigenization, mass tourism could develop only through a significant intervention of external resources. Foreign capital, foreign hotels, foreign airlines, foreign tourism personnel, foreign tourism operators and agents, foreign food, foreign provided infrastructure, and foreign ways of providing tourism services are mandatory to develop tourism under such conditions. In effect, foreign control and ownership is the only way to develop mass and conventional tourism under the conditions produced by the colonial conduit. The consequences are high tourism revenue leakage and virtually no multiplier effect of tourism in the tourist destinations, as demonstrated in African countries such as Kenya and Gambia (Adu-Febiri 1997). These consequences are what the cautionary platform sees as a globalization-induced exploitation of the periphery of the world system by the core.

THE CAUTIONARY PLATFORM: GLOBALIZATION IS THE PROBLEM

This paradigm of tourism, akin to dependency theory *a la* Gundre-Frank (1966), postulates that globalization creates exploitative tourism in the peripheries of the world capitalist system. International tourism, according to this perspective, operates through an exploitative hierarchical structure linking metropolitan capital in the West, through comprador capitalists and small businesses in the periphery countries, to their destination communities (Briton 1982). Sub-Sahara Africa is a typical periphery of the world capitalist economy, and therefore, international tourism could only produce exploitation and contribute to underdevelopment, although the local comprador capitalists and small tourism business owners may benefit financially. Moreover, it is argued that because tourism in the periphery is usually owned by Western capitalist corporations, profit from tourism is siphoned from the periphery to Western metropolis. The cautionary platform uses the massive importation of goods and food for tourist hotels and restaurants; repatriations of tourism profits and salaries of expatriate managers; and payments of high hotel management and foreign architect fees, which decimate the tourist dollar in the destination countries, to buttress its case (Lea 1988). Extreme examples are found in the Gambia, the Caribbean, and Mauritius, which lose as much as 80 percent, 81 percent, and 90 percent of their tourism receipts, respectively (Lea 1988). In addition, the exploitative and unequal structural relations in the global tourism industry prevent substantive connections between tourism and other sectors of the periphery economies to develop; give the high paying tourism jobs to expatriates; commodifies local lifeworlds; and sometimes causes cultural genocide in destination communities (Jafari 1989). This cautionary platform paradigm does not demonize mass tourism development in the periphery, per se, but contends that under the condition of the unequal structural relations in the areas of ownership and control of the industry, tourism would remain exploitative. What it fails to stress is that the contemporary hierarchical structural relationships between the center and the periphery (call it globalization or any other name) does not necessarily create exploitation; rather, it deepens preexisting exploitative structures and processes produced by colonialism. If the conditions created by colonization are removed, the interaction between globalization and indigenization could facilitate nonexploitative tourism.

THE ADAPTANCY PLATFORM:
MASS TOURISM IS THE PROBLEM

The adaptancy platform problematizes the advocacy platform's insistence on the adoption of Western models of mass tourism development in developing countries. Its basic argument is that mass tourism is not a viable model in developing countries because, by its nature, mass tourism is insensitive to the economies, cultures, and environments of these countries. The adaptancy platform highlights the havoc, injustices, human rights abuses, loss of dignity, and so on, that mass tourism is believed to cause in tourism destination communities in the developing countries (Holden 1984). Unsurprisingly, the adaptancy platform seeks to replace mass tourism with alternative tourism development models, which are variously termed appropriate tourism, sensitized tourisms, responsible tourism, green tourism, controlled tourism, or people-to-people tourism (Jafari 1989, 23).

It is reasoned that alternative tourism would avoid the negative impacts of mass tourism and transform tourism to enrich the lives of host communities in the developing world. The merits of alternative forms of tourism, as identified by the adaptancy platform, include the fact that they are community centered, employ local resources, and are less destructive to the environment (Jafari 1989, 23). Additionally, it is emphasized that alternative tourism, unlike mass tourism, is more labor intensive than capital intensive; generates reasonable foreign exchange and retains most of it in destination communities; thrives on existing local infrastructure, facilities, and services; utilizes local foods and products; integrates well with other economic sectors of the destination area; and ultimately creates high multiplier effects in the destination (Jafari 1989, 22). Alternative tourism is theoretically appealing, but does not easily translate into a viable indigenization project that makes tourism work for the developing countries. What the adaptancy platform seems to overlook is the fact that alternative tourism projects have generally been initiated by foreign entrepreneurs, consultants, governments, tourism ministries, and NGOs, rather than local, grassroots people in the developing countries. When alternative forms of tourism are locally initiated (as in the cases of Costa Rica; Bali, Indonesia; and in the Casamance Villages project in Senegal), the initiators are usually the elite business people, most of whom are corrupt and do not work for the overall interest of the local communities. Not surprisingly, the proliferation of alternative forms of tourism in these countries has not yielded corresponding socioeconomic improvement in these countries (Adu-Febiri 1996).

Jafari (1989, quoted in Adu-Febiri 1996, 79) is therefore right in concluding "that the collective propositions of the advocacy, the cautionary, and the adaptancy platforms provide only a partial view of the tourism phenomenon."

THE KNOWLEDGE-BASED PLATFORM: HOST CULTURES MUST ADAPT, NOT BE ELIMINATED

Proposed by Vienna Center Tourism Studies, and popularized by the likes of Jafari (1989), the knowledge-based platform contends that existing tourism theoretical frameworks lack adequate knowledge to construct a comprehensive theory of tourism development. It argues that in order to formulate first principles of tourism, systematic multicountry and cross-cultural tourism studies are required (Jafari 1989). It is suggested that for such systematic studies to create the knowledge base for tourism theorizing, they should be very comprehensive, focusing on the place of tourism in the larger contexts of the society that accommodate it; examine the functions and values of tourism at the personal, group, business, and government levels; and identify the factors that influence, and are influenced by, tourism (Jafari 1989, 24). Unlike the advocacy platform, which argues for the elimination of the host indigenous culture in order for tourism to thrive in non-Western societies, the knowledge-based platform believes that the host culture has to be adapted to external variables of tourism for healthy tourism development to occur. Moreover, the Vienna Center Tourism Studies insists that the dynamics of the host culture that need to be adapted to external variables could be known through existing anthropological studies on destination countries.

The knowledge-based platform fails to recognize that, first, adapting host cultures to neoliberal globalization-driven tourism makes mass tourism exploitative and alternative forms of tourism unfeasible; and second, that the existing anthropological knowledge on many non-Western societies is imperialistic and Eurocentric, and, therefore, problematic—to put it mildly. It is well-documented that when host cultures adapt to the requirements of tourism, indigenous elements of these cultures become commoditized, lose their social control qualities, and lose their ability to creatively relate to external variables to enhance the lifeworlds of the host communities (McKean 1976, Mathieson and Wall 1982, Graburn 1984, Jules-Rosette 1984, Urry 1990, Hewison 1987 and 1996). Furthermore, foreign ownership and control intensify the ecological vulnerability in the host country.

We now know from the works of postcolonial theorists such as Kwame Anthony Appiah (1992), Achie Mafeje (1997), and Achillle Mbembe (2001) that the validity of the bulk of the existing anthropological knowledge on host countries is simply questionable. Anthropologists have failed to identify the core cultural elements that could facilitate tourism development in non-Western countries. While the knowledge-based platform has the potential to resolve some of the flaws in the other platforms, it has its own weakness, as it looks for knowledge in the wrong places—existing anthropological knowledge on tourism destinations is suspect.

Clearly, the preceding platforms of tourism, either separately or together, fail to provide convincing explanations of the development problems of sub-Sahara Africa tourism. Indigenous African cultures are not the problem, neither is mass tourism or globalization. The knowledge-based platform comes close to identifying the main problem by focusing on the lack of knowledge. However, it misses the point by focusing on wrong knowledge, specifically anthropological knowledge on host cultures, instead of a sociological knowledge of the colonial and colonized cultural and structural dynamics that dominate the interface of globalization and indigenization. The main source of the sub-Saharan Africa's tourism development problems is the colonial legacy ignored in existing tourism theorizations. The solution, therefore, does not lie in mass tourism, alternative forms of tourism, elimination of indigenous cultures, adaptation of host culture to tourism, or halting of globalization. Rather, the solution lies in the elimination of the colonial legacy and how it relates to globalization and indigenization processes in sub-Sahara Africa.

THE WEAKEST LINK IN SUB-SAHARAN AFRICA'S TOURISM DEVELOPMENT

The weakest link in the sub-Sahara Africa tourism problematic is not sub-Sahara Africa's failure to eliminate its indigenous cultures, as the neoliberal advocacy platform postulates; it is not attributable to globalization, as the cautionary platform wants us to believe; neither is it due to mass tourism, as posited by the adaptancy platform. Also, the failure of host cultures to adapt to external variables of tourism is not the cause of the development problematic, as the knowledge-based platform highlights. Rather, the extent to which colonial legacy interacts with the processes of globalization and indigenization is the root cause of problems faced by sub-Sahara Africa's tourism.

Sub-Sahara Africa's colonial legacy is manifested in failed governance, political violence, the demise of community, widespread corruption, the colonial mentality of undervaluing anything indigenous and the wholesale acceptance of everything Western, inferiority complex, and so on. Colonization produced this legacy in sub-Sahara Africa through the simultaneous displacement of indigenous governance, spirituality, socialization, modes of production, and intergroup relations and the imposition of foreign political systems, consumer culture, religion, and educational systems.

Many precolonial sub-Sahara African societies operated indigenous governance systems that were "democratic" and integrative. There were enough checks and balances to prevent autocracy and totalitarianism. For example, in chieftaincy, the major political institution, it took the approval of not only the king makers, but also the unanimous approval of the various social and interest groups in the community, to establish a person as a chief (Busia 1968). Also, the chief was not central to the day-to-day administration of the community; rather, administration was decentralized as much as possible through the lineage and interest group systems. This legitimization of indigenous governance engendered loyalty of the ruled to the political system. This loyalty, in turn, produced internal political stability, security, and peace in many sub-Sahara African societies. This is the indigenous governance that the colonial political system displaced. The imposed oppressive, centralized political system alienated Africans from governance and forced them to work in the unrewarding colonial enterprise. In addition, it took away their land, and brutalized them physically and psychologically by demonizing their religions and cultures.

Africans, therefore, saw the colonial state as an enemy to sabotage, rather than an entity worthy of their support. In effect, many Africans developed negative attitudes "towards government institutions and property" (Mensah 1997, 52). As Mensah (ibid.) puts it: "It is no insight to say that for practically everyone, apart from a privileged few, the colonial system became an object of intense hatred. Consequently, many Africans saw nothing wrong with stealing, embezzling, and misappropriating the resources of the colonial government."

This attitude toward government continues in postcolonial Africa, making the state an arena of plunder and misappropriation. The various factions of the African ruling elite constantly fight for control over this plunder, thereby generating political instability and violence with their attendant cultures of fear and silence that are inimical to democratic governance. Furthermore, the colonial government overcentralized administrative and government services, and thereby contributes to bribery and corruption. As Amoako-Tuffour (1996, 33, quoted in Mensah 1997, 53) noted: "The historical locational concentration of administrative authorities, often in the capitals, enhances the monopoly power of civil servants in the allocation and control of resources. For those who travel long distances to apply for any form of licensing, or to seek bureaucratic approval, bribery seems obligatory in order to overcome the time cost of delay."

Paralleling this administrative concentration is skewed physical infrastructure in colonial and postcolonial societies. The colonial enterprise thrived on extraction of primary resources from the colonized societies and dumping imported manufactured goods on them. The colonial commercial capitalism systematically undermined industrialization of the colonies, and facilitated excessive consumption of cheap, imported commodities. It is this situation that has developed into the petty trading or buy-and-sell pandemic in many postindependent African countries.

Another impact of commercial capitalism is skewed infrastructural development in colonial and postcolonial Africa. Ports and administrative facilities were established in the coastal towns to facilitate the exportation of raw materials and importation of cheap manufactured commodities. Roads and railways were normally constructed from the coast to only the hinterland areas that produced the raw materials. "The result," as Mensah 1997, 53) points out, "is the polarized pattern of development common in most African countries." In fact, outside the transportation and administrative "nodes and corridors," infrastructure such as good road and rail networks, water and sewage, electricity, decent hotels and restaurants, entertainment and sports facilities, well-equipped hospitals, and so on, are virtually nonexistent. These are the centrifugal and centripetal forces that underpin the massive rural-urban migration and abject poverty in both rural areas and urban fringes of sub-Sahara Africa.

The removal of the indigenous moral and spiritual training mechanisms contributed to the moral decay that seems to prevail in many parts of sub-Sahara Africa. The colonial religion took emotions out of worship and out of education; African celebratory worship songs and percussions were stigmatized as heathen and replaced with Western church hymns and piano accompaniments. Also, colonial education did not only produce literary scholars devoid of practical skills and ability to transform knowledge into wisdom, but also alienated the graduates from their indigenous cultures that emphasized the importance of loyalty to community, caring, sharing, accountability, responsibility, and respect for human dignity and the natural ecology.

It is these dynamics of the colonial legacy, acting as the link between globalization and indigenization, which account for the failure of sub-Sahara Africa tourism to develop. Until recently, when a few attempts are being made to disrupt this influence through indigenization of tourism in sub-Sahara Africa, tourism development plans were either constructed to adapt host ecologies to tourism (what has been dubbed Type I Tourism), or integrate tourism into the colonial legacy (Type II Tourism). The former approach occurred in Eastern and Southern Africa, where Safari and beach tourism was developed by the colonists as part of the colonial enterprise. The latter is found in Ghana's tourism industry before the 1990s.

Neither Type I nor Type II tourism could be a catalyst of development for sub-Sahara Africa. The Type I strategy is what the advocacy platform encourages and the cautionary platform criticizes. This strategy locks sub-Sahara Africa tourism in the hierarchically structured global tourism industry, owned and consumed primarily by corporations and citizens of the metropolitan Western countries. Local ecologies are constructed as tourism resources, silencing the lifeworlds of the local people of these ecologies. This strategy of tourism development was initiated by colonization and reproduced by the colonial legacy in the postcolonial era, and is now facilitated by neoliberal globalization. Kenya is renowned as the world capital of Safari Tourism, an economic activity that is the country's "largest single source of foreign exchange, ahead of any single agricultural product. But little of that money directly benefits the local people" (Christie and Crompton 2001, 39, cited in Lusigi 1992). This is mainly because of the Western owned and controlled type of tourism operating through the colonial legacy of Kenya. The airlines and ground transportation carrying tourists are owned and controlled by Europeans; most of the foods the tourists eat are imported from Europe and prepared by European chefs; and tourist accommodation in entry points of Kenya and those in the game parks are the properties of Europeans. Consequently, the bulk of the tourism receipts is siphoned back to Europe, and a little left in Kenya as revenue for the government, often ends up in the pockets of corrupt tourism officials and politicians (Adu-Febiri 1997). Tourism indigenization that could contribute to transforming this situation is not on the radar of Kenya's tourism development agenda. The local people who may be the repositories of what is left of the indigenous are excluded from tourism planning and development. This Type I tourism is a product of colonization, recreated by colonial legacy in the context of neoliberal globalization.

The Type I tourism development strategy was consciously avoided in Ghana until the late 1980s. Ghana adopted the Type II tourism strategy that integrates tourism development into the colonial legacy. Under this strategy, tourism development begins after the colony has gained political independence, as a way of diversifying economy of the newly independent country. Unlike the Type I tourism, the tourism infrastructure and facilities are initiated, constructed, owned, and controlled by the postcolonial host state. In the specific case of Ghana, a Ministry of Tourism, a Tourist Board, and a Hotels Corporation were established to facilitate tourism development. However, tourism infrastructure and facilities hardly went beyond the colonial transportation and administrative nodes and corridors. Basically, key aspects of the colonial legacy were left virtually intact, and tourism was integrated into this colonial legacy—a situation that virtually choked tourism to death right from the beginning. Most Ghanaians transferred their disloyalty for the colonial state to the postcolonial state. State owned and controlled tourism infrastructure and facilities were woefully mismanaged, misappropriated, and plundered.

Added to this has been the perennial problem of political instability that scares away international conventional tourists (Teye 1988). And domestic tourism in the form of purely leisure travel hardly exists in Ghana because of cultural and economic constraints (Wyllie 2000). Just as the development of tourism seems to fail, neoliberal globalization emerges to "rescue" the industry through privatization of tourism facilities and services. Ghanaian leaders respond favorably to privatization by offering generous financial incentives, particularly fiscal and profit repatriation, to foreign investors for many years. Since the colonial legacy prevents internal capital accumulation and long-term capital-intensive investment in the postcolonial society, local Ghanaians are unable to buy the state tourism assets being privatized. Furthermore, because of the methodologies and stereotypes imbedded in the colonial legacy, the foreign companies that buy these assets do not trust local (Ghanaian) professionals to manage them, and expatriate management is imported. In effect, former colonial masters are invited to come and own, control, and manage tourism and freely transfer their profits back to the metropolitan West. Thus, the colonial plunder is revisited.

Sub-Sahara Africa tourism, however, is not without its development potential. The relics of sub-Sahara Africa's indigenous epistemologies, philosophies, pedagogies, cosmologies, knowledge, and skills could be reactivated to develop a sustainable tourism for sub-Sahara Africa. The important role of indigenization in transforming tourism in the developing world is being gradually recognized, as in the now-popular "The Mitchell Formula" (Wyllie 2000, 173). The Mitchell Formula was formulated by the Mitchell government of St. Vincent in 1972 "to create an indigenous and integrated tourism industry, one that would ensure greater local participation and control, allow for gradual expansion, and minimize adverse environmental and sociocultural impacts" (Wyllie 2000, 173). Britton (1977) argues that although Mitchell's tourism plan was impressive and tourist arrivals increased by 25 percent in 1974, it leveled off afterwards because of a number of unresolved difficulties, including the lack of proper market research; inadequate funding for promotional campaigns; the problem of physical accessibility, as St. Vincent could be reached only indirectly, with flight transfers at either Barbados or St. Lucia; and the fall of Mitchell's government in 1974.

Like the St. Vincent's model, Senegal's tourism indigenization project began in 1971 as a response to "concern over mass tourism's impact and a desire for greater local involvement" (Wyllie 2000, 175). Unlike the St. Vincent's tourism indigenization program that covered virtually the whole country, Senegal's project left the existing Club Med resort and other conventional tourism untouched, and rather focused on one rural region, the Lower Casamance, with qualities right for alternative tourism development—i.e., attractive rivers, lagoons and inlets, together with the intriguing cultures of the local Diola people (Wyllie 2000, 175). The Senegalese project created a form of tourism antithetical to mass tourism. It used simple accommodations, which were run by the Diola people, and provided opportunities for intimate contact between tourists and the local people. In fact, tourists participated in the daily activities of Diola villagers—they traveled by canoe, with local villagers, on fishing trips along the region's many waterways (Wyllie 2000, 175).

The colonial legacy of Senegal undermined the initial implementation of this project. For instance, the colonial mentality of the Diola villagers compelled them to initially opt for foreign architecture for constructing tourist accommodations. Indeed, most of the villagers had to be persuaded to use their traditional architectural materials, which obviously have some attraction for tourists, instead of cement blocks, sheet metal roofs, and glass windows, and even air conditioning (Wyllie 2000, 175).

Following intense negotiations, nine tourist villages with a total accommodation capacity of 310 beds were completed by 1983, using indigenous Diola building materials and architectural styles. As with many (neo)colonial situations, the tourist villages housing the foreigners and expatriates were physically separated from the Diola villages where the indigenes resided. Thus, instead of tourism being integrated into the indigenous community, as tourism indigenization requires, the indigenous has been adapted to tourism as recommended by the knowledge-based platform. In traditional African societies of sub-Sahara Africa, visitors were accommodated in the houses of the local people, and hardly ever offered a separate accommodation outside.

Although the tourism camps are operated by village cooperatives and the Senegal Department of Tourism markets the camps to Westerners, the camps are not necessarily indigenous. The Senegalese inhabiting the center of these projects are products of the colonial legacy, and lack the know-how in constructing and operating indigenized tourism. It is not surprising, therefore, that the Lower Casamance tourism project has failed to break out of the conventional tourism mold. The project "depends heavily on established international air connections and an official tourism structure for its success" (Wyllie 2000, 175).

Other examples of tourism indigenization projects in sub-Sahara Africa include the ecotourism schemes of Ghana and the Communal Areas Management Program for Indigenous Resources (CAMPFIRE) pioneered by Zimbabwe and replicated in other Southern African countries. Undoubtedly, international demand for these "alternative" forms of tourism has grown in recent years (Christie and Crompton 2000, 41). However, because they are initiated and managed against the backdrop of colonial legacy within neoliberal globalization, these projects are bound to suffer a fate similar to the Lower Casamance project in Senegal.

CONCLUSION: THE DESTINY OF SUB-SAHARAN AFRICAN TOURISM

What historical processes have made sub-Sahara Africa the weakest player in the growing global tourism industry, and to what extent would these processes affect the future prospects of tourism in the region? Neoliberal globalization and indigenization, operating against the background of the region's colonial legacy, render the development of sub-Sahara Africa's tourism ineffective. Local cultures are subordinated to tourism, which is, in turn, integrated to the social structures and cultural dynamics of the colonial legacy. Adapting host cultures to tourism is part of the colonial enterprise that makes conventional tourism exploitative, and alternative forms of tourism unfeasible. Similarly, integrating tourism into the colonial legacy makes it a "cash cow" for the postcolonial elite and their expatriate financiers; neoliberal globalization reproduces these weaknesses of sub-Sahara Africa tourism.

Existing attempts at indigenizing tourism as a way of counteracting its exploitative impacts and removing its developmental constraints are unsuccessful because they are framed in the region's colonial legacy, instead of the indigenous skills, epistemologies, philosophies, and methodologies. In precolonial sub-Sahara Africa, indigenous cultural practices were used to connect with foreign cultures to achieve some successes in commerce. However, indigenous cultural practices are hardly utilized in contemporary sub-Sahara Africa's search for economic and social emancipation. Sub-Sahara Africa's indigenes hold the key to disrupt the colonial legacies that are holding back progress in the region's tourism industry. Systematic studies into the dynamics of sub-Sahara Africa's indigenous strategies for sustainable tourism development should form a critical component of any tourism program aimed at making the region a competitive player in the global tourism industry.

REFERENCES

Ackah, C. A. 1988. *Akan ethics: A study of the moral ideas and the moral behaviour of the Akan tribes of Ghana.* Accra: Ghana Universities Press.

Adjibolosoo, Senyo. 1995. *The human factor in developing Africa.* Westport, CT: Praeger.

Adu-Febiri, Francis. 1996. Tourism and socioeconomic transformation in developing countries. *Review of Human Factor Studies* 2 (1): 73–92.

———. 1997. The human factor, tourism dollar leakage, and multiplier effects in developing countries. *Review of Human Factor Studies* 3 (2): 20–36.

———. 2003. Putting the human factor to work in African tourism: A human factor competency model. In *Management and the human factor: Lessons for Africa,* ed. Victor N. Muzvidziwa and Paul Gundani. Harare: University of Zimbabwe Publications.

Amoako-Tuffour, J. 1996. Public sector corruption, embezzlement, and economic Reform. *Review of Human Factor Studies* 2 (1): 27–48.

Appiah, Kwame Anthony. 1992. *In my father's house: Africa in the philosophy of culture.* New York: Oxford University Press.

Asomaning, Hannah. 2003. Boabeng-Fiema Monkey Sanctuary. GNA Feature. http://www.ghanaweb.com/GhanaHomePage/features/artikel.php?ID=44060.

Backmann, P. 1988. *Tourism in Kenya: A basic need for whom?* Berne: Peter Lang.

Britton, S. G. 1977. Making tourism more supportive of small state development: The case of St. Vincent. *Annals of Tourism Research* 6:268–78.

———. 1982. The political economy of tourism in the Third World. *Annals of Tourism Research* 9 (3): 331–58.

Busia, K. A. 1968. *The position of the chief in the modern political system of Ashanti: A study of the influence of contemporary social changes on Ashanti political institutions.* London: Cass.

Christie, Iain T., and Doreen E. Crompton. 2001. *Tourism in Africa.* World Bank Working Paper Series No. 2. http://www.worldbank.org/afr/wps/wp12.pdf.

Coser, Lewis. 1956. *The functions of social conflict.* London: Free Press.

Crowne, Thomas. 2005. The New World Order: Segment III. http://www.abovetopsecret.com/pages/weekly_012_thomascrowne.html.

Dahrendorf, Ralf. 1958. Toward a theory of social conflict. *Journal of Conflict Resolution* 2:170–85.

Esh, T., and I. Rosenblum. 1975. *Tourism in developing countries—trick or treat? A report from the Gambia.* Uppsala: The Scandinavian Institute of African Studies.

George, Jim. 2001. Creating globalization: "Patriotic internationalism" and symbiotic power relations in the post WW2 era. Centre for the Study of Globalization and Regionalization CSGR Working Paper N0. 66/01, Coventry, UK: Center for the Study of Globalization and Regionalisation (CSGR).

Ghana News Agency. 2003. Boabeng-Fiema monkey sanctuary. Accra: Ghana News Agency, October 3, p.1 http://www.ghanaweb.com/GhanaHomePage/features/artikel.php?ID=44060.

Giddens, Anthony. 1990. *The consequences of modernity.* Cambridge: Polity

Graburn, N. H. H. 1984. The evolution of tourist arts. *Annals of Tourism Research* 11:393–419.

Gundre-Frank, Andre. 1966. The development of underdevelopment. *Monthly Review* 18 (4): 17–30, 425.

Hewison, R. 1987. *The heritage industry: Britain in a climate of decline.* London: Methuen.

———. 1996. Cultural policy and the heritage business. *The European Journal of Cultural Policy* 3:1–13.

Jafari, J. 1989. Socioeconomic dimensions of tourism: An English language literature review. In *Tourism as a factor of change: A sociocultural study*, ed. J. Bystrzanowski, 19–32. Vienna: Center for Research and Documentation in Social Sciences.

Jommo, R. B. 1987. *Indigenous enterprise in Kenya's tourism industry.* Geneva: Institut Universitaire d'Etudies du Developpement.

Jules-Rosette, B. 1984. *The messages of tourist art: An African semiotic system in contemporary perspective.* New York: Plenum.

Lea, J. 1988. *Tourism and development in the Third World.* London: Routledge.

Lusigi, Walter J. 1992. *Managing protected areas in Africa.* Report from a workshop on protected area management in Africa. Mweke, Tanzania: UNESCO–World Heritage Fund.

Mafeje, Archie. 1997. Who are the makers and objects of anthropology? A critical comment on Sally Falk Moore's anthropology and Africa. *African Sociological Review* 1 (1): 1–15.

Maluga, A. P. 1973. Tourism and the Arusha declaration: A contradiction. In *Tourism and socialist development*, ed. I. G. Shivji. Dar-es-Salaam: Tanzania Publishing House.

Mathieson, A., and G. Wall. 1982. *Tourism: economic, physical and social impacts.* London: Longman.

Marx, Karl. 1867. *Capital: A critical analysis of capitalist production.* Vol. 1. New York: E. P. Dutton, 1967.

Mbembe, Achille. 2001. *On the postcolony.* Berkeley: University of California Press.

McKean, P. F. 1976. Tourism, culture change and culture conservation in Bali. In *Changing identities in modern southeast Asia*, ed. J. D. Banks. The Hague: Mouton.

Mensah, Joseph. 1997. Colonization and human factor degradation in Africa. *Review of Human Factor Studies* 3 (1): 48–64.

Orr, D. W. 1999. Education for globalization. *The Ecologist* 29 (3): 166–68.

Robertson, R. 1992. *Globalization: Social theory and global culture*. London: Sage.

Rojek, Chris. 1995. *Decentring Leisure: Rethinking Leisure Theory*. London: Sage.

Teye, V. B. 1988. Coup d'etat and African tourism: A case study of Ghana. *Annals of Tourism Research* 15: 329–56.

Urry, J. 1990. *The tourist gaze: Leisure and travel in contemporary societies*. New York: Sage.

Wiesel, E. 1990. Remarks before the global forum. Moscow.

World Tourism Organization. 1998. *Tourism market trends in Africa*. WTO.

Wyllie, Robert. W. 2000. *Tourism and society: A guide to problems and issues*. Pennsylvania: Venture Publishing.

CHAPTER 6

AFRICA AND THE POLITICAL ECONOMY OF TIME-SPACE COMPRESSION AND SPACE OF FLOWS

UNFASHIONABLE OBSERVATIONS

Joseph Mensah

That contemporary globalization is characterized by a "speed-up in the pace of life" (Harvey 1990, 240), or the shrinking of the world into a global village, is hard to deny. The dynamic time-space compression that underpins this characteristic feature of globalization has generally been presented in the available literature as though it applies evenly across all regions of the world. But can the image of a shrinking world, with unbridled mobility and "space of flows" (Castells 2000a) stand rigorous empirical scrutiny? Is the almost "obligatory use in the literature of terms and phrases such a speed-up, global village, overcoming spatial barriers" (Massey 1999a) really justified? Is everyone's world actually getting smaller?

We know from the works of Hirst and Thompson, for instance, that by 1996, national economies were no more opened in terms of capital flows or trade than they were during the time of the gold standard. Not only that, according to Hirst and Thompson (1996a, 1996b), as much as 91.5 percent of the foreign direct investments then were made in parts of the world that contained only 28 percent of the global population. The situation may very well be different in 2008, with the world continuously shrinking over time.

But has the ensuing "shrinkage" gotten to a point of justifying our hyped assumptions of a universal *placelessness*, or a homogenizing global village in which labor and capital are freely crisscrossing the world? In fact, there are strong indications of growing inequalities in income, living standards, and access to mobility and time-space compression technologies between and within nations, even since the late 1990s (Hoogvelt 2001; McNally 2002; UNDP 2006). Agnew (2001, 5) was even more emphatic on this point with his observation that: "What we do know for sure is that divergence between rich and poor countries has increased significantly during the globalization era compared to previous periods; so much for the world becoming an economic pinhead as time conquers space." At the very least, our excitement about a homogenizing world needs to be qualified with some acknowledgment of its socio-spatial unevenness and heterogenizing undercurrents.

This chapter examines the extent to which Africa, in particular, is adversely positioned in relation to the flows and circulations of time-space compression in our globalizing world. Dwelling on the spatial theorization of political economy—and with insights from David Harvey's (1990) "time-space compression," Manuel Castells' (2000a) "space of flows" and "timeless time," and Doreen Massey's (1999a, 1999b) "power geometries"—the chapter shows how Africa is marginalized in the network society. Moreover, it draws attention to the exorbitant costs wrought upon Africans (by way of Internet charges, air travel costs, phone charges, etc.) as a result of the acute dearth of time-space compression technologies on the continent. The discussion is grounded in the following rhetorical question: If, indeed, globalization entails not only homogenization, but also discernable heterogenization (in the form of uneven geographic development, power imbalances, and social differentiations), why, then, are suppositions of a unifying, global village so *fashionable* in the available literature? Put differently, why are categorical assertions of a shrinking, homogenizing world of unbridled mobility, time-space compression, and space of flows so fashionable in the prevailing discourse on globalization? On the contrary, why are discussions concerning the "power-geometries" (Massey 1999a), the "translocational positionalities"[1] (Anthia 2001), and the "uneven and combined development" (Bond, in this volume) in globalization so *unfashionable*? The term *unfashionable observation* is used in the subtitle to pay homage to Friedrich Nietzsche,[2] who completed a series of four studies that offered a critique of modernity in the context of European and German culture. Like Nietzsche's critique, this chapter seeks to highlight what has been *unfashionable* in the public and academic discourse, except the discourse at stake here relates to contemporary globalization, and, more specifically, to the marginalization of Africa in its attendant time-space compression. The chapter does not seek to identify the causal factors behind Africa's weak attachment to the network society, *per se*,[3] but to show the extent to which the continent is "falling out" of the shrinking world, as a way of drawing the attention of the powers that be in Africa to the urgent need to redress the situation.

DAVID HARVEY'S "TIME-SPACE COMPRESSION"

Popularized by the geographer David Harvey in his well-acclaimed *The Conditions of postmodernity,* "time-space compression" refers to the processes that have reduced spatial barriers and accelerated our experience of time. Put differently, it is the shortening of time and the shrinking of space, or what Marx once called "the annihilation of space by time." According to Harvey (1990, 240), time-space compression has so revolutionized the "objective qualities of space and time that we are forced to alter, sometimes in quite radical ways, how we represent the world to ourselves." Harvey writes that he uses the term *compression* "because a strong case can be made that the history of capitalism has been characterized by speed-up in the pace of life, while so overcoming spatial barriers that the world sometimes seems to collapse inwards upon us" (*ibid.*, 240). For the most part, the compression alluded to here is attributable to advances in transportation and telecommunication technologies such as cell phones, blackberries, faxes, the Internet, and high-speed automobiles, trains, and airplanes.

Harvey (1990, chap. 15) illustrates how these technological innovations have compressed the globe with maps of the world that shrink over time in proportion to the increasing speed of the available transportation. These maps show, in a heuristically-appealing fashion, that between 1500 and 1840, the average speed of horse-drawn coaches and sailing ships was a mere 10 mph. Between 1950 and 1930, the average speed available to humans had increased to 65 mph, through the use of the steam locomotive, and to 36 mph via steam ships. By the 1950s, propeller aircraft had increased the average speed to between 300 and 400 mph, and by the 1960s, jet passenger aircraft had taken humans to an average speed of between 500 and 700 mph. Thus, the world shrunk by about seventy times between 1500 and the 1960s, since the average speed of the horse-drawn coaches and sailing ships in 1500 was a mere 10 mph compared to the top speed of 700 mph attained through jets by the 1960s. Add the speed and instantiation attained through modern devices such as the Internet and cell phones to the equation, and one would be understandably mesmerized by the notion of "a global village" (or "electronic cottages"[4]) in which spatial barriers have been virtually obliterated.

Harvey traces the contemporary round of time-space compression to the period from about 1965 to the early 1970s, when the capitalist mode of production shifted from Fordism to post-Fordism, or what he calls "flexible accumulation." According to Harvey, during this period, the Fordist mode of production was unable to contain its inherent contradictions typified by "spatial rigidities" in which capital was held loyal to a place, or a nation, with ever-increasing spatial barriers to be overcome by the capitalist. Thus, it is the dismantling of the Fordist regime of accumulation by the early 1970s that ushered in the present era of time-space compression. Under the ensuing compression, "the time horizons of both private and public decision-making have shrunk, while satellite communications and declining transport cost have made it increasingly possible to spread those decisions immediately over an ever wider and variegated space" (1990, 147).

With the "collapse" of space by time, money can move around the world—from Algiers to Brisbane or Accra to Zimbabwe—at the press of a button. Goods can be shipped over equally great distances at a relatively low cost through containerization and other modern haulage technologies. People in the Caribbean can be watching the same teledrama or soccer match in real time as their counterparts in Western Europe. Children can communicate with several friends instantaneously, exchanging digital photographs and music files across the globe. Not only that, "Kenyan haricot beans, Californian celery and avocados, North African potatoes, Canadian apples, and Chilean grapes all sit side by side in a British supermarket" (Harvey 1990, 300). Of course, such consumer items as blue jeans, coke, and cell phones are readily recognizable and used in nearly all corners of the world. And, as Agnew (2001) notes, with stealth technology, the ability of any territorial military power to police its airspace is easily undermined; evidently, the old rules and models of "spatial organization based on linear distance-decay of transportation cost and territorial containing of external effects by states have been broken down" (Agnew 2001, 6).

This breakdown, "or disruptive spatiality" (Harvey 1990), has yielded an intriguing paradox: Yes, the power of speed and pace seems to outstrip the power of place (Luke and Tuathail 1998); yes, space is seemingly annihilated through the rapidity of time; yet, space is no less significant now than before; and the spatialization of social theory is even on the rise (Lefebvre 1991; Harvey 1990; Soja 1989, 1996; and Massey 1992). As Harvey shrewdly points out:

> But the collapse of spatial barriers does not mean that the significance of space is decreasing. . . . Heightened competition under conditions of crisis has coerced capitalists into paying much closer attention to relative locational advantages, precisely because diminishing spatial barriers give capitalists the power to exploit minute spatial differentiations to good effect. Small differences in what the space contains in the way of labour supplies, resources, infrastructures, and the like become of increased significance. . . . We thus approach the central paradox: the less important the spatial barrier, the greater the sensitivity of capital to the variations of place within space and the greater the incentive for places to be differentiated in ways attractive to capital (1990, 293–96).

A corollary of this spatial paradox is a situation where the ever-increasing economic and cultural homogenization across the globe—attributable, as least, in part to the time-space compression underway—is simultaneously accompanied by rising regionalism, cultural pluralism, religious fundamentalism, and ethno-fetishism. By the same token, just as time-space compression seems to intensify *placelessness*—or the making of a world that is increasingly alike—there is strong evidence of deepening patterns of uneven development both within and between nations (Agnew 2001, 2).

Time-space compression—and the associated "sense of immediacy and simultaneity about the world" (Brah *et al.* 1999, 3) and "disruptive spatiality" (Harvey 1990, 301)—is behind the ontological instabilities, sociocultural disorientations, and the "confused political, cultural and philosophical movements" (*ibid.*, 284) so prevalent in this postmodern era. As Harvey points out: "Space of very different worlds seem to collapse upon each other, much as the world's commodities are assembled in the supermarket and all manner of sub-cultures get juxtaposed in the contemporary city. Disruptive spatiality triumphs over the coherence of perspective and narrative in postmodern fiction, in exactly the same way that imported beers coexists with local brews, local employment collapses under the weight of foreign competition, and all the divergent spaces of the world are assembled nightly as a collage of images upon the television screen" (*ibid.*, 301–2). According to Gregory (2000), these experiential dimensions set Harvey's time-space compression apart from the fairly similar concepts of *time-space convergence* and *time-space distantiation*, developed by the geographer Daniel Janelle (1969) and the sociologist Anthony Giddens (1984), respectively.

Manuel Castells' "Space of Flows" and "Timeless Time"

In a recent and, arguably, more encompassing formulation, Manuel Castells (2000a) uses the terms of *space of flows* and *timeless time* within his "logic of informationalism" to describe the emergence of a network society. Starting from the premise that "space is the expression of society," it did not take much for Castells to talk of new spatial forms and processes within the context of the structural transformations engendered by the ongoing time-space compression.

According to Castells, social theorists cannot define space outside of social practices, just as physicists can hardly talk of space outside of the dynamics of matter. For Castells, space is essentially borderless, timeless, circuitry of electronic impulses (as per telecommunication and microelectronic technologies) that provide the "material support for time-sharing social practices that work through flows" (*Castells 2000a*, 442). Thus, in this theorization, space is basically about flows: flows of capital, information, images, sounds, and so on. This idea of space chimes well with Castells' logic of informationalism—i.e., a new paradigm of a network society based on information technologies.

Castells' space of flows has three major layers of material support. First, there are "circuits of electronic exchanges" (e.g., microelectronic devices, telecommunications, broadcasting systems, high-speed transportations, computer processing, etc.) that form the material base of the network society. Secondly, there are "nodes and hubs," or places with well-defined social, cultural, physical, and functional characteristics. Some of these places serve as telecommunication exchangers, coordinating the smooth running of the elements in the network. The nodes and hubs are hierarchically arranged, based on their relative significance in the network. Castells notes that his space of flows is not placeless, even though its structural logic is. Thirdly, the space of flows entails "spatially organized, technocratic-financial-managerial elites" who direct the operations of the network. According to Castells, the fundamental form of domination in the network society is based on two main spatial maneuvers: first, the elites find ways to seclude themselves (and their privileges) from the masses, through real estate pricing and other residential security controls and surveillances. Secondly, they create lifestyles, and design corresponding spatial forms, that unify them, accentuate their cultural distinctiveness, and segregate them from the masses around the world. These distinctive symbolic environments come in the form of international hotels, VIP lounges at the airports, first class seating in airplanes, special car rentals and limousine facilities, and so on. Regardless of which country the elites find themselves, they seem to enjoy fairly similar/familiar services. We thus have the phenomenon of the "global traveler" whose access to the Internet, CNN, the "top ten" on the pop chart, cola drinks and beer, Hollywood movies, sitcoms, and the so-called adult entertainment can only be denied at a very high cost to the hotel industry.

Another intriguing term coined by Castells to reinforce his "space of flows" is the concept of *timeless time*. In Castells' logic of informationalism, time is not linear, irreversible, measurable, but rather a relative phenomenon that can be cyclical, random, and even reversible, depending on social context. His basic argument posits that time has compressed in the network society to the point where temporal sequence seems to disappear, and cultures seem to "escape from the clock" (Castells 2000a, 464). Nowhere is Castells' timeless time more evident than in the operations of the global financial market. Here, the whole wide world seems to be working in unison, with financial transaction moving across the globe almost instantaneously, by a press of a button. With trades in futures, options, and other derivatives, transactions are not only about the present timeless time, or real time, but indeed, about capturing the future in the present transactions. Just like the insecurities, confusions, and ontological instabilities engendered by Harvey's time-space compression, Castells' space of flows and timeless time are also associated with increasing volatility, instability, and turbulence, especially in the world financial market. No wonder, no less a bank than UK's Barings Bank could collapse in a day through the speculative exploits of a single employer on futures contract.[5]

To be sure, this theorization of temporality is not that different from what Jameson articulated earlier, in his *Postmodernism, or the cultural logic of late capitalism* (1991), to the effect that there has been a disjuncture in the "signifying chain" between the past, present, and the future, with the present becoming increasingly "autoreferential" (Jameson 1991, xiii, 127). One can also find similar assertions in the patently provocative writings of Jean Baudrillard (1994a, 1994b), who talks of the "multiplication and saturation of exchanges" as a result of simulation and simulacra in a society that is "condensed back into itself" (1994a, 3–13). According to Baudrillard, through endless reproductions of images and symbols, contemporary society has reached an "energetic impasse," unable to go beyond the present, unable "to transcend itself" to make history through the production of new images, symbols, and metaphors. In Baudrillard's view, the United States, in particular, is so caught up in speed, images, symbols, and simulation that it seems to find itself in a crisis of explanatory logic: with "the triumph of effects over cause, of instantaneity over time as depth, the triumph of surface and of pure objectivization over the depth of desire" (Baudrillard 1984, quoted in Harvey 1990, 291). To argue that society is living in some form of "perpetual presents" Dodgshon (1999, 619) as a result of globalization, time-space compression, electronic mediation, or the proliferation of simulation is not that contentious. However, to go as far as to assert the end of history, or to argue that we "no longer grasp history as a flow of meaning"—as Baudrillard (1994a) seems to imply—is to push the theoretical envelop beyond intuitive limits (Dodgshon 1999, 619).

Several noteworthy points can be distilled from Castells' space of flows and timeless time and Harvey's time-space compression elaborated upon here, but the following two are particularly noteworthy for our impending discussion on how Africa is connected to the processes of globalization. First, the global restructuring underway is driven primarily by advances in transportation and telecommunication technologies (e.g., e-mails, cell phones, blackberries, and high-speed trains, and airplanes); and, that these technologies have facilitated the movement of people, commodities, and information around the globe at such a fast pace that even our very experience of time and space has been compressed into *timeless time* and *space of flows*. Secondly, even though spatial barriers are being annihilated through time, spatial differences are no less significant in the contemporary economy. Indeed, locational differences are more consequential in this era of flexible accumulation than it used to be under Fordism. And once we move beyond our generalized assumptions of time-space compression into a spatially differentiated narrative, it becomes clear that matters of positionality, inequities, and power imbalances are embedded in the processes of globalization. More pointedly, time-space compression and space of flows are not geographically uniform, especially given the deepening "patterns of global uneven development in recent years" (Agnew 2001, 2).

POLITICAL ECONOMY OF TIME-SPACE COMPRESSION AND SPACE OF FLOWS

Notwithstanding its long-standing usage in the social sciences—going back to the writings of Montchrétien de Watterville in the seventeenth century[6]—no unified theory of political economy exist. What there is, as Hoogvelt (2001) points out, is a set of questions regarding the relationship between power, the state, or what is political, on the one hand, and wealth, economics, or the market, on the other. Depending on how this nexus is conceived, different theorizations of political economy have held sway at different epochs and for different analysts. For the mercantilist thinkers of the seventeenth and eighteenth centuries and their contemporary advocates, political economy connotes the strengthening of political power through economic means. The various methods used by mercantilists in pursuance of their idea of political economy are discussed at length by Julius Kiiza in Chapter 9 of this volume.

For the neoclassical economists, *a la* Adam Smith and David Ricardo, political economy is used the other way around to imply the deployment of political power in the service of the market. For them, the primacy belongs to the market, as against politics. Bent on providing a "critique of political economy," Marx and his followers use the term to highlight the negative, exploitative undertones of capitalism, and its attendant free market enterprise hailed by the neoclassical economists. For the Marxist, then, the focus is on how social and class relations affect, and are affected by, modes of production.

The preceding conceptualizations underpin different accounts of political economy in the international context (Hoogvelt 2001). Unsurprisingly, for mercantilists, the international political economy entails a competition between nation-states, or units, with each using its power to interfere with the (inter)national market for greater economic and political power *vis-à-vis* other nations. Mercantilists see the international political economy as a zero-sum game in which one nation gains only at the expense of others in a competitive environment (Hoogvelt 2001). For neoclassical economists, the international political economy involves trade liberalization and international interdependence. In their view, free trade is ultimately beneficial to all nations. Marxian thinkers, on their part, subsume political and economic relations between nations under the overarching workings of capitalism on the global scale. For them, the international political economy is structural, in the sense that nations are not isolated, independent units, but are all woven into a structural relationship, predetermined by the capitalist mode of production. Additionally, the structural relationship is hegemonic, with some nations systemically exploiting and dominating others in the ensuing networks of material exchange and capital accumulation. Unlike the neoclassical economists, who are more optimistic about the workings of the international political economy, the Marxists, like the mercantilists, see it as a tension-ridden contestation in which the strong gains at the expense of the weak.

Following the Marxian structural perspective, we define "international political economy" as the overall configuration of power—and the associated social contestations over material exchange and capital accumulation—within and between nations. Recognizing that social and economic life is geographically constituted, we borrow from the Marxist geographical tradition of the likes of Harvey (2006), Peet (1977, 2007), and Smith (1984) to examine the power dynamics beneath the uneven geographies of globalization. More importantly, we use Doreen Massey's (1999a, 1999b) notion of "power-geometries" to underline the fact that the social inequalities of globalization are not solely attributable to class, or the workings of capitalism, but also to other intersections of social domination, including gender, race, ethnicity, age, and geography.

While Harvey and Castells write remarkably about social and spatial inequalities of time-space compression and the space of flows, respectively, their positions on this matter are, arguably, not as pointed as that of Massey (1999a, 1999b), who uses her neologism "power-geometries" to specifically tease out the nuanced power dynamics embedded in the network society.

Hoogvelt (2001), for one, takes Castells to task on grounds that while the latter devotes one volume of his trilogy (Castells, 2000a, 2000b, 2000c) and a sizeable part of another to the interconnections between technology, economy, and patterns of social exclusions, he still fails to clarify the over-arching processes that make exclusion an integral part of globalization.[7] In a similar vein, Massey (1999, 60) criticizes Harvey (1990) for placing too much emphasis on class and money in accounting for variations in time-space compression to the virtual neglect of other social locations such as gender ethnicity, and race.

A careful synthesis of the works of these scholars (i.e., Harvey, Castell, Hoogvelt, and Massey) suggests that the power imbalances in the network society are wrought by a complex admixture of variables, of which class and gender relations, ethnicity, and international racism, and the legacies of colonialism are worthy of note. With this basic realization, it becomes almost axiomatic that not everyone's world is getting smaller. As Kirsch (1995, 536) metaphorically puts it: there are "those who cannot afford the rent in the 'global village' in the first place." Perhaps no one captures this differential positionality in globalization better than Massey (1999, 61) in the following God trick-like allegory:

> Imagine for a moment that you are on a satellite, further out and beyond all actual satellites; you can see 'planet earth' from a distance and, rare for someone with only peaceful intensions, you are equipped with the kind of technology that allows you to see the colours of people's eyes and the number on their number-plates. You can see all the movement and tune-in to all the communications that is going on. Furthest out are the satellites, then aeroplanes, the long haul between London and Tokyo and the hop from San Salvador to Guatemala City. Some of this is people moving, some of it is physical trade, some is media broadcasting. There are faxes, e-mail, film-distribution networks, financial flows and transactions. Look in closer and there are ships and trains, steam trains slogging laboriously up hills somewhere in Asia. Look in closer still and there are lorries and cars and buses and on down further and somewhere in Sub-Saharan Africa there's a woman on foot who still spends hours a day collecting water.

With other intriguing examples of time-space compression—including those of refugees from El Salvador heading to the United States; of migrants from India and Pakistan held up in Heathrow airport for interrogation; of a pensioner in a British inner city; and of people living in the favelas of Rio de Janeiro—Massey (1999a) has shown that almost every individual, or social group, is connected to the space of flows, but in different ways and with varying degrees of intensity.

Therefore, the main issue relates not merely to who is connected and who is not, but to the variations in the *nature* of these connections. Some—notably, the "jet-setters" (Massey 1999a, 61) or the "club-class migrants" (Brah *et al.* 1999, 6)—have the power to be in charge of their space of flows, while others are powerless (or disempowered), and can only participate minimally. Similarly, some people are leaders in the flows, while others are followers; some are positioned only at the receiving end of the flows, while others are at the opposite end, and still others are at both ends. Also, while some participate in the flows of globalization voluntarily, there are others, such as political or "economic" refugees, who are impelled by dire circumstances to be involved. Similarly, while the spatial mobility of some people are reinforced by the capitalist mode of production, and even by the instruments of state control and governmentality, those of others are severely weakened by these same practices. And, finally, as the two chapters by Wisdom J. Tettey in this volume clearly demonstrate, there are those whose involvement in globalization is primarily criminogenic.

A core issue in all this—given our particular interest in how Africa is connected to globalization—is whether or not the relative mobility of people in one region of the world reinforces the immobility of people in other parts, in a zero-sum manner? Does the power of mobility and communication enjoyed by many in the global North in any way undermine the spatial mobility of people in Africa? Put differently, do the first class international air travel privileges enjoyed by the technocratic-financial-managerial and academic elites of the network society feed into the spatial imprisonment of the masses, in, say, Africa? Even though a direct cause-and-effect link is hard to establish here, we do not have to probe too deeply into the matter to realize that the continued use (and overuse) of resources to fulfill the time-space compression needs of people in the global North invariably diminishes, or somehow affects, what is available for people in Africa or the global South, in general. In the specific case of Africa, it is not hard to envisage how the intense, long-standing looting and exploitation perpetrated on the continent by Westerners and their African cronies—as documented in this volume by Patrick Bond (Chapter 1)—will ultimately weaken Africans' access to, and capabilities in, time-space compression technologies. This position becomes even more appealing once we accept the concept of spatial dependence which underpins contemporary geostatistics and Tobler's (1970) so-called first law of geography: "Everything is related to everything else." Additional support for this argument can be distilled from Marx's (1987, 586) observation that "capital grows in one place to a huge mass in a single hand because it has in another place been lost to many."

A fairly similar zero-sum dynamic is behind the dialectical tensions between labor and capital in the space of flows. There are indications that "capital's ability to roam the world further strengthens it in relation to relatively immobile workers" (Massey 1999a, 62). The works of Hirst and Thompson (1996), Potts (1990), and Miles (1999) indicate that globalization has not led to an internationalized market in labor migration, the same way it has facilitated the cross-border mobility of capital worldwide. "In many ways, for the world's underprivileged and poor," write Hirst and Thompson (1996, 31), "there are fewer international migratory options nowadays than there were in the past." In fact, the migration policies of many countries in the global North have been decidedly exclusionary to people of the global South. (Un)surprisingly, with all the talk about time-space compression and unbridled mobility, we still "have sniffer dogs to detect people hiding in the hoods of boats, people die trying to cross the Rio Grande, and boatloads of people precisely trying to 'seek out the best opportunities' go down in the Mediterranean" (Massey 1999b, 39). Robert Miles (1999) in his analysis of the "political economy of migration" demonstrates how airports are spatially organized to assert national identity, reproduce sexism and racism, and reinforce the differential status of people in the international *order of things*.[8] Evidently, time-space compression harbors structural unevenness not only between social groups or regions, but also between labor and capital.

Clearly, globalization exhibits power imbalance, but has the imbalance in the *processes* of globalization produced a corresponding imbalance in the prevailing *discourse* and knowledge production on globalization? We need to draw a fine line between the process(es), or phenomenon, of globalization, on the one hand, and the discourse of globalization, on the other. The former refers to the actual, day-to-day workings of globalization (as per the mechanics of time-space compression and space of flows), while the letter denotes how scholars have discussed, theorized, and produced knowledge about globalization. If one accepts the argument that the world of unbridled mobility and high-speed emails and blackberries are not the world of more than half of the world's population, then are not some Foucauldian power-knowledge dynamics (or some false consciousness) at play in the prevailing discourse on globalization? As Massey (1999b) questions: Whose globalization do we keep hearing about in such *fashionable* mantras as space of flows, global village, electronic cottages, annihilation of space by time in the ever-burgeoning literature on globalization?

With the exception of few studies—notably those of Massey (1999a, 1999b) and Miles (1999)—the available literature has steered clear of discussing the political economy of time-space compression—such discussions have been *unfashionable*. One can reasonably envisage a mutually reinforcing connection between this lacuna and the power imbalance in the actual processes of globalization on the ground. After all, as Foucault (1980) has long theorized: power reproduces knowledge, just as it is based on, and utilizes, knowledge—hence, the Foucauldian power-knowledge. The recurrent globalization talk of a shrinking world is arguably not so much about how the world actually is, as an image in which the world is being painted in the discursive practices of the powers that be. As we shall soon see, "the world is not yet totally globalized (whatever that might mean); the very fact that some are striving so hard to make it so is evidence of the project's incompleteness" (Massey 1999b, 36).

AFRICA IN THE CONTEXT OF GLOBALIZATION
AND TIME-SPACE COMPRESSION

Our upbeat assumptions about how the world is shrinking into a global village in which people are becoming alike (socioculturally and economically)
seem to "rest on a large element of imagination or wishful thinking without
empirical substance" (Agnew 2001, 2). There is enough evidence to suggest
that the "global village" is divided between streets of "haves" and "have-
nots." Still, unlike the socioeconomic polarization of the past, what one finds
under contemporary globalization is a complex reconfiguration of the world
order into a formation that does not readily submit to simple, bipolar catego-
rizations, such as core/periphery or First World/Third World, without any
caveat. At a very broad theoretical level, one can still deploy such binaries,
but they are certainly of limited utility in any nuanced analysis of the contemporary global architecture.

Hoogvelt (2001, 239–40), for one, describes the new world order not
as the traditional pyramid—with the core countries on top, followed by the
semi-periphery, and then the periphery at the base—but as three-tier con-
centric circles. At the core of Hoogvelt's schema is about 20 percent of the
world's elite population, dubbed "bankable"—i.e., people whose economic
contributions are such that any investments made on them payoff; followed
by the "employable tier" of about 20–30 percent of the world population,
people who are in insecure jobs, constantly thrown into competition in the
global labor market; and then the zone of the "excluded," made up of about
50 percent of the world's population, who are "performing neither a productive function, nor presenting a potential consumer market in the present stage of high-tech information-driven capitalism." All three circles in
this concentricity cut across national, continental, and regional boundaries,
albeit in different proportions to their respective position in the international
political economy.

Similarly, Agnew (2001, 2) likens the contemporary geography of uneven
global development to "a complex mosaic of interlinked global city-regions,
prosperous rural areas, resource sites, and 'dead lands' increasingly cut off
from time-space compression." As with Hoogvelt's schema, Agnew's mosaic
cuts across national and regional boundaries. As he puts it, "even if there is
a basic global north-south structure to the world economy . . . some of the
prosperous areas, for example, can be found within even the poorest countries [and *vice versa*]" (Agnew 2002, 2–3; mine in brackets). Castells makes
a similar point in his *End of millennium* to the effect that: "The ascent of
informational capitalism is indeed characterized by simultaneous economic
development and underdevelopment, social inclusion and exclusion, in a process very roughly reflected in comparative statistics. There is polarization in
the distribution of wealth at the global level, differential evolution of intra-
country income inequality, and substantial growth of poverty and misery in
the world at large, and in most countries, both developed and developing"
(82). Notwithstanding this dialectical interpenetration of the global North

and South, and regardless of how one slices the proverbial global pie, the vast majority of sub-Saharan Africans are among the "excluded" or those in the global "dead lands," virtually "falling out" of the network society. Castells writes extensively about the exceptional case of sub-Saharan Africans, whose very low technological base inhibits their functional involvement in the new high-tech economy. The same theme permeates the pages of the *2006 Human development report*. In fact, almost any mention of sub-Saharan Africa in this report alludes to a situation where the human condition on the sub-continent is in reverse of, or exception to, the general global trend. Consider the following excerpts from the report: "Since the mid-1970s almost all regions have been progressively increasing in HDI score. . . . The major *exception is Sub-Saharan Africa*. . . . Over the past three decades developing countries as a group have been converging on developed countries in life expectancy . . . the *exception again is Sub-Saharan Africa*. For the region as a whole life expectancy today is lower than it was three decades ago. . . . Income poverty has fallen in all regions since 1990, *except in Sub-Saharan Africa*. . . . While the world as a whole is on track for achieving the 2015 target of halving extreme poverty, *Sub-Saharan Africa is off track*" (UNDP, 2006, 265–69, emphasis mine).

How does the sub-continent fare in terms of time-space compression innovations, then? From Tables 6.1 and 6.2, it is clear that not only are sub-Saharan African countries worse off in Human Development Index (HDI),[9] but they have very low time-space compression innovations as well. Of the 177 countries ranked in the 2006 HDI, Niger came in dead last, and a whopping twenty-eight (of the thirty-one) low human development countries are in the region. Furthermore, with the exceptions of Botswana, Namibia, and the tiny islands of Seychelles, Mauritius, and Cape Verde, no sub-Saharan African country had more than fifty mainline phones per one thousand people by 2004. The fact that so many countries in the region, including Cameroon, Uganda, Rwanda, Angola, Chad, Central African Republic, Burkina Faso, Sierra Leon, and Niger, had fewer than ten mainland phones per one thousand people (or one per one hundred) in as recently as 2004, is simply astounding in this era of time-space compression. In a more dramatic fashion, Castells (2000c, 92) notes that "there are more telephone lines in Manhattan or in Tokyo than in the whole of Sub-Saharan Africa." The figures for cell phone are slightly encouraging, with many countries jumping from having virtually none in 1990 to more 50 or more cell phones per 1000 people by 2004 (Table 6.1).

Arguably, no other technology underpins the operations of the network society of today more than the Internet. In 1990, sub-Saharan African countries had virtually no Internet connectivity, as can be seen from Table 6.1. By 2004, the region has some connections, but very rudimentary, with most countries having less than 50 Internet users per 1000 people. In fact, as Table 6.2 shows, in 2004, sub-Saharan African had merely 19 Internet users per 1000 people, compared with 115 per 1000 for Latin American and the Caribbean; 55 per 1000 for the Arab States; and 91 per 1000 for East Asia and the Pacific Region (Table 6.2). Clearly, "Africa remains, by and large,

Table 6.1 Sub-Saharan Africa: HDI[1] and time-space compression technologies

HDI Ranking in Sub-Sahara Africa	2004 HDI (Rank)[2]	Phone Mainlines (per 1,000 people)		Cell Subscribers (per 1,000 people)		Internet Users (per 1,000 people)	
		1990	2004	1990	2004	1990	2004
High HDI							
1. Seychelles	0.842 (47)	124	253	0	589	0	239
2. Mauritius	0.800 (63)	53	87	2	413	0	146
Medium HDI							
3. Cape Verde	0.722 (106)	23	148	0	133	0	50
4. Eq. Guinea	0.653 (120)	4	—	0	113	0	10
5. South Africa	0.653 (121)	94	—	(.)[3]	428	0	78
6. Gabon	0.633 (124)	22	28	0	359	0	29
7. Namibia	0.626 (125)	38	64	0	142	0	37
8. S. Tome & Principe	0.607 (127)	19	—	0	—	0	131
9. Botswana	0.570 (131)	18	77	0	319	0	34
10. Comoros	0.556 (132)	8	—	0	—	0	14
11. Ghana	0.532 (136)	3	14	0	78	0	17
12. Congo	0.520 (140)	6	4	0	99	0	9
13. Sudan	0.516 (141)	2	29	0	30	0	32
14. Madagascar	0.509 (143)	3	—	0	18	0	5
15. Cameroon	0.506 (144)	3	7	0	96	0	10
16. Uganda	0.502 (145)	2	3	0	42	0	7
17. Swaziland	0.500 (146)	18	—	0	101	0	32
Low HDI							
18. Togo	0.495 (147)	3	—	0	—	0	37
19. Lesotho	0.494 (149)	8	21	0	88	0	24
20. Zimbabwe	0.491 (151)	12	25	0	31	0	63
21. Kenya	0.491 (152)	7	9	0	76	0	45
22. Mauritania	0.486 (153)	3	—	0	175	0	5
23. Gambia	0.479 (155)	7	—	0	118	0	33
24. Senegal	0.460 (156)	6	—	0	90	0	42
25. Eritrea	0.454 (157)	—	9	0	5	0	12
26. Rwanda	0.450 (158)	1	3	0	16	0	4
27. Nigeria	0.448 (159)	3	8	0	71	0	14
28. Guinea	0.445 (160)	2	—	0	—	0	5
29. Angola	0.439 (161)	7	6	0	48	0	11
30. Tanzania	0.430 (162)	3	—	0	44	0	9
31. Benin	0.428 (163)	3	9	0	—	0	12
32. Cote díIvoire	0.421 (164)	6	13	0	86	0	17
33. Zambia	0.407 (165)	8	8	0	26	0	20
34. Malawi	0.400 (166)	3	7	0	18	0	4
35. Congo, D. Rep	0.391 (167)	1	(.)	0	37	0	—
36. Mozambique	0.390 (168)	4	—	0	36	0	7
37. Burundi	0.384 (169)	1	—	0	—	0	3
38. Ethiopia	0.371 (170)	2	—	0	3	0	2
39. Chad	0.368 (171)	1	1	0	13	0	6
40. Cítral Africa Rep	0.353 (172)	2	3	0	15	0	2
41. GuineañBissau	0.349 (173)	6	—	0	—	0	17
42. Burkina Faso	0.342 (174)	2	6	0	31	0	4

Table 6.1 (*continued*)

43. Mali	0.338 (175)	1	6	0	30	0	4
44. Sierra Leone	0.335 (176)	3	5	0	22	0	2
45. Niger	0.311 (177)	1	2	0	11	0	2

Notes: [1]HDI = Human Development Index. [2]Global rankings in parentheses. [3](.) = The figure is greater or less than zero but small enough that the number would round to zero at the displayed number of decimals points; and—= Data not available.

Source: UNDP 2006 [Derived from Tables 1 and 13].

the switched-off region of the world" when it comes to Internet connectivity (Castells 2000c, 94). The IT lacuna in the region is far more systemic, going beyond mere shortage of Internet connectivity to a debilitating lack of computer infrastructure, training facilities, and consequently, basic computer skills among the bulk of the population.

Electricity consumption is another area where sub-Saharan Africans lag behind people in other parts of the world, feeding into the unflattering image of Africa as "the dark continent." Whether it is in the running of computers for the Internet and emails or television for news programming or for powering up schools, clinics, airports, and factories, electrical energy is virtually indispensable. It is hard to envisage how sub-Saharan Africa can be integrated into the network society without increasing the availability of affordable electricity or energy supply. Table 6.3 shows that whereas the average person living in the OECD countries uses as much as 8,777 kilowatt-hours of electricity, the comparable figure for sub-Saharan Africa is just 522 kilowatt-hours—this is less than what is used by people in other regions of the world. In fact, with the notable exception of the Republic of South Africa, where the electricity consumption per head is in the thousands of kilowatt-hours, most countries in the region have consumption rates in the hundredths of

Table 6.2 Time-space compression technologies by world regions

World Region	Regional Population (million) 2004		Telephone Mainlines *(per 1,000 people)*		Cellular Subscribers *(per 1000 people)*		Internet Users *(per 1,000 people)*	
	#	%	1990	2004	1990	2004	1990	2004
Developing Countries	5,093.6	—	21	122	(.)	175	(.)	64
Sub-Saharan Africa	689.6	10.5	10	—	(.)	77	0	19
Arab States	310.5	4.7	34	91	(.)	169	0	55
East Asia & the Pacific	1,944.0	29.5	18	199	(.)	262	(.)	91
Lat. America. & Carib	548.3	8.3	61	179	(.)	319	0	115
South Asia	1,528.1	23.2	7	35	(.)	42	0	29
Cítral & E. Europe & CIS	405.3	6.1	125	—	(.)	455	0	139
OECD	1,164.8	17.7	390	491	10	714	3	484
World	6590.6	100.0	98	190	2	276	1	138

Source: UNDP 2006 [Derived from Table 13].

Table 6.3　Electricity consumption by selected sub-Saharan African countries & world regions

Selected Countries & World Region	Electricity Consumption per capita (kilowatt-hours)		
	1980	2003	% Change: 1980-2003
Selected Sub-Saharan African Countries			
Cameroon	168	226	25.7
Chad	10	11	9.1
Ghana	450	285	-57.9
Kenya	109	154	29.2
Mali	15	38	60.5
Nigeria	108	162	33.3
Senegal	115	192	40.1
South Africa	3,181	4,595	30.8
Tanzania	41	78	47.4
Zambia	1,125	631	-78.3
Developing Countries	388	1,157	66.5
Sub-Saharan Africa	434	522	16.8
Arab States	626	1,977	68.3
East Asia & the Pacific	329	1418	76.8
Lat Amer & Caribbean	1019	1932	47.2
South Asia	171	598	71.4
Cítral & East Europe & CIS	3284	3432	4.3
OECD	5,761	8,777	34.4
World	1573	2490	36.8

Source: UNDP 2006 [Computed from Table 21].

kilowatt-hours per capita. People in countries such as Chad, Mali, and Tanzania use less than 100 kilowatts-hour of electricity per capita. Castells could not have put it any shrewder with his observation that: "Not only is Africa, by far, the least computerized region of the world, but it does not have the minimum infrastructure required to make use of computers, thus making nonsense of many of the efforts to provide electronic equipment to countries and organizations. Indeed, before moving into electronic, Africa first needs a reliable electricity supply" (2000c, 92).

Given that the high-speed, high-tech world of today runs on technological innovations, an apposite measure of how sub-Saharan Africa compares with the *Rest* is the level of research and development in the region, as measured by the number of researchers, the number of patents, and receipt of royalties and license fees. As Table 6.4 shows, sub-Saharan Africa does very poorly in these indicators, with many of them even lacking any official data. The available data on receipt of royalties and license fees suggest that sub-Saharan Africa had only US$0.5 per person in 2004, compared with the global average of US$17.3 per person. It bears noting, though, that the poor performance of sub-Saharan Africa in the receipts of royalties and license fees is

Table 6.4 R & D and technology creation by world regions

World Regions	Patent Granted to Residents (per million people) 2004	Receipt of royalties and license fees (US$ per person) 2004	Research and Development (R & D) expenditure (% of GDP) 2000-03	Researchers in R & D (per million people) 1990-2003
Developing Countries	—	0.7	1.1	416
Sub-Saharan Africa	—	0.5	—	—
Arab States	—	0.4	—	—
East Asia & the Pacific	—	1.3	1.7	740
Lat Amer & Caribbean	—	1.0	0.6	306
South Asia	—	(.)	0.7	132
Cítral & East Europe & CIS	75	2.5	1.0	2,204
OECD	266	92.4	2.5	3,108
World	138	17.3	2.4	1,153

Source: UNDP 2006 [Derived from Table 13].

not unusual among regions of the developing world—which has an average of mere US$0.7 per person in 2004, compared with US$92.4 for OECD countries in the same year (Table 6.4).

The perturbation in all this is not merely that sub-Saharan Africa has extremely low infrastructural and technological base, vis-à-vis time-space compression, but also that the little available comes with exorbitant price tags, given the usual econometric tensions between supply, demand, and selling price. Time-space compression facilities, including airline connections, Internet access, phone lines, cable television services, and even international travel visas, are hard to come by in many parts of the region. This scarcity creates avenues for price gorging and other exploitative tendencies among supplies. The difficulties black Africans go through in procuring visas are almost legendary in the unwritten annals of international travel. Beside high—and, arguably, bad-faith[10]—visa application fees, African nationals seeking to travel overseas are routinely subjected to exceptionally excessive interrogations and medical examinations by various embassies. And the international racism often meted out to these people at major international airports (such as Skipol in Amsterdam, Heathrow and Gatwick in London, Frankfurt International Airport in Germany, and Toronto International Airport in Canada) are only now receiving some attention in the literature (Mile 1999).

We learned from Harvey's (2003, 109) notion of "spatial fix" that as the general contradictions of capitalism produce crises of overaccumulation (in the West), the capitalist often resorts to "capital switching," or "spatial displacements through opening up new markets, new production capacities, and new resources and labor possibilities elsewhere." There are indications that some capital switching—from Western Europe, the Middle East, and Newly Industrializing Countries (NICs)—are underway in the airline, Internet, and cell phone businesses in sub-Saharan Africa. The exploitative maneuvers of some of these foreign companies are likely to engender yet new rounds of accumulation by dispossession on the African continent (see Patrick Bond's chapter in this volume for more insight on the dynamics of accumulation by dispossession). As with Harvey's (1990) thesis of "capital switching," Smith (2000) opines that to the extent that underdevelopment creates conditions for development (e.g., in the form of cheap labor), there is always the tendency for capital to move from developed regions to under-developed ones. Undoubtedly, the low technological base in Africa could create the conditions for such capital oscillation from the West to the continent, but at what cost to the environment, to national sovereignty, and to the overall development of the continent?

CONCLUSION

Without doubt, since the early 1970s, there has been an increased mobility and internationalization of social, economic, and cultural practices, with different scholars zeroing in on different aspects of the ensuing phenomenon in the available literature (Dodgshon 1999). With the concepts of time-space compression, space of flows, and timeless time, Harvey and Castell (and many others) have highlighted the dramatic restructuring of our spatiotemporal dimensionality and of our experience of it. Ironically, just as time seems to conquer space in the time-space compression underway, emphatic assertions of the *end of history* are not uncommon in the literature (Fukuyama 1992; Baudrillard 1994a). But as Agnew (2001, 8) sarcastically puts it: "History has not ended in instant electronic simulation. History is not the same as the History Channel." In a similar ironic vein, with the annihilation of space (by time)—and the attendant talk of an emerging placelessness—has come a growing concern about space and geographic differences, not only among social theorists, but also among capitalists, for whom miniscule spatial differences have assumed even greater importance.

With the aid of empirical data on time-space compression technologies, such as telephones, the Internet, and electricity, we have shown that the processes of globalization are hardly uniform across space. The character(istics) of individual places or regions interacts with globalization to yield specific outcomes in the network society (Dickens 2000). Different social groups and regions are differently positioned on the axis of globalization, with race, ethnicity, class, gender, age, and other variables of social domination (and their permutations) influencing people's ability to negotiate the topographies of time-space compression. Africa as a whole—and sub-Saharan Africa, in particular—lags behind the rest of the world in nearly all the major indicators of the network society, with some even describing the continent's tie to the global economy as one of *ex*corporation rather than *in*corporation (Terlouw 1992). Still, we must note that not all African, or for that matter sub-Saharan African, countries have "fallen out" of the network society. The sheer size and complexity of the continent make any such generalization patently facile.

Inter- and intranational variations abound on the continent, as one would expect of any part of the world. Similarly, it would be erroneous to paint an image of sub-Saharan Africans as though they are totally powerless in the network society, with no human agency of their own. As Foucault (1980) has taught us, power is indeed everywhere, because it hails from everywhere, and without resistance, defiance, and subversion, power becomes impotent. As several chapters in this very volume, including those of Mensah (Chapter 2), Tettey (Chapters 8 and 12), and the late Prempeh (Chapter 3) demonstrate, Africans have not only participated actively in globalization, but have mounted various forms resistance, when need be, to protect their individual and collective interest. Unfortunately, some aspects of this agency have been criminogenic—then, again, Africans are hardly the only people implicated in criminal activities in the network society.

The human agency exhibited by Africans in this context should not impair our vision of the power imbalance inherent in globalization and its space of flows. As we saw through the works of Doreen Massey, in particular, while almost everyone is somehow caught up in the processes of globalization, some are more in charge than others. This power imbalance even extends into the discursive practices surrounding globalization, making particular observations about globalization more (un)fashionable than others. To the extent that the prevailing knowledge about globalization paints a picture of an unfettered mobility of goods, services, and labor in a shrinking world—an image which is evidently far from what exists in Africa, and perhaps the global South in general—there seems to be some element of what Gayartri Spivak (1999) might call "a successful cognitive failure" (if not false consciousness) in operation.

It has not been our intent to tease out the fine-grained variations in time-space compression innovations or to uncover the root causes of sub-Saharan Africa's weak attachment to the network society. Still, it would not take much forensic theorization to establish that the usual "suspects"—including political instability and cronyism, deteriorating terms of trade, rampant tribalism and ethnic conflicts, excessive foreign debt burden, and subtle and not-so-subtle looting by Westerners and their African allies, and so on—are all implicated, in one way or the other. Our aim here is to sound the alarm bell to the powers that be in sub-Saharan Africa to reverse Castells' prediction of an impending "market deepening"[11]—in which about one-fifth of the world's population continues to do better, while about 40 percent of the world's population, many of whom are very likely to be sub-Saharan Africans, continue to be excluded from the network society.

REFERENCES

Agnew, John. 2001. *The new global economy: Time-space compression, geopolitics, and global uneven development.* Lecture presented at the Center for Globalization and Policy Research, UCLA.

Anthia, Floya. 2001. New hybridity, old concept: The limit of "culture." *Ethnic and Racial Studies* 24 (4): 619–41.

Baudrillard, Jean. 1986. *L'Amérique*. Paris: B. Grasset.

———. 1994a. *The illusion of the end*. Cambridge: Polity.

———. 1994b. *Simulacra and simulation*. First published in French in 1981, trans. Sheila Faria Glaser. Ann Arbor: University of Michigan Press.

Brah, A., M. J. Kickman, and Martin M. Ghaill. 1999. Introduction: Wither 'the global'? In *Global futures: Migration, environment, and globalization*, ed. A. Brah, M. J. Hickman, and M. M. Ghail, 3–26. Basingstoke, Hampshire: Palgrave Macmillan.

Castells, Manuel. 2000a. *The rise of the network society*. Vol. 1 of *The information age: Economy, society, and culture*, Malden MA: Blackwell.

———. 2000b. *The power of identity*. Vol. 2 of *The information age: Economy, society, and culture* Malden MA: Blackwell.

———. 2000c. *End of millennium*. Vol. 3 of *The information age: Economy, society, and culture* Malden MA: Blackwell.

Dickens, Peter. 2000. Globalization. In *Dictionary of human geography*, ed. R. J. Johnston, D. Gregory, G. Pratt, and M. Watts, 315–17. Malden, MA: Blackwell.

Dodgshon, Robert A. 1999. Human geography at the end of time? Some thought on the notion of time-space compression. *Environment and planning D: Society and space* 17:607–20.

Evans, Peter. 2000. Fighting marginalization with transnational networks: Counter-hegemonic globalization. *Contemporary Sociology* 29 (1): 230–41

Foucault, Michel. 1980. *Power/knowledge: Selected interviews and other writings*. New York: Pantheon.

Fukuyama, F. 1992. *The end of history and the last man*. Harmondsworth: Penguin.

Giddens, Anthony. 1984. *The constitution of society*. Cambridge: Polity.

Harvey, David. 1990. *The condition of postmodernity*. Cambridge, MA and Oxford, UK: Blackwell.

———. 2003. *The new imperialism*. Oxford: Oxford University Press.

———. 2006. *The limit of capital*. London and New York: Verso.

Hoogvelt, Ankie. 2001. *Globalization and the postcolonial world: The new political economy of development*. Baltimore: John Hopkins University Press.

Hirst, P., and Thompson, G. 1996a. *Globalization in question: The international economy and the possibilities of governance*. Cambridge: Polity.

———. 1996b. Globalization: Teen frequently asked question and some surprising answers. *Soundings* 4:47–66.

Jameson, F. 1991. *Postmodernism, or the cultural logic of late capitalism*. London: Verso.

Lefebvre, H. 1991. *The production of space, t*rans. D. Nicholson-Smith.Oxford: Blackwell.

Luke, T. W., and G. Tuathail. 1998. Global flowmations, local fundamentalisms, and fast geopolitics: American in and accelerating world order. In *An unruly world? Globalization, governance, and geography*, ed. A Herod, G. Tuathail, and S. M. Roberts, 72. London and New York: Routledge.

Marx, K. 1987. *Capital*. Vol. 1. New York: International.

Massey, Doreen. 1992. Politics and space/time. *New Left Review* 196:65–84.

———. 1999a. Power-geometry and a progressive sense of place. In *Mapping the futures: Local cultures, global change*, ed. Jon Bird *et al*. London and New York: Routledge.

———. 1999b. Imagining globalization: Power-geometries of time-space. In *Global futures: Migration, environment and globalization*, ed. A. Brah, M.J. Hickman, and M. M. Ghaill, 27–43. Basingstoke, Hampshire: Palgrave Macmillan.

McNally, D. 2002. *Another world is possible: Globalization and anti-capitalism*. Winnipeg: Arbeiter Ring.

Miles, Robert. 1999. Analysing the political economy of migration: The airport as an "effective institution of control." In *Global futures: Migration, environment, and globalization*, ed. A. Brah, M.J. Hickman, and M. M. Ghaill, 161–84. Basingstoke, Hampshire: Palgrave Macmillan.

Peet, Richard. 1977. *Radical geography: Alternative viewpoints of contemporary social issues*. Chicago: Maarouta.

———. 2007. *Geography of power: Making global economic policy*. London and New York: Zed Books.

Potts, L. 1990. *The world labour market: A history of migration*. London: Zed Books.

Robins, K., and M. Hepworth. 1988. Electronic spaces—new technologies and the future of cities. *Future* 20:155–76.

Smith, Neil. 1984. *Uneven development: Nature, capital, and the production of space*. New York: Blackwell.

Soja, Edward. 1989. *Postmodern geographies: The reassertion of space in critical social theory*. London: Verso.

———. 1996. *Thirdspace: Journeys to Los Angeles and other real and imagined places*. Oxford: Blackwell.

Spivak, Gayatri C. 1999. *A critique of postcolonial reason: Toward a history of the vanishing present*. Cambridge, MA: Harvard University Press.

Terlouw, C. P. 1992. *The regional geography of the world system: External arena, periphery, semiperiphery, core*. Utrecht: Netherlands Geographical Studies.

The Economist. The bank that disappeared, February 27, 1995.

Tobler, W. R. 1970. A computer model simulation of urban growth in the Detroit region. *Economic Geography* 46 (2): 234–40.

UNDP. 2006. *Human development report, 2006*. New York: UNDP.

NOTES

1. Anthia (2001) uses the concept of "translocational positionality" to show that all the talk of hybridity glosses over the fact that there are unequal relations, cultural hierarchies, and hegemonic practices embedded in the ongoing cultural mixing. The term "power geometries" was coined by Massey (1999a, 1999b) to denote the power imbalances in time-space compression.

2. The four studies include: *David Strauss, the confessor and the writer* (1873); *On the uses and disadvantages of history for life* (1874); *Schopenhauer as educator* (1874); and *Richard Wagner in Bayreuth* (1876).

3. With Patrick Bond's biting exposé on the long-standing "looting of Africa" in this volume, it would not be that difficult to identify the factors implicated in the continent's weak attachment to the network society.

4. The metaphor "electronic cottages" is borrowed from the futuristic work of Robins and Hepworth (1988).

5. Established in 1762, the Barings Bank was Britain's oldest merchant bank. It collapsed in 1995 when one of its employers, Nick Leeson, lost a whopping £827

million (about US$1.4 billion, then) of the bank's money through speculations on futures contracts.

6. According to Hoogvelt (2001, 3). The French writer, Montchrétian de Watterville, was the first to use the term political economy in his work; it was used to describe the science of the acquisition of wealth by the state and individuals.

7. Admittedly, it is hard to fault Castells when it comes to documenting the marginalization of Africa, in particular, in the network society. Castells' *End of millennium* (2000c) offers an extensive account of how Africa is increasingly becoming a Fourth World continent, especially when it comes to information technology.

8. This last slant pays homage to Foucault's "The order of things: An archeology of human sciences."

9. The HDI is a composite measure of human development that incorporates the following three dimensions: life expectancy; adult literacy, and enrollment at the primary, secondary, and tertiary levels; and PPP, or purchasing power parity income (UNDP 2006, 263).

10. "Bad-faith" is used decidedly here: informal, personal interactions with, and interviews of, visa applicants at the British, Dutch, and Canadian embassies in Accra, Ghana, suggest that these visa fees are charged in bad faith, in the sense that the vast majority of the applicants are not only rejected, but rejected on the flimsiest of excuses. Even the rejection letters from the Canadian embassy were, indeed, generic, with the applicants' names filled-in (in ink). Not only that, until recently, visa applicants for the Canadian family unification class were subjected to DNA, as well as bone density, tests—to presumably verify their genetic lineage and age.

11. Castells made this prediction in a 1999 interview in *New Political Economy* 4, no. 3: 385.

CHAPTER 7

AFRICAN STATES'
NEPAD PROJECT

A GLOBAL ELITE NEOLIBERAL SETTLEMENT

Eunice N. Sahle

Current discourses on international political economy generally contend that the decade of the 1970s generated significant shifts in economic, intellectual, and political spheres that continue to shape national and global developments. On the economic level, these discourses claim that the period saw the emergence of a serious global recession characterized by decline in production, high inflation, crisis of profits for the majority of firms, technological developments, rise in government deficits, and massive layoffs for workers. These economic developments and major changes in the political landscape of major countries in the global North in the late 1970s and early 1980s—the rise of Margaret Thatcher in the UK, Helmut Kohl in Germany, and Ronald Reagan in the United States—and intellectual shifts that called for the dismantling of the global Keynesian economic framework are highlighted as core factors that ushered in a new phase of globalization underpinned by neoliberal economic discourse.

In the context of African countries, analysts argue that these global economic, political, and intellectual shifts have had a significant influence on the continent's development process. In the economic realm, for instance, the core features of the neoliberal economic globalization are said to have contributed to an economic downward spiral in most African countries. These countries, however, are not the only ones that have faced major economic crisis, for as John Rapley has argued, the crisis of capital accumulation has been a core feature of the current phase of globalization in all parts of the world (Rapley 2004). In essence, the onset of this phase of globalization marked the end of the post-1945 "golden age" of global capitalism, which had seen significant economic growth in the global North and various parts of the global South. In Africa, the crisis of postcolonial capitalism has been characterized by a serious economic crisis, evidenced by decline in economic surplus, levels of investment and savings, inability of African states to meet their debt obligations to public and private lenders, and failure of these states to maintain what Yusuf Bangura has termed as the postcolonial social contract (Ihonvbere 2000; Bangura 1992).[1] The developments that emerged globally in the 1970s have, over the years, seen states institute various economic and political strategies as a response to the economic conditions and contradictions generated by neoliberal economic strategies. This chapter's objective is to examine the ways in which African states have responded to neoliberal globalization, with a specific focus on their New Partnership for Africa's Development (NEPAD) initiative. In the main, African states, like other states elsewhere, have not been bystanders in the evolution of the contemporary phase of globalization and other global shifts that characterize the current global conjuncture. Consequently, the launching of NEPAD demonstrates the political agency of these states. Nonetheless, and contrary to dominant approaches to the study of Africa's political economy, it is argued that their agency is nonetheless mediated by local and global factors.

With respect to the emergence and promotion of the NEPAD project, the chapter's underlying argument is that its transformative concepts such as "ownership," "partnership" notwithstanding, it represents a global elite neoliberal settlement aimed at the consolidation of the neoliberal project in Africa. This global elite comprises local political-economic elites and leading actors of what we have termed elsewhere as the transnational development historical bloc (Sahle 2008) whose members are powerful institutions of global governance—World Bank, International Monetary Fund (IMF), and World Trade Organization (WTO)—the dominant states in the world system, and private capital. The chapter has three sections. In efforts to contextualize the discussion on NEPAD, section one highlights the ways in which the constitutive ideas framing neoliberal economic globalization shaped Africa's development discourse in the pre-NEPAD era. Section two critically examines the core features of the NEPAD initiative, while section three demonstrates the limitations of the initiative as a blueprint for Africa's political-economic processes in the conjuncture of neoliberal capitalist strategies.

CONTEXUALIZING NEPAD:
GLOBAL NEOLIBERALISM AND THE EMERGENCE OF A NEW DEVELOPMENT DISCOURSE IN AFRICA

Over the last two decades, the emergence and evolution of neoliberal globalization has greatly shaped Africa's economic and political processes. On the economic front, this development has seen the rise of a new development paradigm that borrows heavily from the constitutive ideas that underpin neoliberal thought and practice, such as calls for a limited role of the state in the economic arena, cuts in social spending, valorization of private capital, and the promotion of international free trade. In specific terms, this discourse has explained Africa's economic crisis and stagnation as being a result of the state's extensive role in economic affairs, especially through the expansion of publicly owned enterprises in the postcolonial period (World Bank 1981, 37). Other contributing factors to the continent's economic crisis, as articulated by advocates of neoliberal restructuring, are extensive trade protection measures, such as high tariffs and licensing procedures, and overvalued currencies. In addition, agricultural policies, especially the practice of paying small-scale producers limited returns for their products, and the decline of agricultural exports in the 1970s, are also highlighted as contributing to economic stagnation and crisis. The expenditure patterns followed by postcolonial governments of providing subsidies in agriculture and in social sectors such as education and health, and the expansion of the civil service, are also highlighted as factors.

With the rise of a neoliberal development paradigm, and in response to the serious economic crisis that came to a head in most African countries in the late 1970s, African states have, over the last two decades, implemented core elements of the economic strategies advocated by the neoliberal development framework. In line with neoliberal development thought, these states, at serious cost to many people, especially women and children, have cut spending in various social sectors. In the health sector, for instance, neoliberal reforms that call for the introduction of a market-based approach to health service provision have resulted in increases in health costs—a process that has, in the case of the Democratic Republic of Congo, seen a decline in women seeking prenatal care and hospital visits for young children (Turshen 1994, 81). Neoliberal economic strategies have also been implemented in education, a development that has facilitated the deepening of the gender gap that has historically existed in this sector (Tsikata and Kerr 2000).[2] Other reforms have included layoffs of public sector workers in the effort to achieve what various reports from the World Bank on Africa term as the "rationalization" of the civil service (World Bank 1981, 1989, 1994).[3]

Privatization of publicly owned enterprises is another element of neoliberal economic strategies. As African countries entered a period of serious economic crisis, their reliance on public enterprises as engines of economic growth came under heavy criticism by scholars working within the new development paradigm of neoliberalism and the international lending community and its leading institutions, such as the World Bank and the International Monetary Fund. According to supporters of neoliberal economic strategies, public enterprises were largely responsible for the African continent's limited development and economic crisis because they were inefficient, created rent-seeking opportunities, and stifled the entrepreneurial spirit.

These core measures of neoliberal economic restructuring described above were, by the late 1980s, deemed inadequate for the transformation of African economic development along modern capitalist lines. Consequently, by the late 1980s, advocates of the neoliberal development paradigm began to call for reforms in Africa's political arena. As a World Bank seminar report declared in 1989, the economic problems of the continent were also due to political practices: "Underlying the litany of Africa's development problems is a crisis of governance . . . [a] deep political malaise [that] stymies action in most countries" (World Bank 1989, xii). The discourse on political reforms highlighted the lack of good governance as a factor that had led to economic crisis, extensive personalized forms of rule, human rights abuses, and limited foreign investment, due to an inefficient judiciary that had failed to "protect property and enforce contracts" (World Bank 1989, 9). This trend, according to this line of thought, also led to high levels of corruption, waste, and lack of economic development in most of Africa. Thus, according to advocates of good governance, changes to regime structures were necessary for the economic and political recovery of the continent. By the late 1980s, the debate on political reforms had evolved beyond calls for good governance practices to include the promotion of the establishment of multiparty democratic states. In contrast to their earlier development paradigm, which supported the establishment of "developmental dictatorships" in the periphery, their new discourse no longer upheld dictators as the foundation for economic development. Consequently, multiparty democracy (along with other terms such as governance, human rights, and free markets) in Africa and other parts of the global South occupied a prominent place in the development discourse of the international lending community who utilized foreign aid as a powerful tool in the push for its establishment. While advocating political reforms as a cornerstone of good governance the underlying frame of the World Bank's definition of the latter is adoption of neoliberal economic strategies by African states: "Good governance includes the creation, protection, and enforcement of property rights, without which the scope for market transactions is limited. It includes the provision of a regulatory regime that works with the market to promote competition. And it includes the provision of sound macroeconomic policies that create a stable environment for market activity. Good governance also means the absence of corruption, which can subvert the goals of policy and undermine the legitimacy of the public institutions that support markets" (World Bank 2002, 99).

While the global elite-driven twin project of promoting market-led capitalism and democracy in Africa in the current phase of globalization continued to shape development discourse in Africa and elsewhere in the global South, by the late 1990s, this project was increasingly being challenged from various sites. In the main, for analysts of Africa's development, the nirvana that advocates of the neoliberal development model had promised had not emerged. Instead, study after study of Washington Consensus policies in Africa demonstrated the failure of these policies as a model for equitable and democratic development. As one analyst has stated, "the anticipation [economic recovery and development] proved to be false. Balance-of-payments gaps were often narrowed, but by less than expected and only temporarily. The benefits of reforms were often overwhelmed by the effects of adverse external shocks-like the collapse of export prices. New investment failed to appear. Indeed, the demand-restraint policies encouraged by the IMF depressed investment instead of increasing it, and many African economies continued to stagnate in the 1980s" (Lancaster 1993, 16).

The evident failure of the neoliberal development model did not deter its advocates from claiming that this model had benefited African societies, especially the poor. From the perspective of the World Bank, for instance, "the poor are mostly rural, and as producers, they tend to benefit from agricultural, trade and exchange rate reforms. . . . As consumers, both the urban and the rural poor tend to be hurt by rising food prices. But adjustment policies have seldom had a major impact on food prices in either the open or the parallel market, which supplies most of the poor" (Bond 2001, 25).[4] This claim contradicts empirical evidence from various parts of Africa, and the fact that most of the IMF riots in the continent, whether in Zambia, Sudan, or Tunisia, emerged following the hiking of food prices due to other Washington Consensus policies of currency devaluation and cutting food subsidies. It is in the context of increasing local and global discontent with neoliberal economic restructuring (notably, the anti-globalization riots in Seattle, among many others, as discussed by Edward Prempeh in Chapter 4 of this volume) that African states emerged with the NEPAD initiative that they claimed would lead not only to economic recovery but to an African Renaissance characterized by sustainable economic growth and democratic politics. We now turn to a discussion of NEPAD.

Response to Neoliberal Globalization: African States' NEPAD Initiative

NEPAD emerged in October 2001 when African Presidents launched it at the Organization of African Unity (now, African Union) meeting in Abuja (NEPAD 2001). Prior to this launch, however, ruling elites had not shared this new initiative with citizens in the various social formations in Africa. These elites, however, especially Thabo Mbeki the current President of South Africa, had consulted widely with global North political elites, such as Tony Blair, and had presented a draft version of NEPAD (New African Initiative) to G8 leaders at their meeting in Genoa in July 2001.

The NEPAD initiative outlines what it conceives as the origins of Africa's underdevelopment and offers an economic and political roadmap geared to addressing the continent's perpetual crisis of development and "exclusion in a globalising world" (NEPAD 2001, 1). The document highlights five developments as being the sources of Africa's underdevelopment. First, it claims that the evolution of the world economic system has resulted in Africa being relegated to the role of producing primary commodities for international markets and as a reserve for cheap labor. This global division of labor has contributed greatly to the continent's economic stagnation since, "of necessity, [it] has meant the draining of Africa's resources rather than their use for the continent's development. . . . Thus, Africa remains the poorest continent despite being one of the most richly endowed regions of the world" (NEPAD 2001, 5).

Second, the document argues that the nature of colonial economic and political structures laid the foundation that would haunt the continent's development for a long time. The era of European colonialism led to the deepening of the continent's integration into the global system, on unequal terms, as mainly a producer of primary commodities for the industrial needs of the colonizing powers, and to the establishment of weak state structures. In the main, "colonialism subverted hitherto traditional structures, institutions and values or made them subservient to the economic and political needs of the imperial powers. It also retarded the development of an entrepreneurial class, as well as a middle class with skills and managerial capacity" (NEPAD 2001, 5). Third, postcolonial political and economic developments did not usher in a new period of democratic and sustained economic growth. According to NEPAD, "At independence, virtually all the new states were characterised by a shortage of skilled professionals and a weak capitalist class, resulting in a weakening of the accumulation process. Post-colonial Africa inherited weak states and dysfunctional economies, which were further aggravated by poor leadership, corruption and bad governance in many countries. Africa's experience shows that the rate of accumulation in the post-colonial period has not been sufficient to rebuild societies in the wake of colonial underdevelopment, or to sustain improvement in the standard of living. . . . This has had deleterious consequences on the political process and led to sustained patronage and corruption" (NEPAD 2001, 5–6).

Fourth, while emphasizing the role of local historical conditions in facilitating structural dependency and the emergence of undemocratic and weak states, the document argues that international conditions in the immediate postcolonial era were no less important. In particular, "the divisions caused by the Cold War hampered the development of accountable governments across the continent" (NEPAD 2001, 5). Fifth, even after twenty years of neoliberal reforms, the document declares that the fundamental characteristics of African states remain: weak, underpinned by corruption and patronage, and thus "a major constraint on sustainable development" (NEPAD 2001, 5). According to NEPAD, while the neoliberal economic restructuring of the 1980s-90s was meant to reconstitute African political economies, leading them to a dynamic capitalist path, it did not lead to a fundamental shift in the continent's economic structures thus there remains an "urgent need to implement far-reaching reforms [since]. . . . Structural adjustment programmes . . . provided only a partial solution. They promoted reforms that tended to remove serious price distortions, but gave inadequate attention to the provision of social services. Consequently, only few countries managed to achieve sustainable higher growth under these programmes" (NEPAD 2001, 5).

Architects of NEPAD do not stop at articulating the historical developments that have generated obstacles for the continent's development—they are keenly looking forward and asking, "What is to be done?"—to borrow a pertinent phrase from Vladimir Lenin. On this front they see the current phase of globalization as offering an opening not only for the continent's economic development, but also for it to join and take on an important role in the "global body politic." So what is to be done for African countries to make a sound transition to capitalist modernity? According to NEPAD, the measures that are needed to address the continent's underdevelopment encompass reforms in the economic and political arena and the formation of "a new partnership" between African states and their global North counterparts. In the main, the NEPAD initiative proposes several economic and political measures to facilitate not only Africa's economic recovery but also the emergence of sustainable economic growth. Here we concentrate on four measures.

A first measure is a rethinking of the continent's integration into the world economic system in the contemporary phase of globalization. For African ruling elites, African countries can benefit from developments generated by neoliberal economic globalization, such as new technologies and economic production methods. In order for this to happen, they argue that the integration of Africa countries needs to be rethought since, historically, the process has generated inequality between the continent and the industrialized North. In their view, what is needed is a new integration framework that views this process from a global interdependence perspective. Such an approach to global economic integration would take as its starting point the reality of "global interdependence with regard to production and demand, the environmental base that sustains the planet, cross-border migration, [and] a global financial architecture that rewards good socio-economic management" (NEPAD 2001, 8).

A second measure, which, in a way, derives from NEPAD's call for an interdependence approach to economic globalization, is the redefinition of the relationship between African states and their global North counterparts, which NEPAD argues has historically been marked by inequality due to the global power asymmetry that has characterized the evolution of the world economic system. For African states, what is needed is "a new partnership" between African countries, the global North, and the leading institutions of global governance. In this respect, such a partnership would require the global North "to reverse the decline in ODA flows to Africa and to meet the target level of ODA flows equivalent to 0.7 per cent of each developed country's gross national product (GNP) within an agreed period" (NEPAD 2001, 53). Further, the partnership would involve a more progressive approach to addressing development problems generated by the debt overhang that most African countries face, by having countries in the global North and multilateral institutions increase "aid flows [that would] be used to complement funds released by debt reduction for accelerating the fight against poverty" (NEPAD 2001, 54). In addition, this new partnership would seek to address the unequal nature of the contemporary international trading system by having global North countries admitting goods from African countries to their markets and seeking "more equitable terms of trade for African countries within the WTO multilateral framework" (NEPAD 2001, 53). Last, but not least, this partnership would see African political elites working collaboratively with their counterparts in the North in efforts to push and encourage private capital involvement in African countries with the World Bank and other international financial institutions playing a central role in this process (NEPAD 2001, 53–54).

Taking "ownership" of the development process by African peoples and their leaders is a third measure proposed by NEPAD advocates. In this regard, NEPAD declares that a time has come for Africans to be agents of their own destiny and to "understand that development is a process of empowerment and self-reliance," which requires that Africans "not be wards of benevolent guardians" but "the architects of their own sustained upliftment" (NEPAD 2001, 6). This spirit of ownership, argue African ruling elites, is embodied in NEPAD, for the initiative "centres on African ownership and management of its development process including its relationship with the global North." For these elites, the NEPAD initiative is a bold turn in their development thought and practice as it represents their first step in taking responsibility for the continent's development. According to them, NEPAD is their pledge, which is "based on a common vision and a firm and shared conviction, that they have a pressing duty to eradicate poverty and to place their countries, both individually and collectively, on a path of sustainable growth and development . . . an agenda for the renewal of the continent. The agenda is based on national and regional priorities and development plans that must be prepared through participatory processes involving the people" (NEPAD 2001, 17)."

A fourth measure is the *Peace, Security, Democracy and Political Governance Initiatives* that is aimed at the promotion of democracy, good governance, and peace. While the various components of this initiative are all important, here, we will highlight the core elements of the *Democracy and Political Governance Initiative* since it takes centre stage in the NEPAD framework. Like the transnational lending community, the architects of NEPAD claim to strongly endorse political reforms that are underpinned by democratic political practices. In this respect, African ruling elites claim that they are aware and acknowledge that development will only occur in the context of a political framework that embraces "democracy, respect for human rights, peace and good governance" (NEPAD 2001, 17). NEPAD also states that African leaders pledge "to respect the global standards of democracy, the core components of which include political pluralism, allowing for the existence of several political parties and workers' unions, and fair, open and democratic elections, periodically organised to enable people to choose their leaders freely" (NEPAD 2001, 17).

According to NEPAD advocates, embracing global democratic practices and other political reforms is the only political option for African countries, since with the end of the cold war, the world community will tolerate nothing else. In this respect, they claim that the post-1989 world has seen the definition of core political concepts such as "democracy and state legitimacy," which must now be accompanied by a demonstration of good governance, "a culture of human rights and popular participation." With this development, African ruling elites claim that they have instituted political reforms that are widely "recognized by governments across the world"—a development that, according to them, has led key players in the world political-economic system to view Africa through a new lens as evidenced, they claim, by developments such as the: "The United Nations Millennium Declaration, adopted in September 2000." The latter, in their view, confirms the global community's readiness to support Africa's efforts to address the continent's underdevelopment and marginalisation (NEPAD 2001, 9).

NEPAD AS A BLUEPRINT FOR AFRICA'S POLITICO-ECONOMIC TRANSFORMATION

As the preceding discussion indicates, the central message of the proponents of NEPAD, both on the continent and outside, is that it provides a blueprint for Africa's economic and political transformation that will lead to an "*African Renaissance*," characterized by sustainable economic growth and democratic political practices. But does the NEPAD initiative provide an economic and political framework that will facilitate such a renaissance? Does the framework represent a transformative move in Africa's development discourse or a consolidation of the contemporary hegemonic neoliberal development paradigm with an indigenous imprint? The chapter contends that, as it stands, the NEPAD framework has several limitations as a blueprint for, and explanation of, political and economic processes in Africa. These limitations emerge from: its underestimation of forces that underpin the global system; the neoliberal theory that informs NEPAD's economic framework; its neglect of the class foundations of African states; and its narrow definition of democracy.

In terms of Africa's economic development, NEPAD's discussion on the historical origins of the continent's underdevelopment illuminates an important historical development that has had a great influence on Africa's development and that challenges the ahistorical tendencies of some of the dominant approaches in studies of the continent's political economy. To argue, as some analysts do, that the roots of the continent's economic stagnation lie in postcolonial patterns of accumulation, especially the neopatrimonial basis of the African state, which it is claimed are the "essential operating codes for politics" in the continent, offers only partial insights (Bratton and Van de Walle 1997, 63). The neopatrimonial foundations of these states have their roots in the evolution of colonial political economy whose hallmarks were to limit both the emergence of an independent capitalist class not dependent on the state for its reproduction, and the development of diversified economic structures. NEPAD's historical approach to the question of underdevelopment further challenges the hegemonic neoliberal development perspective, which considers colonialism and other local-global structural and political conditions irrelevant to our understanding of Africa's so-called development crisis.

NEPAD's foregrounding of the historical roots of Africa's development crisis leads to its call for a rethinking of the relationship between African countries and the global North. As it astutely argues, this relationship has been marked by inequality, with the global North forcing its own development visions on African countries and supporting an international economic architecture that has continually deepened the continent's marginalization. What is needed then, as mentioned earlier, is a new framework that outlines responsibilities and obligations for African and global North states. The call for "a new partnership" may be all very well and good on paper, but it reflects a major departure from NEPAD's grasp of the profound ways in which the economic, political, and ideological foundations that underpin the world political-economic system shape Africa's political and economic processes. After stating how Africa's integration into the world economic system has been marked by "exclusion," NEPAD's architects now envision a new era whereby the modalities of global capitalism can be tamed by a civil dialogue and "gentlemen's" agreements between African elites and their global North counterparts.

The notion that, at this global conjuncture, the forces of global capital can be persuaded to become partners with African states and contribute to the continent's recovery and development demonstrates the many limitations and contradictions that pepper the NEPAD initiative. For instance, the initiative does not explain how the competition that has marked the evolution of global capitalism would suddenly not set structural limits for Africa's development, and why forces of global capital would be willing, given their search for expansion and profits, to facilitate the continent's development. Global capitalism involves competition, not only among local firms, but international ones, and also among nations. As an early analyst of the rise of global capitalism astutely observed: "the development of capitalist production makes it constantly necessary to keep increasing the amount of capital laid out in a given industrial undertaking, and competition makes . . . competition to be felt by each individual industrial capitalist as external coercive laws . . . compels him to keep constantly extending his capital, in order to preserve it, but extend he cannot except by means of progressive accumulation" (Marx 1961, 592). Thus, capitalism, as a mode of production, remains a spectre of competition that continues to incorporate various parts of the world into the world capitalist economy unevenly and on unequal terms. Consequently, the rhetorical of free trade, global village, and interdependence notwithstanding, the process continues deepening the historical economic divide between the global North and global South, a reality that is captured by one of NEPAD's organic intellectuals, Thabo Mbeki, in his constant critique of the contemporary global system as being marked by "global apartheid"—a system that "has pity neither for beautiful nature nor for living human beings" (Mbeki 2002).

NEPAD supporters' underestimation of how the imperatives of global capital limit the emergence of "a new partnership" between African countries and the global North extends to its claim that a partnership can emerge between African states and institutions of global governance. As mentioned earlier, these supporters claim that the embrace of market-led development and good governance measures have resulted in institutions of global governance viewing African countries through a new lens. But the empirical evidence stemming from the efforts of global South states and civil society actors to craft a democratic dialogue on development as a global and a social justice issue with the global North and institutions of global governance demonstrate otherwise and make the claims of African states ring hollow. A few examples will suffice here. In the last decade or so, civil society groups have been involved in a persistent struggle for the democratization of leading institutions of global governance to address what they deem as a serious case of their undemocratic underpinnings. In addition, the promotion of "unregulated economic globalization" by these institutions, a process that is generating deep social dislocations, is another source of discontent between these institutions and groups in civil society (Murphy 2000, 789). It is important to note the nature of civil society's engagement with leading international institutions varies depending on the institution, the nature of issues that frame the dialogue, and the global political conjuncture. In the specific case of the World Trade Organization's involvement with transnational civil society, the process has been generated through major critiques by groups in transnational civil society and by intellectuals who have highlighted the asymmetrical nature of the international trading regime. From its establishment in the immediate post-1945 period, this regime has served and reflected the needs and interests of dominant transnational interests drawn mainly from the industrialized North at the expense of countries in the developing world. Thus, contemporary challenges presented by transnational civil society to the WTO—from the ministerial meetings in Singapore and beyond—have a long history, but the intensity of the undemocratic and unjust nature of this international trading regime has been shaped by the nature of the current stage of globalization.

Since its inception in 1994, the World Trade Organization has used an inclusion/exclusion strategy in its involvement with transnational civil society. The founding moment of the WTO's strategy with transnational civil society was in 1996, when the institution issued guidelines that were to govern its relationship with this community. As Rorden Wilkison's argues, the six guidelines stipulated that, first, the WTO's association with non-state actors was to be at the "discretion of the organization, and the latter would only be involved in a dialogue with non-state actors who showed concern" with the central issues of the WTO. Second, non-state actors involved in the dialogue had to play an important role in disseminating information about the

WTO; and third, the latter would become more transparent by making its documents increasingly available on its Web site. The fourth guideline spelled out specific ways in which the relationship between the WTO and non-state actors would develop, mainly through the WTO's organized "issue-specific symposia" (Wilkinson 2005, 163). Fifth, WTO staff who participated in dialogues with non-state actors would do so in a "personal" capacity, and the last guideline stipulated that "under no circumstances" would non-state actors be engaged in "the work of the WTO or its meetings" (Wilkinson 2005, 165). The preceding clearly indicates the limited room for maneuver for transitional civil society actors in their engagement with the WTO. What has occurred since the establishment of the guidelines is that non-state actors whose agenda is closer to that of the WTO are legitimized and those that raise questions are delegitimized.

The other institutions of global governance, the World Bank and the IMF, have also increasingly adopted the strategy of engaging transnational civil society. These two institutions have been criticized mainly for their lack of accountability and their endorsement of global political-economic neoliberalism strategies. In terms of representation, for example, countries that have what Ngaire Woods terms the most "intensive" relationship with these organizations are inadequately represented on their executive boards (Woods 2001, 84). In the context of representation in these two institutions, African countries are the most underrepresented. For example, "The 21 anglophone members of the IMF, 11 of whom have 'an intense' relationship with the IMF, are represented by one Executive Director" (Woods 2001, 85). The same countries, including the Seychelles, are represented by one Executive Director at the World Bank. This power asymmetry has led transnational civil society to call for reforms in the structure of these two institutions. The IMF and the World Bank have, in the past few years, opened up spaces for dialogue with members of transnational civil society. Both institutions have made attempts to provide information on their activities and to hold biannual meetings with some members of transnational civil society. While these efforts mark a significant development given the history of secrecy in these institutions, it would be naïve to think that their practices will become democratic in the near future. As Ngaire Woods declares, even with recent developments, non-state actors "have not taken a place as major 'stakeholders' in the institutions: they have not acquired control, nor a formal participatory role in decision-making" (Woods 2001, 96).

Moving beyond the limits of NEPAD's doctrine calls for the formation of a new partnership for Africa's development. NEPAD has other limitations as a blueprint for African countries' politicoeconomic development along capitalist lines. While its aims are to institute measures that would result in the deepening of capitalist economic structures in the continent, NEPAD's vision is riddled with contradictions. To begin with, its conceptualization of capitalist transformation of African countries falls within the same narrow parameters advocated by the Washington Consensus. The latter deems the transition of the continent to capitalist economic modernity as involving merely the introduction of "market incentives" in all the key sectors of the economy, and limited investment in social sector development. NEPAD goes even further and claims that what African countries need is "far-reaching" neoliberal reforms, since SAPs did not go far enough, especially in the restructuring of the social service sector along market lines. This limited view of the capitalist economic development model stems from the ahistorical and reductionist nature of the neoliberal theory of development that frames NEPAD and Washington Consensus development frameworks. Such an approach ignores the brutality, social dislocation, structural, and historical conditions, such as, "enclosure movement" (Polanyi 1946) imperialism and slavery, that have marked the evolution of capitalist development trajectories. Historical evidence of societies undergoing capitalist transformation demonstrates a radical and brutal dislocation of core aspects of social life and the central role of states and dominant classes in this process. Yet these factors are ignored by advocates of neoliberal economic development in Africa and elsewhere in their representation of capitalism in a historical, benign, apolitical and technical terms. As Joseph Stiglitz, a former steward of global neoliberalism at the World Bank, states in a forward to Karl Polanyi's seminal text:

> The advocates of the neoliberal Washington consensus emphasize that it is government interventions that are the source of the problem; the key to transformation is 'getting prices' and getting the government out of the economy through privatization and liberalization. In this view, development is little more than the accumulation of capital and improvements in the efficiency with which resources are allocated—purely technical matters. This ideology misunderstands the nature of the transformation itself—a transformation of society, not just of the economy, and a transformation of the economy that is far more profound than their simple prescriptions would suggest. Their perspective represents a misreading of history, as Polanyi effectively argues (Stiglitz 2001, xiv).

Further, NEPAD's approach to politico-economic change is deeply reductionist and leads it, like its Washington Consensus counterpart, to conceptualize transition to market-led capitalism as a unilinear process, leading all societies to the last stage of economic development, as W. Rostow articulated almost fifty years ago in his "stages of growth" argument (Rostow 1960). Such an approach to political-economic change neglects to acknowledge that even the transformation to capitalism in the global North involved complex social processes that took different trajectories. European transitions to capitalist economic modernity, for instance, took various paths, and were highly mediated processes. Consequently, in the context of Africa and elsewhere, it would be fruitful to think of these processes of social change as being complex and taking different trajectories, albeit within structural constraints set by local structures and the world system. As Henrique Cardozo and Enzo Falleto have argued, capitalist transformations are mediated by local class structures, cultural practices, colonial history, and of course, the nature of the global political and economic conjuncture (Cardoso and Faletto 1979). Taking such a complex view of politico-economic change will not only historicize Africa's development trajectories, but also Europe's and North America's transformation to their own forms of capitalism.

NEPAD's advocates also misrepresent the transformative potential of the social forces closely linked to African states. In essence, their claim that African states are committed to leading their societies to a new era of development marked by equality and "people-centered" development ignores the social bases of these states. This approach to African states represents them as institutions that float above history and class dynamics. In the case of the latter, for instance, the class foundations of the initiative were embedded from the beginning, for the process leading to the adoption of the NEPAD framework was initiated and framed by members of the continent's ruling classes. Throughout the framing process, for instance, civil society groups and other social actors were never consulted. Further, like the architects of earlier and contemporary hegemonic theories of development, modernization and neoliberalism, respectively, proponents of NEPAD represent ruling elites as the benevolent, and the only, agents and guardians of political and economic processes in Africa.

In the political arena, NEPAD claims, as mentioned earlier, that the continent has entered a new political age marked by democracy, respect for human rights, and search for peace. Yet, from Malawi to Nigeria and places in between, Africa's so-called democratic regimes have the markings of "illiberal" democracies (Zakaria 1997). In the case of Nigeria, the return of President Obasanjo to office was characterized by what internal and external observers termed as "massive irregularities." Electoral records in the southern River State, for instance, indicated "a near 100 per cent turnout with 2.1 million of 2.2 million registered voters supporting President Obasanjo," a result that contradicts the low turnout trend recorded by observers in the state; and in Obasanjo's home region he "won 1,360,170 votes against his opponent's 680" (Bond 2004, 18).[5] Confronted with questions about the legitimacy of the election results, given the irregularities that characterized them, not just in his home state but in others as well, President Obasanjo offered a "cultural" explanation: "Certain communities in this country make up their minds to act as one in political matters. . . . They probably don't have that kind of culture in most European countries" (Bond 2004, 18). These comments roll off the tongue of one of the framers of NEPAD and a self-proclaimed leading force in the African Renaissance project. The same undemocratic trend and return to authoritarian tendencies is also evident in Kenya. In 2006, for example, facing a major political crisis generated by questions surrounding his response to corruption in his government with the emergence of Githongo's report, Mwai Kibaki's regime returned to the old repressive ways of Kenyatta and Moi eras. In the middle of the night in early March, the regime had workers of the media outlets of *The Standard Group* attacked by hooded men. During these raids, workers at *The Standard* newspapers were ordered to lie down by men carrying AK-47s, who went on to burn newspapers meant for delivery the following day and arrest three journalists. Yet, the regime's response through its Internal Security Minister, John Michuku, was that "the raids were designed to protect state security" (BBC News, March 2, 2006; *The Standard*, March 3, 2006). With national and global criticism of this incident and the increasing intolerance of independent media and dissent in the country, Kibaki's regime responded by stating that it was committed to the "promotion of responsible jour- nalism" (BBC News, March 2, 2006).[6] The neoauthoritarian tendencies of the Kenyan state continued in December 2007, as indicated by the brutal response of its security apparatus following the questioning by a range of social forces on the validity of the results of the December 27 presidential vote, given the reported irregularities characterizing the process.[7]

The class foundations of African ruling elites' commitment to democratic politics and their disrespect of the popular will is also clearly evident in their stipulation in the NEPAD blueprint that they hold each accountable for the deepening of democracy and other good governance practices. According to NEPAD, this is to be achieved through the African Peer Review Mechanism (APRM). Thus far, African leaders have ignored their much-touted APRM framework. The support of Robert Mugabe's autocratic rule in Zimbabwe by Mbeki and other African ruling elites demonstrates how rhetorical their support for democracy and respect for human rights is. For several years now, Mugabe has consolidated his power in an authoritarian political structure that has no regard for basic human rights, let alone the broader human rights embodied in second and third generation human rights discourses. Yet, at the Commonwealth Heads of Government meeting, Mbeki had no qualms stat- ing that the push to suspend Zimbabwe from the Commonwealth was noth- ing but sheer racism on the part of the leaders of the White Commonwealth. This resorting to claims of White Commonwealth racist conspiracy ignores facts pertaining to the March 2002 presidential elections in Zimbabwe. As various observers have stated, intimidation and other forms of state-spon- sored terror characterized these elections. According to one report: "The Presidential election was marred by a high level of politically motivated vio- lence and intimidation. . . . We were concerned that the legislative framework within which the elections were conducted, particularly certain provisions of the Public Order and Security Act and the General Laws Amendment Act, was basically flawed. Limitations on the freedom of speech, movement and of association prevented the opposition from campaigning freely" (*Star* [Johan- nesburg], March 31, 2002).

While Mugabe continues to deepen his autocratic rule, his NEPAD col- leagues are silent or, like Mbeki, claim they believe in "quiet diplomacy." In 2005, for instance, Mugabe continued his policy of gross violation of human rights by ordering the destruction of homes of the most marginalized com- munities in Harare under his regime, so-called "Operation Murambatsvina- Shona or "drive out trash" (Byers 2005). But African elites have thus far not called for political sanctions or any other disciplinary measure, nor have their global "partners" in development called for regime in Zimbabwe.

The emergence of limited forms of democracy is not surprising if one takes a careful look at the nature of the democracy that is being promoted in the era of neoliberal economic and political globalization. Elites drawn from government and business sectors are deemed by members of the transnational development historical bloc to be the central players in the establishment of democracy in the developing world. As the World Bank declared in 1989, "A common mistake is to ignore local leadership, often on the grounds that it is exploitative. . . . On the contrary, studies show that working with existing leaders" (quoted in Sahle 2008) yields better results. The intellectual and political origins of the international lending community's democratization campaign make it clear that underlying the push for peripheral democratization is the stabilization of the existing economic and social system, and hence, the interests of capital at both the local and international levels (Robinson 1996; Sahle 2008). In addition, like its view of market economic reforms, the community's view of democratization in Africa and elsewhere in the global South is not that of a historical and social process; rather, their idea is that as long as there are local elites who are interested in implementing procedural democracy, liberal democracy can generally operate (Huntington 1991).

Given the significant limitations of the emergence of "a new partnership" for Africa's development, and other elements embodied in the NEPAD framework, what are some of the factors underpinning the latter? Two possible factors inform the emergence and promotion of framework. To begin with, in the current age of neoliberal capitalism, the world system has set structural limits on African states as far as their capital accumulation strategies are concerned. In the era of "disciplinary neoliberalism" (Gill 2003, 130–32), very few states, especially those whose economic structures are underpinned by "petrol-capitalism" (Watts 199), have room to maneuver in terms of mapping out economic strategies and containing the hegemony and pressures from the leading states in the world political-economic system. Second, at the political level, the need for political legitimacy—given the serious crisis of legitimacy that African states have had to contend with from the late 1970s due to internal and global developments—has resulted in the majority of African states adopting neoliberal economic strategies in the hopes of accessing international financial flows from institutions such as the World Bank and the International Monetary Fund, and from dominant states in the North. From the perspective of these states, the era of seeking development paths that diverge from the global norm, as epitomized by Julius Nyerere or Thomas Sankara political-economic projects in an earlier period, is not entertained in this global conjuncture marked by a neoliberal regime of truth.

While seeking external legitimacy, ruling elites have also engaged in political strategies aimed at gaining consent and legitimacy at the local level. What has emerged in Africa in the era of neoliberalism and NEPAD strategies is that the leading lights of African ruling bloc "talk left and walk right," as Patrick Bond has argued in various works. Mbeki's scathing critiques of market-led development—e.g., "The critically important task to end the poverty and underdevelopment, in which millions of Africans are trapped, inside and outside our country, cannot be accomplished by the market. If we were to follow the prescriptions of neoliberal market ideology, we would abandon the masses of our people to permanent poverty and underdevelopment," while referring to himself as a Thatcherite (Mbeki 2003)—exemplify the phenomenon that Bond articulates. In their promotion of NEPAD, African ruling elites and their Northern counterparts embrace Lady Margaret Thatcher's mantra: "There is no alternative" to neoliberal capitalism. Given these political and structural realities, African states have, through NEPAD, constructed global capitalist expansion as a process that can be civilized through the forging of a partnership with the global North and the dominant institutions of global governance, among other measures outlined in the NEPAD framework.

At the local level, African states' embrace of global neoliberalism through NEPAD has enabled the reproduction of their legitimacy—at least for the dominant classes, factions of which have benefited from neoliberal economic strategies, such as privatization—even though the continent continues on the same economic downward spiral that marked its pre-NEPAD era. With the launching of NEPAD, African leaders claim that they can deliver the long awaited "development cake" since they "own'" the continent's development process. Further, they claim that "a new partnership" with the global North has emerged, since their NEPAD initiative has been endorsed by leaders of the global North, as evidenced by the enthusiastic support it has received from various northern quarters, especially in Canada, under Prime Jean Chrétien, the G8 meetings in Genoa, the European Union, and in Washington, where one commenter stated, "NEPAD is philosophically spot-on. The U.S. will focus on those emerging markets doing the right thing in terms of private sector development, economic freedom and liberty" (Bond 2004, 15).[8] How long the hegemony of the transnational elite neoliberal settlement will last is difficult to tell for the regime of truth embodied in the NEPAD framework, and other neoliberal inspired political-economic projects in the continent are increasingly contested, as evidenced by social movements and organizations linked to the African Social Forum and local critical groups in civil society (Sahle and Bond, forthcoming). The ability of African states to contain these movements, however, cannot be ruled out, given what has gone on in Zimbabwe in the last several years, and given the efforts in Malawi to contain critics of the neoliberalizing state through the enacting of punitive laws (Sahle, 2006).

CONCLUSION

This chapter has attempted to demonstrate the ways in which Africa states have responded to the current phase of globalization. As the discussion has indicated, these states have been heavily involved in the process and have used their political agency in efforts to reproduce themselves given the nature of the contemporary global conjuncture. The chapter has also challenged the claims by African states as outlined in the NEPAD initiative and has demonstrated its limitations as a tool for Africa's transformation along democratic and equitable lines. Finally the discussion has also highlighted how, in very profound ways, the NEPAD initiative represents the recycling of the hegemonic neoliberal development and thus offers not a new start for the continent, but a deepening of neoliberal political and economic practices in the continent as advocated by global political and economic elites.

REFERENCES

Amin, S. 1997. *Capitalism in the age of globalization: The management of contemporary Society*. London: Zed Books.

———. 1998. *Spectres of Capitalism: A critique of current intellectual fashions*. New York: Monthly Review Press.

Bangura, Yusuf. 1992. Authoritarian rule and democracy in Africa: A theoretical discourse. In *When democracy makes sense*, ed. Lars Rudebeck. 69–104, Uppsala, Sweden: Uppsala University.

BBC News. March 2, 2006. http://news.bbc.co.uk.

———. Scores dead in Kenya poll clashes, December 31, 2007. http://news.bbc .co.uk.

Bond, Patrick. 2001. *Against global apartheid: South Africa meets the World Bank, IMF, and international finance*. Cape Town: University of Cape Town Press.

———. 2004. Talk Left, Walk Right: South Africa's Frustrated Global Reforms. London: The Merlin Press, Ltd.

Bratton, Michael, and Nicolas Van de Walle. 1997. *Democratic experiments in Africa: Regime transitions in comparative perspective*. Cambridge: Cambridge University Press.

Byers, Michael. 2005. Are you a "global citizen"? Really? What does that mean? *The Tyee*.

Cardoso, F. Henrique, and Enzo Faletto. 1979. *Dependency and development in Latin America*. Berkeley: University of California Press.

Daily Nation. Violence erupts after Kibaki sworn in, December 31, 2007. http:// www.nationmedia.com/dailynation/nmgindex.asp.

Friedman, M. 2002. *Capitalism and Freedom*. Chicago: University of Chicago.

Gill, Stephen. 2003. *Power and resistance in the New World*. Houndmills: Palgrave Macmillan.

Hayek, A. F. 2001. *Road to Serfdom*. Routledge.

Huntington, Samuel. 1991. *The third wave: Democratization in the late twentieth century*. Norman: University of Oklahoma Press.

Ihonvbere, Julius. 2000. *Africa and the New World order*. New York: Peter Lang.

Lancaster, Carol. 1993. *United States and Africa: Into the twenty-first century*. Washington, DC: Overseas Development Council.

Marx, Karl. 1961. *Capital: Volume 1*. Moscow: Foreign Language Publishing House.

Mbeki, Thabo. 2002. Address by President Mbeki at the welcome ceremony of the world summit on sustainable development, Johannesburg.

———. 2003. Letter from the president, African National Congress Today, October 31. http://www.anc.org.za.

Murphy, N. Craig. 2000. Global governance: Poorly done and poorly understood. *International Affairs* 76 (4): 789–804.

New Partnership for Africa's Development (NEPAD), http://www.nepad.

Rapley, John. 2004. *Globalization and inequality: Neoliberalism's downward spiral.* Boulder: Lynne Rienner.

Robinson, I. William. 1996. *Promoting Polyarchy: Globalization, US Intervention, and Hegemony.* Cambridge: Cambridge University Press.

Rostow, W. Whitman. 1960. *The stages of economic growth: A non-communist manifesto.* Cambridge: Cambridge University Press.

Sahle, N. Eunice. 2006. Human rights dialogue: A conversation with Ollen Mwalubunju. *Societies Without Borders* 1:123–37.

———. 2008 (forthcoming). *World orders, development and transformation.* Houdmills, UK, Palgrave Macmillan.

Sahle, N. Eunice, and Patrick Bond, eds., with a foreword by Samir Amin. forthcoming. *Social movements and collective action in Africa: Development, democracy, human rights and environmental justice.* Lexington Books and Rowman and Littlefield.

Star (Johannesburg), March 31, 2002.

Stiglitz, E. Joseph, with a foreword by Karl Polanyi. 2001. *The great transformation: The political and economic origins of our time.* Boston: Beacon.

The Standard, March 3, 2006.

Tsikata, Dzodzi and Joanna Kerr. 2000. *Demanding dignity: Women confronting economic reforms in Africa.* Ottawa: The North-South Institute.

Turshen, Meredeth. 1994. Impact of economic reforms on women's health and health care in sub-Saharan Africa. In *Women in the age of economic transformation*, ed. Nahid Aslanbeigui, Steven Pressman, and Gale Summerfield, 77–94. London: Routledge.

Watts, M. 2006. Empire of Oil: Capitalist Dispossession and the Scramble for Africa. *Monthly Review* 58 (4).

Wilkinson, Rorden. 2005. Managing global civil society. In *The idea of global civil society*, ed. Randall D. German and Michael Kenny,156–74. London: Routledge.

Woods, Ngaire. 2001. Making the IMF and the world more accountable. *International Affairs* 77 (1): 83–100.

World Bank. 1981. *Accelerated development in sub-Saharan Africa.* Washington: World Bank.

———. 1989. *Sub-Saharan Africa: From crisis to sustainable growth.* Washington: World Bank.

———. 1994. *Adjustment in Africa.* Oxford: Oxford University Press.

———. 2002. *World development report 2002: Building institutions for markets.* New York: Oxford University Press.

Zakaria, Fareed. 1997. The rise of illiberal democracy. *Foreign Affairs*, November.

NOTES

1. For detailed discussions of the various elements of this crisis, see Julius Ihonvbere, *Africa and the new world order* (New York: Peter Lang, 2000); and Yusuf Bangura, "Authoritarian Rule and Democracy in Africa: A Theoretical Discourse," in Lars Rudebeck, *When democracy Makes Sense* (Uppsala University, Sweden, 1992).

2. For extended discussion on the impact of neoliberal based reforms on the education sector in various African countries, see Dzodzi Tsikata and Joanna Kerr with Cathy Blacklock and Jocelyne Laforce, *Demanding Dignity: Women Confronting Economic Reforms in Africa* (Ottawa: The North-South Institute, 2000).

3. For seminar reports from the World Bank on neoliberal restructuring in Africa, see *Adjustment in Africa* (Oxford: Oxford University Press, 1994); *Accelerated Development in Africa* (Washington: The World Bank, 1981); and *Sub-Saharan Africa: From Crisis to Sustainable Growth* (Washington: World Bank, 1989).

4. Quoted in Patrick Bond, *Against Global Apartheid: South Africa meets the World Bank, IMF and International Finance* (Cape Town: University of Cape Tow Press, 2001).

5. IRIN news service, May 12, 2003 and *Mail and Guardian*, April 26, 2003, respectively, quoted in Bond 2004, 18.

6. For detailed comments, see Mutahi Kagwe, Kenya's Information Minister, BBC News, March 2, 2006.

7. See, "Scores dead in Kenya poll clashes," *BBC news*, December 31, 2007 (http://news.bbc.co.uk); and "Violence erupts after Kibaki sworn in," *Daily Nation*, December 31, 2007, http://www.nationmedia.com/dailynation/nmgindex .asp.

8. D. Gopinath, "Doubt of Africa," *Institutional Investor Magazine*, May 2003, quoted in Bond, 2004, 15.

PART II

COUNTRY CASE STUDIES

CHAPTER 8

GLOBALIZATION, CYBERSEXUALITY AMONG GHANAIAN YOUTH, AND MORAL PANIC

Wisdom J. Tettey

INTRODUCTION

Irrespective of where one stands with regard to the benefits, or otherwise, of the processes of globalization, there is no denying the fact that they have had tremendous transformative impacts on socioeconomic, cultural, and political dynamics around the world (Petras and Veltmeyer 2001; Pettman 2003). These transformations have produced qualitative shifts in how transnational interactions are organized, as they reconfigure the spatiotemporal environment within which those interactions occur (McGrew 2000, 48). Part of the reason behind the developments noted above are technological innovations that allow the flow of capital and information to traverse physical boundaries with alacrity and to be integrated at an unprecedented level. As we witness what Giddens (1991) describes as the emptying of time and space, there have emerged new challenges that are raising widespread concern. O'Grady (2001, 132), for example, contends that: "Two of the key contributors to *globalization*—tourism and the Internet—have provided an unexpected bonus to child abusers, making the opportunity for child abuse more accessible. One could draw a partial causal relationship between the rapid expansion of *globalization* and the growth of child sex trade. Tourism has become the world's largest industry and its long arms reach out into ever more obscure parts of the planet."

Hughes (2000) argues that, as part of the process of globalization, women and children have become commoditized on the global market for various interests, including organized crime, tourists, and military personnel seeking to satisfy concupiscent desires of one form or another. She further opines that "through financial and technological independence, the sex industry and the Internet industry have become partners in the global sexual exploitation of women and children" (Hughes 2000, 35). While sexual exploitation is not new, the emergence of new technologies has expanded the coterie of actors involved (both victims and beneficiaries), and the sophistication and geographical scope of such activities (Shah 2007). As Chow-White (2006, 884) observes, "increasingly, information and communication technologies, such as the Internet, are playing a particularly significant role, not only in the promotion and packaging of sex tourism but also of a new type of global surveillance of bodies, race and desire." Bernstein (2001) also explicates the connection between globalization and the commodification of the body, arguing that capitalist restructuring of the international political economy that we have experienced over the last three decades has manifested itself at the most intimate levels.

Studies from various parts of the world have contributed to these fears as the Janus-faced nature of the Internet leads to the conclusion that it is not only a useful resource, but also "a 'Pandoras Box' of criminal opportunity" (Schneider 2003, 374). O'Grady (2001, 124) argues that "for all the benefits the Internet provides, it also has its drawbacks, especially providing a vehicle to spread child *pornography* quickly. . . . Increasing ties among nations provides the pedophile with the opportunity to hide from the immediate community, to operate within residence, to encounter a global network of like-minded individuals and worst of all, to discover an endless supply of victims." Some researchers reveal potentials for "cybersexual compulsivity" among Internet users and the erosion of other areas of youth activity and responsibility that result from social pathologies referred to as technological addictions (Griffith 2000). A study by the Pew Internet Research Center (2001) shows that 57 percent of parents worry that strangers will contact their children online; close to 60 percent of teens have received a message from a stranger; and 50 percent report communicating with someone they have never met. A national survey of youth, aged ten to seventeen, in the United Kingdom suggests that about one-quarter of respondents had had unwanted exposure to sexual material on the Internet (Mitchell et al., 2003). What makes the situation even more worrisome is the fact that most teens acknowledge that they do not tell their parents when a stranger contacts them online. One said, "I wouldn't tell about it to my parents, they'd flip out and probably restrict my access to the Internet" (Pew Internet Research Center 2001; see also Mitchell 2003, 343).

There is growing concern that Internet use in Ghana may reflect Cooper et al.'s (1999) study that sexual pursuits, ranging from visiting Web sites with sexual themes to intense online sexual interactions may be the most common use of the Internet. The Ghana Health Survey in 2002 revealed the "disturbing . . . rate at which kids are watching porno via the Internet. Some of these kids are so smart that they have obtained addresses of websites of porno all over the world and after classes they dash to the nearest Internet café to watch nude pictures on the Internet" (2002a). My own observations indicate that it is not unusual to find young adult males in Internet cafes trying to discretely browse through sexually explicit Web sites or engage in cybersex, which involves the textual exchange of erotic material. Several respondents who were surveyed or interviewed during field research for a larger study on cybersexual activity in Ghana that I am working on, intimated that they use, and or know others who use, the Internet for these purposes. One interviewee disclosed thus: "The Internet allows me to entertain myself in ways that will not lead to trouble . . . such as STDs or pregnancy." There is concern among the public that too much engagement with the Internet may lead to addiction to the lascivious world of Internet sex, which could significantly distract the youth from more "productive endeavors," such as school, community service, and so on. As the World Youth Report 2003 (UN 2004, 302–3) notes, "the impact of the global media on young people is perhaps a metaphor for the broader impact of globalization, in so far as the apparently liberating technologies such as mobile phones and Internet computer games actually alienate young people by creating a world of individualistic hyperstimulation in which more mundane activities such as school simply cannot compete."

It is in the context of the preceding developments that this chapter examines cybersexual activity among the youth in Ghana. In this study, I adopt the United Nations' (n.d.) definition of "youth," meaning those between fifteen and twenty-four years of age. With the expansion in the number of Internet cafes, and the subsequent access that youth have to the technology, there is anxiety about the negative moral, social, and psychological impacts that it can have. These concerns are predicated on the relatively free access that the youth have to adult Web sites; the potential risks that they face, vis-à-vis solicitations in chat rooms and relationships that they develop with cyber pen pals; and their vulnerability to sexual marketing on the World Wide Web. It is important to note that some of the individuals who lure these youth pretend to be online pen pals, and then demand nude pictures with promises of financial reward, helping to bring the girls abroad, or finding them partners for marriage (see Taylor 2002, 3). These developments have resulted in a moral panic among the public at large, leading to calls for action by legislators, religious leaders, and various civic groups (see Ghanaweb 2002b). One senior Christian cleric intimated that "something grave is going to happen to this country if steps are not taken to fight this abomination [which is] undermining efforts to control the HIV/AIDS scourge." The government has responded by cautioning "Ghanaian women against participation in such obscenities and pornographies which go against the very grain of the culture and training of the Ghanaian" (Ghanaweb 2002a).

Having provided an insight into the moral panic that the intersection of the Internet and sexual activity has generated, through the social construction of this online danger (Kuipers 2006), the next section provides an analysis of the theoretical framework within which the study is situated, followed by a discussion of the methodology that guided the research. The chapter then proceeds to analyze the socioeconomic situation confronting Ghanaians, and the youth, in particular, after which it focuses on how Ghanaian youth are negotiating their participation and survival in the context of the economy of desire that has resulted from processes of globalization and the information technology revolution that facilitates them. It specifically explores the involvement of youth in the transnational space of Internet-related sex and sexuality. It interrogates how economies of desire intertwine with desperate economic circumstances in Ghana, to turn Ghanaian youth into objects and seekers of desire in the spaces created by the Internet. It examines how these spaces facilitate ethno-sexual consumption through "racial, ethnic, and national self-imaginings and constructions" (Nagel 2003, 21) and reproduce patterns of domination and inequality in the global system.

ECONOMY OF DESIRE, THE INTERNET, AND TRANSNATIONALIZATION OF SEXUAL COMMERCE

I use a political economy of desire framework to engage with the issues that are the object of this project. "Lack and scarcity are the main characteristics of the economy of desire. . . . This scarcity is not restricted to economic resources. It also applies to the gratification, bodily well-being, sexual desire and body commitment" (Epele 2001, 161). It draws from political economy (Mosco 1996), critical race theory (Ahmed 2000; Wing 2000; Delgado 1995, xiv; Bhaba 1994), gender and class analyses (Böhme 2003; Riordan 2001; Kempadoo 1999; Chapkis 1997; Bell 1994) to examine the relationships among global forces, technological advances, and the transnational manifestations of cybersexual activities and their off-line impacts.

Over the last few decades, neoliberal economic policies have defined the socio-economic trajectories of many countries in the world. Among those who have been significantly affected by these policies are developing societies that have been compelled by circumstances to adopt policy prescriptions whose repercussions on their populations have been very harsh (World Bank 2004; Saul 2001). The neoliberal policies have significantly eroded access to public goods, exacerbated unemployment, and resulted in the creation of despondent populations. These circumstances, combined with Internet-facilitated sexual commerce, have produced conditions that reveal "the relationship among capitalism's disruptive, restructuring activities: powerful images, fantasies, and desires (produced both locally and globally) that are inextricably tied up with race and gender; the emergence of young, poor black single mothers, married women and single young women, who are willing to engage in the sex trade; and a strong demand for these women's services on the part of white, foreign male tourists" (Brennan 2001, 621).

Related to this is Nagel's (2003, 22) observation that "the Internet is a symbolically rich domain for cruising sites of ethno-sexual desire" (see also

Moore and Clark 2001). The expression of this desire is shaped by structural inequalities in the global political economy, which, in turn, influence access to exotic bodies or compels a search for "opportunities" presented by the privileged. An interesting dimension of Internet-facilitated sexuality, therefore, is the extent to which it has expanded possibilities for sex to be racialized, and for race to be sexualized. The Internet not only combines with a competitive global market of sexual desire (Böhme 2003) to make access to the cheapest bodies very easy; it also reflects how racialization of those bodies feeds the desires of privileged groups (Gossett and Byrne 2002; see also Cheek 2003). It is significant to note, for example, that one area of global sexual exchanges (i.e., sex tourism) involves mostly economically better-to-do white men as the seekers of desire, and poor women, mostly of color, as the objects of desire (Richter 1998). For the women involved in this market, the feminization of poverty makes the transnational sex trade more enticing. Entering a relationship with men from the developed world presumably provides an opportunity for them to escape the economic hardships of their homeland—what Brennan (2001) calls the "opportunity myth." Thus, interactions among actors in this transnational sexual space are premised on culturally and racially based imaginings, which stem from essentialized representations of "the other" (Schaeffer-Grabiel 2004).

The active way in which some Third World women seek Western men, or "play along" in pursuit of the "opportunity myth," poses a challenge to feminist theory. There is a tendency by some feminist scholars and other women's rights activists seeking to address "Third World" women's engagement in the commercial sex industry, to frame such involvement exclusively in terms of patriarchal systems of oppression and subordination (see Bell 1994; Chapkis 1997; Robinson 1998). However, as the narratives by some Ghanaian women in the ensuing discussion, and those of some "Third World" prostitutes (see Wojcicki 2002; Brennan 2001), reveal, the concept of the "sex worker," which suggests entrepreneurship within a capitalist economy, aptly describes their motivations. These motivations, and the actions pursued to actualize them, reflect active agency on the part of the women. There is the need, therefore, to move beyond the discourse of victimology that exclusively characterizes many feminist analyses of "Third World" women's engagement in sex-related activities—both in the public and domestic spheres (see Jeffreys 2004). A more apposite approach should recognize women's agency as an intrinsic part of the commodification of sex in the era of globalization, as actors make various choices, even as they are constrained by systemic structures of one kind or another (see also Kempadoo 1999, 226).

The preceding argument is not to diminish the reality of power inequalities in the relationships described above. Indeed, the location of the interactants, and their societies, in the global capitalist structure shapes the power that they exert or exude, and hence their bargaining power. There are clearly different degrees of power between Third World women and their clients from the industrialized world whose privileged location in the global capitalist structure gives them an upper hand in fulfilling their objectives within the economy of desire.

The theoretical framework adopted for this study, thus, allows us to approach the sexual uses of the Internet from a perspective that is not encumbered by an exclusively patriarchal and dichotomized problematization of women's position in the global sex trade, but rather recognizes the multiple spaces occupied by various actors in these contexts, as they negotiate a plurality of, sometimes contradictory, locations. It facilitates analyses not only of the class-based exploitation of the economically vulnerable, but also the racialization that characterizes the myth of the sexualized "other," and the agency that African actors exhibit even as they are constrained by systemic structures of one kind or another. As Zook (2002, 1261) points out, "The roles of these actors . . . are not simply determined by a spaceless logic of cyber-interaction but by histories and economies of the physical places they inhabit. In short, the 'space of flows' cannot be understood without reference to the 'space of places' to which it connects. This geography also provides a valuable counterpoint to mainstream electronic commerce and highlights the ability of socially marginal and underground interests to use the Internet to form and connect in global networks."

It is worth noting that while much of the literature tends to focus on the eroticization of the female body and the satisfaction of male desire, the objects of desire in Ghana, as in other places, are sometimes males and the exploiters/beneficiaries female (Nagel 2003, 204–9; Schaeffer-Grabiel 2004; *Daily Graphic* 2002). The relationships are both homo- and hetero-sexual in nature. This chapter will, nevertheless, focus on the latter types of relationship because they are the most dominant. Moreover, the former type tends to be more difficult to assess because it is culturally unacceptable and could attract stringent social and legal sanctions when it is detected.

METHODOLOGY

The study is mainly qualitative and, as alluded to above, is part of a larger study on cybersexual activity in Ghana. Our interest was not in churning out statistical data about number of respondents, frequency distributions, and so on, that can be generalized across all Ghanaian youth or sex tourists, but to get insights into the lived experiences of our subjects, their mindsets, and the motivations that drive them as they engage with the Internet. These insights provide a basis for more extensive research on the issues addressed in the study, and for rethinking theoretical, conceptual, and analytical approaches to understanding them.

We employ the "global ethnography" methodology put forward by Burawoy et al. (2001; see also Gottfried 2001), which allows us to transcend the local focus of traditional ethnography to embrace analyses that incorporate broader geographical and historical processes which influence, and elicit responses from, the local. In the context of the time-space compression that defines the ICT-globalization nexus, it is important that the ethnographic scope of the study be global, even as it focuses on the study of specific locales. This requires engaging not only with those in Ghana who are agents and victims of the economy of desire, but also those who are implicated in those processes in places beyond the country. For this latter purpose, the research draws on Ghana-focused sexually oriented Web sites and sexual activities by tourists who are drawn to Ghana by narratives that they have accessed on the Internet.

Narratives of reality are socially constructed (Esposito and Murphy 2000). We, therefore, adopted methodologies and forms of evidence and interpretation that allowed for "storytelling, counterstory telling, and the analysis of narrative . . . [because they enable one to contest] myths, presuppositions, and received wisdoms that make up the common culture" in one locale or another (Wing 2000; see also Delgado 1995, xiv). In a global context where the dominant narratives reflect the positions of the powerful, this method also gives subalterns the opportunity to voice their interpretation of realities, their location within them, how they negotiate them, and why they relate to them the way they do.

To get at the various narratives, we purposively sampled sex-related Web sites/forums/chat rooms that contained information on Ghana in order to gain perspectives on the global ethnography of cybersexual activities (see McClelland 2002). This was done between January 2003 and August 2004, and involved content analyzing discussions on the sites (see Phua and Kaufman 2003; Phua 2002). We also conducted field research in Ghana between May 2003 and August 2003, and during the same period in 2004. During the fieldwork, we analyzed secondary data on cybersexual activity such as police, court, and news reports. Interviews were conducted with representatives of various organizations interested in cybersexuality (e.g., law enforcement, religious, educational, community based, and human rights/advocacy) to gain an understanding of their knowledge of the issues, as well as the nature and extent of the problem and responses to it. A sample of Internet café operators and Internet Service Providers (ISPs) were interviewed for the same reason. Two clubs identified on the Web sites referred to above, as locations where sex tourists can meet potential clients, were visited. The research team had conversations with tourists at the clubs. Through this method, key informant contacts, and a process of snowball sampling, we identified those who had used the Internet to facilitate or inform their trip to Ghana. We interviewed ten of them and nine of their clients. The interviews helped to understand why they engage in these activities and to give voice to their personal experiences.

In addition to the above methods, an in-depth ethnographic case study of cybersexual activity was conducted in Swedru, a commercial town in the Central Region of Ghana, between May and August 2004. The region is one of the most deprived in the country, and certain towns there (particularly Swedru) gained notoriety as physical locations where virtual actors arrange in-person rendezvous to fulfill their desires (Ghanaweb 2002c). Swedru, thus, became a transnational meeting ground, both in a physical sense and in the context of the boundlessness of cyberspace. The case study, thus, provides insights as to why the town is a destination of choice and the impact that cybersexual activity has had on the community and individuals. We organized two focus group discussions with a representative sample of community members (including the youth, parents, and community leaders) to elicit their views on these matters. We also interviewed some women who were advertently or inadvertently involved with cybersexual activities, family members of the women who were involved, key informants, and some young men who served as mediators of the transnational spaces facilitated by the Internet.

POLITICAL ECONOMY OF DEPRIVATION AND THE SOCIOECONOMIC CONTEXT FOR CYBERSEXUAL ACTIVITY

Ghana went through intense economic crises over the course of the 1970s and early 1980s. The crisis was precipitated by both internal and external factors. Among the internal triggers were economic mismanagement, political corruption, severe drought, and the deportation of about a million Ghanaians from Nigeria. Externally, the country had to contend with deteriorating terms of trade, falling export prices for its primary commodities, and consequent balance of payment problems. The implications of these developments were far-reaching. By the early 1980s, inflation was hovering at over 100 percent, per capita GDP had plummeted to US$739 from its 1960 level of US$1009, real export earnings stood at only half of 1970 values, and import volumes had shrunk by over 33 percent (Konadu-Agyemang 2000, 473).

In response to this economic morass, the country underwent International Monetary Fund (IMF) and World Bank dictated Structural Adjustment Programs (SAPs), which involved reductions in government expenditure, devaluation of the currency, retrenchment of workers, privatization of state enterprises, and removal of price controls. Consequently, 300,000 workers in the public service were laid off and deep cuts were made to government support to social services, such as health care and education.

While these policies have helped address some of the macroeconomic problems that the country was facing, they have not extricated the country from its economic doldrums. Inflation continues to be high "with wild fluctuations that over the course of [the 1990s] saw prices increase more than ten times," eventually settling at 50 percent in 2000 (Canagarajah and Pörtner 2003, 5). Total debt has continued to rise from US$1.39 billion in 1980, to US$5.87 billion in 1995, to its current level of over US$6 billion. The country, thus, spends over 60 percent of its export earnings on debt-servicing, thereby redirecting resources away from sectors and groups in desperate need (Tsikata 2000). The result of the economic crisis, and the policies implemented to deal with it, was extreme deprivation for large segments of the population. By 1999, about 40 percent of Ghanaians were living below the poverty line, while 27 percent faced extreme poverty (Government of Ghana 2003a, 13). The situation in Ghana reflects the trend in much of

Africa, where "around 55% of all people employed are not earning enough to lift themselves and their families above the US$1 a day poverty line" (International Labor Organization 2005 60; see also Teale 2000).

The failure of the SAP to alleviate Ghanaians' economic privation is borne out by the fact that the country is now implementing the Highly Indebted Poor Countries' (HIPC) Initiative under the guidance of the IMF and World Bank. Konadu-Agyemang (2000) notes the increased regional, class, and gender disparities that have resulted from the deplorable economic conditions that many Ghanaians live under. Many citizens have responded in a variety of ways, including the exodus of both skilled and unskilled workers to other countries, mainly in the industrialized world (see Tettey 2002). The country's agricultural sector, which constitutes the mainstay of the economy, has seen the greatest reduction in productivity registered by any African country between 1980 and 2001 (International Labor Organization 2005, 61). Total expenditure on education, between 1992 and 1998, dropped significantly by about 10 percent (Canagarajah and Pörtner 2003, 8). The overall prognosis for Ghana does not seem different from the following bleak assessment for the continent as a whole: Africa: "The high share of working poor and total poverty is likely to persist given the region's high unemployment rates, insufficient capacity for job creation, rapidly expanding labor force and huge overall decent work deficit" (International Labor Organization 2005, 64; see also International Labor Organization 2004; Government of Ghana 2003b, 6). This portentous picture has severe implications for the country's youth, who constitute 21.4 percent of the population (United Nations 2002). Generally, the youth tend to be poorer than the older generation, thereby compounding their susceptibility to other socioeconomic problems, which leads to disillusionment and or risky behavior aimed at extricating themselves from poverty (World Bank 2002; see also Sigudhia 2004; African Development Forum 2004, 3; Mufune 2000). The World Bank (2002) notes that African youngsters are growing up in a time of both heightened peril and unprecedented opportunity. More than ever before, adolescents—particularly those in cities—are connected to the world at large through communication, information, and transportation technologies. Yet, the cycle of poverty, inadequate education and work opportunities, and civil unrest stunts the development of too many millions of young people (see also Government of Ghana 2003a, 28). The gendered nature of poverty means that the situation is even worse for young women, thereby increasing their vulnerability to exploitation (Government of Ghana 2003a, 25; Glover et al. 2003, 35–36; Okojie 2003). It is clear that at the same time as globalization is bringing the world together in a variety ways, we are also witnessing significant disparities in the circumstances of people in different regions of the world. It is in this respect that the UN (2004, 302) observes that "the global culture has become a fundamental building block in many young people's lives. However, their relationship with it is very fragile because youth, more than any other, are exposed to and have come to rely on the global consumer culture but probably have the fewest resources and the most to lose should global culture not provide the satisfaction they demand of it."

In the midst of the deprivation discussed above, and the disparities that define the global political economy, globalization and information technology are teasing Ghanaian youth with images of the consumerist lifestyle that characterizes the industrialized world. Unfortunately, however, most of them do not have the wherewithal to replicate that lifestyle. Consequently, many young people are compelled to be ingenious, through processes of "globalization from below" (Falk 1993), in order to survive within the new reality. For female youth, some unpleasant, yet compelling, options include prostitution, both at home and abroad (Taylor 2002; Aghatise 2002). As Chapkis (1997, 29–30) observes, in the context of sex workers, "practices of prostitution, like other forms of commodification and consumption, can be read [in] more complex ways than simply as a confirmation of male domination. They may also be sites of ingenious resistance and cultural subversion . . . the prostitute cannot be reduced to . . . a passive object used in male sexual practice, but instead it can be understood as a place of agency where the sex worker makes active use of the existing sexual order" (see also Schaeffer-Grabiel 2004).

The Internet has also become one of the mechanisms by which African youth are exploring opportunities for personal advancement (see World Bank 2002).

CONSUMPTION OF THE VIRTUAL HUMAN CORPUS, SEX TOURISM, AND SEXUAL COMMERCE

In the new transnational social space made possible by ICTs, one does not have to cross physical boundaries in order to engage directly with the center or periphery of the world capitalist system. Developments in Internet-enabled sexual commerce, and the concerns that they have engendered, are complicated by processes of globalization with which they are intricately intertwined. The consumerism that is characteristic of globalization, and of the capitalist economic system that undergirds it, is not limited to material goods but has been extended to the consumption of people as well (Firat and Dholakia 1998). This latter consumption pattern involves deriving satisfaction from the human body itself as opposed to concrete products of human endeavor. The Internet facilitates the practice in a variety of forms, including viewing sexually explicit material and fostering on-line and, and subsequently, off-line amorous or sexual relationships.

Beyond just accessing lewd material, which was referred to earlier, some Ghanaian youth, principally female, have become recruiting targets for advertising on sexually explicit Web sites. Interviews with some young women at nightclubs noted for sex tourism in Accra revealed that they make contact with their clients via the Internet. These women, some of whom are secondary school and university students, are registered with online services located abroad (see, for example, Africanprincess.com 2004; One-and-only 2004a; One-and-only 2004b). Prospective clients obtain contact numbers from dating services online and make contact with the women when they arrive in the country. In other cases, the men contact the women prior to leaving their home countries, and arrangements are made for different kinds of romantic or sexual activity when the men arrive in Ghana. One man claimed that he bought a list from "africonnections," a dating service, for $17.50 that had twenty-five phone numbers with photographs of the girls.

While some young women, especially urban and secondary school/university educated women, engage with the technology directly, this is not the case with all the women who appear on the Internet by way of texts or images. Most of the women outside the major cities, who are involved in cyber-facilitated sexual activity, are not conversant with the Internet, and hence do not directly engage with the technology. This became clear during the ethnographic research in Swedru, when it was revealed that the encounter between young women from the area who appear on the Internet and their prospective clients is mediated not only by the technology, but by an organized group of local young men. The young men's *modus operandi* are captured by one of them in the following statement:

> We normally approach the beautiful girls in town and tell them that we can find them pen pals abroad who can help them leave the country. We ask them for their pictures to accompany their profile. Sometimes the girls are not interested, but after we give them money, they agree. About one month later, we tell them that some men abroad are interested in marrying them, but want to see them naked so that they can be sure . . . that they meet their standards. . . . Many of the girls are not comfortable with this, but we tell them that they will receive between $100 and $300 for doing that. After they take the pictures, we send them to our contact people who use them on their websites.

Based on interviews with key informants in the community, it looks like the money that the young women receive for taking the nude photographs is a very small percentage of what the gendered agents get from the Web site operators. This mirrors inequities in resource distribution evident in economic transactions between men and women within the larger society. Nevertheless, in a community characterized by high levels of poverty, unemployment, and little prospects, the offer of a couple of hundred dollars can be a very enticing proposition. The gendered agents for the transnational cybersex networks also serve as go-betweens, when the men who respond to the ads arrive in Ghana, and get paid for their services. The revulsion toward these cyber and real-life pimps is vividly illustrated by the following criticism from one key informant: "some young men in our own community are assisting these sex maniacs to destroy our daughters and our community."

What the above discussion makes clear is the potential for an expanding sex tourism network that has been significantly facilitated by the Internet. As Wonders and Michalowski (2001, 545) point out, "'sex tourism' highlights the convergence between prostitution and tourism, links the global with the local, and draws attention to both the production and consumption of sexual services." There are networks on the Internet where people exchange experiences about sexual exploits in Ghana and offer advice about how to satisfy members' concupiscence. A sixty-one-year-old from Australia wrote: "Ghanaian babes are uninhibited, e.g., some [write in online ads] openly seeking 'broad-minded, sexy men; [saying] I am interested in erotic pictures . . . making love. . . . Well, after $2500 for a round-trip 38-hour flight . . . I arrived inn [sic] Accra the capital. I found my way to Swedru . . . the workd [sic] soon got around that an eligible 'obroni' [white man] had arrived; . . . I had to schedule them. . . . Each was gorgeous, like the best coffee: hot, strong, black and full of flavour." The operation of these networks confirms Chow-White's (2006, 884) assertion that "cyberspace enables sex tourists to build deeper connections between the racialization, sexualization and commodification of sex workers' bodies and Western masculinity."

Some sex tourists target young teenage girls. Not only do they have sex with them; they also take nude photographs of them, presumably for child pornography Web sites, Listservs, chat rooms, and other exchange networks. The case of Morgens Riber Nielsen, a Danish man based in Norway, helps to put the issue of Internet-facilitated pedophilia into perspective. The Criminal Investigation Department (CID) of the Ghana Police Service worked in collaboration with the Norwegian Police to arrest Nielsen. At the time of his arrest in Norway, he had in his possession pictures of twelve teenage girls amongst 3,000 films that he had produced (Ghanaweb 2002c).

It is not inaccurate to say that the economic hardships that a lot of Ghanaians face turn these young women into vulnerable preys for marauding sexual predators whose egos are presumably fanned by the Ghanaian women whom they encounter. As one sex tourist said: "Oh, how nice to be a big slob of an American and be fawned over by the wayward college females that would just do anything for a few dollars!" Another intimated that "every Ghanaian girl's dream is to catch a white man from the western world" (World Sex Guide Forum 2004). Nevertheless, the sweeping generalizations presented by the sex tourists, in the foregoing narratives about Ghanaian women's ambitions, reflect the condescending attitudes of these privileged Westerners toward the subaltern "other" that they exploit. It is also an insult to Ghanaian womanhood as a whole to have the ambitions of all the country's women reduced to the perceptions contained in these inflammatory and egotistical, self-gratifying discourses of white men. The views expressed by these sex tourists corroborate the observation that "most global sex tourism . . . arises from the linkage between the political economic advantage enjoyed by affluent men from developed countries and the widespread cultural fantasy in those nations that dusky-skinned 'others' from exotic southern lands are liberated from the sexual/emotional inhibitions characteristic of women (and/or men) in their own societies" (Wonders and Michalowski 1998, 549–50).

By and large, white men are the targets of those women who engage in cybersexual activities, whether directly or mediated, as well as their off-line manifestations. This preference is based on a general, and sometimes erroneous, impression that white men are wealthy and generous. For these women, a relationship with a white man provides an opportunity to overcome the vicissitudes of life in Ghana, and an avenue to lift their families out of poverty and squalor. A relationship with a white man could also mean an opportunity to migrate to Europe or America, the dream destination of many a Ghanaian youth. They are suffused with the "opportunity myth," and crave the glamorous images of these places that are painted in the media, or peddled by certain compatriots returning from there. Furthermore, the economic success of some Ghanaians resident abroad, which is reflected in buildings, cars, and conspicuous consumption, fuel these perceptions of the metropole. The social status that comes with conspicuous consumption of foreign goods is another motivation for seeking links to foreigners who can provide such symbols of perceived upward mobility. This status then gives them the power to upset the existing dominant structures of power (Friedman 1990; see also United Nations 2004, 302). Nyamnjoh and Page (2002, 612–13) outline similar motivations in the Cameroonian context, where "young ladies . . . [who] comb the beaches in search of whiteness are interested in more than prostitution; they are interested in a gateway to fulfilling their fantasies, thus making sense of the promises of modernization in a context where the reality of its implementation has failed woefully."

The narratives above also illustrate how interactions among actors in this transnational sexual space created by the Internet and its off-line relative derive from culturally- and racially-based and essentialized imaginings of the "other." It is, moreover, clear that the relative power of the interactants in these relationships is dependent on their own, and their countries', location within the global capitalist structure. The sex tourists are driven by a desire for the cheap and the exotic, while the women are motivated by the need to escape economic despondency by becoming entrepreneurs in the global marketplace of sexual consumerism, and/or by hopes of a fantasy marriage and relocation to the metropole.

Another dimension of cybersexual activity that needs to be highlighted is the way in which its organizers exploit victims without their consent, whether latent or manifest. Some of the Ghanaian women on the Internet claim that they did not consciously choose to be there. One woman in Swedru whose semi-nude picture appeared on the Internet asserted that she was unaware that it would end there when a photographer offered to take a picture of her at a nearby beach. Some women the research team talked to at a popular beach in Accra expressed concern about people at the beach with cameras. They were concerned that these individuals may take pictures of them in compromising situations that may end up in one medium or another, thereby creating the impression that they are selling their bodies. What the Swedru woman's assertion and the concerns of others in Accra show is the emergence of a group of savvy local entrepreneurs who are responding to the market for exotic images by exploiting unsuspecting women and their bodies for their own pecuniary gain.

There is no gainsaying the exploitation that characterizes the women's relationship with local, Ghanaian, male agents who manipulate them, and are complicit in the exploitation and violation of their bodies. As processes of globalization and their intersection with advances in information technology facilitate the fulfillment of needs and desires for different actors, these young men in Ghana are taking advantage of the situation by acting as agents within the interstices of ethno-sexual desire, sex tourism, and economic deprivation. This is their own way of addressing the socioeconomic deprivation that they face, by taking advantage of the opportunities that the economy of desire and the Internet present. There were suggestions in the Swedru area that the local agents had gained financially from their involvement in these activities, and some of them are said to have built houses and bought cars with the monies that they made from their activities.

Socioeconomic Impacts of Cybersexual Activity

The activities described above have affected individuals, families, and communities in a variety of ways. One of the biggest impacts on Swedru, as a result of the cybersex related stories, is the stigma that has engulfed the town. It has assumed a reputation among many Ghanaians and Internet chatroom participants as a haven for immorality and promiscuity. The reputation goes back to 1998, when, out of the seventy-seven women showcased in Ghanaian newspapers as unashamedly selling their naked bodies on the Internet, fifty-four came from the town. This stigmatization of a whole community angers many residents of the town and makes them uncomfortable. The reaction has created resentment and strong antagonism not only toward those women and men who are accused of bringing the name of the town into disrepute, but their relatives as well. Consequently, fissures have emerged within the town's social structure, thereby upsetting the hitherto existing social balance. According to the parents of some of the young women whose pictures were featured on the Internet site in 1998, their families have had to face untold hardships, including social isolation, as a result of the social stigmatization that comes with engagement in what most Ghanaians consider to be shameful, indecent, and immoral activities. One mother lamented that right after the story broke, others thought of them as "an *ashawo* family [i.e., family of prostitutes]. People pointed at us wherever we went, scorned us, and called us all sorts of names."

Among some of the microlevel effects is "virtual infidelity" that is impairing or devastating real life relationships. Marriages have also fallen apart as a result of the revelations. One woman was reported to have had a miscarriage when pictures of her on the Internet were published by the local media (Attah 1998). Further investigations, in the course of this study, revealed that her shock was due to the fact that she was unaware that the picture, which was ostensibly meant for a potential suitor abroad, had ended up on the Internet, in the full glare of the world. One woman disclosed that her planned marriage to her fiancé was ruined because of the ridicule that the publication of the pictures in the newspapers brought him. He was pressured by friends and family not to go ahead with the marriage. According to her, "they said they did not want to bring into their family a girl who had exposed herself to the whole world."

It is interesting to note that despite the widespread condemnation, among the Ghanaian public, of cybersexual activities, their off-line corollaries, as well as sexual commerce in general, many of the female youth interviewed intimated that they understood why their peers would engage in such activities. They contended that the socioeconomic challenges they face makes their bodies the only asset they could use as a means of survival. A young woman, operating at one of the clubs frequented by sex tourists, confided thus: "If I am hungry and a white man is willing to take me abroad for sex, what is wrong with that? After all, I will not be the first to do that. I know girls who have met foreign men through the Internet and are enjoying life abroad now, or getting money sent to them from there." This disclosure corroborates Freeman-Longo's (2000, 79) observation that "it is easy for young people to recognize that many of these 'models' are close to their age, thus legitimizing in the minds of the youth online that people their age are also involved in real life and online sexual activities. It normalizes the experience." Thus, while various individuals and organizations have appealed to moral values as a means of curbing the youth's involvement in cybersexual and other forms of sexual commerce, these appeals do not seem to be an easy sell. The clash between the "feel good" appeal of moral rectitude and the expedience of engaging in the economy of desire, however risky, is a difficult dilemma for a lot of youth tethering on the brink of economic survival, but the likelihood that they will resolve it in favor of expedience is very high.

Unfortunately, however, while sex tourists and those who feed on the exoticized bodies of these Ghanaian women and girls are, by and large, able to fulfill their desires, a vast majority of the latter tends to be disappointed in the long run. This is because they are hardly able to realize the dreams that have been promised by the "opportunity myth." There are reports of girls and young women who have been impregnated by sex tourists and left to fend for themselves. This fate is vividly illustrated by the case of a young teenage single mother who was taken from Swedru and abandoned in Accra by a sex tourist after she got pregnant. Narrating the story, her mother recalled that "she was only 13 years old and in JSS-1 [Junior Secondary School – grade 1]. She was introduced to Morgens Riber [the Danish man referred to earlier] by boys in the town. After that she left Swedru with him and she did not come back again. After she got pregnant, he left the country and now she is struggling to look after the child in Accra."

Stories like this mirror Brennan's (2001) accounts of women in the Dominican Republic who have fallen victim to the world of sex tourism.

CONCLUSION

The neoliberal economic agenda that underpins economic globalization holds sway over the economies of developing countries, and the prescriptions of that agenda impose tremendous hardships on many young people in those locations. Neoliberal prescriptions also claw back, to a significant degree, the public goods that citizens had enjoyed in the past. Consequently, the youth are compelled to be ingenious in order to survive within the new reality. That ingenuity takes a variety of forms, including forays into the Internet-enabled global sex market, which can be described as part of the process of "globalization from below" (Eaton et al. 2003; Falk 1993).

This chapter argues that the interaction of Ghanaian youth with the global, as an avenue for economic redress, has been facilitated in unprecedented ways by the new information technologies. In the new transnational social space made possible by these technologies' capacity for time-space compression, one does not have to cross physical boundaries in order to engage directly with the center or periphery of the world capitalist system. Processes of globalization intricately intertwine with developments in Internet-enabled sexual commerce to introduce a sophistication to transnational sexual engagement that has created a moral panic in Ghana.

The nexus of interactions that have been enabled by the Internet help to extend the reach and scope of processes that intensify consumerism as well as the commodification of women's bodies and male desire (Wonders and Michalowski 2001). The Internet combines with a competitive global market of sexual desire to target the cheapest bodies and to facilitate access to them. Moreover, it has provided a mechanism for ingenuity among Ghanaian youth who take advantage of innovations in the global capitalist market, a market that, ironically, simultaneously perpetuates their economic peripheralization and/or sexual exploitation. The Ghanaian case also points to the racialization that characterizes the myth of the sexualized "other" and the consciously class- and gender-based exploitation of the economically vulnerable.

For the Ghanaian women involved in this market, the feminization of poverty intensifies the allure of the transnational sex trade, and increases their vulnerability to exploitation in the context of the exchange relations that characterize the market. Their engagement with the market is, however, not bereft of agency, and calls for analytical frameworks that transcend the victimology of an exclusively patriarchal and dichotomized problematization of women's position in the global sex trade. More appropriate approaches must recognize the ingenuity and activism of women in these exchange relationships, as they negotiate their locations within multiple, and sometimes contradictory, spaces. The foregoing analysis of the Ghanaian experience supports Chapkins (1997, 29–30) observation, in the context of sex workers, that "practices of prostitution, like other forms of commodification and consumption, can be read [in] more complex ways than simply as a confirmation of male domination. They may also be sites of ingenious resistance and cultural subversion . . . the prostitute cannot be reduced to . . . a passive object used in male sexual practice, but instead it can be understood as a place of agency where the sex worker makes active use of the existing sexual order."

ACKNOWLEDGEMENT

Research for this chapter was made possible, in part, by a grant from the Social Science and Humanities Research Council of Canada. I am grateful for this support.

REFERENCES

African Development Forum. Youth in Africa: A major resource for change. Issue Paper. African Development Forum, October 11–15, 2004. http://www.uneca .org/adf/pre-symposium/issue-paper.pdf.

Africanprincess.com. Ghana. http://www.africanprincess.com/least/ghan01.html.

Aghatise, Esohe. 2002. Trafficking for prostitution in Italy: Concept paper. Prepared for the United Nations Expert Group Meeting on Trafficking in Women and Girls, New York.

Ahmed, Sara. 2000. *Strange encounters: Embodied others in post-coloniality*. New York: Routledge.

Attah, Haruna. 1998. Letter from Africa. *Sunday Times*, May 17. http://www .suntimes.co.za/1998/05/17/insight/in12.htm.

Bell, Shannon. 1994. *Reading, writing, and rewriting the prostitute body*. Bloomington: Indiana University Press.

Bernstein, Elizabeth. 2001. *Economies of desire: Sexual commerce and post-industrial culture*. PhD diss., University of California, Berkeley.

Bhaba, Homi. 1994. *The location of culture*. London and New York: Routledge.

Böhme, Gernot. 2003. Contribution to the critique of the aesthetic economy. *Thesis Eleven* 73:71–82

Brennan, Denise. 2001. Tourism in transnational places: Dominican sex workers and German sex tourists imagine one another. *Identities* 7 (4): 621–63

Burawoy, Michael, J. A. Blum, S. George, Z. Gille, T. Gowan, L. Hanney, M. Klawiter, S. H. Lopez, S. O. Riain, and M. Thayer. 2000. *Global ethnography: Forces, connections, and imaginations in a postmodern world*. Berkeley: University of California Press.

Canagarajah, Sudharshan and Claus C. Pörtner.2003. *Evolution of poverty and welfare in Ghana in the 1990s: Achievements and challenges*. Africa Region Working Paper Series, no. 61. Washington, DC: World Bank.

Chapkis, Wendy. 1997. *Live sex acts: Women performing erotic labor*. New York: Routledge.

Cheek, Pamela. 2003. *Sexual antipodes: Enlightenment globalization and the placing of sex*. Stanford: Stanford University Press.

Chow-White, Peter A. 2006. Race, gender and sex on the net: Semantic networks of selling and storytelling sex tourism. *Media, Culture & Society* 28 (6): 883–905

Cooper, A., C. R. Scherer, S. C. Boies, and B. L. Gordon. 1999. Sexuality on the Internet: From sexual exploration to pathological expression. *Professional Psychology: Research and Practice* 30 (2): 154–64.

Daily Graphic, "Expose Foreign Sex Racketeers" – Prof. Dzobo, February 12, 2002.

Delgado, Richard. 1995. *Critical race theory: The cutting edge*. Philadelphia: Temple University Press.

Durham, Deborrah. 2000. Youth and the social imagination in Africa. *Anthropological Quarterly* 73 (3): 113–20.

Eaton, L., A. Flisher, and L. E. Aaro. 2003. Unsafe sexual behavior in South African youth. *Social Science and Medicine* 56: 149–65.

Epele, Maria E. 2001. Excess, scarcity, and desire among drug-using sex workers. *Body and Society* 7 (2–3): 161–79.

Esposito, Luigi, and John W. Murphy. 2000. Another step in the study of race relations. *The Sociological Quarterly* 41 (2): 171–87.

Falk, Richard. 1993. The making of global citizenship. In *Global visions: Beyond the new world order*, ed. J. Brecher, J. Childs, and J. Cutler. Boston: South End Press.

Firat, A. Fuat and N. Dholakia. 1998. *Consuming people: From political economy to theaters of consumption*. London: Routledge.

Freeman-Longo, Robert. 2000. Children, teens, and sex on the Internet. *Sexual Addiction and Compulsivity* 7 (2): 75–90

Friedman, Jonathan. 1990. Being in the world: Globalization and localization. *Theory, Culture and Society* 7 (2–3): 311–28.

Ghanaweb, 2002a. Gov't condemns porno site with Ghana's flag, August 27 http://www.ghanaweb.com/GhanaHomePage/NewsArchive/artikel.php?ID=26785.

———. 2002b. Pornographic material still a crime – Jake, December 18, 2002. http://www.ghanaweb.com/GhanaHomePage/NewsArchive/printnews.php?ID=30719.

———.2002c, Police uncovers pornographic syndicate, October 24, 2002. http://www.ghanaweb.com/GhanaHomePage/NewsArchive/printnews.php?ID=28649

———. Giddens Anthony. 1991. *Modernity and self-identity: Self and society in the late modern age*. Stanford, CA: Stanford University Press.

Glover, E. K., A Bannerman, B. W. Pence, H. Jones, R. Miller, E. Weiss, and J. Neequaye-Tetteh. 2003. Sexual health experiences of adolescents in three Ghanaian towns. *International Family Planning Perspectives* 29 (1): 32–40.

Government of Ghana. 2003a. *Ghana poverty reduction strategy 2003–2005: An agenda for growth and prosperity, volume 1*. Accra: Assembly Press.

———. 2003b. *Implementation of the Ghana poverty reduction strategy: 2000 annual progress report*. Accra: National Development Planning Commission.

Gossett, Jennifer L., and Sarah Byrne. 2002. "Click here": A content analysis of Internet rape sites. *Gender and Society* 16 (5): 689–709

Gottfried, Heidi. 2001. From "manufacturing consent" to "global ethnography": A retrospective examination. *Contemporary Sociology* 30 (5): 435–38.

Griffiths, Mark. 2000. Excessive Internet use: Implications for sexual behavior. *Cyber Psychology and Behavior* 3 (4): 537–53.

Hughes, D. M. 2000. The Internet and sex industries: Partners in global sexual exploitation. *IEEE Technology and Society Magazine* Spring: 35–42.

International Labor Organization. 2004. Economic security strengthens tolerance and happiness as well as growth and development, news release, Geneva.

———. 2005. *World employment report 2004–05: Employment, productivity, and poverty reduction*. Geneva: International Labor Organization.

Jeffreys, Elaine. 2004. *China, sex, and prostitution*. London: Routledge Curzon.

Kempadoo, Kamala. 1999. Slavery or work? Reconceptualizing third world prostitution. *Positions* 7 (1), 225–37.

Konadu-Agyemang, Kwadwo. 2000. The best of times and the worst of times: Structural adjustment programs and uneven development in Africa: The case of Ghana. *Professional Geographer* 52 (3): 469–83.

Kuipers, Giselinde. 2006. The social construction of digital danger: Debating, defusing, and inflating the moral dangers of online humor and pornography in the Netherlands and the United States. *New Media and Society* 8 (3): 379–400.

McLelland, Mark J. 2002. New directions in thinking about sexualities research. *Sexualities* 5 (4): 387–406.

McGrew, A. 2000. Sustainable globalization? The global politics of development and exclusion in the new world order. In *Poverty and development into the 21st century*, ed. T. Allen and A. Thomas. Oxford: Oxford University Press, 345–64.

Mitchell, Kimberly J., David Finkelhor, and Janis Wolak. 2003. The exposure of youth to unwanted sexual material on the Internet: A national survey of risk, impact, and prevention. *Youth and Society* 34 (3): 330–58.

Moore, Lisa J., and Adele E. Clark. 2001. The traffic in cyberanatomies: Sex/gender/sexualities in local and global formations. *Body and Society* 7 (1): 57–96

Mosco, Vincent. 1996. *The political economy of communication*. London: Sage.

Mufune, Pempelani. 2000. Street youth in southern Africa. *International Social Science Journal* 52 (164): 233–43.

Nagel, Joane. 2003. *Race, ethnicity and sexuality: Intimate intersections, forbidden frontiers*. New York and Oxford: Oxford University Press.

Namnjoh, Francis B., and Ben Page. 2002. *Whiteman Kontri* and the enduring allure of modernity among Cameroonian youth. *African Affairs* 101: 607–34.

O'Grady, Ron. 2001. Eradicating pedophilia: Toward the humanization of society. *Journal of International Affairs* 55 (1): 123–40.

Okojie, Chistiana E. 2003. Employment creation for youth in Africa: The gender dimension. Prepared for the Expert Group Meeting on Jobs for Youth: National Strategies for Employment Promotion, Geneva, Switzerland.

One-and-only. Show Profile. 2004a. http://search.msn.com/results.aspx?srch=105 &form=as5&q=(http%3a%2f%2fwww.one-and-only.com%2foando%2fqsearch%2fs howprofile.asp%3fsid%3dddc8fdbd-6ba7–447D-907A-06862F221AD2%26Track ingID%3d201298%26Theme%3d3%26Us.

———. 2004b. http://www.one-and-only.com/oando/qsearch/showprofile.asp?SID =DDC8FDBD-6BA7–447D-907A-06862F221AD2&TrackingID=201298&Th eme=3&UserID=46454A464B464E&RN=15589&POS=4&Handle=attractiveb lackl&i=1.

Pettman, Jan J. 2003. International sex and service. In *Globalization: Theory and practice*, ed. Eleonore Kofman and Gillian Youngs, 157–73. New York: Continuum.

Petras, James, and Henry Veltmeyer. 2001. *Globalization unmasked: Imperialism in the 21st century*. Halifax: Fernwood; London: Zed Books.

Pew Internet Research Center. 2001. Teenage life online: The rise of the instant-message generation and the Internet's impact on friendships and family relationships. http://www.pewInternet.org/report_display.asp?r=36.

Phua, Voon C. 2002. Sex and sexuality in men's personal advertisements. *Men and Masculinities* 5 (2): 178–91.

Phua, Voon C., and Gayle. Kaufman. 2003. The crossroads of race and sexuality: Date selection among men in Internet "personal ads." *Journal of Family Issues* 24 (8): 981–94.

Richter Linda K. 1998. Exploring the political role of gender in tourism research. In *Global tourism*, ed. William F. Theobald, 391–404. Oxford: Butterworth-Heinemann.

Riordan, Ellen. 2001. Commodified agents and empowered girls: Consuming and producing feminism. *Journal of Communication Inquiry* 25 (3): 279–97.

Bishop, Ryan, and Lillian S. Robinson. 1998. *Night market: Sexual cultures and the Thai economic miracle.* New York. Routledge.

Saul, John. 2001. Cry for the beloved country: The post-apartheid denouement. *Review of African Political Economy* 28 (89): 329–344.

Schaeffer-Grabiel, Felicity. 2004. Cyberbrides and global imaginaries: Mexican women's turn from national to the foreign. *Space and Culture* 7 (1): 33–48.

Schneider, Jacqueline L. 2003. Hiding in plain sight: An exploration of the illegal? Activities of a drugs newsgroup. *The Howard Journal* 42: 374–89.

Shah, Nishant. 2007. Subject to technology: Internet pornography, cyber-terrorism, and the Indian state. *Inter-Asia Cultural Studies* 8 (3): 349–36.

Taylor, Ernest. 2002. Trafficking in women and girls. Prepared for the United Nations Expert Group Meeting on the Trafficking in Women and Girls, New York.

Teale, Francis. 2000. *Private sector wages and poverty in Ghana: 1988–98.* Centre for the Study of African Economies Working Paper Series, no. WPS/2000–6, 1–22.

Tettey, Wisdom J. 2002. Africa's brain drain: Networking diaspora communities for socio-economic development. *Mots Pluriels* 20 (February). http://www.arts.uwa.edu.au/MotsPluriels/MP2002wjt.html.

Tsikata, Yvonne M. 2000. *Globalization, poverty and inequality in sub-Saharan Africa: A political economy appraisal.* Paris: OECD Development Centre.

United Nations. n.d. Youth at the United Nations. http://www.un.org/esa/socdev/unyin/qanda.htm.

———. 2002. *World population prospects.* New York: United Nations.

———. 2004. *World youth report 2003: The global situation of young people.* New York. United Nations.

Wing, Adrien K. 2000. *Global critical race feminism: An international reader.* New York: New York University Press.

Wojcicki, Janet M. 2002. Commercial sex work or Ukuphanda? Sex-for-money exchange in Soweto and Hammnaskraal area, South Africa. *Culture, Medicine, and Psychiatry* 26:339–70.

Wonders, Nancy A., and Raymond Michalowski. 2001. Bodies, borders, and sex tourism in a globalized world: A tale of two sities—Amsterdam and Havana. *Social Problems* 48 (4): 545–71.

World Bank. 2002. Focusing on youth in Africa: African officials, youth discuss adolescent health and development. News, June 27, http://web.worldbank.org/WBSITE/EXTERNAL/NEWS/0,,contentMDK:20050339~menuPK:34459~pagePK:64003015~piPK:64003012~theSitePK:4607,00.html.

———. 2004. *Country assistance strategy for Ghana: 2004–7.* Report No. 27838-GH. Washington, DC: World Bank.

World Sex Guide Forum. 2004. Ghana. http://www.wsgforum.com/vforum/showthread.php?s=a30b32266539d70a23dd3227b8adbd43&threadid=863&highlight=ghana.

Zook, Matthew A. 2002. Underground globalization: Mapping the space of flows of the Internet adult industry. *Environment and Planning* 44: 1261–86.

CHAPTER 9

MERCANTILISM AND THE STRUGGLE FOR LATE INDUSTRIALIZATION IN AN AGE OF GLOBALIZATION

A COMPARATIVE ANALYSIS OF TAIWAN AND UGANDA*

Julius Kiiza

Any nation which owing to misfortunes is behind others in industry, commerce, and navigation, while she nevertheless possesses the mental and material means for developing those acquisitions, must first of all strengthen her own individual powers, in order to fit herself to enter into free competition with more advanced nations

—Friedrich List, 1885

* An earlier draft of this chapter appeared as a Center for Basic Research (CBR) Working Paper. The CBR draft was revised and presented at the Annual Conference on Development and Change in Neemrana, India in December 2005. The comments I received from the CBR researchers and the Neemrana conference participants are gratefully acknowledged. I alone am responsible for the contents of this chapter.

INTRODUCTION

The last few decades have witnessed a spirited debate over globalization and the real or perceived impact of global economic integration on the performance of national economies (Weiss 1998, 1999; Rodrik 2001; Chang 2007). The debate appeared, for a time, to be polarized between the theorists of global market integration (e.g., Ohmae 1995, Dollar 2001) and those that are critical of the globalization orthodoxy (Weiss 1998; Rodrik 1999; Chang 2002; Amsden 2005). The former group celebrated the convergence of different species of capitalism on the Anglo-American norm of "free trade"; the latter underscored cross-national variations in capitalist development. One group announced the rise of the "borderless world" signifying the sovereignty of private capital over sovereign states; the other documented the enduring significance of nation-states in the "global" political economy. One team celebrated the "death" of industrial policy; the other appreciated the changing, but *not* ending, significance of industrial policy (Rodrik 2004; Chang 2007).

By the end of the 1990s, some degree of consensus had emerged. That effective industrialization is strongly associated with developmentalist institutions is no longer debatable (Chang 2007; Reinert 2007). That the economic dynamism of the Northeast Asian tigers—or even Ireland (Chang 2003)—is linked to distinctly national economic policies is not debatable either. What is debatable is the vitality of country-specific industrial policies for latecomers (such as Uganda) that seek to industrialize in the current era of globalization. Do policies of economic nationalism—what I unashamedly call *economic mercantilism*—make sense in the current age of globalization?

It is the purpose of this chapter to examine the functionality of economic mercantilism as an instrument of late industrialization in Africa. The focus is on Uganda, against the backdrop of "early" industrialization (in Britain and the United States), and effective "late" industrialization in Taiwan and other East Asia tigers. The rationale for examining Uganda in the light of the Asian economic miracles is simple, but not obvious. The Asian tigers (such as Taiwan and South Korea), and to a lesser extent, Singapore, were, in several respects, comparable to Uganda five decades ago. Taiwan, for example, had gross domestic product (GDP) per capita of US$199 in 1950, comparable to Uganda's $200 at the time of independence (1962). Taiwan is a former colony (of Japan), just like Uganda, which is a former colony of Britain. Both suffered colonial exploitation and plunder. Both are economies of small-to-medium enterprises (SMEs). Both Taiwan and Uganda are tiny nation-states of about twenty-five million people. Moreover, both emerged from colonialism with strong wishes to industrialize and transform the national economy. Yet, today, the two are substantially different. Uganda is still a commodity economy, with the agricultural sector employing 88 percent of the total labor force, accounting for 85 percent of total foreign exchange earnings and contributing 54 percent of GDP. By contrast, Taiwan is a high-tech economy known for the manufacture and export of computers, electronics, and other high value-added industrial products. How does one explain the effectiveness of the Asian tigers (such as Taiwan) and the inability of sub-Saharan African countries (such as Uganda) to attain industrialized nation status in the current age of globalization?

The central claim of this chapter is that globalization is a distinctive form of economic nationalism—that of the dominant industrial economies. It is simultaneously beneficial to the competitive industrial economies and detrimental to the commodity latecomer economies. This is not to suggest that late industrializers have absolutely nothing to gain from a "global" economic order. Globalization has undeniably increased the flow of information, the diffusion of technology, and the cross-border movement of capital goods needed for late industrialization. The international flow of foreign direct investment (FDI) also seems to have facilitated specific categories of late industrialization, particularly in China and other Asian tigers. But, this restates the problem. Why are some countries more effective than others in benefiting from global market integration? Why does globalization foster late industrialization in East Asia and not in sub-Saharan Africa when both regions are "globally" integrated? This chapter contends that cross-national variations in the levels of economic performance primarily spring from the capacity of domestic political institutions—particularly the state—to mediate the external pressures of globalism and pursue the long-term developmental goals of the national economy. As Friedrich List (1885, xxvi) argued, any country that is "behind others in industry, commerce, and navigation . . . must first of all strengthen her own individual powers, in order to fit herself to enter into free competition with more advanced nations."

The chapter first conceptualizes economic mercantilism. The major objections to economic mercantilism are outlined with reference to the constraining role of today's contextual variables, such as the WTO rules.[1] Evidence is then presented to show that effective "early" *and* "late" industrialization took place via the active use of economic mercantilism. The chapter then outlines the industrialization outcomes of two cases—Taiwan (representing successful use of economic mercantilism) and Uganda (representing premature global market integration). The analysis ends by stressing the changing, but not ending, significance of economic mercantilism.

CONCEPTUALIZING ECONOMIC MERCANTILISM

The term "mercantilism" never entered the political economy lexicon till the later part of the eighteenth century (Wilson 1967, 3–10). This was centuries *after* the practice of economic mercantilism had been tested, trusted, and institutionalized, or even amended to suit the changing tasks of governing the national economy. In other words, mercantile economic policies developed first. The "system" or "theory" of economic mercantilism came later. As a corollary, "mercantilism" has been a controversial term in both liberal and Marxian political economy analysis. In the liberal economics tradition, Adam Smith (1776/1937) decried the "mercantile system."[2] Smith was enraged by the heavy customs duties erected by England from about 1688 onwards, which, he argued, would never have been imposed "had not the mercantile system taught us, in many cases, to employ taxation as an instrument, not of revenue, but of monopoly" (Smith, 1776/1937: 833; cf. Coleman 1969, 6). Following the Smithian tradition, rational choice theory conceptualizes economic mercantilism as the polar opposite of economic liberalism or "globalization." State involvement in the economy is pejoratively associated with rent-seeking business behavior. The claim is that state policies such as protective tariffs prop up inefficient firms, undermine innovation, and *distort* the free markets, nationally and internationally.

Marxist economic analysis is not kind to mercantilism either. Mercantilism, it is alleged, is "a system of State-regulated exploitation through trade. ... [It is] essentially the economic policy of an age of primitive accumulation."[3] Neither Marxism nor liberalism appreciates the *dynamic* character of mercantilism—the fact, that is, that mercantilism as an instrument of economic development changes in character, depending on the changing needs of the national economy.

This chapter contends that the *substance* of mercantile economic nationalism is an adjustable set. The tools used might involve *direct* state involvement in industrialization via public companies or *indirect* approaches to wealth creation such as offering tax holidays to selected industries. It might involve infant industry protection at one time and economic openness (or globalization) at another, depending on the concrete demands of national economic governance (Kiiza 2007).

Researched evidence shows that today's industrialized economies used mercantilistic policies to grow (Chang 2002). In his seminal work entitled *Power and plenty as objectives of foreign policy*, Jacob Viner (1948) documents several policies that were of "nearly universal importance" in early industrialization. First, the hemorrhage of gold or silver (a mercantilist measure of wealth) was discouraged.[4] Second, importation of raw materials was encouraged while the export of raw materials to rival nation-states was prohibited. (King James I, England, for example, banned the export of unfinished cloth to the Netherlands, which was the economic hegemon of the time. Third, importation of manufactured or luxurious products was discouraged (via high tariffs or even a total ban). Fourth, importation of capital goods and skilled workers was encouraged. Fifth, "exports" of skilled industrialists and machinery were restricted. (Often, "defection" by local industrialists to rival states was treated as a treasonable offence punishable by death). Sixth, navigation laws were formulated to promote domestic shipbuilding and create jobs for local people. And seventh, strong navies (or armies) were built by all visionary monarchs. The ultimate goal of these mercantilist policies was to strengthen the state (that is, the coercive apparatus) and enrich the nation (i.e., the people).

The policies of economic mercantilism—or what the German historical school calls *Merkantilismu*—historically took roots in countries that deliberately embarked on a *Staatsbildung* (state-building) program. For the German nationalists, *Merkantilismus* was no ordinary economic policy. It was above everything else, "a policy of state-making (*Staatsbildung*) carried out by wise and benevolent rulers" (Cameron 1989, 129). Gustav (von) Schmoller (1896, 69) argued that mercantilism "in its innermost kernel is nothing but state-making—not state-making in a narrow sense but state-making and national-economic-making at the same time." Central to this double-edged *Staatsbildung* project was the centralization of the state. This involved the transfer of power from small political units of the medieval period to centralized states. (The classic example was the centralization of Hohenzollern Prussia.)[5] Additionally, *Staatsbildung* involved creating a merit-based bureaucracy or civil service to serve as an engine of modern economic policymaking (Toye 2007). It involved using state power to create political stability, abolish interstate tariffs, and harmonize foreign "commercial" policies.

Evidence suggests that effective late industrialization borrowed heavily from economic mercantilism. Japan, Korea, and Taiwan, for example, derived great benefits from global market integration *without* renouncing the strategic role of the state in the domestic economy (Johnson 1982, 1999; Noland and Pack 2003, xii). According to Rodrik (2001), the East Asian tigers "were free to do their own thing, and did so, combining trade reliance with unorthodox policies—export subsidies, domestic content requirements, import-export linkages, patent and copyrights infringements, restrictions on capital flows (including direct foreign investments), directed credit, and so on" (28). The key question today is whether mercantilism is still feasible, given the restrictive WTO rules and other dynamics in the global political economy. It is these dynamics that are invoked in today's objections to mercantilism.

OBJECTIONS TO ECONOMIC MERCANTILISM

The main objection to mercantile economic nationalism today is couched in the language of globalization. The view of the intellectual orthodoxy is that the world economy has gone through substantial or even "epochal" changes over the last two decades. Globalization has allegedly rendered industrial policy irrelevant. Globalization theorists do not deny the continued existence of states as political entities. What they question is the economic role of states in the current era of economic openness. Infant industry protection, subsidization, and other industrial policy tools are rejected as pointless aberrations from the Anglo-American norm of economic liberalism. The claim is that deepening economic integration has led to the rise of "ungovernable" markets, the deterritorialisation of economic activity, and the convergence of national varieties of capitalist development on the Anglo-American norm of free markets (cf. Reich 1992).

A key obstacle to the use of mercantilism in "late" industrialization lies in the restrictive WTO rules. The official WTO ideology of economic liberalism has rendered protectionism difficult. Under the Agreement on Subsidies and Countervailing Measures, export subsidies are now illegal—except for poor countries with per capita income below US$1,000. Local content requirements (which were pivotal in indigenizing foreign capital and technology to Asia) are now disallowed. The WTO norm of "national treatment" mandates developing countries to treat foreign capital and imported goods "no less favorably" than national capital or locally produced goods. Most importantly, infringements on foreign patents and copyrights—which were crucial for both early industrializers, such as the United States (Ben-Atar 1995; Chang 2002) and latecomers such as the Asian tigers (Rodrik 2001, 28) is now illegal under the TRIPS Agreement. In the light of the restrictive WTO rules and the North-South free trade agreements (FTAs), the global context of industrialization has arguably changed dramatically. The tempting conclusion is that economic mercantilism and country-specific industrial policies are dead.

Another major obstacle to economic mercantilism is the rising importance of bilateral trade agreements, particularly between the advanced knowledge economies of the North and the primary commodity producers of the global South. Oftentimes, the rich countries—labeled "Bad Samaritans" by Ha-Joon Chang (2007)—actively push for issues that have been resisted within the WTO framework. The Economic Partnership Agreements (EPAs) between the EU and the ESA countries illustrate the point at issue. The EU argued that the EPAs had to be concluded by December 31, 2007. The aim was to have the EPAs enforceable by January 2008. The substance of EPAs includes trade liberalization, protection of intellectual property, competition policy, investment, and government procurement. The last three of these are the core elements of the "Singapore Issues" (Khor 2004) that were resisted by the BRICs (Brazil, Russia, India, China), backed by the small and vulnerable economies (SVEs). This suggests that EPAs may be alternative avenues for advanced economies to actualize their national interests that could not be accepted in the WTO framework.

This chapter accepts the observations, but finds loopholes in the conclusions, of the critics of modern economic mercantilism. As Irfan ul Haque (2007, 4) observes, "simple copying of past policies and practices is now neither feasible nor altogether desirable for countries striving to catch up with the more advanced countries." This, however, is not to suggest that there are "no alternatives" to free market fundamentalism. Globalization has changed, not ended, the significance of economic mercantilism. As Rodrik (2004, 29) suggests: "The reality is that industrial policies have run rampant during the last two decades—and nowhere more so than in those economies that have steadfastly adopted the agenda of orthodox reform." Indeed, effective early and late industrialization typically involved building viable domestic institutions, designing innovative policies, and marshalling domestic capacities to reclaim development "policy space" from both local and foreign obstacles. This suggests that catch-up industrializers such as Uganda can, and should, draw insights from the history of effective industrialization. Below, I present five pieces of evidence that appear to underscore the centrality of economic statism in both "early" and "late" industrialization.

Economic Mercantilism in Seventeenth-Century France

The earliest prototype of institutionalised economic mercantilism is perhaps seventeenth-century France under Jean-Baptiste Colbert. Colbert was the economic affairs czar of King Louis XIV. Like twentieth-century Japan or Taiwan, Colbert established a high quality economic bureaucracy that became pivotal to France's economic transformation. Colbert was politically insulated from the French *Parlement* and other short-termist interests. Yet, somewhat ironically for absolute monachism, he was "embedded" in the productive sectors of society, particularly the merchant and industrial community. Contrary to the prognosis of rational choice theory, Colbert used his political insulation and discretionary powers in pursuit of the national interest, not personal gain. He used economic *etatisme* (statism) to construct a distinctly French economic nation in the face of formidable economic pressures from rival nation-states, particularly the Netherlands (which was the economic hegemon of the time). Colbertian France not only established state monopolies such the *La Campagnie des Indes Occidentales* (the French West India Company). It worked as an investment banker along the lines later proposed by Hirschman (1958) and Gerschenkron (1962). Like the developmental states of East Asia, the French monarchy socialized the risks of key enterprises, gave tariff protection to priority industries (such as textiles), and encouraged exports by means of bounties or export rebates.

While Colbert had no theory of rent-seeking business behavior to guide his industrial policy, he undoubtedly knew how to guard against it. Privileges to industrialists were granted with meticulous care. Colbert demanded evidence that privileged industrialists "were really going to endow France with a new invention or a new type of manufacturing" (Cole 1939/1964, 135). Once the privilege was granted, he exhorted his corps of quality bureaucrats to ensure that "the entrepreneur lived up to the terms imposed upon him. . . . When public policy seemed to demand it, when an enterprise did not succeed, when a manufacture failed to comply with the terms he had agreed to, Colbert did not hesitate to revoke the privilege" (Cole 1939/1964, 135–36). By the time of Colbert's death in 1683, France was "perhaps the richest, most populous, and strongest nation of western Europe" (Scoville 1960, 155). The covariation of *colbertisme* and France's level of economic performance is damaging to the liberal and Marxist claim that economic mercantilism is antithetical to national economic vitality. If anything, Colbertian France strongly suggests that economic nationalism is a crucial variable in the development of capitalism.

Economic Mercantilism and Pioneer Industrialization in Britain

The second case that illustrates the historical significance of economic nationalism is the rise of Britain to industrial supremacy in the eighteenth and nineteenth centuries. The literature (both rightist and leftist) predominantly asserts that Britain's economic transformation took place in the context of *free* markets.[6] The orthodox claim is that the efficiency logic of Smithian-Ricardian markets is *the* primary causal explanation of Britain's industrialism. The counterfactual claim is that Britain would *not* have advanced if it were not for its free market regime. This claim is, at best, simplistic. The "Workshop of the World" was no doubt a capitalist economy. But it was *not* a free market economy. For one thing, Britain used state power to politically construct a reliable domestic market *and* capture overseas markets (in the United States, India, and Africa), for *British* manufacturers. For another thing, protectionism, war, and foreign policy were all shrewdly used in the service of the British economic nation (in a typical mercantilist fashion). The genesis of English mercantilism is associated with the Tudor monarchs (named after Henry Tudor), particularly Queen Elizabeth I who reigned from 1558–1603 (Kiiza 2001, chap. 2, for details). Prior to 1600, England routinely used state power to import technology from continental Europe. It recruited "German miners, Dutch engineers specialised in drainage, French civil engineers and architects" (Kindleberger 1996, 109). In the seventeenth century, England used state laws and other nationalistic institutions for governing the domestic economy. The Navigation Act of 1651, for example, simultaneously *protected* English merchant capital and sought to deprive the Dutch of their shipping and fishing supremacy. Under this act, trade from one British port to another became an exclusive preserve of *British* ships. *British* ships were not permitted to sail through an intermediate port. Even when merchandise originated from, or was destined for, another country, it had to go through Britain. The aim was to undercut Amsterdam as Europe's entrepot, and create business for *British* merchants (Cameron 1989, 157).

It must be emphasized, however, that British economic mercantilism was not static. In the eighteenth and nineteenth centuries, it took the form of economic openness. This was apparently because of Britain's first mover advantages in the race to industrialization. Bolstered by the likes of Adam Smith and David Ricardo, British economic ideology espoused the virtues of god-given comparative advantages and free trade. Free trade was, nevertheless, a double-edged sword. It was simultaneously beneficial to Britain, the "Workshop of the World" *and* detrimental to continental Europe and the United States—the contemporaries of Britain that had not yet developed the competitive muscles to match Britain's manufacturing might. Indeed, the United States denounced free trade as *Britain's economic imperialism* (cf. Semmel 1970). To America, free trade ideology was shrewdly crafted to enhance Britain's supremacy and condemn agricultural states like the United States to structural underdevelopment. In the last part of the nineteenth century, Italy, Germany, and France followed suit. The argument of continental Europe, just like the United States, was that the long-term *national* interests called for state intervention to protect infant industries (Kiiza 2001).

Once America and other rival nation-states insulated their national economies from British manufacturers, Britain strategically changed its economic gears. It encouraged domestic firms to shift from the relatively low value-added textile manufacturing to the higher value-added capital goods (where an expanding niche market existed) and the services sector (particularly banking and insurance). By grabbing "protectorate" markets and settler colonies in Africa in the late nineteenth century, Britain also demonstrated its willingness to amend its laissez-faire ideology to suit the changing needs of the imperial economy. Britain's laissez-faire regime completely collapsed in the 1930s (thanks to the damaging effects of World War I and the Great Depression), only to be revived in the postwar era under U.S.-led economic liberalism. Today, the United Kingdom has virtually no objection to economic globalization and other policies initiated by the "Bigger Brother"—the United States.[7] The point worth emphasizing is that Britain's changing economic regime does not signify the irrelevance of economic nationalism. It is, in fact, more consistent with the changing priorities of the national economy.

Economic Mercantilism and Early "Late" Industrialization in the United States

The third and most interesting case of economic nationalism is the United States. America's transformation into a modern industrial and IT-driven economy is informative for two reasons. The first reason is the United States' historical rejection of free trade ideology as a distinctive form of *British* economic imperialism. Second is America's commitment to neoliberal globalism as the most "sensible" strategy of governing the economy today.[8] In its early stages of industrialization, America was unmistakably mercantilist. It was isolationist and ultranationalistic. The guiding political ideology was *America for Americans*. American mercantilism was, in effect, an applied philosophy of economic statism, comparable to German economic nationalism. Like German nationalism, American nationalism was a distinctive species of economic policy. It was nothing but state-making (*Staatsbildung*) in a broad political economy sense (Schmoller 1896, 69; Wilson 1967, 6). The policy was theoretically justifiable for the Untied States, as for Germany, or any other country, past or present, that seeks to attain industrialized nation status in the face of substantial *inter-national* competition. According to Friedrich List (1885), such a country must use domestic political institutions to protect the *nation-alokonomie* from the harmful pressures of the "cosmopolitical" (or "global") economy. This implies substantial economic regulation and control. The aim is to enrich the nation and strengthen the state. If the peaceful *Staatsbildung* measures prove ineffective, war becomes an inevitable option (see Tilly 1985). It is precisely those countries that "put the might of their fleets and admiralties, the apparatus of customs laws and navigation laws, with rapidity, boldness and clear purpose, at the service of the economic interests of the nation and state, which obtain . . . thereby the lead in the struggle and in riches and industrial prosperity" (Schmoller, quoted in Wilson 1967, 6). This Schmollerian-Listian political economy philosophy was central to America's rise to industrial, technological, and military supremacy.

American nationalism assumed a critical stage with the overthrow of British colonialism, the Declaration of Independence (July 4, 1776), and the establishment of the "United States" of America. The struggle was cemented by the national consciousness of the U.S. revolutionaries and their political will to build a rich and strong nation "that stretched from ocean to ocean" (Crapol 1973, 10). In July 1776, the United States was only 369,000 square miles. By 1860, it had expanded nearly eight times to 3,022,387 square miles. This "continental" empire was pivotal to America's industrial revolution. Yet, neither territorial expansion nor political independence answered the crucial question of America's *economic* sovereignty. To Alexander Hamilton, Mathew Carey, and other economic nationalists, the United States was still a victim of British economic imperialism. As late as the time of the American Civil War (1861–65), the Untied States was dependent on Britain as a source of investment capital and a market of agricultural exports. The prices of America's wheat and cotton exports were set by the buyers "in the Liverpool and London commodity markets" (Crapol 1973, 14). America's status in that system was semi-vassal at best, and neocolonial, at worst. If the United States was to effectively transform the national economy and realize its mission as "a nation of great wealth and power," it had to delink itself from Britain's economic hegemony. This meant assisting local industrialists to erect "the workshops of the world" on American soil. It also meant using protective tariffs, transport subsidies, and other nationalistic policies to develop the national economy. This is exactly what America did *for centuries*. In the 1884 Berlin Conference, for example, while Britain and other "G8" powers of the day were designing "global" mechanisms of sharing out Africa amongst themselves, America's commitment to economic nationalism was firm. Newton Nutting eloquently asserted: "Let free trade remain on the banners of England, but let our policy be in all the years to come what it has been in the past. Let us seek to make a market here for all our products . . . let us stand by the idea that America is a Government for Americans and American ideas and principles" (Nutting 1884, quoted in Crapol 1973, 20).

In short, after 110 years of political independence, the United States was not ready to go global. The national economy was still paramount. American firms had to be protected from foreign competitors.

American nationalism, however, was ambivalent in character. It was characterized by xenophobia for Britain's commercial and naval supremacy, coupled with "admiration and respect for British industry and enterprise" (Crapol 1973, 9). The aim of Americanism was not to create a fairer system of global capitalism. The aim was to *replace* the economic hegemon—Britain. Theirs was a struggle to dismantle pax Britannica *and* erect pax Americana. This appears to explain why the United States is the most articulate zealot of free trade today. In virtually all the recent international forums—from WTO's Seattle Conference of 1999 to UNCTAD's Bangkok Conference of February 2000; from the IMF annual conference in Prague (September 2000) to the bloodstained G8 summit in Genoa (July 20–22, 2001)—U.S.-led economic liberalism has dominated agenda setting. In Uganda and other

African countries (which have hardly been independent for forty years!), Americanism is actively pushing for liberalization and other orthodox adjustment programs. Through the agency of the IMF/World Bank fraternity, the United States and other industrial powers have exerted leverage on African governments to privatize state-owned enterprises. Africa's trade and industrial policies must be liberalized. Protective tariffs and subsidies must also be dissolved. The claim is that these tools of economic nationalism "prop" up inefficient firms, promote rent-seeking business behavior, and interfere with the "American conception of free enterprise" (Aikman 1986, 116). The solution is supposedly to institutionalize a regime of economic liberalism premised upon the virtues of market efficiency. America's push for a global regime of unbridled capitalism is significant for two reasons. First, it is *inconsistent* with its own history of economic mercantilism. Second, it upholds List's (1885) proposition that free trade is the natural view of a dominant industrial economy, particularly one seeking to prevent the rise of competitors abroad. This suggests that economic liberalism or "globalization" is not necessarily the polar opposite of economic nationalism. Rather, it is a distinctive form of economic nationalism—that of the giant industrial powers.

Economic Mercantilism and Late Industrialization in Japan

The fourth case of economic nationalism—which is perhaps the most relevant for "late, late" industrialization—is Japan. Japan's rapid transformation from a backward economy of the nineteenth century to a globally competitive industrial economy of the twentieth century is a compelling case of economic statism. It is a prototype of rapid "late" industrialization propelled by economic nationalism. Japan's developmentalism sprang from a distinctly nationalistic economic ideology. Meiji Japan wanted to enhance domestic production, boost the balance of payments, and immunize the nation against the economic and military threats of other states, particularly the United States. As early as the 1880s (and between 1937 and 1964), all state agencies "were required to prepare a foreign exchange budget as well as their normal yen budget" (Tiedemann 1974, 138). According to Johnson (1982), "control of the foreign exchange budget meant control of the entire economy" (25). The aim was to enhance national economic vitality *and* strengthen the state. Japan's developmentalism begins in 1868 with the overthrow of the Tokugawa dynasty and the restoration of power to Emperor Meiji. This militant transfer of power was sparked by two crucial developments—one internal and the other, external. The internal crisis is associated with the Tokugawa establishment, more specifically, the struggle between the *shogunate* (central authority) and *daimyo* (territorial feudal authorities) over the allocation of political and economic power. This was particularly explosive in three economically and militarily strong daimyo—Satsuma, Choshu, and Tosa. The *external* threat emanated from the crystallization of America's economic interests in the Asia Pacific region. In 1853, the United States sent Commodore Mathew Perry to Japan on a distinctly mercantilist mission (Wall 1971,

10–11; Hane 1986, 67). Perry had to open the doors of seclusionist Japan by force, if need be. Accordingly, belligerent Perry forced Japan to sign the unequal treaties of 1854 and 1858.

The combined effect of the internal and external tremors was a national crisis. Tokugawa Japan was at the crossroads. Japan's seclusion and its sovereignty were under threat. The *samurai* (warrior-scholars) became key players in the ensuing debates and social struggles. The most important outcome of the Japanese crisis was *sonno-joi*—the nationalist movement to "revere the Emperor and repel the barbarians." This meant overthrowing the Tokugawa regime and restoring power to the emperor—the power that had been "usurped" by the Tokugawa dynasty. Unlike Chairman Mao's China or Kim Il Sung's North Korea, Japanese nationalists knew the importance of Western technology in their struggle to build an economic nation. But, unlike Uganda and other economic laggards of Africa, Japan drew a distinction between modernity and westernization: one signified economic progress and the other, Western cultural imperialism. The Japanese wanted modernity, not westernization. They needed Western technology *without* the greed, individualism, and social Darwinism of Western capitalism (Hane 1986, 73). Thus, technology that was imported from the West had to be mediated by Asian ethical values. The overriding aim was to build a distinctly *Japanese* economic nation. Thus, where Germany had the Listian political economy tradition, and where the Americans had the *America for Americans* doctrine, the Japanese developed *fukoku-kyohei*—the movement to enrich the nation and strengthen the state. This became the dominant goal of Meiji Japan's economic statism.

Japan's nationalists were aware that *fukoku-kyohei* would be unproductive unless they uprooted the key institutional obstacles to economic progress. There was the need to centralize power and strengthen state structures. Meiji Japan subordinated the local authorities to the central government institutions. This involved the abolition of the *han*, their replacement with prefectures, and the unification of the Japanese state. Second, the unequal treaties of 1854 and 1858 (which legislated against the use of state power to nationalistically regulate the economy) were repealed. Japan had to use tariffs as instruments of economic nationalism. Third, the caste system of the Tokugawa regime and other antidevelopment feudal institutions, such as *kuge* (court aristocrat) or *daimyo* (feudal lord), were abolished. Fourth, legal reforms were carried out, closely modeled on the French legal system. The aim was not to adopt a Western culture of "rule-of-law." The aim was to shift from the Tokugawa "rule-by-status" to a new regime of "rule-*by*-law," defined as the "rule of bureaucrats" (Hendeson 1968, 415). This meant transforming the Tokugawa tradition of samurai-bureaucrats into an institutionalized system of "administrative guidance" (Johnson 1982, chap. 7). Japan also carried out land reforms guided by the "land-belongs-to-the-cultivator" philosophy. The ultimate objective of these institutional reforms was to transform the nation into a rich, strong, and prosperous industrial economy.

Japan's late industrialization is significant in two respects. First, Japan attained *in a few decades*, outcomes that took *centuries* in Britain's early industrialization. Second, Japan developed a capitalist economy that is nonetheless *unlike* Anglo-American capitalism. The nationality of Japanese capitalism is underpinned by a distinctly homegrown institution—the capitalist developmental state (Johnson 1982, 1999). At the core of this institution are several ingredients of effective economic statism. The paramount goal of state activism is economic transformation. Second, the state guides the market using a pilot agency (such as METI). The pilot agency is staffed with high quality economic bureaucrats who, among other things, perform intelligence gathering functions needed to transform the national economy. Third, the state does not "kick" private entrepreneurs out of the economy. It instead forges strategic alliances with the business community. Yet, the state does not succumb to the short-termist profit maximization ideology of private businesses. In other words, the state is simultaneously "embedded" in society and "autonomous" (Evans 1995). Finally, power and authority acquire a distinctive character. The politicians merely "reign"; state bureaucrats actually "rule." Put differently, formal authority is in the hands of politicians; real power in the bureaucracy.[9] It is these developmental credentials that enabled Japan to attain rapid and structural economic transformation. To what extent is "late, late" industrialization in Taiwan and Uganda consistent with, or different from, the experiences of *earlier* industrializers?

"LATE" INDUSTRIALIZATION IN TAIWAN AND UGANDA

As already indicated, both Taiwan and Uganda are former colonies (of Japan and Britain, respectively). Japanese colonialism in Taiwan was no doubt more developmental than British colonialism in Uganda (Ho 1978, 101; Mamdani 1976, 30–36). But Taiwan, like Uganda, emerged out of colonialism with an agricultural economy that was structured to supply food and other farm products to the former colonial power. More importantly, both Taiwan and Uganda emerged out of colonialism with strong wishes to industrialize and transform the national economy. Today, the two economies are substantially different. Taiwan is a high-tech economy known for manufacturing computers, electronics, and other high value-added products. It has risen to become the third leading exporter of IT products (after the United States and Japan). Uganda is still a Ricardian economy, with the agricultural sector employing 88 percent of the total labor force, accounting for 85 percent of total foreign exchange earnings, and contributing 54 percent of GDP. How does one account for Taiwan's effectiveness and Uganda's incapacity to translate its "wish" to industrialize into durable economic outcomes? The answer, I contend, defies modernization theory, dependency analysis, and other traditional theories of development. It primarily lies in the sphere of institutional political economy, privileging developmental ideologies and political institutions (particularly the developmental state) as the *primary* explanation of economic transformation, or the lack thereof.

In Taiwan, the dominant postwar ideology has been economic nationalism. Taiwan's postcolonial economic history started with massive agrarian reforms that redistributed land to the tiller (cf. Wade 1990). This not only removed a major obstacle to increased agricultural productivity—that is, landlordism. It effectively created a domestic market for local industries (particularly the textile industries). Taiwan also implemented substantial institutional innovations evidenced in the use of high quality economic bureaucrats, the strategic formulation of national economic goals, and the mobilization of long-term investment capital (Wade 1990, 240). By contrast, postcolonial Uganda implemented no structural institutional reforms. The main obstacle, it would seem, was the independence constitution (made in England) that created competing centers of authority between the central government and kingdom-states like Buganda (where *mailo*-landlords controlled both land and political power). Attempts by the first independence government (1962–71) to centralize political power and institute other nationalistic reforms faced bitter resistance from the local elites (Mamdani 1976). Today, after four decades of political independence, Uganda has not overcome its developmental obstacles. The Local Councils (LCs) of the current regime (1986–to date) undoubtedly represent a structural reform of the postcolonial state. But land reforms—the most crucial reforms in an agrarian economy—have not been carried out. This is because of two reasons. First, the armed struggle (1981–86) that brought Yoweri Museveni to presidency (1986–to date) obtained massive political and logistical support from the people of Buganda. President Museveni apparently found himself in a more difficult position than Chiang Kai-shek who had no political ties to the local landed elites.[10] Secondly, under the ongoing structural adjustment programs (SAPs) of the IMF/World Bank fraternity, the dominant economic ideology prioritizes "land markets" over nationalistic agrarian reforms. The claim is that the ownership and use of land, like other forms of property, must be based on the free market economics principle of *willing-seller, willing-buyer*. This is substantially different from Taiwan's state-guided "land-to-the-tiller" program.[11]

In the current era of globalization, the Taiwan-Uganda differences have widened, not narrowed. In Uganda, the dominant framework for national economic management has been economic liberalism, more specifically, *orthodox* adjustment. The "structural" adjustment programs of the IMF/World Bank fraternity have involved the replacement of state-managed foreign exchange rates with market-determined rates; the removal of state controls on product and factor prices; and the equalization of sales tax on imports and domestic products. These were the key elements of orthodox adjustment in the early to mid-1980s. Under the current regime of President Museveni, Uganda has implemented more far-reaching economic reforms. Public servants have been retrenched from 320,000 in 1993 to 150,000 in 2000 (Kiiza 2000). The economy has been fully liberalized. The capital account and foreign exchange markets have been deregulated. A liberalized regime of trade and industrial policy has also been institutionalized. Most importantly, several state-owned enterprises (like Nile Hotel Complex) have been privatized.

The problem is not necessarily the sale of *public* enterprises to "private" individuals. The problem lies in the theoretical rationale of privatization and the long-term developmental implications of the new regime. The orthodox claim is that the state is an inefficient economic manager and must, *ipso facto*, be kicked out of the economy. Yet, from an "efficiency" perspective, privatization in Uganda defies economic logic. The divestitures completed so far have achieved *less* than their asset value. This is largely because the "for-sale" parastatals (such as the five-star Nile Hotel Complex) were grossly undervalued. Second, government is injecting *more* moneys in the enterprises (prior to divestiture) than it is realizing from the sales. By June 30, 1997, "the net accumulated sales proceeds from privatization amounted to Shs $90 billion, leaving a net deficit of Shs 5.6bn."[12] Third, by the beginning of the year 2000, only twenty-eight of the fifty-five privatized enterprises had been fully paid for. Yet, the moneys from divestiture have been "borrowed" by politically connected "predators" (such as Salim Saleh, brother to President Museveni). These and other internal flaws of privatization question the "efficiency" claims of economic liberalism. It must, nevertheless, be emphasized that Uganda's focus on free market reforms is "rational," for the alternative Taiwan-style reforms are risky, politically. They, therefore, require a state that has political *autonomy* from vested interests. Far-reaching reforms are also difficult to implement precisely because they call for a committed, meritocratic state bureaucracy—the very opposite of Uganda's underpaid, demotivated, and demoralized civil service (which is typically recruited via the politics of "who-knows-whom").[13] How, then, does Uganda's economic liberalism compare with Taiwan's species of adjustment?

In the 1980s and 1990s, Taiwan undoubtedly implemented important economic reforms. The Little Tiger *formally* shifted from a fixed exchange rate to a flexible rate in February 1979. Thereafter, a regime of liberalized interest rates and capital flows has been *officially* encouraged (although in practice, the central bank has operated some form of managed exchange rate). In trade and industrial policy, both tariff and non-tariff barriers have been relaxed (Kuo and Liu 1998, 181). Between 1982 and 1989, the average nominal tariff rate declined from 31.0 percent to 9.7 percent. By 1995, the rate had declined further to 8.6 percent (DGBAS 1998). Today, "further liberalization," "adjustment," and "globalization" are common terminologies in Taiwan's political economy lexicon. The orthodox conclusion is that Taiwan has embraced Anglo-Americanism and globalization (Schive 1999, 47–48). Evidence, however, suggests that Taiwan's economic reforms are *unlike* the globally integrated liberal policies of Anglo-American ideology. In contrast with Uganda's donor-driven programs, adjustment in Taiwan has been distinctly *mercantilist*. While the trigger of economic reform has oftentimes come from abroad, the object of adjustment has never been global market integration. The object has invariably been to strengthen the Taiwanese national economy in the face of both internal and external challenges of economic governance. In the event of the petroleum crisis (1970–73 and 1979–80), Taiwan responded by actively restructuring *and* upgrading its industrial base. The aim was to acquire cutting-edge technology (via increased R&D investment) and transform the economy into a high value-added industrial and information economy. In the face of American protectionism (under the Omnibus Trade Act) in the 1980s, Taiwan's response was distinctly nationalistic. The Little Tiger strategically allowed the NT dollar to appreciate from 39.85 to 35.50 to the U.S. dollar. It also sent a state-led "purchasing mission" to the United States to buy American goods. The aim was *to appear* to be doing something to reduce the United States' trade deficit with Taiwan.[14] Faced with the healthy but real problem of *trade surplus* in the mid-1980s, Taiwan, again, strategically adjusted its tools of economic nationalism. Some form of adjustment was encouraged to cool down the rising economic temperature. The rise of President Chen Shui-bian to power (in May 2000) undoubtedly broke the long postwar regime of the KMT. But the economic bureaucracy appears to have remained intact. Today, Taiwan continues to grapple with capital surpluses, trade surpluses, rising wages, and other problems of a mature industrial economy. So how does Taiwan's response to its economic challenges compare with Uganda's approach?

In contrast with Uganda's "big-bang" adoption of economic liberalism, Taiwan has typically taken a calculated, cautious, and coordinated approach to economic reform. Taiwan also continues to set long-term industrial priorities for the national economy. In the 1980s, these were defined on the basis of a *2-high, 2-large, 2-low* formula. This meant that Taiwan would prioritize industries that were "*high* in technology intensity, *high* in value-added; *large* in market potential, *large* in industrial linkage (forward or backward), *low* in energy consumption, or *low* in pollution" (CIER 1995, 12). More recently, the state has prioritized ten new millennium industries. "telecommunications, information, consumer electronics, semiconductors, precision machinery and automation, aerospace, advanced materials, specialty chemicals and pharmaceuticals, medical and health care, and pollution control and treatment" (IDB/MOEA 2001). These industries were prioritized "because they cause little pollution, have strong market potential, are technologically demanding, but not heavily energy reliant, and have high value-added products" (IDB/MOEA 2001). Moreover, in contrast with Uganda's erosion-of-the-state scenario, economic reform in Taiwan has not precluded the use of state power to construct development enhancing institutions. The Hsinchu Science-based industrial park, for example, was set up in 1980 at the very dawn of the current era of globalization. By the year 2001, "a total of 88 well-planned industrial parks covering a total area of 11,895 hectares were completed, and 23 new parks with a total area of 18,414 hectares" were under construction (IDB/MOEA 2001). The aim of these developmental institutions is to transform the island into a *higher* technology and knowledge intensive economy.

What difference, one might ask, has *mercantile* adjustment made in Taiwan in comparison with *orthodox* adjustment in Uganda? If one measures economic performance in terms of GDP growth rates alone, one could confidently declare that there is no substantial difference. Uganda has registered growth rates of 7.4 percent a year since 1987 and is now growing at 5.7 percent. This rapid growth—attained under a liberal economic regime—is comparable to Taiwan's postwar rates of GDP growth (CEPD, various years). If, however, one measures economic performance in terms of *structural* transformation, a different picture emerges. Two crucial variables will be highlighted to illustrate the point at issue. First is the sectoral source of GDP; second is the share of higher value-added products in total exports.[15]

Sectoral Distribution of GDP

Taiwan and Uganda have had substantial differences in their sectoral sources of GDP. In Taiwan, the share of agriculture in total GDP declined from 32.2 percent in 1952 to 7.7 percent in 1980. By 1999, this figure had declined further to only 2.6 percent. Today, it is estimated to be about 2.5 percent (CEPD 2000, 52). Closely related to the decline in the importance of agriculture is the rapid expansion of the higher value-added industrial and services sectors. The share of industry (liberally defined to include manufacturing, construction, and electricity, gas, and water) more than doubled from 19.7 percent in 1952 to 45.7 percent in 1980. This figure reached an all-time high of 47.1 percent in 1987 and thereafter declined consistently to 41 percent in 1990 and 33 percent in 1999 (CEPD 2000, Table 3–8b, 52). Two issues are worth emphasizing. One is that the bulk of industrial expansion took place in the higher value-added "manufacturing" subsector. The share of manufacturing in total GDP increased from 12.9 percent in 1952 to 36 percent in 1980. It reached a peak of nearly 40 percent in 1986, and gradually declined to 33.2 percent in 1990 and 26.4 percent in 1999 (Kiiza 2002, Table 5.2). Second, the relative fall in the importance of the industrial sector after 1987 is closely associated with the substantial expansion of the services sector. Between 1987 and 1999, as the relative importance of industry fell, that of the services sector increased from 48 percent to 64.3 percent. In short, beginning with the second half of the 1980s, Taiwan acquired the symptoms of a mature developed economy with a hi-tech industrial sector whose significance was, nevertheless, being replaced by high quality services. It is this type of Taiwan that embarked on "structural" adjustment in 1988. Taiwan's new economic ideology was consistent with the changing priorities of economic nationalism rather than the external pressures of the global political economy.

In the case of Uganda, the share of agriculture in total GDP declined marginally from 53.4 percent in 1963 to 51.7 percent in 1980 (MOFPED 2000, A12). By 1985, it had *increased* again to 54.8 percent. Between 1990 and 2000, agriculture's share declined gradually from 53.5 percent to about 42 percent. Over the same period, the share of "manufacturing" (defined broadly to include the low value-added processing activities) oscillated between 7.8 percent in 1963 to 8.7 percent in 1970. Thereafter, it declined to 4.4 percent in 1980, and gradually increased to nearly 10 percent in 1999 (a level that is lower than Taiwan's 12.9 percent in 1952). This underscores a substantial distinction between Taiwan and Uganda. Taiwan implemented some form of liberalization in the late 1980s *after* it had attained industrialized nation status. By contrast, Uganda's globally integrated liberalization in the 1980s and 1990s took place in a predominantly Ricardian *agricultural* economy with a low value-added industrial sector. Uganda's liberalization, it seems, was premature. It was, in effect, an exposure of the local embryonic firms to the competitive pressures of the global marketplace. This is antithetical to the logic of durable economic nationalism.

Share of High Value-Added Products in Total Exports

The share of high value-added manufactured products in total exports is a useful proxy of *the value* that is exported by the national economy into the competitive world markets. In Taiwan, the share of "processed" agricultural products in total visible exports declined substantially from about 70 percent in 1952 to 5.6 percent in 1980 (CEPD, various issues). The value of unprocessed agricultural exports increased from 22.4 percent in 1952 to the all-time high level of 27.6 percent in 1955. It then declined remarkably to 3.6 percent in 1980. By 1999, agricultural exports (0.3 percent) and processed agricultural products (1.3 percent) were insignificant in Taiwan's export basket. What had happened?[16] The share of industrial products increased from less than 10 percent in 1952 to 50.5 percent in 1962 (Uganda's year of independence). By 1980, the industrial products accounted for 90.8 percent of Taiwan's exports, a figure that expanded further to 98.4 percent in 1999 (CEPD 2000, 208). This suggests that Taiwan's international competitiveness has substantially increased since the 1950s.

In Uganda, the no-value-added "food and live animals" subsector accounted for 64 percent of the net domestic exports in 1968. By 1974, the share of this subsector in total domestic exports had *increased* to nearly 80 percent, with coffee and tea accounting for 78 percent of total domestic exports. By the 1990s, no structural change had taken place. The share of coffee exports oscillated between 64.2 percent in 1991, 74.6 percent in 1994, and 55.1 percent in 1998 (UBS 1999, 86). Over the same period, the share of the traditional exports (coffee, cotton, tea, and tobacco) fluctuated between 76.4 percent in 1991, 80 percent in 1994, and 65.9 percent in 1998. In comparison with Taiwan, and with the sole exception of 1995 and 1996, Uganda's traditional exports have been fetching less dollar values than Taiwan's *agricultural* exports in the 1980s and 1990s. It is also important to note that Uganda's export basket has no *industrial* products. The competitiveness of Uganda's primary commodity exports in the global markets is therefore highly suspect.

CONCLUSION

This chapter set out to examine the link between mercantilism and the struggle for late industrialization in the current era of globalization. Comparative historical evidence strongly suggests that no country—early or late industrializer—has ever developed in the context of free "global" markets. Virtually all effective developers have used domestic institutions, particularly the state, to mediate the external political economy pressures and govern the national economy *in the national interest*. On the basis of concrete historical evidence, it seems reasonable to conclude, with Dani Rodrik (2001) that there is "no convincing evidence" that globalization boosts late industrialization. Global market integration is *no* recipe for late economic transformation. This is not to deny the potential benefits of "global" information flows, technological diffusion, and FDI flows for late development. The point, rather, is that effective late industrialization is unlikely unless a developing country participates in the world economy on its own terms, not the terms dictated by the external political economy pressures.

The WTO rules and the now ubiquitous free trade agreements (FTAs) have undoubtedly changed the context of late industrialization. However, serious developing countries still have room to maneuver. For example, the use of regional integration as an avenue for late industrialization is still permissible under the WTO rules. Second, neither the WTO rules nor the FTAs can uproot innovative industrial policies. The struggle for late industrialization now needs to be launched more shrewdly in the domestic economy—via high quality education; scientific and technological innovation; the establishment of development enhancing institutions (such as Export Processing Zones); and innovative industrial policies (such as tax holidays for priority industries).

Evidence suggests, thirdly, that developing countries *voluntarily* accept the restrictive WTO and FTA rules. This is not to downplay the subtle economic diplomacy of the advanced countries. The Economic Partnership Agreements (EPAs) between the EU and the African, Caribbean, and Pacific (ACP) countries are a case in point. The EU is offering EUR 22 billion to the ACP countries over the period 2008 to 2013, as an "incentive" for signing the FTAs with the EU. The official rhetoric is that this money would help ACP countries "prepare new structural reforms and trade policies," European Union [EU] 2008, 1). What is not explicitly stated is that the "aid-for-trade" is meant to make ACP countries WTO compliant, that is, adopting freer trade with the ultracompetitive economies in the North and in Asia. Nor is it explicitly stated that the EU is reintroducing (via the FTAs) the key elements of the "Singapore Issues" that were resisted by developing countries in the WTO framework. My fundamental point, however, is that developing countries are not as helpless as they often claim. Rather than blindly endorsing the WTO rules and FTAs, developing countries need to do their homework. Rather than endlessly blaming the EU for using subtle diplomacy to advance their *national* interests, developing countries need to strengthen the team that negotiates with foreign officials. We need to recruit the best and brightest national skills to take charge of our national developmental affairs. We also need to reclaim the state from neoliberal state elites and transform government into a key strategic player in the economy. The ultimate goal is to attain the two-pronged objective of economic mercantilism—strengthening the state and enriching the nation. The struggle is difficult but no impossible.

The overall conclusion of this study is simple. Globalization is not the polar opposite of economic mercantilism. It is *a distinctive form of economic nationalism*—that of the dominant industrial economies. From a developing country's perspective, strategic state intervention in the national economy makes a difference. Economic nationalism matters. Catch-up industrializers, like Taiwan, that politically construct national competitive advantages deliver more substantial economic outcomes than nation-states, like Uganda, that place their hopes on neoliberal globalism.

REFERENCES

Amsden, Alice. 2001. *The rise of "the rest": Challenges to the West from late-industrialising economies.* Oxford: Oxford University Press.

Calleo, D. P. et al. 1973. *America and the world political economy: Atlantic dreams and national realities.* Bloomington and London: Indiana University Press.

Cameron, R. 1989. *A concise economic history of the world: From Paleolithic times to the present.* New York, Oxford: Oxford University Press.

CEPD (Council for Economic Planning and Development). *Taiwan statistical data book.* Taipei: ROC. Various Years.

Chang, H-j. 2001. Intellectual property rights and economic development: Historical lessons and emerging issues. *Journal of Human Development* 2 (2): 289–311.

———. 2002. *Kicking away the ladder: Development strategies in historical perspective.* London: Anthem Press.

———. 2007. *Bad samaritans: Rich nations, poor policies & the threat to the developing world.* London: Random House.

Chang, Han-yu, and H. Myers Ramon. 1963. Japanese colonial development policy in Taiwan, 1895–1906: A case of bureaucratic entrepreneurship. *Journal of Asian Studies* 22 (4): 143–83.

CIECD (Council for International Economic Cooperation and Development). 1965. *Fourth four-year plan for economic development, 1965–68.* Taipei: ROC.

CIER (Chung-hua Institute for Economic Research). 1995. *Technology support institutions and policy priorities for industrial development in Taiwan, R.O.C.: A country report.*

Cohen, S., and Zysman, J. 1987. *Manufacturing matters: The Myth of a post-industrial economy.* New York: Basic Books.

Cole, C. W. 1964. *Colbert and a century of French mercantilism.* Vol. 2. London: Frank Cass, 1939.

Crane, G. T. 1998. Economic nationalism: Bringing the nation back in. *Millennium Journal of International Studies* 27 (1): 55–75.

———. 1999. Imagining the economic nation: Globalization in China. *New Political Economy* 4 (2): 215–32. http://www.usyd.edu.au/ovidweb/ovidweb/cgi.

Crapol, E. P. 1973. *America for Americans: Economic nationalism and anglophobia in the late twentieth century.* Westport, CT: Greenwood.

Das, B. L. 1998. *The WTO agreements: Deficiencies, imbalances, and required changes.* Penang: Third World Network.

DGBAS (Directorate-General of Budgeting and Statistics) 1998. *Statistical abstract of national income, Taiwan area.* Taipei: ROC.

EC (European Commission). 2007. Trade and Development. http://ec.europa.eu/trade/issues/global/development/index_en.htm.

EU (European Union) 2008. Trade policy in practice: Interim economic partnership agreements http://www.delsen.ec.europa.eu/fr/telechargements/interim_economic_partnership_agreements.pdf.

Evans, Peter. 1995. *Embedded autonomy: States and industrial transformation.* Princeton, NJ: Princeton University Press.

Gann, L. H. 1984. Western and Japanese colonialism: Some preliminary comparisons. In *The Japanese colonial empire, 1895–1945, ed.* R. H. Myers and Mark R. Peattie. Princeton, NJ: Princeton University Press.

Gerschenkron, Alexander. 1962. *Economic backwardness in historical perspective.* Cambridge: Harvard University Press.

Gold, T. 1988. Colonial origins of Taiwanese capitalism. In *Contending approaches to the political economy of Taiwan,* ed. E. A. Winckler and S. Greenhalgh, 101–17. Armonk and New York: M. E. Sharpe.

Greider, W. 1997. *One world, ready or not: The manic logic of global capitalism.* New York: Simon and Schuster.

Hane, M. 1986. *Modern Japan: A historical survey.* Boulder and London: Westview.

Haque, Irfan ul. 2007. Rethinking industrial policy. *UNCTAD Discussion Papers* 183.

Hirschman, Albert O. 1958. *The strategy of economic development.* New Haven, CT: Yale University Press.

Hirst, P., and G. Thompson. 1996. *Globalization in question: The international economy and the possibilities of governance.* Cambridge: Polity.

Ho, S. P. S. 1978. *Economic development of Taiwan, 1860–1970.* New Haven, CT: Yale University Press.

Hobsbawm, E. J. 1968. *Industry and empire: An economic history of Britain since 1750.* London: Weidenfeld and Nicolson.

Hoekman, Bernard, and M. M. Kostecki. 2001. *The political economy of the world trading system: The WTO and beyond.* 2nd ed. Oxford: Oxford University Press.

IDB/MOEA (Industrial Development Bureau/Ministry of Economic Affairs). 2001. *Course of industrial development.* http://www.moeaidb.gov.tw/idb/indintro/etext/1.htm.

IPC (International Food & Agricultural Trade Policy Council). 2007. Economic partnership agreements between the EU and Africa: The importance of trade and development. *IPC Issue Brief* 23.

Ismail, Faizel. 2006. How can least developed countries and other small, weak, and vulnerable economies also gain from the Doha development agenda on the road to Hong Kong? *Journal of World Trade* 40 (1): 37–68.

Johnson, C. 1982. *MITI and the Japanese miracle: The growth of industrial policy, 1925–1975.* Stanford: Stanford University Press.

Khor, Martin, 2004. *The Singapore issues in the WTO: Implications and recent developments.* Penang: Third World Network.

Kiiza, Julius 2001. *Does economic nationalism make sense in an era of globalization? A comparative analysis of Taiwan and Uganda,* PhD diss., University of Sydney.

———. 2007. Developmental nationalism and economic performance in Africa: The case of three "successful" African economies. In *Institutional change and economic development,* ed. Ha-Joon Chang, 281–300. New York: United Nations University Press; London: Anthem.

Kumar, Nagesh, and Kevin Gallagher. 2006. Relevance of "policy space" for development. implications for multilateral trade negotiations. *ICTSD draft paper.*

Kindleberger, Charles P. 1996. *World economic primacy: 1500 to 1900.* New York and Oxford:. Oxford University Press.

Kuo, S. W. Y., and C. Y. Liu. 1998. Taiwan. In *East Asia in crisis: From being a miracle to needing one?*, ed. R. H. McLeod and R. Garnaut. London and New York: Routledge.

List, Friedrich. 1885. *National system of political economy*, trans. Samson S Lloyd. London: Longmans.

Mamdani, M. 1976. *Politics and class formation in Uganda.* London and Nairobi: Heinemann.

Mann, Michael. 1997. Has globalization ended the rise and rise of the nation-state? *Review of International Political Economy 4 (3): 472–96.*

McLeod, R. H., and R. Garnaut. 1998. *East Asia in crisis: From being a miracle to needing one?* London and New York. Routledge.

Michalak, Wieslaw, and Richard Gibb. 1997. Trading blocs and multilateralism in the world economy. http://jstor.org/jstor/gifcvtdir/.

MOFPED (Ministry of Finance, Planning, and Economic Development). 2000 *Background to the budget, 2000/01: Increasing efficiency in poverty reduction service delivery through output oriented budgeting.* Kampala, Uganda.

Mokyr, J, ed. 1999. *The British industrial revolution.* Boulder, CO: Westview.

Ohmae, Keinichi. 1995. *The borderless world.* New York: Collins.

Peattie, 1984. Introduction. In *The Japanese colonial empire, 1895–1945*, ed. Myers and Peattie, 3–52. Princeton, NJ: Princeton University Press.

Preparata, G. G., et al. 1996. Protecting the infant industry: Cosmopolitan versus nationalist economists. *International Journal of Social Economics* 23 (2): 4–34. http://www.usyd.edu.au/ovidweb/ovidweb/cgi.

Reich, R. B. 1992. *The work of nations.* New York: Vintage.

Reinert, Eric. 1999. The role of the state in economic growth. *Journal of Economic Studies* 26 (4–5): 268–326.

———. 2007. Institutionalism ancient, old and new: A historical perspective on institutions and uneven development. In *Institutional change and economic development*, ed. Ha-Joon Chang, 53–72. New York: United Nations University Press; London: Anthem.

Rodrik, Dani. 2001. The global governance of trade as if development really mattered. *UNDP research report.* New York.

———. 2004. Industrial policy for the twenty-first century. Paper prepared for UNIDO.

Schive, C. 1999. How was Taiwan's economy opened up? The foreign factor in appraisal. In *The political economy of Taiwan's development into the 21st century: Essays in memory of John C. H. Fei, vol. 2, ed.* Ranis, G.; Hu, Sheng-Cheng; and Chu, Yun-Peng, 31–50. Cheltenham, United Kingdom: Edward Elgar.

Schulman, S. 2000. Nationalist sources of international economic integration. *International Studies Quarterly 44 (3):* 365–90.

Schwartz, Herman. M. 2000. *States versus markets: History, geography, and the development of the international political economy.* New York: St Martin's.

Semmel, B. 1970. *The rise of free trade imperialism.* Cambridge: Cambridge University Press.

Smith, A. 1776/1937. *An inquiry into the nature and causes of the wealth of nations*, ed. E Cannan. New York. Modern Library Edition.

Tiedemann, A. E. 1974. Japan's economic foreign policies, 1868–93. In *Japan's foreign policy, 1868–1941, ed*. James W. Morley. New York. Columbia University Press.

UBS (Uganda Bureau of Statistics). 1999. Statistical abstract. Entebbe. UBS.

Uganda, 1998. *Vision 2025. A strategic framework for national development*. Vol. 1. Kampala: Ministry of Finance, Planning, and Economic Development.

———. 1999. *Vision 2025. A strategic framework for national development*. Vol. 2. Kampala: Ministry of Finance, Planning, and Economic Development.

Viner, Jacob. 1948. Power versus plenty as objectives of foreign policy in the seventeenth and eighteenth centuries. *World Politics*, 1–29.

Wade, Robert. 1990. *Governing the market: Economic theory and the role of government in East Asian industrialization*. Princeton, NJ: Princeton University Press.

———. 1996. Globalisation and its limits: Reports of the death of the national economy are greatly exaggerated. In *National diversity and global capitalism*, ed. Suzanne Berger and Ronald Dore. Ithaca, NY: Cornell University Press.

Wall, R. F. 1971. *Japan's century: An interpretation of Japanese history since the eighteenfifties*. London: The Historical Association.

Weiss, Linda 1998. *The myth of the powerless state: Governing the economy in a global era*. Cambridge. Polity Press.

———. 1999. Globalization and national governance: Antimony or interdependence? *Review of International Studies* 25 (5).

———. 2000. Developmental states in transition: Adapting, dismantling, innovating, not "normalising." *The Asia Pacific Review* 13 (1): 21–33.

Wilson, C. 1958/1967. *Mercantilism*. Cambridge. Historical Association.

NOTES

1. The WTO Agreements have been described as "Unequal Treaties," *unequal* in the sense that they disproportionately favour the powerful OECD economies at the expense of the less industrialized countries (cf. Das 1998, viii, 1–9; Khor 2000, 27–39; Chang 2001, 289). Developing countries are legally bound to change their national policies "in such diverse areas as services, agriculture, intellectual property and investment measures" (Khor 2000, 32). The aim is to "harmonize" their economic policies with the WTO regime. This implies "rolling back" infant industry protection and other national strategies of economic governance. Such initiatives are likely to undermine the economic performance of countries (like Uganda) that have competitive disadvantages in value-added industrial and information activities.

2. The earliest use of the term mercantile system appears in Victor Riquetti's (1763) *Philosophie Rurale*, in which he talks of the "absurd inconsistency of the mercantile system" (*systeme mercantile*) (329). This was an attack on the view that a nation benefits from the importation of money, an earlier theoretical perspective that understood mercantilism as that "system of economic doctrine . . . based on the principle that money alone is wealth," (*Oxford English Dictionary*, quoted in Coleman 1969, 1).

3. Dobb 1946, 209, quoted in Coleman 1969, 7. I hasten to point out, though, that mercantilism does not figure much in Karl Marx's treatment of history.

4. Spain, for example, declared the export of gold and silver punishable by death in the early sixteenth century. France declared the export of gold and silver illegal in 1506, 1540, 1548, and 1574 (Frieden and Lake 1987, 67).

5. In the fifteenth century, the Hohenzollern dynasty ruled over the Electorate of Bradenburg, whose capital city was Berlin. These rulers expanded and eventually brought Eastern Prussia under their control in 1618. Beginning with the rise of Frederick William, the "Great Elector," in 1640, these rulers were effective mercantilists. They built Brandenburg-Prussia into one of the most powerful nations in Europe. It is this Prussia that is described by historians as the precursor to modern Germany. The strategies that were used include some of the standard mercantilist policies—protective tariffs, grants of monopoly and subsidies to industry, and attracting skilled entrepreneurs and artisans to migrate and settle in their territory. More important was the internal organization of the state. Prussia's rulers centralized their administration, hired corps of professional civil servants, and demanded that their bureaucrats meet high standards of accountability. They deepened their tax-collection infrastructure, and were frugal in revenue expenditure, compared to the luxury and splendor of Spain, for example. In short, Prussia "created an efficient state mechanism that was quite exceptional in the Europe of its day" (Cameron 1989, 143).

6. For a growing, but still limited, body of scholarship that attempts to "reinvent" economic history, see Hobsbawn 1968; Weiss and Hobson 1995; Reinert 1999; and Chang 2002.

7. The G8 summit that recently took place in Genoa, Italy (July 20–22, 2001) is a case in point. Prime Minister Tony Blair of the United Kingdom, like President George Bush of America, criticized the "anti-globalization" riots of individuals and groups that appear to be threatened by global economic integration. Tony Blair, like the American president, argued that an increase in free trade is the best way to go (BBC News, "G8 leaders focus on world poverty," http://newsvote .bbc.co.uk/hi/english/business/newsid_1448000/1448241.stm. A notable exception to this unquestioning "followership" position is the Kyoto protocol of March 2001. George Bush rejected the protocol, arguing that controlling green gas emissions/global warming was antithetical to America's *national* (read "business") interests. Tony Blair and other G8 leaders have objected to this.

8. In a key speech to the World Bank prior to the G8 summit in Genoa (July 20–22, 2001), President George Bush asserted: "Those who protest free trade are no friends of the poor. . . . What some call globalization is in fact the triumph of human liberty stretching across national borders" (see BBC News, "Bush's agenda for Genoa" on http://newsvote.bbc.co.uk/hi/english/business/newsid _1448000/1448241.stm.

9. These elements of the developmental state are under review in the light of Japan's economic troubles (since 1992), the unemployment crisis that hit "a post-war high of 5 per cent" (*The Sydney Morning Herald, September 6, 2001*), and other challenges facing the national economy. The transformation of Japan's postwar superministry MITI into METI (Ministry of Economy, Trade and Industry) was itself precipitated by the need to address "not the reform of individual policies and systems," but rather planning a "major transformation of the entire post-war Japanese socio-economic system" (Takeo Hiranuma, Minister of Economy, Trade and Industry, on http://www.meti.go.jp/english/topic/data/ eMETIStarte.html.

10. Indeed, while Chiang initiated massive land reforms, thereby removing a major institutional fetter to increased agricultural productivity, Museveni *restored* the monarchy in Uganda (in 1993). In effect, Uganda's president gave a "thumbs-up" to the institution of landlordism. The aim, it would seem, was to build political

capital in Buganda where the monarchy is supported by a substantial number of people.

11. For a discussion of other alternatives to the "willing-seller, willing-buyer" principle (e.g., land taxes on unused land designed to encourage productive land use), see Mazibuko Jara 2001, RDP [the Reconstruction and Development Program of South Africa] Gave Land Remedy, in *The Sowetan* (Johannesburg) http://allafrica.com/stories/printable/200107130248.html.

12. Ddumba-Ssentamu, 2001. The privatization process and its impact on society, cited in *The Monitor*, March 14, 2001 on http://www.monitor.co.ug/news.

13. Taiwan's unfaltering commitment to economic nationalism was also shaped by two crucial geopolitical factors: U.S. interest in Taiwan (for ideological and strategic reasons) and the perennial threat of invasion from mainland China. Uganda has had no overwhelming national crisis to trigger long-term institutional reforms.

14. The actual economic outcomes favored Taiwan, not America.

15. Other crucial variables have been omitted because of limited space. They include. the sectoral distribution of employment; the relative trends and levels of per capita GDP; the structure of foreign trade; the value of imports and exports; plus the institutions (the developmental state in Taiwan and the "predatory" state in Uganda) underpinning the Taiwan-Uganda variations in economic performance. For a detailed analysis, see Kiiza (2002).

16. It is worth noting that the value of Taiwan's agricultural exports was actually *higher* in the 1980s and 1990s than it was in the 1950s and 1960s. It is the *share* of these products in total exports that had substantially fallen, relative to the high value-added manufactured exports.

CHAPTER 10

ZIMBABWEAN LAND REDISTRIBUTION!

GLOBALIZATION AND NEOLIBERAL NARRATIVES AND TRANSNATIONAL CONNECTIONS

Blair Rutherford

INTRODUCTION

Zimbabwe has been at the forefront of the debates and contestations concerning the intersection of Africa and the world since 2000, at least in the Anglophone media, academic, and policy discourses. Major continental institutions, such as the African Union and its African Commission on Human and People's Rights; regional bodies, such as the Southern African Development Committee (SADC); significant pan-African initiatives to engage with the outside world, such as the New Partnership for Africa's Development (NEPAD); multilateral institutions, such as United Nations and the Commonwealth; and the recent European Union-Africa Summit in Portugal (in December 2007) have seen recent meetings and initiatives founded on different interpretations of what has been happening in Zimbabwe.

* I want to thank Joseph Mensah and Edward Osei Kwadwo Prempeh for my inclusion in this book; I was involved as an editor for their excellent articles in the journal *SPE*.

Whereas policy-makers, politicians, and media commentators in North America, Europe, and many non-African Commonwealth countries have generally been highly critical of the Zimbabwean government's conduct concerning elections, upholding the rule of law and human rights abuses, many African leaders argue such concerns are either mistaken or should not be used to undermine continental initiatives. As the Senegalese foreign minister, Cheikh Tidiane Gadio, a strong proponent of NEPAD, lamented in 2002, "How can the Senegalese people, the Malian people be held accountable for what happened in Zimbabwe?" (cited in Amosu and Cobb Jr. 2002; see also Taylor 2002). Five years later, there was a similar diplomatic flurry over the invitation of President Mugabe to Lisbon to attend the second EU-Africa summit. British Prime Minister Gordon Brown and a few other European heads of state refused to attend, and human rights groups in Europe and Zimbabwe condemned the invitation. In contrast, many African leaders rallied around President Mugabe, including when he was criticized at the conference by, amongst others, the German chancellor, Angela Merkel. During this conference, President Abdulaye Wade of Senegal rebutted such criticism, saying, "What Ms. Merkel said is on the basis of her information. Sadly her information is not correct" (cited in Mock 2007).

The lines of division over Zimbabwe are not always clear-cut—there are many African critics of President Mugabe and his government, not the least of all in Zimbabwe itself, and there is a minority of those in North America, Europe, and elsewhere outside of Africa who support the actions of the Zimbabwean government. But overall, the division between "Africa and the West" has become greatly mobilized in regards to debates concerning the Zimbabwean government. Whereas President Mugabe and his supporters can take some credit in framing the national crises and disputes as a "West versus Africa" issue (see, e.g., Freeman 2005a, 2005b), it is a frame that comes easily for many analysts who draw on this dichotomy to understand contemporary and historical political economy processes on the continent. It is a dichotomy that easily blends into a contrast between imperialism (and its current manifestations, such as globalization and neoliberalism) and sovereignty, be it continental or, more commonly, national.

For example, the well-known media champion of "free markets," *The Economist*, gloatingly held up the horrendous economic conditions that have visibly emerged in Zimbabwe since 2000 as the sign of what happens when "anti-globalization" rhetoric begins to control the policy levers of a national economy: To the foes of globalisation, President Robert Mugabe's views are unexceptional. He argues that "runaway market forces" are leading a "vicious, all-out assault on the poor." He decries the modern trend of "banishing the state from the public sphere for the benefit of big business." What sets him apart from other anti-globalisers, however, is that he has been able to put his ideas into practice (*The Economist* 2002).

Following from its ideological project that free markets promoted by the neoliberal agendas of the International Monetary Fund (IMF) and the World

Bank do no harm, the magazine concludes with its syllogism that "greater efficiency leads to greater wealth, and vice versa, as Zimbabwe so harrowingly shows. Nowhere has withdrawn so swiftly from the global economy, nor seen such a thorough reversal of neoliberal policies. The results—an economy that has contracted by 35% in five years, and half the population in need of food aid—are hard to paper over" (*The Economist* 2002). For this influential magazine, Zimbabwe's *economic* crisis—inflation in late 2007 in the five digits, official unemployment over 80 percent, and the scarcity of most commodities from the store shelves—is simply due to defiance of so-called rational and universal economic principles (see also Richardson 2005).

In contrast, President Mugabe and his supporters are defiant against "Western imperialism" and its Zimbabwean "stooges." Since 2000, President Mugabe has frequently characterized the main Zimbabwean opposition party, the Movement for Democratic Change (MDC), as "a tool of Western imperialism" (cited, e.g., in Itano 2005). He portrays the economic problems of the country as caused by "Western sanctions" and the meddling of "imperialist interests," that is, the U.K. and U.S. governments. As he (2007) eloquently declared in his September 2007 speech to the General Assembly of the United Nations in New York City, the problems of Zimbabwe lie in its colonial history and the continuing inequalities on the world scale. Accordingly, President Mugabe reasoned, the Zimbabwean government is merely protecting the sovereignty of Zimbabwe in the face of the hostile West:

Mr President,

Zimbabwe won its independence on 18th April, 1980, after a protracted war against British colonial imperialism which denied us human rights and democracy. That colonial system which suppressed and oppressed us enjoyed the support of many countries of the West who were signatories to the UN Universal Declaration of Human Rights.

Even after 1945, it would appear that the Berlin Conference of 1884, through which Africa was parcelled to colonial European powers, remained stronger than the Universal Declaration of Human Rights. It is therefore clear that for the West, vested economic interests, racial and ethnocentric considerations proved stronger than their adherence to principles of the Universal Declaration of Human Rights.

The West still negates our sovereignties by way of control of our resources, in the process making us mere chattels in our own lands, mere minders of its trans-national interests. In my own country and other sister states in Southern Africa, the most visible form of this control has been over land despoiled from us at the onset of British colonialism.

That control largely persists, although it stands firmly challenged in Zimbabwe, thereby triggering the current stand-off between us and Britain, supported by her cousin states, most notably the United States and Australia. Mr Bush, Mr. Blair and now Mr Brown's sense of human rights precludes our people's right to their God-given resources, which in their view must be controlled by their kith and kin. I am termed dictator because I have rejected this supremacist view and frustrated the neo-colonialists.

Mr President,

Clearly the history of the struggle for our own national and people's rights is unknown to the president of the United States of America. He thinks the Declaration of Human Rights starts with his last term in office! He thinks she can introduce to us, who bore the brunt of fighting for the freedoms of our peoples, the virtues of the Universal Declaration of Human Rights. What rank hypocrisy!

This current, mass-mediated political and policy contestation over Zimbabwe thus appears to fall along a familiar division: pro-West and pro-globalization against pro-national sovereignty and anti-imperialism. Yet, such a contestation rests on significant contradictions—the non-African critics often do so in the name of the Zimbabwean people, a claim of sovereignty they do not possess other than in the name of universal human rights. In turn, the proponents of sovereignty, be it continental or national, will be doing so in terms of clamoring for Zimbabwe's participation in international events or mechanisms, including those like NEPAD that are strongly associated with neoliberalism and globalization (Bond 2002). However, I content that this familiar and, for some, comforting dichotomy of pro-/anti- globalization and West/African sovereignty misses particular transnational and national dimensions of the conflict in Zimbabwe, hindering both analyses and politics.

Such contradictions suggest that basing one's analysis on a singular characterization of globalization or sovereignty misses out the varied dimensions of controversies concerning the intersections between Africa's development and neoliberal globalization, at both the continental and national scales (see Chapter 1 of this volume). I argue here that "globalization" is neither something that has yet to come to Africa, due to the intransigence of leaders such as Mugabe, nor an all-dominating pressure that such African leaders are valiantly resisting. Rather, following the analysis of James Ferguson (2006, 41), I suggest that the case of Zimbabwe shows how "specific forms of 'global' integration on the continent coexist with specific—and equally 'global'—forms of exclusion, marginalization, and disconnection." Providing a situated understanding of the Zimbabwe land crisis vis-à-vis transnational and national processes and influences entails examining both the forms of interconnections as well as "the material inequalities and spatial and scalar disjunctures that such interconnections both depend on and, in some ways, help to produce" (Ferguson 2006, 49). In so doing, I seek to go beyond this paralyzing dichotomy of "West versus Africa," which channels responses to Zimbabwe and the global (dis-)order today.

To illustrate my argument, I focus on the politics of land in Zimbabwe. Most commentators agree that the government-enabled and -abetted occupations of white-owned commercial farms, starting in February 2000, has helped to catapult Zimbabwe into the center of the Anglophone debates concerning Africa and the world. The massive and, as even confirmed now by its promoters and supporters (e.g., News24, 2007), chaotic land redistribution activities have led to the removal of nearly four thousand white, predominantly Zimbabwean, commercial farmers from the land, and their commercial farms being parceled out amongst tens of thousands of black Zimbabweans. I examine some of the particular transnational interconnections and their material inequalities and disjuncture that are occluded by the simple pro-/anti-globalization division, before turning to the situation of farmworkers and the politics of land to rethink the analytical utility of the concept of national sovereignty. Before doing so, I will briefly discuss my theoretical perspective concerning globalization and sovereignty.

Theoretical Interlude

As noted in other chapters of this book, there is much debate and analysis of what globalization entails and when it began. Rather than entering into the fray here, I am more interested in examining transnational activities—be they uneven "flows" or "hops" of ideas, money, bodies, institutions, and/or technologies—and how they intersect with other projects and activities at different scales of action. Some of these transnational activities are labeled "global" by those involved and/or by those affected or commenting on them. But rather than assume that these activities are necessarily the same or have a singular effect, I aim to examine how the labeling of them as such may miss out on other dimensions, understandings, and effects of such activities. In making this argument, I draw on the work of James Ferguson, Anna Tsing, and Donald Moore.

In his recent book, Ferguson (2006) examines how Africa is an "inconvenience" to theorists, advocates, and detractors of "globalization," as its political economies do not simply follow either the successful or the negative portrayals of the spread of neoliberal capitalism. Rather, he argues that current forms of international investment and projects into Africa largely take place in the form of enclaves (e.g., particular mining operations or wildlife conservancies), with great emphasis on securing their boundaries against the surrounding African locales and peoples. As he contends (Ferguson 2006, 47), the "'global' does not 'flow,' thereby connecting and watering contiguous spaces; it hops instead, efficiently connecting the enclaved points in the network while excluding (with equal efficiency) the spaces that lie between the points."

Analogous to what Ferguson does to the term "modernity," I take "globalization" to not be a stable category with a universal set of meanings, but rather as a "native category" that does particular work in different contexts for differentially situated social actors. Ferguson argues that for many Africans, "modernity" is not a goal that can easily be achieved through planning and markets, but rather a global status of rank and privilege from which most Africans are excluded or, for some, have lost over time. With the fragmentation and dissolution of the promises of international and national development in many parts of Africa, and for the majority of Africans, such ranks have "become not stages to be passed through but non-serialized statuses that are separated from each other by exclusionary walls, not developmental stairways" (Ferguson 2006, 189). Accordingly, "globalization" as a "native category" means its semantic work can entail the assumption that it will usher in great wealth, or, perhaps, it is the new cover for Western imperialism against which stalwarts of sovereignty need to defend. This is not a nominalist position, but rather an ethnographic one, trying to understand what categories do in particular social projects.

Anna Tsing's (2005) work is instrumental here. Tsing argues against assuming a separation between "the local" and "the global," as many social science engagements with globalization end up doing as they try to understand specific responses to planetary activities. Such analytical perspectives tend to assume a homogeneity and uniformity of "global" processes and motion toward the "local" for social and cultural heterogeneity. This leads to what she calls the dilemma of falling into a tired dichotomy, invoking "distinctions between local reactions and global forces, local consumption and global circulation, local resistance and global structures of capitalism, local translation and global imagination" (Tsing 2005, 58). Instead, she suggests examining activities that are global (or "local" or "national") as "scale-making projects"—political and social efforts that seek to bring spatial dimensionality into being, often by becoming entangled in other scale-making projects of, say, national or regional scales. In short, successful "global" projects may come to fruition only through their involvement with particular "local" or "national" scale projects. In turn, national-scale projects such as sovereignty are inevitably dependent on transnational activities and projects, even if the latter are not explicitly noted or actively downplayed (Mitchell 1991).

Such attention to spatializing practices also dislodges the common suturing of sovereignty to the nation-state. Rather, such a coupling is the result of particular national-scale projects that may become entangled in other selective sovereignties, all of which "pivot on the production of scale, subjection, and territory" (Moore 2005, 223). Moore carefully examines such intertwining and historically situated sovereignties between the colonial and postcolonial states and chiefly rule and other sovereign dynamics (such as coming from rainmakers): "Fusing together anthropological and administrative models of polity and social evolution, indirect rule constructed one sovereign slot, a chief, mapped to a singular African landscape, a tribal territory. Postcolonial administrators largely followed this institutional [model]" (Moore 2005, 222). Below I will follow a similar analysis by sketching out the sovereign space of European farmers in regard to farmworkers (see also Rutherford 2008).

Accordingly, what some may call global processes in regard to Zimbabwe may have much more specific dimensions as they become "entangled" (Moore 2005, 4) in other social and political projects of varying scales. My aim here is not to identify what is properly "global" or "national," but rather to examine how such analytical evaluations miss the complicated cultural politics concerning land and labour in rural Zimbabwe.

GLOBAL (DIS-)CONNECTIONS AND LAND

Land politics in Zimbabwe have been intimately connected to global connections and disconnections since 1890 when Queen Victoria granted the British South African Company a Royal Charter to administer the new territory of Southern Rhodesia. The postcolonial configuration of land divisions between commercial farms and communal areas emerged directly from the policies, laws, and practices of the colonial state as it reserved generally the best agricultural land for those classified as "European," and forced those they identified as "indigenous Natives" onto native reserves with generally the worst agricultural land in terms of soils and rainfall. The actual focus on land as the object of localized politics, the territorialization itself, emerged under colonial rule (Hughes 2006). By the 1930s at least, the colonial government and European farmer groups actively cultivated transnational connections with companies, policy-makers, and purchasers to support agricultural production on these farms, resulting in a post-World War II agricultural boom for this sector, particularly in export tobacco. While transnational ties were sought out for white farmers, the policies regarding African farming in the Native Reserves were more about penalizing their marketing opportunities and seeking to intervene in, and actively control, their land use activities through state interventions (Moore 2005; Alexander 2006).

Whereas transnational connections and export opportunities for African farmers were actively discouraged, many of the land policies and programs directed toward the Native Reserves during the colonial period, from conservation to community development, came from transnational linkages with ideas, institutions, and particular experts from other European colonies in Africa, the United Kingdom, and the United States (Beinart 1984; Drinkwater 1991; Alexander 2006). Such transnational ties have continued in the postcolonial period after 1980 when the ruling ZANU (PF) government engaged with international experts, consultants, and donors concerning land resettlement, land tenure, and wildlife conservation, amongst other fields of intervention (e.g., Cusworth 2000; Ranger 1993; Duffy 2000). Such transnational connections have always been shaped by other projects as they forged effective or ineffective scale-making projects of interventions regarding land in the colonial and postcolonial periods (e.g., Beinart 1984; Alexander 2006). National-scale projects and interventions regarding land have thus been energized by particular transnational ties regarding development and conservation.

These transnational connections and ruptures are elided by a focus simply on the putative "onrush" of globalization. Colonial rule was definitely part of globalizing initiatives, but its actual configuration depended on how it articulated with specific national-scale and localized-scale activities. The changing land uses in Zimbabwe in the 1990s is a great example of promotion of neoliberal globalization. Unlike the ideological projections by its uncritical supporters such as *The Economist*, the entanglement of neoliberal globalization with national and localized scale-making projects in Zimbabwe did not lead to "greater wealth" for the majority, but rather was a factor in increasing tensions in the country, which, in turn, contributed to the emergence of the current political conflict and economic crisis in Zimbabwe.

After 1980, commercial agriculture became the dominant economic sector in Zimbabwe until 2000, with its share of the Gross National Product going from 14.0 percent in 1980 to 20.1 percent in 1999. Productivity almost doubled between 1980 and 1996. Agriculture's backward and forward linkages to the domestic manufacturing sector made it a crucial sector in the national economy (Rukuni and Jensen 2003). But given the colonial history of racial segregation that was in law until 1979, the vast majority of the commercial farmers in Zimbabwe continued to be white. In 2000, around 4,100 of the 4,800 or so commercial farmers were white Zimbabweans (Selby 2006).

While much of the profitable commercial farms were involved in export agriculture, particularly flue-cured tobacco, the ZANU (PF) government's introduction of the Economic Structural Adjustment Program (ESAP) in the 1990s saw growing pressure and opportunities to move into export agriculture. Market deregulations and financial incentives, including access to off-shore credit, fueled this expansion into other foreign exchange earning land uses. With the introduction of export-processing zones in the commercial farming areas, direct foreign investment increased in commercial farming.

Sam Moyo (2000) identified significant land use changes in agriculture during this decade, as government support for domestic food production was replaced by credit facilities and market opportunities for export agriculture. In the 1990s, more and more commercial farmers moved into horticulture (particularly flowers, vegetables, and fruit), wildlife farming (for sale, tourism, or hunting), and ostrich raising. However, only those farmers with access to resources, credit facilities, and technical know-how were able to actively take advantage of these opportunities. By 1995–96, an estimated 30 percent of commercial farmers devoted some or all of their lands to these new land uses. Elite black commercial farmers and parastatals were also involved. Although various attempts were made to revalue land use activities in the Communal Areas (the former Native Reserves) and other smallholder farmer areas to involve more of them in the export activities. Moyo (2000, 163) notes less than 5 percent of these smallholder farmers were involved in these new land uses.

Commercial farming was one of the few sectors in Zimbabwe that actively benefited from the Economic Structural Adjustment Programs (ESAPs). The manufacturing sector and government social services, such as health and education, were adversely affected by the standard package of neoliberal policies prescribed by the International Financial Institutions in the 1980s and 1990s. Bond and Manyanya (2002, 60) capture the broadly devastating consequences of ESAPs for the majority of Zimbabweans:

> As a direct result of funding cuts and cost-recovery policies, exacerbated by the HIV/AIDS pandemic, Zimbabwe's brief 1980s rise in literacy and health indicators was dramatically reversed. . . . More steadily, manufacturing sector

output crashed from peak 1991 levels, and the standard of living for the average Zimbabwean worker was devastated. Comparing other indices of pre-*Esap* and *Esap*-era economic activity, total formal-sector jobs (including agricultural) rose from just under a million at independence to 1.244 million in 1991 and then remained flat. Urban unemployment (not commercial farmwork) rose from 454 000 in early 1980 to 620 000 in 1991 before falling back to 590 000 by year-end 1995. Average earnings (after inflation) rose a half-percent each year from 1980–1990, but fell by more than 10% annually from 1991–1995. Between 1980 and 1990, the Zimbabwe dollar lost 70% of its value against the US dollar; between 1991 and 1995 (half as long a period), it lost 67%. Inflation averaged 13.4% from 1980–1990, and 27.6% from 1991–1995.

As commercial farmers, on the whole, did very well economically during the 1990s, an even greater share of the profits went to the farm owner (and shareholders) rather than the farmworkers, compared to the 1980s (Kanyenze 2001). Moreover, the growing wealth of predominantly white farmers, in comparison to the deepening immiseration of more and more black Zimbabweans under ESAP, made them stand out even greater than their already tainted reputation in African nationalist discourses, given their general support to, and great benefits from, the colonial and Rhodesian Front regimes (Rutherford 2004). A report prepared for the IMF in 1998 summarizes the growing inequality nicely when it observed that commercial "farmers gained almost all the share [of the GDP] that wage earners lost" (Botchwey et al. 1998, 180, cited in Brett 2005, 10).

When combined with shifts in government policies that actively downplayed land resettlement for the land poor and landless and rather supported land distribution to the black elite, the neoliberal policies and the "free market" directly fed into grievances against white farmers and was an issue that helped to facilitate the direct targeting of white farms by ZANU (PF) after 2000 (Rutherford 2008).

But did this exacerbation of economic inequalities by ZANU (PF)'s adoption of neoliberal policies mean that President Mugabe is right in defying "globalization"? While a few commentators may make such an argument (e.g., Moyo and Yeros 2005, Gowans 2007), it neglects the Mugabe government's desperate search for international investors for the vast declining agricultural sector. The ZANU (PF) government's putative defense of national sovereignty against Western imperialism has not prevented it from desperately seeking other international actors to invest and acquire its land, particularly given the collapse of its export agricultural industry.

Much of the over ten million hectares taken from nearly four thousand white commercial farmers have been nominally given to about fifteen thousand black commercial farmers and over one hundred thousand smallholder farmers (Ncube 2007). Yet, there is great uncertainty with regard to this land, as many black Zimbabweans who were initially given smallholdings after 2000 have subsequently been evicted by black Zimbabweans with ties to ZANU (PF), compounded by politicized violence and looting (Wolmers

2007; Rutherford 2008), occasional droughts, and the increased inflation and economic "meltdown." For example, the horticultural sector, which grew on average by 15 percent per year during the 1990s, contracted by 40 percent from 2000 to 2005 (Selby 2006, 177). Only 55 million kilograms of tobacco were sold through the Harare auction floors in 2006, compared to 250 million in 1999 (*Mail & Guardian* 2006a; *The Zimbabwean* 2006). Every year since 2000, Zimbabwe has required food aid to feed at least a million people a year as its own domestic maize production has declined, given the great uncertainties racing through economic distribution, production, and consumption networks. The government itself has admitted that living standards for Zimbabweans have declined by 150 percent between 1996 and 2005 (IRIN 2006).

I will give a brief example of government attempts to court international investors, noting extensive handover of land to Chinese investors, though there are other examples of such attempts of forging different types of transnational connections concerning the land.[1] In early 2003, as part of the Mugabe government's "look East" foreign policy initiative (see, e.g., Brown and Sriram 2008), the government gave over 100,000 hectares in the southeastern Lowveld to a Chinese state company to grow maize. The Nuanetsi Irrigation Project was using land owned by the Development Trust of Zimbabwe, an organization established under the leadership of the then Vice President (and now late) Joshua Nkomo in 1989 (ZWNEWS 2001). Although by the 1990s, the leaders of the Development Trust of Zimbabwe and others envisioned that this land would be used as an irrigated land resettlement scheme growing cotton and sugar, the infrastructure to develop such an enterprise was never put into place (Wolmers 2007, 205–6). Despite this history, with great fanfare, the government touted the Chinese company's project as "the panacea to restore food security in a country where large commercial irrigation projects have been decimated by the disorderly resettlement programme" (cited in Kahiya 2003). The Chinese company was paid to clear the land, subdivide it into smaller plots, while the ZANU (PF) government sought to resettle the 10,000 families that had settled on the farm during the start of 2000 land occupations, though in the words of the state controlled newspaper, they were now viewed as "unlawfully staying at the ranch" (Maponga 2003). The hope was that the smallholder farmers would grow three maize crops per year, with the anticipated harvest of seven tonnes per hectare (Zim Online 2006). Instead, a few months later, the Chinese company abandoned the project (Mukaro 2003). A Zimbabwean parastatal tried to carry out the project, but three years later, it, too, abandoned the project (Zim Online 2006), like many of the other grand irrigation schemes the ZANU (PF) government has initiated, including the use of the Zimbabwean army to brutally manage them (SPT 2006). In 2005, the ZANU (PF) government aimed to transfer thousands of more hectares of land to Chinese firms, in this case commercial farmland confiscated after 2000, but it is unclear what success, if any, this transnational initiative will have (Zim Online 2005a; Marawanyika and Mukaro 2005).

In short, the ZANU (PF) government has been desperately seeking transnational allies in its so-called defense of the "national sovereignty" project. Although under the increasingly racial discourse of the ruling party and its supporters, this postcolonial, anticolonial, nationalist project is said to be explicitly for black Africans (Ranger 2004; Raftopoulos 2007), the ZANU (PF) government has also actively excluded a large number of black Africans born and living in Zimbabwe from its definition of who belongs to the nation.

THE MARGINS OF SOVEREIGNTY: FARMWORKERS AND LAND

Since 2000, much of the international media has focused its attention on the Mugabe government's forced removal of most white farmers, helping to frame Zimbabwe as a "white versus black" or "West versus Africa" conflict, and enabling ZANU (PF) and its supporters to confirm its loyalty to this very same narrative (Willems 2005). Although black "victims" of the ZANU (PF) government's actions are frequently highlighted, particularly after Operation Murambatsvina—the so-called urban "clean-up" operation that began in May 2005 that has destroyed the homes and livelihoods of hundreds of thousands of Zimbabweans (Potts 2006)—the main globalized mass-mediated characterization of the Zimbabwean crisis is principally through the lens of race. But in the hands of ZANU (PF), this racialized lens has also contributed to the active devaluing of claims of belonging to the nation of commercial farmworkers.

In 2000, there were over 300,000 men and women (and some children) working on the commercial farms in Zimbabwe. Most of them also lived with their dependents on the farms in workers' compounds, making this group total close to two million people out of a national population of around eleven million. Like many black Zimbabweans, farmworkers have also largely suffered through the economic meltdown and uncertainty since 2000. Yet the ZANU (PF) government has also actively marginalized this demographically large grouMany farmworkers have been targets of ruling party violence, including killings, have been actively discriminated against in getting access to any of the "fast-tracked" land redistribution, and many have also had their actual Zimbabwean citizenship removed. To understand the reasons for this targeting of farmworkers, one needs to go beyond simple invocations of national sovereignty and examine how farmworkers have been emplaced through the cultural politics of citizenship in this country.

As I have written elsewhere (e.g., Rutherford 2001a, 2007), since the colonial period, government policies and administrative structures strongly tied commercial farmworkers to white farmers. From the 1940s to 1960s, many of the farmworkers on European farms were from the neighboring colonies of Nyasaland (Malawi), Northern Rhodesia (Zambia), and Portuguese East Africa (Mozambique). White farmers became the main administrative authority over their lives, with minimal role for colonial officials and no role for trade unions, which were banned from operating in the agricultural industry until 1979. In relation to farmworkers, white farmers became recognized by the colonial state as a form of sovereign power, which I have called "domestic government" (Rutherford, 2001a, 2001b). Although much of the legislative discrimination against farmworkers was removed after independence in 1980, farmworkers were still largely neglected in the expansion of social services in the countryside. Instead, government ministers explicitly identified white farmers as those who should "look after" farmworkers, relying on the colonial practices of domestic government. Although ZANU (PF) ministers and the state media periodically demonized white farmers as racist settlers who stole land from black people during the first twenty years of postcolonial rule, particularly during elections, they also explicitly prioritized their rights over that of farmworkers. For example, when the possibility of black farmworkers getting the vote in local government elections was publicly discussed in 1988, the then Minister of Local Government and Housing, Enos Chikowore, declared in Zimbabwe's parliament that farmworkers should be refused the electoral franchise, for if they "were to vote, then 200 workers could vote out their employers or their bosses for whatever reasons, et cetera. So these are the considerations that we've had to take into account" (cited in Rutherford 2001a, 52). Farmworkers only received the franchise to vote in local government elections in 1997.

Why this discrimination? Partially, it has to do with the transnational heritage of farm labor in Zimbabwe. Most estimates have suggested only about 25 percent or so of farmworkers were foreign-born by the 1990s, compared to over half in the 1960s (Sachikonye 2003, 57). Yet there has been a widespread assumption held by many Zimbabweans that farmworkers are "foreigners" by birth or by descent, even though the Citizenship Act at that time would have made any farmworkers born of a foreign parent a Zimbabwean (Rutherford 2007). But such a designation could also have included mine workers, since historically, many mine workers in the colonial period also came from neighboring colonies, albeit at a much smaller percentage than farmworkers by the 1950s. Rather, I argue that farmworkers have been treated as suspect citizens by many Zimbabweans because of the moral evaluation of their job and for their close association with white farmers control vis-à-vis domestic government.

Farmwork is a low status job for most Zimbabweans. This is not only because of the hard work involved, but also because, in the colonial period, it involved very low remuneration and potentially punitive labor conditions (Rubert 1998). Moreover, many Zimbabweans negatively evaluated those who worked for a long time on commercial farms as having moral laxity and unable to farm for themselves as a (smallholder) farmer (Rutherford 2007). Due to such evaluations of farmwork, the preferences of many colonized Zimbabweans were to work in other jobs in the colony or to go to South Africa. As a consequence, white farmers and the colonial administrations had to actively recruit Africans from neighboring colonies to work as farmworkers.

The close, paternalistic ties between white farmers and black farmworkers also led to the representation of the latter as the "servants" of the former. In some cases, evaluating such dependencies has led to declarations that farmworkers must be "liberated" from the control of white farmers. But some politicians and others have often claimed that farmworkers have not been truly committed to the African nationalist cause as defined by ZANU (PF), and thus not part of the Zimbabwean nation (Rutherford 2001b). This is most clearly seen in how farmworkers have been positioned in policies and debates concerning land redistribution.

In the first onrush of the ZANU (PF) government's land resettlement program in the early 1980s, former and current farmworkers were included. But starting in the late 1980s, as officials and policy-makers began to emphasize more technical criteria and notions of agricultural expertise and existing resources (Alexander 2006) farmworkers began to be actively discriminated against. They were viewed as lazy and too resource poor to be selected as settlers for resettlement programs (Moyo, Rutherford, and Amanor-Wilks 2000). This coincided with a general slowdown in land redistribution and the government's prioritization of establishing indigenous commercial farmers more than increasing the number of smallholder farmers on any commercial farms purchased for land redistribution (Moyo 2000; Alexander 2006).

Therefore, government policies, political discourse, and hegemonic sentiment in Zimbabwe had placed farmworkers on the margins of sovereignty: they were viewed as belonging more to white farmers rather than the nation at large. When land occupations began in February 2000, many of the ZANU (PF) land occupiers thus saw farmworkers as being more in support of white farmers than wanting to receive land themselves, despite the actual varied responses of farmworkers to land occupations and the political mobilization for the opposition MDC (Rutherford 2001b, 2007; Sachikonye 2003; Waeterloos and Rutherford 2004; Moyo and Yeros 2005). More than white farmers, farmworkers have been targeted by much political violence, as ZANU (PF) cadres have seen them not only as potentially supportive of the MDC, but also as a potential voting block for ZANU (PF), to be nurtured through intimidation and violence (HRW 2002; Rutherford 2008). Not only have the vast majority of farmworkers lost their jobs through the removal of most commercial farmers (and due to the slow pace of actual farming by the new farmers), but they also have actively been discriminated against receiving any land by (competing) land distribution authorities, driven off by new settlers, or subject to coercive attempts to make them work for the new African settler farmers (Sachikonye 2003; Rutherford 2008).

At the same time, the government's amendment of the Citizenship Act in 2001 (just before the presidential election held in March 2002) disenfranchised untold tens of thousands of farmworkers and other Zimbabweans from citizenship on the grounds that (at least) one of their parents or grandparents was foreign-born. Although the government implemented a complicated process for renunciation of this putative foreign citizenship, and the courts and politicians and some policy-makers have claimed the amendment to be null and void for at least those whose parents were born in southern Africa, in practice, many farmworkers or former farmworkers and others are now literally placed outside the margins of sovereignty by having no citizenship (see, e.g., DPA 2005; Manwere 2007a, 2007b; Manyukwe 2007; Rutherford 2007).

In summary, farmworkers who generally had poor working and living conditions before 2000 have lost out even more as ZANU (PF) has pursued its violent campaign in holding onto power in the name of national sovereignty.

CONCLUSION

The Zimbabwean crisis is illustrative of how actions being carried out in Africa can become a lightening rod in the contestation over globalization on the continent. Through examining transnational linkages and ruptures and particular national-scale formations of citizenship, and sovereignties neglected by the main contours of the mass mediated policy and political debate over Zimbabwe, I have raised questions concerning the helpfulness of conventional understandings of globalization and sovereignty in analytically and politically grasping the particular political and social dimensions of the unfolding crisis in this southern African country. Drawing on recent theoretical works, I have put forward a slightly different analysis of how the land conflict in Zimbabwe can be understood in relation to both transnational and national activities and processes. Although those wedded to the comfortable and comforting dichotomy of the West and Africa, pro- or anti-globalization, may not be interested in moving beyond their positions, I find the increasing discomfort of the majority of Zimbabweans to the ongoing meltdown there compels one to move beyond the entrenched lines to seek other ways of understanding and potentially addressing the crisis other than simply calling for greater market penetration or the absolute defense of national sovereignty. Given their limits in grasping what has been happening there, it is time to find alternative analytics.

REFERENCES

Alexander, Jocelyn. 2006. *The unsettled land: State-making and the politics of land in Zimbabwe, 1893–200.* Oxford: James Currey.

Amosu, Akwe, and Charles Cobb, Jr. 2002. Africa: Don't hold NEPAD hostage over Zimbabwe says Minister. *AllAfrica.com*, March 27. http://allafrica.com/stories/200203270498.html.

Beinart, William. 1984. Soil erosion, conservationism and ideas about development: A southern African exploration 1900–1960. *Journal of Southern African Studies* 11 (1): 52–83.

Bond, Patrick, ed. 2002. *Fanon's warning: A civil society reader on the new partnership for Africa's development.* Trenton, NJ: Africa World Press.

Bond, Patrick, and Masimba Manyanya. 2002. *Zimbabwe's plunge: Exhausted nationalism, neoliberalism, and the search for social justice.* Trenton, NJ: Africa World Press.

Brett, E. A. 2005. From corporatism to liberalisation in Zimbabwe: Economic policy regimes and political crisis (1980–1997). *Crisis States Programme working papers series* 58. London: London School of Economics.

Brown, Stephen, and Chandra Lekha Sriram. 2008 (forthcoming). China's role in human rights abuses in Africa: Clarifying issues of culpability. In *China in Africa: Geopolitical and geoeconomic considerations*, ed. R. Rotberg. Washington: Brookings Institution.

Cusworth, John. 2000. A review of the UK ODA evaluation of the land resettlement programme in 1988 and the land appraisal mission of 1996. In *Land reform in Zimbabwe*, ed. T. A. Bowyer-Bower and C. Stoneman. Aldershot, UK: Ashgate.

DPA (Deutsche Presse-Agentur). 2005. More than 150,000 voters disqualified ahead of Zimbabwe senate poll, *DPA* (Germany), October 30. http://news.monstersandcritics.com/africa/news/printer_1058425.php.

Drinkwater, Michael. 1991. *The state and agrarian change in Zimbabwe's communal areas*. New York: St Martin's Press.

Eager, Angela. 2001. Gaddafi sends thugs to help Mugabe fight election battle. *The Telegraph* (United Kingdom), October 14. http://www.zimbabwesituation.com/oct14_2001.html#link4.

Evans, Michael. 2002. Zimbabwe facing "colonial bankruptcy." *Mashada forums*, September8.http://www.mashada.com/forums/politics/1146-zimbabwe-facing-colonial-bancruptcy.html.

Ferguson, James. 2006. *Global shadows: Africa in the neoliberal world order*. Durham, NC: Duke University Press.

Freeman, Linda. 2005a. South Africa's Zimbabwe policy: Unravelling the contradictions. *Journal of Contemporary African Studies* 23 (2): 147–72.

———. 2005b. Contradictory constructions of the crisis in Zimbabwe. *Historia* 50 (2): 287–310.

Gowans, Stephen. 2007. What's really going on in Zimbabwe? Mugabe gets the Milosevic treatment. *Counterpunch*, March 23. http://www.counterpunch.org/gowans03232007.html.

HRW (Human Rights Watch). 2002. *Fast track land reform in Zimbabwe*. New York: HRW.

Hughes, David McDermott (2006). *From enslavement to environmentalism: Politics on a southern African frontier*. Seattle: University of Washington Press.

IRIN. 2006. Government reports 150% drop in living standards. *IRIN*, December 6. http://www.alertnet.org/thenews/newsdesk/IRIN/8bbcf651901501fb1ecb9e4b0984d43e.htm.

Itano, Nicole. 2005. Mugabe lashes out at "half-wit" archbishop. *Mail & Guardian* (South Africa), March 29. http://www.mg.co.za/articlePage.aspx?articleid=200408&area=/zim_elections/zim_news.

Kahiya, Vincent. 2003. Irrigation projects no solution to food security. *Zimbabwe Independent*, February 21. http://www.zimbabwesituation.com/feb21b_2003.html#link19.

Kanyenze, Godfrey. 2001. Zimbabwe's labour relations policies and the implications for farm workers. In *Zimbabwe's farm workers: Policy dimensions*, ed. D. Amanor-Wilks, 86–114. Lusaka, Zambia: Panos Southern Africa.

Mail & Guardian (South Africa). 2006a. Zimbabwe reports lowest tobacco yield, February 16. http://www.mg.co.za/articlePage.aspx?articleid=264409&area=/breaking_news/breaking_news__business/.

————. 2006b. Rautenbach ordered to vacate Zim farm, February 20. http://www.mg.co.za/articlePage.aspx?articleid=264782&area=/breaking_news/breaking_news_africa/.

Manwere, Orirando. 2007a. Declared stateless in country of birth. *Zimbabwe Independent*, October 26. http://www.kubatana.net/html/archive/opin/071026om.asp?sector=OPIN.

————. 2007b. Citizenship law to prejudice many of voters. *Zimbabwe Independent*, November 2. http://allafrica.com/stories/200711020722.html.

Manyukwe, Clemence. 2007. Mudede: I'm under pressure. *Financial Gazette* (Zimbabwe), September 6. http://www.zimbabwesituation.com/sep6b_2007.html#Z12.

Maponga, George. 2003. 10,000 families resettled on Nuanetsi Ranch. *Herald* (Zimbabwe), August 5.

Marawanyika, Godfrey, and Augustine Mukaro. 2005. Govt to cede land to Chinese. *Zimbabwe Independent*, November 3. http://www.zimbabwesituation.com/nov4c_2005.html#Z5.

Meldrum, Andrew. Tycoon flees Zimbabwe after falling foul of Mugabe. *The Guardian* (United Kingdom), June 9. http://www.guardian.co.uk/zimbabwe/article/0,,1793719,00.html.

Mitchell, Timothy. 1991. The limits of the state: Beyond statist approaches and their critics. *American Political Science Review* 85 (1): 77–96.

Mock, Vanessa. 2007. Zimbabwe dominates and divides at EU-Africa summit. *Radio Netherlands*, December 9. http://www.zimbabwesituation.com/dec10_2007.html#Z7.

Moore, Donald. 2005. *Suffering for territory: Race, place, and power in Zimbabwe*. Durham, NC: Duke University Press.

Moyo, Sam. 2000. *Land reform under structural adjustment in Zimbabwe*. Uppsala: Nordiska Afrikainstitutet.

Moyo, Sam, Blair Rutherford, and Dede Amanor-Wilks. 2000. Land reform and changing social relations for farm workers in Zimbabwe. *Review of African Political Economy* 27 (84): 181–202.

Moyo, Sam, and Paris Yeros. 2005. Land occupations and land reform in Zimbabwe: Towards the national democratic revolution. In *Reclaiming the land: The resurgence of rural movements in Africa, Asia, and Latin America*, ed. S. Moyo and P. Yeros, 165–205. London: Zed Books.

Mugabe, Robert. 2007. Speech to the 62nd session of the United Nations general assembly, September 26. http://www.newzimbabwe.com/pages/un34.16973.html.

Mukaro, Augustine. 2003. Chinese firm abandons Nuanetsi project. *Zimbabwe Independent*, August 1. http://www.zimbabwesituation.com/aug2a_2003.html #link 15.

News24. 2006. Zim loan claim "total fiction." *News24* (South Africa), January 20. http://www.zimbabwesituation.com/jan21_2006.html#Z9.

————. 2007. Land reform was chaotic—Zim VP. *News24* (South Africa), July 19. http://www.news24.com/News24/Africa/Zimbabwe/0,,2-11-1662_2150133,00.html.

Ncube, Njabulo. 2007. Mugabe admits cronies also part of the rot. *Financial Gazette* (Zimbabwe). http://www.fingaz.co.zw/story.aspx?stid=1826.

Potts, Deborah. 2006. "Restoring order"? The interrelationships between Operation Murambatsvina in Zimbabwe and urban poverty, informal housing, and employment. *Journal of Southern African Studies* 32 (2): 273–91.

Raftopoulos, Brian. 2007. Nation, race, and history in Zimbabwean Politics. In *Making nations, creating strangers: States and citizenship in Africa*, ed. S. Dorman, D. Hammett, and P. Nugent, 161–80. Leiden: Brill.

Ranger, Terence. 1993. The communal areas of Zimbabwe. In *Land in African agrarian systems*, ed. T. J. Bassett and D. G. Crummey, 354–85. Madison, WI: University of Wisconsin Press.

———. 2004. Nationalist historiography, patriotic history, and the history of the nation: The struggle over the past in Zimbabwe. *Journal of Southern African Studies* 30 (2): 215–34.

Richardson, Craig. 2005. The loss of property rights and the collapse of Zimbabwe. *Cato Journal* 25 (3): 541–65.

Rubert, Stephen. 1998. *A most promising weed: A history of tobacco farming and labor in colonial Zimbabwe, 1890–1945*. Athens, OH: Ohio University Center for International Studies.

Rukuni, Mandivamba, and Stig Jensen. 2003. Land, growth, and governance: Tenure reform and visions of progress in Zimbabwe. In *Zimbabwe's unfinished business: Rethinking land, state, and nation in the context of crisis, ed*. A. Hammar, B. Raftopoulos, and S. Jensen, 243–62. Harare: Weaver.

Rutherford, Blair. 2001a. *Working on the margins: Black workers, white farmers in postcolonial Zimbabwe*. London: Zed Books.

———. 2001b. Commercial farm workers and the politics of (dis)placement in Zimbabwe: Liberation, colonialism, and democracy. *Journal of Agrarian Change* 1 (4): 626–51.

———. 2004. Desired publics, domestic government, and entangled fears: On the anthropology of civil society, farm workers, and white farmers in Zimbabwe. *Cultural Anthropology* 19 (3): 122–53.

———. 2007. Shifting grounds in Zimbabwe: Citizenship and farm workers in the new politics of land. In *Making nations, creating strangers: States and citizenship in Africa*, ed. S. Rich Dorman, P. Nugent, and D. Hammett, 105–22. Leiden: Brill.

———. 2008 (forthcoming). Conditional belonging: Farm workers and the cultural politics of recognition in Zimbabwe. *Development and Change*.

Sachikonye, Lloyd. 2003. *The situation of commercial farm workers after land reform in Zimbabwe*. London: Catholic Institute for International Relations.

Selby, Angus. 2006. Commercial farmers and the state: Interest group politics and land reform in Zimbabwe, PhD diss., University of Oxford.

SPT (Solidarity Peace Trust). 2006. *Operation Taguta/Sisuthi. Command agriculture in Zimbabwe: Its impact on rural communities in Matabeleland*. Port Shepstone, South Africa: SPT.

Sunday Mirror (Zimbabwe). 2004. Cunning methods to sway you, December 12. http://www.zwnews.com/issuefull.cfm?ArticleID=10776.

Taylor, Ian. 2002. Zimbabwe and the death of NEPAD Alternative Information and Development Centre. http://www.aidc.org.za/?q=book/view/183.

The Economist (UK). 2002. The Zimbabwean model, November 28. http://www.zimbabwesituation.com/dec5_2002.html#link14.

The Zimbabwean. 2006. Tobacco floors close, October 25. http://www.zimbabwesituation.com/oct26a_2006.html#Z12.

Tsing, Anna. 2005. *Friction: An ethnography of global connection*. Princeton: Princeton University Press.

Waeterloos, Evert, and Blair Rutherford. 2004. Land reform in Zimbabwe: Challenges and opportunities for poverty reduction among commercial farm workers. *World Development* 32 (3): 537–53.

Willems, Wendy. 2005. Remnants of empire? British media reporting on Zimbabwe. *Westminster Papers in Communication and Culture* (Special Issue, November), School of Media, Arts, and Design. London: University of Westminster, 91–108.

Wolmers, William. 2007. *From wilderness vision to farm invasions: Conservation & development in Zimbabwe's south-east Lowveld.* Oxford: James Currey.

Zim Online. 2005a. Chinese to take over former white-owned farms. *Zim Online*, May 18. http://www.zimbabwesituation.com/may19_2005.html#link1.

———. 2005b. Zimbabwe weeds out 18 white farmers from district, spares Mugabe ally, *Zim Online*, November 10. http://www.zimbabwesituation.com/nov10a_2005.html#Z2.

———. 2006. Zimbabwe abandons multibillion dollar irrigation project, *Zim Online*, February 27. http://www.zimbabwesituation.com/feb27_2006.html#Z3.

ZWNEWS. 2001. Development Trust of Zimbabwe *ZWNEWS*, January 1. http://www.zwnews.com/issuefull.cfm?ArticleID=85.

NOTE

1. For example, there have been reported deals, particularly in the early 2000s, with Colonel Gaddafi of Libya involving the transfer of Zimbabwean commercial farms, amongst other property, in exchange for oil and financial support (see e.g., Evans 2002; Eager 2001). I also heard rumors from farm workers in Mashonaland East province in 2002 of Libyans coming to inspect farms. White businessmen, such as the Zimbabweans Billy Rautenbach and John Bredenkamp, or the British Nicholas van Hoogstraten (all of whom with extensive and often controversial transnational ties), who have had close business ties with various leaders of ZANU (PF) have also had their landholdings exempted from confiscation, unless they, too, saw the tides turn in their political alliances, given the often ferocious jockeying for influence in the senior ranks of the ruling party (see e.g., *Sunday Mirror* 2004; Zim Online 2005b; News24 2006; *Mail & Guardian* 2006b; Meldrum 2006).

CHAPTER 11

THE SOUTH AFRICAN PEOPLE'S BUDGET CAMPAIGN AS A CHALLENGE TO NEOLIBERAL POLICY FRAMEWORK AND METHODOLOGY

Carolyn Bassett

The notion of public input on government budgets predates the current period, but interest has grown in response to the widespread adoption of neoliberal economic restructuring programs over the past three decades (Krafchik 2006; Brautigam 2004). The notion of popular or participatory budgets has gained currency in many parts of the world as popular sector organizations seek ways to influence government policy in an era of spending cuts that seem to fall disproportionately on the poor. This chapter examines one example of popular budgeting involving the People's Budget Campaign in South Africa. I suggest that this popular budget project reflects a complex interaction with neoliberal ideas about policies and policy processes. On the one hand, the campaign offers a critique of the content of neoliberal policies, showing that balanced budgets need not reduce social services designed to improve the lives of the poor. The campaign advances alternative policies, both on the expenditure and on the revenue side, that still meet the strictures of "fiscal responsibility." It also simultaneously incorporates, at least implicitly, a critique of the policy processes associated with neoliberalism—specifically, the tendency to advocate a closed policy process, driven by experts. The People's Budget Campaign reasserted the right of citizens to help shape policy, drawing on their intelligence, creativity, and capacity to accept trade-offs in pursuit of the public good.

At the same time, people's budgets can be understood, at least in part, as products of neoliberalism, in that they operate within a discourse of fiscal conservatism and balanced budgets. The realism of the People's Budget Campaign, which seeks to subvert neoliberalism using some of the latter's core principles as the basis for an alternative vision, paradoxically may advance the legitimacy of neoliberalism by opening spaces for critique within the government's policy parameters, rather than reforming the economic framework overall. Implied in this approach is the possibility that even where neoliberal restructuring has been highly contested, as in South Africa, people have begun to become neoliberal citizens, which means even alternatives are increasingly shaped by neoliberal norms. This change in political culture is essential for states and capital to move neoliberalism, which, to date, has been adopted in a rather authoritarian manner, toward hegemony, in the Gramscian sense of being based upon widely held norms that become "common sense." The South African People's Budget Campaign operates within this tricky ground: its critique has opened political spaces for the state to respond to its critics by adopting a slightly more expansive and pro-poor fiscal program. Needless to say, the way the government responds is designed to maintain the neoliberal framework and increase its public acceptance.

POLICY, PARTICIPATION, AND NEOLIBERAL RESTRUCTURING

In the late 1970s and early 1980s, states began to adopt a new economic policy framework influenced by neoliberal prescriptions. Some governments embraced the new framework, while others, especially those that were unable to service their foreign debt, had it forced upon them through structural adjustment programs (SAPs) devised by the International Monetary Fund (IMF) and the World Bank. The policy prescriptions of neoliberal restructuring called for a minimal state that permitted (international) market allocation of resources and setting of prices (Biersteker 1990). The specific policy proposals that flowed from this conceptualization of growth, economic reform, and development included reducing tariffs and non-tariff barriers to international trade, allowing the national currency to be freely traded, reducing direct subsidies to consumers on food and government services (e.g., health care, education, housing, electricity, and water), restricting labor rights, selling state-owned enterprises, entrenching private property rights, and restructuring taxation systems away from corporate and progressive income taxes and toward consumption taxes. Lower government spending, balanced budgets, and accelerated debt payments were at the core of the neoliberal program.

Equally importantly, the neoliberal approach involved a distinct policy-making methodology, which, invariably insists that economic policy matters, such as those relating to budgets, should be "depoliticized" by removing them from the realm of public debate and placing them into the hands of economists and technocrats. As Przeworski (1991) has noted, the meth-odology was based on a profound conviction that there was only one cor-rect approach to economic policy reform, and that any opposition, even any discussion, was self-interested populist reaction. A "shock treatment" approach was favored over gradualism because it was felt that modifications to the prescriptions might undermine their "coherence." Although propo-nents acknowledged that a gradual introduction of neoliberal policies might cause fewer social tensions, they counterargued that gradualism increased the chances that organized opposition would mount and succeed in modifying the program in a way that would negate its effectiveness. Thus, proponents of neoliberal restructuring tended to ignore the question of how states would legitimize the policy program, perhaps assuming that the policies would be so successful that public support would soon follow.

In reality, much of the harshest burden of neoliberal restructuring fell on the poor—the poorest people and the poorest countries—contrary to the prediction of advocates. It was not until the late 1980s that the impact of neoliberal restructuring in poor countries, many of them in Africa, was rec-ognized to any significant extent in global policy circles. Notably, a group of United Nations researchers revealed that poor children were suffering the most under structural adjustment programs, and proposed "adjustment with a human face" to mitigate this apparently unforeseen consequence of neolib-eral restructuring. Their proposals included a more expansionary economic program and special measures targeted to reduce the impact of adjustment on the poor (Cornia *et al.* 1987). Over the short term, "adjustment with a human face" had little real impact on neoliberal restructuring programs, since state officials and international advisors maintained that desirable as such social interventions might be, they were unaffordable. Since the 1990s, however, "adjustment with a human face" perspectives had begun to perme-ate the economic programs of the Bretton Woods institutions.

The Highly Indebted Poor Countries (HIPC) program, which tied debt relief to strict neoliberal conditionality and higher levels of social spending to reduce poverty, was initiated in the mid-1990s (Teunissen and Akkerman 2004). The program was praised, by some, for improving the social content of, and incorporating local input into, economic restructuring programs, but in most cases, failed to reduce debt. The HIPC program was later revised to incorporate the Poverty Reduction Strategy Initiative, with essentially the same goals but a higher element of "national ownership" in developing and implementing poverty reduction programs as an element of neoliberal structural adjustment (Cheru 2006). These initiatives have been disappoint-ing for a variety of reasons. However, for our purposes, what is important about them is what they imply in terms of a new perception that changes had to be made to neoliberal restructuring programs in order to maintain them. Specifically, it has become accepted that neoliberal restructuring needs to be "socially sustainable" (not garner widespread public opposition) and that small-scale social policy interventions, plus a requirement of some public participation in developing and monitoring these poverty reduction programs, may neutralize public opposition. Thus, we have seen changes in both the content and methodology of neoliberal restructuring over the past decade, but within a framework that seeks to maintain the economic liberalization programs.

THEORIZING THE CHALLENGES TO NEOLIBERAL RESTRUCTURING AND THEIR IMPLICATIONS FOR POPULAR MOVEMENTS

The question of whether, and how, neoliberal economic restructuring can become a legitimate program with popular support has long been a source of contestation. As suggested above, proponents of the programs were late in noting the importance of fostering widespread acceptance of neoliberal norms as being in the "general interest" of the population, and not merely beneficial to a few international creditors and local business elites—to achieve what Antonio Gramsci (1971) referred to as hegemonic status. By hegemonic status, Gramsci meant a broad level of cultural acceptance, because otherwise, the state would be forced to govern in an authoritarian manner (domination). The costs of governing through "domination" were high, in the sense that the state would be more vulnerable to fundamental challenges that potentially implied a dramatic shift in their socioeconomic program. Gramsci (1971) argued that capitalism has been so tenacious in places like Western Europe because it has been culturally supported by bourgeois norms that come to permeate many of the institutions and social practices of society—they become "common sense." This is no natural occurrence, as Carroll and Ratner (1994, 5–6) explain: "Consent does not arise spontaneously; it must be won through ideological struggles and material concessions. By these means, a general interest or collective identity is constructed that unites the dominant and subordinate alike as members of the same political community." The early neoliberal reforms failed to achieve hegemonic status because they did not offer the required spaces for dissent and compromise, which posed a problem for states and an opportunity for oppositional movements.

Given states' tendency to pursue neoliberalism by governing through "domination," rather than "hegemony," many opponents of neoliberal restructuring focused on the possibility of moving beyond critiques of specific measures to developing an effective, coherent, democratic, and empowering alternative program for socioeconomic transformation that would capture broad popular support. Pursuing changes of this nature implied questions both of content and of process. Scholars and activists from a range of perspectives found the writings of Gramsci particularly useful in thinking theoretically and methodologically about how to explore these questions. The task of building an alternative basis for the state (socialism for Gramsci, though not all who utilize his analysis seek a socialist alternative) similarly required political engagement and struggle to take place on an ideological and cultural terrain (Gramsci's "war of position") (Sassoon 1982). Neo-Gramscians argue that social movements that seek a genuine alternative must develop a "counter-hegemonic strategy" to draw a number of social actors together into a purposive strategy for social transformation. Counter-hegemonic movements oppose the existing order by unifying class and popular democratic struggles around an alternative set of social practices and norms that reshape society even before the old order has been destroyed (Carroll 1992).

John Saul's (1993) articulation of "structural reform" further explicates this neo-Gramscian approach to dissent and democratic alternatives. Saul explained that structural reform requires programs and practices that are mutually reinforcing and rooted within popular initiatives. To be relevant to the base, it must put forward concrete reforms, but by doing so, draw the system as a whole into question. The leadership must remain accountable to its base through democratic consultation so that the "movement" is grounded in its constituency, which itself remains somewhat autonomous of the leadership. Furthermore, the base must be empowered by the continual strengthening of their capacity for democratic control and collective decision-making. If reforms become ends in themselves, rather than starting points to change cultural practices, they risk being incorporated by the state to strengthen its own rule—i.e., "mere reformism," or elements in the state's hegemonic project.

The question of where "mere reformism" ends, and the kind of cultural change associated with structural reform begins, is easier to identify in theory than in practice. Both the effectiveness of the state and of social movement actors are put to the test, because the state requires dissent that it can manage and incorporate into its overall program in order to achieve hegemonic rule, while alternative movements need *concrete* objectives that will clearly improve peoples' lives in the short term in order to build its base. Indeed, a state that has had some difficulty constructing a hegemonic basis for governance has a strong incentive to reform its program by accepting and incorporating some of the demands of its opposition, while robbing them of their radical, democratizing content. These kinds of political questions are particularly important as we turn to the case study of South Africa's People's Budget Campaign, because the country's economic reform strategy follows the general neoliberal trends outlined above, and the successes and limitations of the campaign may serve to further illuminate the tricky ground on which genuine alternatives may be constructed.

FISCAL POLICY IN SOUTH AFRICA: AN OVERVIEW

Fiscal policy has been central to the neoliberal project, with most restructuring programs insisting that government spending be cut and its priorities changed. In South Africa, the situation was slightly different because when the country finally achieved majority rule in 1994, it was in the advantageous position of holding relatively little debt, even less of it, foreign, and thus was not forced to adopt neoliberal restructuring through a donor-devised structural adjustment program. Nonetheless, the new government embraced most of the same neoliberal policies, with little immediate concern for the impact on the poor. Indeed, in 1993, just a year before they formed the government, the ANC voluntarily cosigned (with the government) an IMF loan agreement that incorporated stringent fiscal policy conditions: reducing the budget deficit to 6 percent of Gross Domestic Product, containing expenditures to avoid increasing taxes, keeping the civil service wage bill under control, and foregoing "excessive" social spending (Padayachee 1994). When nonracial democracy was introduced in 1994, fiscal policy pursued three main objectives: to produce an annual surplus in order to pay down the country's accumulated debt; to cut corporate taxes; and to deracialize public spending. The first two priorities continued the neoliberal approach of the previous government, while the third was a reaction to the racist programs of apartheid.[1]

These three objectives were featured in the ANC government's neoliberal economic restructuring program, *Growth, Employment, and Redistribution* (GEAR), announced in 1996. Changes to government taxation and spending policies played a central role in GEAR. The government committed to a series of changes in fiscal policy that would cut government spending and direct social expenditure toward the poorest. The government deficit was to be cut from 4.5 percent of GDP to 3 percent by 2000, a much lower deficit than agreed to with the IMF. Tax incidence was fixed at 25 percent of gross domestic product (which meant spending could not rise beyond this level), and while the program pledged to retain a progressive tax system, it argued that "international experience confirms that it is on the expenditure side that the budget is most effectively able to contribute to redistribution" (South Africa 1996). Social expenditures were to focus on providing basic services to the poor with the elimination or scaling down of activities which cannot be provided to all or which could be undertaken effectively by the private sector. On paper, the fiscal conservatism of South Africa's neoliberal restructuring program was about more than balanced budgets—it was about the appropriate level of social protection to be accorded to individuals—but in practice, the level of support was very low, as most people were no less impoverished after apartheid than before—and some were worse off (Marais 2001).

South Africa is considered to be a middle-income country, but a large portion of the population, between one-quarter and three-fifths, depending on the measure used, lives in poverty. In fact, the country has one of the widest income gaps in the world, and a 2004 study found that the gap widened in the decade after majority rule (People's Budget Campaign [PBC] 2005). Poverty is most prevalent amongst blacks, women, and rural people. A high level of unemployment and slow rate of job creation were behind the rising poverty among members of these groups. In fact, unemployment rose steadily after majority rule. In 2004, the unemployment rate was between 30 and 40 percent, depending on whether the "narrow" (actively seeking work) or "broad" (wanting work) definition was used. Rural women and youth were disproportionately represented among the unemployed (PBC 2005). Many believe that these statistics are misleading since they include workers who are marginally and temporarily employed in unregulated casual and seasonal jobs, and those people involved in informal, survivalist activities that pay very little (Clarke 2008). Real wages declined after 1994, so many who had jobs were impoverished: in 2004, more than 40 percent of the employed, and half of the employed blacks, had incomes below R1,000 per month (just over US$140), and nearly 20 percent had incomes below R500 (about US$70) (Valodia et al., 2006, 91–92, 95).

The government improved basic services to the poor, but on the basis of high user fees that most could not afford. Those who fell behind on rent or service payments faced armed evictions (Desai 2002). By 1999, the percentage with access to safe water near their homes increased from 70 to 80 percent, but thousands of water connections were cut off every month because people could not pay their bills. The situation improved slightly after 2000, but many poor communities were underserved. Housing subsidies helped build 630,000 homes, but these numbers included both built homes and the transfer of title deeds for tiny serviced plots of land (with a pit latrine and a yard tap) on which people were expected to build their own shacks. Moreover, the housing backlog continued to grow (Marais 2001, 190–91; PBC 2005). School fees and transportation costs have continued to rise, although the quality of publicly provided services in both these areas remains substandard. Access to social grants, which were primarily old age pensions, disability grants, and child support grants, improved substantially, especially after 2003, though many pensioners had to support many family members and there were no programs for long-term unemployed young people (PBC 2005). The rapid spread of the HIV/AIDS virus, and the government's slow response, exacerbated the situation. In short, poverty has remained a serious problem in South Africa throughout the era of majority rule, and the introduction of a neoliberal restructuring program appears to have exacerbated the situation—at best, it failed to noticeably reduce poverty.

In addition to the policy priorities of the new government, the institutional framework of the state also shaped fiscal policy. The budgetary provisions of the 1996 constitution, which affected the 1997–98 and subsequent budgets, introduced a new fiscal federalism framework that accorded the provinces responsibility for social policy under national standards. On paper, the National Council of Provinces has primary responsibility for social policy development and coordination, but in practice, the Budget Council, comprised of the federal and provincial finance ministers, has played the policy negotiation and coordination role (Wehner 2000). The provinces have little taxation authority so they rely on federal funding transfers, making them junior partners in the process. The entire architecture of fiscal federalism is relatively closed to public participation and input—and indeed, has been tightly controlled by the national finance minister.

The budget drafting process takes about fourteen months, proceeding in several distinct phases (Krafchik 2001). In the first phase, spanning roughly November to March, the national and provincial executives and their top advisors negotiate the total annual expenditure; estimate the revenue for the upcoming year; and determine the division of revenue among the levels of government, departments, key programs, and other important spending categories. In phase two, from April to August, the departments draw up their plans. At the next stage, occurring from September to November, the individual departmental plans are brought together and priorities are determined, with national and provincial governments ratifying the agreements. The three-year medium term budget policy statement is released in November, while the entire budget is presented to the National Assembly the following March. It is with these two announcements that the budget is made public, and the national and provincial assemblies have the opportunities to debate and vote on it. The only opportunity structured into the process for public input into the budget is once it has been read in the National Assembly and referred to committee—in other words, when it has largely been finalized.

The national government budget has gradually shifted to be in line with the Growth, Employment, and Redistribution (GEAR) priorities, though it became more expansionary after 2000. By the late 2000s, government spending and taxation accounted for nearly 30 percent of GDP, noticeably higher than the 25 percent limit GEAR set. The shift to a more expansionary fiscal stance after 2001 nonetheless occurred under fiscal stringency; the government was poised to produce its first budget surplus in 2007–8 (Jacobs 2007). In fiscal year 2000–2001, one-fifth of the federal expenditures were allocated to debt payment and other contingency amounts, and the remainder shared between federal-level and provincial-level programs. The provinces, with responsibility for health, welfare, and educational programs, received just over two-fifths of federal budget monies, and the remaining 31 percent was used for federal programs (Wehner 2000). The provinces spend about 40 percent of their budgets on education, one-quarter on health, and one-fifth on welfare (Krafchik 2001, 125). At the federal level, expenditures on basic services, like housing and water, rose, while defense spending declined (Mokate 2000, 66–67). Expenditure on infrastructure associated with transportation and communication declined in the 1990s, but began to rise again after 2001, as did social service expenditures. In a number of cases, however, budget allocations for social services were higher than actual expenditures, especially at the provincial level since state institutions did not have the capacity to spend their entire allocation (Jacobs 2007).

FISCAL POLICY AND POPULAR INPUT

South Africa's labor movement was one of the few popular movements to have regular access to the budget process, but they were deeply dissatisfied with the government's approach to budget consultation. On paper, South Africa has a number of channels for input into fiscal policy, but in practice, the process has been quite closed. The role of the National Assembly is to exercise authority over the government, but under the rules of the national government, money bills must be accepted in their entirety or rejected, which means that once the budget made it to the national budget committee (after it had been introduced in the National Assembly), there was little opportunity for input (Krafchik 2001). Since ANC members dominate the committees, and the ANC has maintained tight party discipline, the committees had little incentive to raise objections to money bills. Short of voting down the entire budget (which could have meant expulsion from the ANC for dissenting members and loss of their seat), the only option was to send the legislation back to the sponsoring department if there were serious concerns. Even this was a rare event, meaning that the annual ritual of the budget committee hearings has been a fairly empty exercise for members of the National Assembly and nongovernmental organizations alike.

Overall, civil society actors, like the labor movement, felt that they had little influence over the government's budget through parliamentary committees and increasingly declined to put much energy into trying to shape fiscal policy in this way. At the 1997–98 parliamentary budget hearings, Zwelinzima Vavi, the Deputy General Secretary of the Congress of South African Trade Unions (COSATU)—the country's largest labor federation and one of the largest non-governmental organizations—reported that: "We are frustrated by the constraining nature of the budget process which renders meaningless both contributions by civil society and the deliberations of the elected people's representatives. For this reason we have, after some deliberation, decided that unless the budget process is fundamentally transformed to accommodate real public input and effective parliamentary oversight, this submission . . . will be our last. We will only participate in future parliamentary budget hearings if meaningful participation is made possible through a reformed budget process" (COSATU 1998). Soon afterward, COSATU anticipated the announcement of the 1998–99 budget by saying they would not participate in that year's or subsequent budget hearings because the Department of Finance was unwilling to permit meaningful public or parliamentary input (COSATU 1998). Since that time, the labor federation has boycotted the parliamentary budget hearings.

Nongovernmental organizations found it equally difficult to influence fiscal policy through the National Economic Development and Labour Council (NEDLAC), created by the government in 1995. NEDLAC is a policy negotiation institution mandated by parliament to consider all major changes to economic, social, and labor market policy. It is comprised of equal representation of business, labor, and government delegates, with a more limited role for community representatives. One of its subcommittees is the Public Finance and Monetary Policy (PFMP) Chamber, which is comprised of delegates of the three main constituents, though not community groups, and has a mandate to consider the monetary and fiscal policy issues that its members deem to be priorities.

In its first year of operation, the finance committee spent much of its time discussing budgetary issues (NEDLAC 1995), but after that, there was little discussion of fiscal policy at NEDLAC. Trevor Manuel, appointed Minister of Finance in 1996, was particularly reluctant to bring fiscal policy matters to NEDLAC, and indeed, public officials under his authority seldom attended meetings.[2] The finance minister said that only inputs based on a consensus between business and labor would be useful—because these two constituencies were unlikely to agree on budget priorities, it meant the minister could ignore NEDLAC (NEDLAC 1997; Heinz 1997). On taxation, the government favored the input of a committee of experts, the Katz Commission, over NEDLAC delegates. Moreover, although NEDLAC incorporated some civil society actors into the policy process, the methodology of discussion made public consultation difficult, even among the constituencies of the represented groups, and to emphasize proposals based on the kind of technical expertise possessed by professional economists (Bassett 2000).

It was not just at NEDLAC that the government's preference for receiving policy advice from experts led to a style of policy discourse that tended to close policy processes to social movements. COSATU complained about the process associated with public input into the Katz Commission. For example, commenting to the Standing Committee on Finance, with regard to its efforts to influence the commission's recommendations, the COSATU noted that:

> We have been constrained not only by the very limited time available to study the report, but also the unnecessarily complex and inaccessible style used by the Commission in presenting its findings. It is of great concern to us that the Commission seems to be under the impression that the task of restructuring our tax system is the exclusive preserve of tax experts and business technocrats. This seriously underestimates the sensitivity with which the majority of South Africans view the question of taxation, and the need for the tax system to be aligned to the tasks of transformation of our country. This requires active participation of ordinary people in the process, as we have had in other processes such as the [Constitutional Assembly]. The virtual total absence of mass-based constituencies in inputs both into the Commission and the Standing Committee, reflects the alienating way in which the Commission has gone about its business (COSATU 1996).

COSATU also criticized the content of the Katz Commission recommendations, saying they would make taxes even more regressive (COSATU 1996).

The unions had expected that the method of developing budgets, expenditure priorities, and the tax structure would have changed substantially after the 1994 elections, due to the ANC's commitment to a common vision of restructuring and due to COSATU's close relationship with the ANC. COSATU wanted fiscal policy to be characterized by transparency, redistribution, and efficiency, as outlined in the Reconstruction and Development Program (RDP), which had been developed by the ANC's broad political constituency (that included COSATU) and served as the ANC's 1994 political platform. The RDP stated that the government should restructure the national budget to support economic growth, improve revenue collection, and target expenditure more effectively to meet basic needs in a way that did not create a macroeconomic crisis (ANC 1994). Budget expenditures should emphasize housing, education, health, jobs, and skill training needs.

The RDP also recommended efficient democratic oversight of budget formulation (ANC 1994).

When the first real ANC budget was announced (1995–96), COSATU
denounced it as failing to shift expenditures decisively to support the RDP,
and the process as lacking consultation (COSATU 1995). In a 1997 report
to NEDLAC's labor delegation, COSATU General Secretary Mbhazima
Shilowa proposed that employment creation and social equity could serve
as simplified assessment criteria for the 1997–98 budget (Shilowa 1997). In
terms of employment creation, the test would be simple: Does the budget
create new jobs? Does the budget destroy current jobs? In terms of social
equity, the budget could reduce apartheid era inequalities, maintain them at
current levels, or increase the inequalities. Reducing inequalities required a
redistributive tax structure and expenditure on public services geared to areas
that disproportionately benefited the poor—e.g., housing, healthcare, and
education. After the announcement of GEAR, government policies moved
farther from labor and other social movement priorities. Though expenditures were deracialized, and social spending directed increasingly to the poor,
low levels of social spending meant the benefits were minimal. Moreover, the
government was less amenable than ever to input from labor or other civil
society groups.

Although structures were in place for labor and other social actors to
engage with the policy process and provide input into the country's budget,
the reality was that the country's economic framework and the government's
budget priorities had already been set by GEAR and were not open for public
input. As a result, labor and other groups looked to other ways of influencing
the policy process and budget formulation. The section below explores a key
initiative for this, the People's Budget Campaign in South Africa.

PEOPLE'S BUDGET PROCESS

In response to being effectively shut out of the policy process in important
areas, coalitions and major civil society organizations like COSATU looked
for new ways to work together and new strategies to influence government
policy. This led to the development of a popular budgeting process called
the People's Budget Campaign (PBC). South Africa's PBC belongs to the
category of citizen budgeting initiatives that Warren Krafchik calls budget
groups, which engage in applied budget analysis independently of the government (Krafchik 2006). Engagement on budgetary issues was particularly
relevant in South Africa, given the tendency of the government to reject
policy proposals originating in civil society on the basis of lack of available
funds, rather than rejecting them based on their merits, and consistently
claiming that new social programs could be introduced only when foreign
investment arrived and the economy began to grow. The PBC was created
in 1999 as an attempt to reorient state policy, via the budget, to support
a range of policy proposals designed to address poverty. The PBC was the

outcome of collaboration by three large coalitions that have campaigned on social justice issues for several decades: COSATU, the South African NGO Coalition (SANGOCO), and the South African Council of Churches (SACC).[3] A steering committee, comprised of the three founding coalitions and coordinated by the National Labour and International Development Institute (NALEDI), produced a People's Budget each year. The People's Budget was a document integrating a range of policy demands into an alternative policy vision, complete with the budget implications of its proposals. Much of its content was based on campaigns developed by the three coalitions and their allies, many of which originated at the grassroots. The PBC played an important role in coalition building among the organizations involved because they had to work together and take the priorities of other organizations on board to achieve a coordinated voice on a range of policy issues. The People's Budget document incorporates new proposals into the existing framework each year, in a cumulative effort.

The idea was to use the announcement of the government's annual budget as an opportunity to engage in a dialogue with the government, within civil society, and with the public about the country's overall policy direction and how it affected the poor. South Africa's Women's Budget has used a similar strategy to engage with the government and society over the gender content of fiscal policy, but operates independently of the PBC (Budlender 2000). The origin of the PBC was the poverty hearings convened by the South African NGOs Coalition (SANGOCO) in 1997 in response to GEAR. Doug Tilton, a representative of the South African Council of Churches (SACC), reported that "it was a response to GEAR and it was meant as an alternative macroeconomic critique and to identify places where public spending could be used in a targeted way to combat poverty, alleviate unemployment and create jobs" (Tilton 2006). A core premise of the PBC was that addressing poverty and inequality immediately would be good for the economy overall and was not just a plea for charity for the indigent. COSATU spokesperson Patrick Craven explained: "We believe that the core of the problem is that the government does not have the right priorities. We think that poverty and unemployment should be seen as the key problems, and not the budget deficit, not the trade deficit, not inflation, all of which are presented as problems that the government has to grapple with. We are not saying that these problems don't exist. But we feel that they are less of a problem [than poverty and unemployment are]" (Craven 2006). The main demands of the PBC have been to reform government policy and processes to emphasize programs designed to meet basic needs, especially through the provision of services; the creation of quality jobs; and access to basic skills development and training for the majority in a democratic setting, paying due attention to the protection of the physical environment. The PBC calls the framework that integrates these proposals a "developmental" approach to the budget—an approach that seeks to eradicate poverty by increasing the capacity of the poor to earn an income, consume adequately to maintain their health, and enjoy a minimum level of social security should they face misfortune. Thus, the state should foster redistribution at a far more fundamental level than the mere provision of pensions for seniors and social grants for families with young children. In effect, the government should not only protect the poor with social services, but should also seek to stimulate the economy in a way that would eliminate poverty (PBC 2005). As the 2005–6 PBC report argued: "Ending poverty is not just about spending more and better. Perhaps even more importantly, it is about economic and political power. The government must step in to empower the poor economically and socially by improving social protection, redistributing wealth and redirecting the economy to create employment. That means that we need measures to give the poor greater access to jobs, productive assets and skills, ensuring greater investment in industries" (PBC 2004, 3). An important aspect of the People's Budget Campaign methodology has been to translate popular demands into technically rigorous policy proposals that includes costing them and presenting them in a format that is designed to permit civil society to have input into the expert-driven policy-making norms favored by the government. The PBC documents have been used by parliamentarians to push for policy changes from the government. The process associated with producing the People's Budget was changed in order to enhance its ability to influence policy-makers—initially, the People's Budget was released in response to the government's budget, but at the urging of the nation's treasury and other government officials, they began to release the document early in the policy cycle, when the treasury department was pulling together the various spending proposals.

The PBC organizers also see the People's Budget process as an opportunity to engage in education and popular mobilization, although there was little consensus on the extent to which it could play this role. The PBC produced shorter, more "popular" versions of the annual people's budget for use within the structures of the three coalitions and other civil society organizations. In 2006, the PBC facilitator, who was on staff at National Labour and International Development Institute (NALEDI), said the PBC document was to be reformatted to a more popular version in response to concerns from the coalition partners that the document, while rigorous, was too technically focused to be useful for campaigning or for education within their constituencies.

The more expansive role of the coalition was not easy to undertake. There were concerns that the People's Budget founding coalitions did not have the capacity to engage in sustained, ongoing popular education on the issue of the national budget. For some, popularizing the People's Budget was not a priority; instead, the document was more useful as a lobbying document. Moreover, there was little sense that the PBC's sponsoring organizations had the capacity or the interest in canvassing the public widely for their views on the content and priorities for futures People's Budget documents—they found it more fruitful to use the document to highlight issues and campaigns already prioritized by social movements within the ambit of the three sponsoring coalitions. The process was far more focused on influencing policy decision-makers than on building a grassroots coalition that actively participated in the People's Budget process. A representative of the South African Council of Churches argued that it was more fruitful to engage the public in individual policy campaigns, like the Treatment Action Campaign's push for widespread public access to antiretroviral treatments, than to attempt to mobilize a broad constituency to understand and engage the state through the national budget. All of the coalitions involved in the PBC suffered from financial constraints that limited the resources they could put into developing the materials and networks needed for popular education, consultation, and mobilization around the budget. Despite these difficulties, there are indications that some of the budget reforms advocated by the PBC have been realized in the government's budget in recent years. For the PBC, there were some hidden dangers in this apparent success, as we shall soon see from the role of the PBC in the state's bid for a hegemonic program.

SOUTH AFRICA'S PEOPLE'S BUDGET PROCESS: WHAT HAS BEEN ACHIEVED?

In terms of public influence and concrete outcomes, PBC representatives noted that the government has adopted a more expansive approach to government spending since 2000, compared to the late 1990s (the so-called GEAR era). Priorities began to shift with the 2000–2001 budget, with more funding allocated to social programs designed to improve the material circumstances of the poor, as well as investing in economic infrastructure, in the hope of "crowding in" more private sector investment (PBC 2006–7). The 2006–7 People's Budget report listed eight specific areas where the national budget had shifted in line with PBC recommendations, including the elimination of sales tax on paraffin, a fuel relied on by the poor; an expanded child welfare grant; tax cuts; a developmental role for state-owned enterprises, rather than privatization; and promises to provide free basic services and anti-retrovirals for HIV/AIDS patients.

While the PBC felt that the sustained pressure from civil society organizations played a major role in the new approach, representatives interviewed did not claim specific victory for the shift in the government's fiscal stance. Certainly, the campaign began to make headway with the media from 2005, the same year that the Minister of Finance spoke at a PBC meeting for the first time. Nonetheless, the South African NGOs Coalition (SANGOCO) representative Hassen Lorgat explained that although the government's fiscal program had become more generous to the poor, the framework remained based on market logic rather than becoming "rights affirming" in the way the PBC envisioned (Lorgat 2007). In other words, the government was situating the rise in social spending and spending on infrastructure as an outcome made possible as a result of the Growth, Employment and Redistribution [GEAR] (and operating within the same broad logic and paradigm) rather than shifting its overall approach to prioritize social rights in an effective repudiation of GEAR.

Apparently, the coalition is not being unduly modest by refusing to take partial credit for the changes, even though their work, and sustained pressure from social movement organizations within and outside the coalition, contributed to the government's shifts in policy. As noted above, the changes adopted by the government have been in line with the prevailing redesign of neoliberal approaches, as discussed with regard to structural adjustment programs. Lorgat's assertion that the government's reforms have taken place within a different framework than that advocated by the PBC is at the core of the matter. As explained in the 2006–7 People's Budget report: "the competitiveness approach is associated with a problematic division of labour in the state. The social service departments focus on fighting poverty while the economics departments, with few exceptions, see their role as driving exports and economic growth. In this context, social programmes do not explicitly prioritise economic engagement by the poor. Meanwhile, economic strategies do not aim primarily to restructure the formal sector to overcome marginalisation and poverty. The social service departments seem to aim narrowly to improve living conditions, rather than ensuring that improvements in basic services help people earn an income themselves" (PBC 2005, 11–12).

Some of the government's reforms may have been advocated by the PBC, but since they are being made within the prevailing neoliberal framework, their implications are fundamentally different. The state is reforming marginal aspects of their neoliberal restructuring program in order to be able to maintain it in the face of growing challenges from civil society and the failure of the program to deliver what it promised—growth and jobs, and thus, higher tax revenues to expand social programs. In many ways, the government has not deviated from its original neoliberal vision—every element of the post-2001 fiscal program had been advocated in GEAR, except that the government used fiscal policy in a more expansionary way after 2001.

As noted earlier on, one of the key elements of a hegemonic program is its ability to incorporate dissent in a way that strengthens the core of the social order—i.e., reform in order to maintain the *status quo*. In this context, social movement representatives are quite right that trumpeting the success of the PBC may actually serve to legitimize, rather than to delegitimize, the government's economic and development strategy, implying that neoliberalism has been adequately reformed to meet the demands put forward by social movement organizations. If the ANC government can be seen to be responding to their critics, this implies that reform within neoliberalism is possible, so there is no need for a fundamental rethinking of the approach.

Moreover, the PBC has not really engaged in a politics that could lead to a counter-hegemonic project. Their efforts have been directed primarily to the state and the government, and have not been part of a broad project to reform political culture at a level of "common sense." There may be good reasons why the PBC has not engaged in such a political project, and perhaps, as one informant suggested, budget issues are not the forum to educate the public, but the point still remains that the PBC, in practice, has been a lobbying strategy (in addition to a coalition building exercise). One of the reasons why popular budgeting became so relevant during the present era has been because the neoliberal state has tended to reject proposals for social reform on the basis of affordability rather than desirability. That makes fiscal policy issues a particularly critical ground on which to engage the state.

CONCLUSION

This chapter has analyzed South Africa's People's Budget Campaign in terms of the ongoing efforts of the state to legitimize its economic program, and of social actors to propose a fundamental alternative. Engaging the state on fiscal policy issues has become common during the neoliberal era, in part because budget cuts have been central to the restructuring program and have hit the poor very hard, and in part because neoliberal discourse tends to address demands for higher levels of social support from the state as requiring growth to take place first, and moreover, to be conceptually separated from the policies designed to promote growth. In more recent years, neoliberal policy advice has accepted that some basic social programs will reduce the impact of economic adjustment on the poor, but these reforms have been made with the same overall restructuring framework. Gramscian theory suggests that, indeed, such reforms are necessary, at least in a democratic context, in order for the state to maintain its core program. By incorporating dissent into minor reforms, the state can actually strengthen its legitimacy with the broader public. For social movements, like the PBC, that are seeking far more fundamental changes than mere reforms of neoliberalism, the challenge will be to use their demands as a starting point to engage in a process of popular education that will foster cultural change such that the state will no longer be able to govern on the basis of the neoliberal program. The PBC has not become such a movement, though related and more straightforward campaigns, such as the one for a Basic Income Grant, which seeks a universal income support grant for South Africans, may offer such possibilities instead.

REFERENCES

ANC. 1994. *Reconstruction and development programme.* Johannesburg: Umanyano Publications.

Bassett, Carolyn. 2000. *Negotiating South Africa's economic future*, PhD diss., York University.

Biersteker, Thomas J. 1990. Reducing the role of the state in the economy: A conceptual exploration of IMF and World Bank prescriptions. *International Studies Quarterly* 34 (4): 477–92.

Brautigam, Deborah. 2004. The people's budget? Politics, participation and pro-poor policy. *Development Policy Review* 22 (6): 653–68.

Budlender, Deborah. 2000. The political economy of women's budgets in the south. *World Development* 28 (7): 1365–78.

Carroll, William K. 1992. Introduction: Social movements and counter-hegemony in a Canadian context. In *Organizing dissent*, ed. William K. Carroll. Toronto: Garamond, 1–19.

Carroll, William K., and R. S. Ratner. 1994. Between Leninism and radical pluralism: Gramscian reflections on counter-hegemony and the new social movements. *Critical Sociology* 20 (2): 3–26.

Cheru, Fantu. 2006. Building and supporting PRSPs in Africa: What has worked well so far? What needs changing? *Third World Quarterly* 27 (2): 355–76.

Clarke, Marlea. 2008 (forthcoming). Challenging labour market flexibilisation: Union and community-based struggles in post-apartheid South Africa. In *The global economy contested: Investment, production, and labour*, ed. Marcus Taylor. New York: Routledge.

Cornia, Giovanni Andrea, Richard Jolly, and Frances Stewart, eds. 1987. *Adjustment with a human face. Vol 1*. Oxford: Clarendon.

COSATU. 1995. Submissions on the 1995/96 budget to the Parliamentary Joint Standing Committee on Finance, Johannesburg.

———. 1996. Submissions to Finance Standing Committee on the 3rd Interim Report of the Katz Commission on Taxation, Johannesburg.

———. 1998. COSATU will not participate in 1998 budget hearings, news release, Johannesburg, March 9.

Craven, Patrick. 2006. Interview with spokesperson, Congress of South African Trade Unions, August 21.

Desai, Ashwin. 2002. *We are the poors*. New York: Monthly Review.

Gramsci, Antonio. 1971. *Selections from the prison notebooks*. New York: International Publishers.

Hassen, Ebrahim. 2006. Interview with senior campaigner, National Labour and Economic Development Institute, August 20.

Heinz, James. 1997. *Interview, monetary policy researcher, National Economic Development and Labour Institute*, November 12.

Jacobs, Peter T. 2007. Pro-poor budgeting and South Africa's "developmental state": The 2007–2008 national budget. *Review of African Political Economy* 34: 505–13.

Krafchik, Warren. 2001. The participation of civil society and the legislatures in the formulation of the budget. In *Public participation in democratic governance in South Africa, ed.* Gregory Houston. Pretoria: HSRC, 83–138.

———. 2006. Can civil society add value to budget decision-making? A description of the rise of civil society budget work. In *Citizen Participation and Pro-Poor Budgeting, ed.* UN Department of Economic and Social Affairs. New York: United Nations, 57–78.

Lesejane, Desmond (Reverend). 2006. Interview, director, Ecumenical Service for Social and Economic Transformation, August 18.

Lorgat, Hassen. 2006. Interview, manager, Campaigns and Communication, South African Non-Governmental Organisation Coalition, August 16.

Marais, Hein. 2001. *South Africa: Limits to change. 2nd ed.* London: Zed Books.

Mokate, Renosi. 2000. Macro-economic context. In *Poverty and inequality in South Africa: Meeting the challenge, ed.* Julian May. Cape Town: David Philips, 51–72.

Naidoo, Mahandra. 1997. *Interview, coordinator of the Public Finance and Monetary Policy Chamber, NEDLAC*, November 19.

NEDLAC. 1995. Public Finance and Monetary Policy Chamber, budget framework for 1996/97, in the Executive Director's Report, 4th Meeting of the Executive Council, Thursday November 30.

———. 1997. Minutes of the Public Finance and Monetary Policy Chamber (*draft*), October 10.

PBC. 2005. *People's budget 2006–2007*. Johannesburg: NALEDI.

———. 2004. *People's budget 2005–2006*. Johannesburg: NALEDI.

Padayachee, Vishnu. 1994. Debt, development, and democracy: The IMF in post-apartheid South Africa. *Review of African Political Economy* 62:585–97.

Przeworski, Adam. 1991. *Democracy and the market*. Cambridge: Cambridge University Press.

Sassoon, Anne Showstack. 1982. A Gramsci dictionary. In *Approaches to Gramsci*, ed. Anne Showstack Sassoon. London: Writers and Readers Publishing Cooperative Society, 12–17.

Saul, John S. 1993. *Recolonization and resistance in Southern Africa in the 1990s*. Toronto: Between the Lines.

Shilowa, Mbhazima. 1997. COSATU General Secretary. Labour's approach to the 1997/8 budget. Presented to the NEDLAC Labour Negotiations School, February 25.

South Africa. 1996. *Growth, employment, and redistribution: A macroeconomic strategy*. Pretoria: Government of the Republic of South Africa.

South African Labour Bulletin. 1993. "Going in with Confidence"—Interview with Ebrahim Patel 17.1: 23–31.

Teunissen, Jan Joost, and Age Akkerman, eds. 2004. *HIPC debt relief: Myths and reality*. FONDAD (Forum for Debt and Development. The Hague: The Netherlands

Tilton, Doug. 2006. Interview, Communications Unit, South African Council of Churches, August 25.

Valodia, Imran, L. Lebani, C. Skinner, and R. Devey. 2006. Low-waged and informal employment in South Africa. *Transformation* 60: 90–126.

Wehner, Joachim. 2000. Fiscal federalism in South Africa. *Publius* 30 (3): 47–72.

NOTES

1. Apartheid was a system of race-based rule that permitted only people categorized as "white" to have full democratic citizenship rights. People who were categorized as belonging to other races were not permitted to vote and were denied many other basic civil and political rights, as well as being deliberately placed at an economic disadvantage. The system of apartheid was eliminated in 1994 after five years of political negotiations, with the first fully democratic elections in the country. The African National Congress, which had been the main political opposition movement inside and outside the country, won a political majority and has ruled the country ever since.

2. Deputy Director of Finance Maria Ramos attended on behalf of the government regularly in 1996, but in 1997, government attendance had become sporadic. (NEDLAC PFMP *Minutes*, 1995–97; see also Heinz 1997 and Naidoo 1997).

3. Unless otherwise referenced, the information for this paragraph was derived from interviews undertaken on my behalf by Sabine Niedhardt in Johannesburg, South Africa, in August 2006, with the following officials who have been actively involved with the People's Budget campaign: Ebrahim Hassen, Senior

Campaigner, National Labour and Economic Development Institute (August 20, 2006); Patrick Craven, Spokesperson, Congress of South African Trade Unions (August 21, 2006); Doug Tilton, Communications Unit, South African Council of Churches (August 25, 2006); Hassen Lorgat, Manager, Campaigns and Communication, South African Non-Governmental Organisation Coalition (August 16, 2006); and Desmond Lesejane (Reverend), Director, Ecumenical Service for Social and Economic Transformation (August 18, 2006).

CHAPTER 12

GLOBALIZATION AND INTERNET FRAUD IN GHANA

INTERROGATING THE POLITICAL ECONOMY OF SURVIVAL, SUBALTERN AGENCY, AND THEIR RAMIFICATIONS

Wisdom J. Tettey

INTRODUCTION

Globalization has had a tremendous impact not only on the speed and organization of transnational interactions among different actors around the world in the social, economic, and political spheres, but has also created, as it interlaces with neoliberalism, constraints on livelihoods as well as new possibilities for subaltern agents to reconfigure their connections to the global (Petras and Veltmeyer 2001). These transformations have produced qualitative shifts in how transnational interactions are organized as they reconfigure the spatiotemporal environment within which those interactions occur (McGrew 2000, 48). "Part of the reason behind the developments noted above are technological innovations that allow the flow of capital and information to traverse physical boundaries with alacrity and to be integrated at an unprecedented level" (Tettey 2006, 33). Granova and Eloff (2004, 7) point out that "one of the most important enabling infrastructures of the globalised economy is without a doubt the Internet. The Internet revolutionized many industries in all corners of the world, with developing countries being no exception." As we witness what Giddens (1991) describes as the emptying of time and space, however, there have emerged new challenges that are raising widespread concern. Chua et al. (2007, 759–66) note, for example, that "Internet auctions are among the most celebrated and successful new business models of the emerging knowledge economy . . . eBay, the largest Internet auction house, has experienced exponential growth in customers, number of items sold, and gross merchandise sales since its incorporation in 1996. . . . In 2005, eBay hosted over 181 million registered users and mediated over 1.6 billion trades worth $44 billion. However, growth in Internet auctions has been accompanied by a steady increase in fraud . . . making Internet auction fraud the leading source of Internet fraud."

The intersection of globalization and Information and Communication Technologies (ICTs) is, therefore, raising concerns about the expansion and complexity of economic crimes being perpetrated via these technologies. Some of these cyber crimes have only been made possible by developments in ICTs, while others predate the technologies but have been significantly facilitated by them. As Durkin (2007, 356) points out, "the Internet has created a fertile opportunity structure for deviant behavior," what Chua et al. (2007, 760) refer to as "highly 'criminogenic' environments."

It is in the context of this development that the present chapter examines cyber fraud in Ghana, particularly since there is a global perception that the scams, especially economic crimes, operate "via a globally dispersed network that nevertheless contains a clear agglomeration of activity in West Africa" (Zook 2007, 65). With the expansion in the number of Internet cafes, and the subsequent access that Ghanaians have to the technology, there is growing concern about the negative moral, social, and psychological impacts that it can have. Recent reports in the local media about Internet-enabled criminal activities in the country and the arrest of suspects in Ghana and elsewhere have also been disconcerting to many citizens, reflecting the perception elsewhere in the world that ICTs, in spite of their positive contributions to society, could also unleash "a 'Pandoras Box' of criminal opportunity" (Schneider 2003, 374). The chapter explores, specifically, the involvement of some Ghanaians, and non-Ghanaians residents of the country, in the transnational space of cyber fraud. Furthermore, I interrogate the socioeconomic impact of these activities and the response that they have generated among various stakeholders, including proprietors of Internet cafes, law enforcement agencies, and legislative bodies in the country.

AN OVERVIEW OF THE CRIMINOGENIC ENVIRONMENT OF THE INTERNET

Cyber crimes cover a whole gamut of activities. These include unsanctioned access; unauthorized tampering of material; implanting viruses; denial of service attacks; identity theft; and fraud (Korsell and Söderman 2001). Increasingly, identity theft has become a major concern as scammers use the above means to collect personal information of victims that they then use to perpetrate all sorts of illegal activity to the detriment of the true owner of that identity. Between January and September 2007, there were 52,167 victims of such activities in the United Kingdom alone (Furnell 2007, 6). One of the ways by which such theft occurs is phishing, a phenomenon that has grown significantly between 2006 and 2007 (see Figure 1, below):

> Phishing is the name often given to the activity of spoofing emails or websites. The two-tier scam—which the [National High Tech Crimes Unit (NHTCU)] says is still ongoing and originated from Eastern Europe last summer—targeted several UK banks, including Lloyds TSB, Nat West and Barclays in the autumn. The first-tier is an email sent to customers purporting to be a security check from their bank, which in reality it is an attempt to trick users in to handing over sensitive account information to fraudsters. The email asks them to 're-register' or 'reactivate' their accounts by inputting their debit card details on a bogus site, whose URL is disguised to hide its identity (Thompson 2004; see also Shelley 2003).

It is estimated that the average time that these sites stay operational is about four days (Goldsborough 2007, 21). Nevertheless, this is enough time for extensive criminal activity, and deception of unsuspecting individuals, to take place. While phishing tends to target individuals a lot of times, it is worth noting that large corporations and institutions are not immune from the wiles of online criminals. A recent report indicates that a large U.S. grocery chain, Supervalu, Inc., "was conned into depositing more than $10 million into two fraudulent bank accounts before it discovered the ruse" (Vijayan 2007, 14).

The phenomenal growth in criminal activity that occurs in cyberspace, and the extent of its global ramifications, is borne out by the fact that the number of cases referred to the Internet Fraud Complaint Center in the United States tripled between 2001 and 2002, ballooning from 16,775 to 48,252. The respective commensurate cost to victims was between US$17m and US$54m (National White Collar Crime Center and the Federal Bureau of

Figure 1   Phishing report—Sept. 2006–Sept. 2007

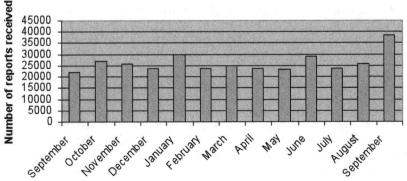

Investigation, 2003; see also, Wolf 2000, 96). By December 2006, the number of complaints stood at 207,492 and "the total dollar loss from all referred cases of fraud was $198.44 million with a median dollar loss of $724.00 per complaint. This is up from $183.12 million in total reported losses in 2005" (Internet Complaint Center 2007, 3).

At the turn of the millennium, the United Nations (2000, 21) reported that consumers lost about a half a billion dollars annually as a result of hackers stealing credit and calling card information. By 2003, estimates suggested that about £4 billion is lost each year through credit card scams, 50 percent of which result from online transactions. Incidentally, online transactions constitute just 2 percent of all transactions (Burden and Palmer 2003, 224; see also Bluestein 2003). The Internet Fraud Complaint Center in the United States (2003) also reports that "for the third straight year, Internet auction fraud was the most reported offense, comprising 46% of referred complaints. Non-delivery of merchandise and non-payment accounted for 31% of complaints, and credit/debit card fraud made up nearly 12% of complaints. Among victims who reported a dollar loss, the highest median dollar losses were found among Nigerian letter fraud ($3,864), identity theft ($2,000), and check fraud ($1,100) complainants" (Internet Fraud Complaints Center of the Federal Bureau of Investigation [IFCCFBI], 2003)

Between 2005 and 2007, over a million people throughout the world lost, altogether, US$2.1 billion, as a result of phishing (Hall 2007, 4). British security agents arrested six men in November 2003 for defrauding three banks to the tune of £350,000 over a two-year period (Thompson 2004). They had used the Internet to obtain false identities, which they then deployed to secure credit cards, checkbooks, and overdraft facilities from the banks. Booty from the fraud was then used to support the culprits' luxurious lifestyle in the United Kingdom and Nigeria. Cyber crimes, on a similar scale, have been reported in the United States as well. Raj Trivedi, for example, was prosecuted for defrauding over 700 people across the world, of amounts totaling US$992,000. He did this by advertising products on the Internet and not delivering them after receiving payment from customers (National White Collar Crime Center and Federal Bureau of Investigation 2003, 15; see also Hillis 2003).

The ubiquity, fluidity, and speed with which these activities are carried out pose challenges that require global collaboration to combat. The perpetrators are not only elusive and difficult to apprehend; the transnational nature of the mediascape within which they are carried out introduce jurisdictional complexities that law enforcement agencies must contend with. The United Nations (1996, 32) observes that "organized crime has become predominantly 'border-free' in character, while leaving law enforcement locked in traditional national legal frameworks." The challenge of containing this phenomenon calls for transnational collaborative efforts, a realization that give birth to the 2001 Convention on Cybercrime, signed by the Council of Europe, Canada, Japan, South Africa, and the United States (Huey and Rosenberg 2004).

METHODOLOGY

The study is mainly qualitative because our interest was not in generating statistical data about flows of cyber crime activity, number of cases, number of people involved, and amounts involved, but rather, to gain insights into the lived experiences of those who engage in these activities, both as victims and perpetrators; their mindsets; and the motivations that drive them as they engage with the Internet. These insights provide the building blocks for rethinking theoretical, conceptual, and analytical approaches to understanding the phenomenon of cyber fraud in a global context.

The research draws on "global ethnography" methodology (Burawoy et al. 2001; see also Gottfried 2001) in order to transcend the local focus of traditional ethnography, thereby enabling us to "incorporate broader geographical and historical processes which influence, and elicit responses from, the local. In the context of the time-space compression that defines the ICT–globalization nexus, it is important that the ethnographic scope of the study be global, even as it focuses on the study of specific locales. This requires engaging not only with those in Ghana who are agents and victims" of cyber fraud, but also those who are implicated, extraterritorially, in those processes (Tettey 2006, 39). In order to achieve this, personal interviews and group discussions were conducted with patrons of Internet cafes, which are the main venues at which people interact with the Internet. A purposive sample of Internet café staff, community leaders, and representatives of institutions concerned with cyber crime, such as law enforcement agencies and the legislature, were also interviewed to get their views on the issues addressed by the study. This field research was conducted in Ghana between May 2003 and June 2006. The study also made use of the author's own collection of e-mail correspondence from scammers, news reports from Ghana, as well as other countries, which refer to instances of cyber fraud connected to Ghana, personal exchanges with people who have discussed these scams with the author, and secondary sources which report on cyber crime in a global context.

I adopted methodologies and forms of evidence and interpretation that allowed for "storytelling, counterstory telling, and the analysis of narratives . . . [because they enable one to contest] myths, presuppositions, and received wisdoms that make up the common culture" in one locale or another (Wing 2000; see also Delgado 1995, xiv). As Tettey (2006, 40) points out: "In a global context where the dominant narratives reflect the positions of the powerful, this method also gives subalterns the opportunity to voice their interpretation of realities, their location within them, how they negotiate them, and why they relate to them the way they do. Through the analysis of content and discourses that are provided by the data collected, we are able to deconstruct these socially constructed narratives of reality from various actors" (see also Esposito and Murphy 2000).

CYBER CRIME IN GHANA AND
ITS GLOBAL RAMIFICATIONS

The fluid intersections created by the dual processes of globalization and information technology, and their appropriation for criminal activities, is borne out by the fact that such activities bring together protagonists in more than one country. It has also been established that while the origins of these scams in Africa can be traced to Nigeria, subsequently extending to several countries in West Africa, perpetrators in contemporary global operations are not limited to these geographical boundaries (Ojedokum 2005, 14). Nodes of activity can be found in every continent, as people form networks that traverse spatiotemporal confines. Thus, "while there remains a notable concentration of 419 spam activities within West Africa, the majority of contact points have shifted to Europe, most notable the United Kingdom and the Netherlands. This . . . supports the idea that 419 spam networks represent a globalizing criminal enterprise that takes little notice of political boundaries that currently define the international system of states. Moreover, the complexity of the global 419 network illustrates the ability of individuals to use cyberspace to warp and distort space while simultaneously remaining tied to specific places and polities" (Zooks 2007, 72).

Ghana is also seeing a spate of Internet frauds, particularly in the capital, Accra, and has become very intricately entangled in the global imaginary of cyber crime. It is significant to note that these crimes are alleged to be most preponderant in the densely populated and economically deprived areas of the city such as Nima, Accra New Town, and Alajo. Thus, while conventional wisdom will suggest that residents of these areas are the most likely to be removed from the knowledge economy, as a result of socioeconomic deprivation, low levels of education, and the attendant location on the less endowed side of the digital divide, the reality is that they have used their ingenuity to exercise agency in a manner that challenges established systems of authority and power. These systems are not only internal to the Ghanaian state but are located in some of the most advanced polities in the world. A recent report from Australia notes that the level of activity in "Ghana is very disturbing— it's possibly 3 to 4 times more than what we've seen in Nigeria" (ITNews 2007; see also Ultrascan 2007, 10, 13).

As indicated earlier, credit card theft is a major and growing global concern. Those who engage in these activities employ a variety of methods to accomplish their goals. They sometimes conspire with employees of certain hotels to gain access to credit card numbers and other financial details of unsuspecting visitors when they stay at these facilities. It has also been suggested that some Internet café operators collude with the fraudsters. These are usually the very small operators with a few computers who are trying to irk out a living out of this emerging market of Internet service provision. They are also mostly located in the deprived communities, and the chance of benefiting from the booty of these fraudsters' activities may be too attractive to resist. But there are certainly other service providers (especially the very big facilities) who are concerned about the impact of the nefarious activities on their business because of the potential for legal liability, and so want to rid their premises of the individuals involved. It was revealed in the course of this study that there are networks of contact people who sell credit card data. In fact, "cybercriminals increasingly operate in an elaborate networked underworld of Web sites and chat rooms, where they sell one another stolen account numbers, tools for making credit cards, scanners to pick up credit card numbers and PINS from ATMs, and viruses and other malicious software" (Consumer Reports 2007, 28).

These contacts, known in Ghanaian Internet fraud circles as "medicine men," manage to collect credit card information on people around the world and then offer them for sale to others who then use them for commercial transactions online. One report revealed that "a visit to many of the Internet cafes show some of the fraudsters at work. Their ages can be as low as 12 and 13, and it is surprising how they are able to make such Internet contacts and to even trick foreign online companies for items like mobile phone" and other consumer items (http://www.accra-mail.com/story.asp?ID=7948). It is instructive to note that on Christmas day 2007, the notoriety of the Ghanaian scammers came into bold relief when the country was identified as one of the most active locations for fraudulent online credit card transactions with companies in the United Kingdom. According to *Times Online* (2007), "a clue to fraudsters' backgrounds can also be found in the most popular flights bought with stolen or cloned credit cards. Kotaka [*sic*] international airport near Accra, Ghana, leads the list, followed by Los Angeles and Amsterdam." The desire to imitate the consumerist ethos that cultural and economic globalization have produced provides an added incentive for the economically marginalized to engage in such activities. Products so acquired are sold cheap on the local market. One negative effect of computer fraud is that it is difficult to stop the perpetrators from indulging in it once they taste its "sweetness." This supports the assertion about "cybercompulsive activity," which has also been reported in Serbia (Todorovic 2000).

What is interesting about these transactions is the extent to which the activities of the Internet fraudsters have been transnationalized, and involve sophisticated processes for delivery of items bought through the scams. Evidence of this is a case involving a woman in Missouri, United States, who served as the conduit through which the goods were delivered from American companies to the fraudsters in Ghana (*Lakes Sun Leader* 2002). The extent to which the coterie of accomplices in Internet scams has been globalized is illustrated by the case of a twenty-four-year-old Russian student who sat in the comfort of his home in Moscow, posted job ads on Monster.com, asking for applications, with promises of huge remuneration and perks for services rendered, and roping applicants into a scheme to defraud some of the richest people in the United States. "Mr Klopv and his accomplices almost succeeded . . . having stolen $1.5 million from four victims before his lust for wealth and an attempt to steal $10.7 million more led him to two truly big fish, who proved his undoing" (*New York Times* 2007).

What the foregoing examples show is the fact that in the new configuration made possible by the confluence of the Internet and globalization, social capital is not premised on a moral economy derived from physical propinquity, shared membership of a territorialized space, and or affinities of firmly established regimes of trust, but on a new imaginary that flows from shared incorporation into an economy of desire promising mutual benefit from purposeful or, for some accomplices, unintended criminality. After all, "the electronic environment of the new economy has universalized the experience of uncertainty and stress as work and occupational structures are reorganized by the logics of global markets" (Sandywell 2006, 43).

Phishing scams are also part of the sophisticated arsenal at the disposal of Ghanaian Internet fraudsters and their international accomplices. In September 2007, for example, two suspects were apprehended for developing Web sites that imitated those of several well-established Ghanaian companies, as well as that of the country's Ministry of Interior. They had used the sites to advertise positions that were, ostensibly, open in these organizations. The target for this recruitment exercise was a non-Ghanaian labor market. Following receipt of applications for these nonexistent jobs, the scammers asked "successful" applicants "to pay various amounts of dollars into an account for the processing of their resident and work permits by the Ministry of the Interior. . . . The Deputy Director-General of the Criminal Investigations Department (CID) of the Ghana Police Service, Deputy Commissioner of Police (DCOP), Patrick Timbillah, told the Daily Graphic that the suspects had so far collected more than $30,000 from their unsuspecting foreign job seekers" (Ghanaweb, 2007a).

In some cases, scammers have developed phished sites that run bogus promotions or lotteries that they use as baits to dupe the public. This was the case when three suspects "developed a parallel website, www .mtnpromotions.com, offering prizes to unsuspecting persons, mostly foreigners, [and informing them] that they had won Mercedez Benz saloon cars as their prizes. The three would then inform the alleged winners to provide details of their contact addresses for the shipment of the cars to them . . . one of the so-called winners was informed that the cost of shipping the car to him was $5,795 but he had to pay an advance processing fee of $950" (Myjoyonline 2007).

Related to the above case is advance fee fraud, Nigerian letter fraud, or 419 schemes (as they are popularly known). It is another criminal activity that has assumed a significant dimension as a result of the Internet (Thompson 2003). The name of the scheme has its provenance in a piece of legislation that was enacted by the Nigerian Government in the early 1990s to deal with fraud. Ironically, 419 schemes also have a connection to a Biblical verse, Philippians 4:19, which seems to provide some kind of spiritual inspiration for the perpetrators. The verse goes as follows: "But my God shall supply all your needs according to his riches in Glory by Jesus." It is noteworthy that the 419 scam predates extensive e-mail use, but the reach and speed of the technology have been appropriated to expand the geographic scope within which potential victims are sought and the rate at which they are contacted. According to the IFCC (National White Collar Crime Center and the Federal Bureau of Investigation 2003, 6–7), "the highest dollar loss per incident is found among Nigerian letter fraud (median loss of $3,400). . . . Of 16,164 complaints, 74 individuals lost money totaling $1.6 million." It is significant that the Nigerian letter fraud (i.e., 419 schemes) has its own category in the IFCC's report. This shows the extent of its global reach and the negative repercussions that it has wrought on the global economy and authority structures.

Perpetrators of the scheme make unsolicited contacts with people domiciled in foreign countries, particularly in Western Europe and North America. The relatively low cost of using the Internet to gain access to many people over a wide geographical expanse makes the technology an effective and efficient tool for the purposes of these individuals. They make promises of mutually beneficial business deals, only to swindle the unsuspecting "partner." The stories about these frauds are exemplified by the case of two U.S. businessmen from Ebiz Infotech who were defrauded out of $32,700 by Ghanaian tricksters who claimed they were in the gold business. The businessmen, after interacting with the con men over the Internet, traveled to Ghana to meet their "partners," only to realize that the whole transaction was a fraud. A couple of Israeli business people were also duped of $678,000 in a transaction that was primarily conducted via the Internet. The con men used a reputable financial institution in Holland, Pyramid Trust Services, to channel the amount into their bank account in Ghana (Ghanaweb, 2003).

Internet solicitations to transfer illegally acquired assets (liquid and otherwise) are another means used by fraudsters to dupe unsuspecting victims. Very tantalizing offers are made in the e-mail requests. Gullible victims are then asked to submit personal account numbers into which the illegal loot could be transferred. Once the tricksters get access to victims' account details, they withdraw significant amounts, and are never heard from again. Here is a verbatim e-mail sent to this author, inviting his participation in such deals:

Dear Sir/madam

I know this is an unconventional way of introducing a transaction, but if you can read my letter carefully, you will understand the necessity for my action, I am Michael Izaghi, 48years from Angola. My consignment of US$7.5Million is right now at Accra Airport, of which the consignment has been cleared and ready for shipment.

It impress me to use this opportunity to explain myself and my situation here in the Accra, Ghana. I am the personal lawyer of the Angolan rebel leader Late Jonas Savimbi who was killed by his opponents. Please view this site for your understandings. (*http://www.empereur.com/angola.html*)

I am seeking for your consent to help/assist me to receive and handle my consignment in your country on my behalf. I contacted you based on trust and confidence, and to also promise never to betray me because I have already suffered to make this a success and moreover it serves as my life at the present, Please Bear in mind that such opportunity comes ones in a life time. However have accepted you as my foreign partner, who is to stand and receive this consignment in your country since I wish to invest this fund in your country into a lucrative business. You also sit to assist/guard me towards investing this fund.

Please reply me with the following information so that I can urgently obtain a Certificate of beneficiary which you have to tender to the diplomat upon his arrival to your country for the release of the Consignment to you as the beneficiary on my behalf will join you immediately the consignment leaves Accra Ghana, for the investment. I have resolved to give you 20% for your assistance towards receiving the consignment on my behalf in your country.

Your full name and address,

Your mobile telephone number and fax number,

Occupation

Age and Religion

However I also wish to inform you that I have taken in full capacity all expense for me here to finalize and get ready for the clearing of the consignment from the Diplomat when he arrive your country. Upon the receipt of the above requested information, Please thank you for your understanding and concern, as l awaits for your urgent response

Regards,

Michael Izaghi.Esq

Producing the correspondence, unedited and with all the grammatical errors, is significant in corroborating the assertion that most of the perpetrators are from the socioeconomically deprived communities in the country, and yet are savvy in the globalized world of Internet fraud. While the earliest 419 messages purported to come from relatives and associates of corrupt politicians or bankers who claimed to hold the key to their loot, there has emerged, over the last few years, a transition to messages related to businessmen who have suffered untimely deaths at the hands of unscrupulous partners. Their relatives are, therefore, looking for people who will help secure the deceased's assets. The following message illustrates this version of the 419 letters, and is tinged with subtle appeals for sympathy for someone orphaned by tragic circumstances.

Dear Friend,

My name in JUDE KAMARA, 21 Years and a citizen of SIERRA-LEONE. I am the eldest son of the late Royal Chief, HARRISON KAMARA of Sierra-Leone, a Gold and DIAMOND merchant before his death. My father, mother, brothers and sisters were killed by rebel, during the war in Sierra-Leone.

Right now, I am at the BUJUGUBURA refugee camp here in Accra, Ghana.

But before the death of my father, he deposited the sum of US$ 18.5 million in a TRUNK BOX at a security company vault as FAMILY VALUABLES here in Accra, Ghana and named me the next –of –kin being the eldest son. I am contacting you because I need a God fearing, trustworthy and reliable individual who will help me receive the consignment in area of investment out of Africa and also help me out of Africa to start a new life.

For your help in helping me receive my fund as the beneficiary, I will offer you 25% of the total sum (US$ 18.5 Million), But you must keep this transaction SECRET because I don't want anybody here in Africa to know that my late father deposited such amount in my name being a refugee here.

Please I will want you to reply me as quickly as possible.

your beloved son,

Jude Kamara.

In a related scheme, fraudsters send notices announcing sudden financial windfalls for the recipient. In these notices, the fraudsters pretend to make a deliberate "mistake" of associating the recipient's name with a bank account or a deposit of one kind or another, and asking him or her to provide certain kinds of information that will facilitate the transfer of funds. Once the individual provides that information, which eventually might include banking details, their legitimate accounts are ransacked. In other cases, they are asked to make some payments prior to the transfer, payments that are then pocketed by the fraudsters. It is clear that the producers of these 419 messages tap into human greed and a psychology of deceit to defraud their victims. It is their hope that people who are willing to claim what is not theirs will swallow the bait and, ironically, end up becoming the swindled. Here is an excerpt from one of such notices, which contains information about an unexpected, and clearly underserved, windfall: "This is a notification that your contract fund, inheritance or Lottery Wining, which was deposited in our bank; BNP Paribas Bank Plc., since 1994–2007 has accumulated an interest sum of £1,800,000.00 GBP only. Based on the joint agreement signed by the board of trustees of BNP Paribas Bank Plc., the management has mandated us to pay you the accrued interest pending when approvals would be granted on the principal contract/inheritance Sum."

Another lure of the 419 letters is premised on moral epiphany that, presumably, emerges in moments where the senders have to come to terms with their mortality. They draw largely on Christian values of generosity and obligation to the less fortunate. As illustrated by the example below, these letters portray the sender as a magnanimous individual interested in spreading good to beneficiaries across the world. Such is the tenor of the following letter received by this author:

My name is Mrs. Mabel Wells I am a dying woman who has decided to donate what I have to charity through you. . . . I am 59 years old and was diagnosed for cancer about 2years ago, immediately after the death of my husband who had left me everything he worked for. I have been touched by the lord to donate from what I have inherited from my late husband to charity through you for the good work of humanity, rather than allow my relatives to use my husband's hard earned funds inappropriately. I have asked the lord to forgive me all my sins and I believe he has, because He is merciful. I will be going in for an operation, and I pray that I survive the operation.

> I have decided to Willing/Donate the sum of (Four Million Three Hundred Thousand United State Dollars)to charity through you for the good work of the lord, and to help the motherless, less privileged and also for the assistance of the widows. . . .
>
> If you are interested to be bless, also willing to bless other's too, I will inform my Family Lawyer so that he can arrange the release of the funds to you. I know I have never met you but my mind tells me to do this and I hope you are sincerely. I will pay you 35% of this money if you will assist me because I am now too weak and fragile to do things myself because of my cancer.

The fraudsters do not only appeal to the victims' shared desire to be part of a moral commitment that transcends geographical boundaries; they also spike that appeal with promises of personal gain for the prospective partner. Through this dual enticement, the scammers are able to resolve the dialectical tension between selflessness and selfishness that many would-be victims might have to contend with, thereby making them vulnerable to the machinations of the fraudsters. Such was the case with a Florida woman who fell for a scheme asking for support for an orphanage in Ghana, with promises of millions in return. She fell for it, thinking that this was the answer to her financial woes.

> At first Susan says she was, indeed, skeptical. But she believed that helping build the orphanage was a good thing to do, and started corresponding with a man down there. 'I asked him for his passport photo, and he sent this. I asked for him his children's passport photos and he sent that," she said. He sent the pictures, as well as some official looking government documents, and she began sending money—thousands at a time. After a few months, and a total of $75,000, Susan . . . thought it was time check on the orphanage and start collecting her promised multi-million dollar payoff—so she flew to Africa, to the country of Ghana. The story began to unravel. There was no orphanage, and there was no multi-million dollar payoff (Ghanaweb, 2007b; Myfoxtampabay 2007).

What is fascinating about some of these messages is their reference to actual events or individuals, tapping into a scintilla of truth about the occurrence or personalities, in order to establish a basis of credibility for their peccadilloes among the uniformed. The following message, as was the case with the Jonas Savimbi reference above, provides a link to a Web site that carries a story that corroborates the claim of the scammer, except that the latter has nothing to do with the victims of the incident referred to.

> One of our accounts, with holding balance of £12.500000,000 (Twelve Million Five Hundred thousand pounds Sterling) has been dormant and last operated for years ago. From my investigations, the owner of the said account is a foreigner by name MR. JOHN SHUMEJDA who died along with his entire family in crash at Birmingham Airport on 4th Jan,2002. View this website for verification *http://www.cwn.org.uk/business/a-z/a/agco/2002/01/020104-air-crash.htm*

Since then, nobody has done anything as regards the claiming of this money, as he has no family member that has any knowledge as to the existence of either the account or the funds; I have confidently discussed this issue with some of the bank officials and we have agreed to find a reliable foreign partner to deal with.

My proposition to you, is to seek your consent to present you as the Next of kin and beneficiary of this late client, So that the proceeds of this account valued a huge sum shall be paid to you, and then we can share the amount on a mutually agreed percentage of 30% for you, While 60% for me and others involved, 10% shall be used for miscelenious expenses while the remainder shall be given to a reputable charity home because the money is owned by a deceased person.

This transaction is totally free of risk and troubles as the fund is legitimate and does not originate from drug, money laundry, terrorism or any other illegal act, funds will be released to you after necessary processes have been followed.

These e-mails, therefore, suggest that the scammers are very much integrated into global flows of information that allows them to pick stories that are likely to resonate with a transnational audience.

The extent to which the ICT-globalization nexus distorts territoriality is borne out by the possibilities offered by flexibilities in telephony. It is now possible for people located in one part of the world to have phone numbers that suggest that they live somewhere else. They may have a United States coded number, but calls to that number get completed in another country. With this possibility, cyber scammers are able to design and change their location as they deem fit for particular transactions, providing phone numbers that are ostensibly for that location in order to convince potential victims that they are indeed operating from that location. A victim can, therefore, have a conversation with a fraudster operating as an employee of a lottery company in Madrid or Amsterdam, when in fact the latter is physically located in Accra.

Another form that these schemes take involves the use of ICT to forge documents to entice and outmaneuver victims (see Ojedokum 2005). Potential victims are not only individuals and corporate entities, but also states. The security authorities in Ghana recently arrested several culprits who had in their possession forged documents purported to have been signed by the country's minister of defense and a senior official of the United Nations in New York, authorizing the movement of large sums of money across international borders. In this arrest, the police seized three "terrorist-free" certificates. The rationale behind issuing the certificates was to vouch that the monies being transported had been established to be free from terrorist activities and so should be allowed at entry points without hindrance. Sometimes,

the scheme targets individuals that use Internet classified ads to sell merchandise. Typically, an interested party located outside the United States contacts a seller. The seller is told that the buyer has an associate in the United States that owes him money. As such, he will have the associate send the seller a cashier's check for the amount owed to the buyer. This amount will be thousands of dollars more than the price of the merchandise, and the seller is told the excess amount will be used to pay the shipping costs associated with getting the merchandise to his location. The seller is instructed to deposit the check, and as soon as it clears, to wire (Western Union) the excess funds back to the buyer, or to another associate identified as a shipping agent. In most instances, the money is sent to locations in West Africa (Nigeria). Because a cashier's check is used, a bank will typically release the funds immediately, or after a one or two day hold. Falsely believing the check has cleared, the seller wires the money as instructed. In some cases, the buyer is able to convince the seller that some circumstance has arisen that necessitates the cancellation of the sale, and is successful in conning the victim into sending the remainder of the money. Shortly thereafter, their bank notifies the victim that the check was fraudulent, and the bank is holding the victim responsible for the full amount of the check. *http:// www.ifccfbi.gov/strategy/11403NigerianWarning.pdf*

Some of these fraudsters have mastered other sophisticated ways by which to take advantage of their victims. One such method is called *superzonda* (Marshall and Tompsett 2005, 135) or *botnets* (Consumer Reports 2007). The latter refers to "networks of hijacked home computers (known as zombies) that criminals can hide behind, and use, to send spam or infect other computers" (Consumer Reports 2007, 30). Fraudsters use compromised computers for fraudulent activity because it helps them elude detection since the proxies make it difficult for authorities to determine their true location. The process works to trick unsuspecting people, with whom the fraudsters come into contact, by taking them to pages they have no idea they had visited, with the possibility of leaving behind digital footprints that could be used to acquire their personal information and deployed for criminal activity. "Typosquatting" or keystroke logging (Consumer Reports, 2007, 29) is another predatory mechanism that is used by Internet fraudsters to ply their identity theft schemes. It involves "digital thieves [using] sophisticated, automated systems to purchase dozens, if not hundreds, of possible misspellings of domain names . . . to build vast networks of Web sites to siphon traffic away from legitimate companies." The reason they siphon that traffic is to steal personal information from clueless visitors" (Hall 2007, 4; Hinde 2005).

SOCIOCULTURAL AND ECONOMIC IMPACTS OF CYBER CRIMINAL ACTIVITIES

The repercussions from the activities described above are far-reaching, with ramifications for individuals, countries, and the international system. These range from the micro-level, where individuals and families are suffering various repercussions, through the meso-level, where Internet facilities and commercial enterprises are threatened with legal suits and/or economic ruin. At the national level, investment opportunities are jeopardized and the country's reputation damaged. The state is thus left to grapple with the socioeconomic consequences that come with such a situation with little ability to deal with the causes. Finally, the credibility of international transactions have been ruptured as the activities of scammers inject tensions in interstate relations, undermine systems of control and authority associated with the Westphalian state architecture, and send these authorities scrambling to find solutions.

Ghanaian Internet cafes have become the targets of retribution by companies and security services outside the country. In the words of a CEO of one large Internet facility, "You can track an IP address so it [i.e., complaints and threats] comes back to me personally. . . . They think we are an office rather than a public centre with an average of 1200 people a day coming through" (http://www.balancingact-africa.com/news/back/balancing-act_158 .html). According to a Yahoo security consultant, "99.99% of purchases from Ghana are fraud. At least 99% of Yahoo stores don't ship internationally anyway. Our fraud orders are up literally about 1000 percent over last year, almost all from Ghana" (http://www.balancingact-africa.com/news/back/ balancing-act_158.html). It is worth noting that local companies are falling victim to these scams as well. A Ghanaian e-commerce setup, eshopAfrica. com, recently lost heavily when a fraudster made a transaction with a stolen credit card. As one analyst remarked: "The e-commerce mountain is already perilously steep for African companies to climb without adding fraud of this kind as a further disincentive"(http://www.balancingact-africa.com/news/ back/balancing-act_158.html).

Reports such as this paint a devastating picture about the country to the global business community. At the national level, therefore, there is increased concern among state officials and business people that Internet economic crimes are a major challenge to economic development. This is because they increase the country's risk profile, which translates into higher costs of doing business with various institutions in the international community, as well as reduced credit ratings (see Furnell 2007, 8). Furthermore, there is a real possibility that citizens', companies', and other agencies' access to the rest of the world could be constrained if service providers decide to block access to the Internet. Edelson (2003, 397) revealed, for example, that "a technical contact at a satellite provider described the problem created by 419 spam. The company provides VSAT services to major ISPs in Africa, who in turn serve dozens of ISPs and cybercafes. . . . At the time of writing, the technical contact had blocked over 270 specific IPs . . . out of their 28 class C networks— manually. The IP address is not unblocked until the cybercafé responds that it has stopped the abuse. One spammer can send out thousands of spams in an hour. At $1/hour, he may not be a money maker for the cybercafé relative to the annoyance he causes" (Edelson 2003, 397).

The repercussions of Ghanaians' inability to engage a world that is significantly characterized by Internet-enabled information and transaction flows can only be devastating. Added to these problems is the concern by users, ISPs, and civil libertarians that governments might use the activities of these criminal elements as an excuse to trample on the privacy rights of citizens through data retention and subsequent intrusion into the lives of other online users who may not necessarily be engaged in these nefarious acts (Huey and Rosenberg 2004).

Incidents in other countries where victims had been lured to the con artists' countries, and eventually murdered, send chills down the spines of prospective investors. These investors may not be sure whether they are dealing with trustworthy partners and may develop cold feet as they wonder about what fate might befall them if they make trips to the country. Kaplan (2001) reveals that at least fifteen business people have suffered fatalities at the hands of advance-fee fraudsters, and that three Americans who were kidnapped by a Nigerian scam ring in Kenya were fortunate to have been rescued by Kenyan police in May 2001. An Irishman had a taste of the dangerous world of Internet fraudsters in Ghana, when he "travelled to the West African state . . . after he apparently became embroiled in an email fraud scam and was taken hostage. He was attempting to recover money he had paid into the investment trap but was taken hostage in the hotel room as kidnappers contacted family and business associates back in Ireland demanding more money" (*Irish Times* 2007).

Nigerians, as indicated earlier, have acquired notoriety for being masterminds of computer fraud in Africa. The chief of the U.S. Secret Service's Financial Crimes Division contends that "nobody comes close to being as good as the Nigerians" (Kaplan 2001). This perception is shared by Ghanaians as well, and is generating resentment against their neighbors whom they accuse of using the country as a base to perpetrate their crimes. Ghanaians are adamant that their country's reputation not be ruined by foreigners who, because they operate from Ghana, bring the country's image into disrepute. This accusation is not without substance, because a large number of the culprits arrested in Ghana are Nigerians. In January 2007, for example, law enforcement agents arrested a Nigerian who, together with his accomplices, pretended to be Ghanaians and defrauded a Canadians businessman to the tune of US$90,000.

> The Police source said investigations revealed that the complainant, a businessman, received series of phone calls during the month of December, 2005 from suspects Basse alias Kojo Williams and Inyang Edem alias Victor Item, now at large to the effect that, he Kojo Williams had an amount of US$6.5 million with a security company in Ghana by name Alliance Security Company and that before this money could be released, they needed a clearance certificate from Ghana's Narcotic Control Board which involved money.
>
> As a result, Basse started receiving remittance in various currencies from the Canadian to the tune of US$50,000. The Police said in October last year, Basse and his accomplices finally lured Mr. Monfared into the country to have the alleged documents signed. On arrival in the country, Basse and his accomplice, Inyang Edem met the victim at the airport and took him to a hotel (Ghanaweb 2007c).

According to the assistant director of Interpol's sub-Directorate for Africa, "crackdowns in Nigeria have caused many . . . practitioners to head to other African countries such as Benin, Togo, Botswana and South Africa" (Ghanaweb 2001). It is instructive to note that these Nigerians are not just targeting foreigners outside Ghana, but are engaged in fraudulent activities against organizations within the country as well. In January 2004, two Nigerians were arrested for attempting to defraud the Bank of Ghana (BoG) of an amount of $48.6 million. The two suspects were alleged to have designed letterheads of the Bank of Ghana, with some bearing information that "$45 million and $3,650,000 had been transferred from two banks abroad into an account at the International Remittance Department of BoG." Another letter which bore the watermark "original" of the BoG and purported to have been signed by the deputy governor confirmed that the bank had successfully taken delivery of the $45 million and $3,650,000 from the Bank of Simpanan Nasional, Kuala Lumpur branch, Malaysia, and the Central Bank of Cote d' Ivoire and that the amount should be released to the owner "The police had information that one of them had been seen at an Internet café photocopying such documents" (Ghanaweb, 2004). The cost of these activities is quite significant for both individuals and organizations. This fact is supported by a 2003 case in South Africa where a hacker gained access to the personal computers of 10 ABSA Internet banking clients and, by means of "typosquatting" or keystroke logging, managed to scoop a total of R530,000 out of their accounts. In spite of the fact that Ghana, as a whole, has not attained the level of ICT mastery that is characteristic of more developed countries, the fact that there is a community of imagination into which these actors can tap and gain relevant knowledge is itself a manifestation of the possibilities created by the Internet, globalization, and their deterritorializing communities of affinity. Indeed, "cybercriminals increasingly operate in an elaborate networked underworld of Web sites and chatrooms, where they sell one another stolen account numbers, tools for making credit cards, scanners to pick up card numbers and PINs from ATMs, and viruses and other malicious software. Such thieves pay $14 to $18 per stolen identity, according to security firm Symantec. They surely get their money's worth. In 2006 alone, identity theft cost consumers and businesses $49.3 billion" (Consumer Reports 2006, 28).

By compromising Internet banking transactions, hackers not only impose huge financial liabilities on banks and their clients, but also erode faith in online banking operations (Kuisma et al. 2007). In the ABSA case referred to above, the bank was compelled to reimburse the victims and to invest in various interventions, such as a one-year offer of free antivirus software. According to the U.S. Federal Trade Commission, about "10 million Americans (4.6%) fall prey to identity thieves every year at a cost of US$11 billion. . . . When the impact on businesses is included, the cost of identity theft increased to more than US$52 billion [in 2004]," according to a recent report from the Better Business Bureau in the United States (Hinde 2005,

19). The CEO of Nigeria Telecom (NITEL) disclosed that "Internal fraud is a huge problem and it's a problem throughout the company. There's a leakage of between 30–40% of our revenue. We think we can stop 70% of that. In the past you took care of your neighbour so that he didn't get a bill. When we started looking at the problem, we analysed the CDRs and found that 30% had not been billed" (http://www.balancingact-africa.com/news/back/balancing-act_209.html). Granova and Eloff (2004, 11) argue that "cases involving identity theft fraud and consequential damages are almost certain to arise in the future in all developing countries. . . . [A]n organization will always carry the risk and be liable for damages or loss that result from an incident similar to that involving ABSA unless it can prove that it has identified all potential risks and took 'all reasonable steps to avoid the risk or at least limit the consequences.'" In order to sustain the ability to address these potential liabilities, it is obvious that these institutions will unload the cost on to customers through various means, including increased bank charges, for example, thereby spreading the liability to all those who use their services. The nefarious activities of these fraudsters and cyber criminals are also putting a heavy burden on government agencies. The Federal Trade Commission in the United States, for example, recently asked for a 10 percent increase in its consumer protection budget in order to combat cyber crime and to make it safer for consumers to go about their activities (Consumer Reports 2007, 34). Clearly the ability of government agencies in Ghana to shore up their budgetary situations, in order to take on cybercrime, is severely constrained by the country's economic predicaments. Consequently, their capacity to deal with the burgeoning instances and forms of cybercrime is equally constricted. There is, therefore, no doubt that "the purveyors of this type of [crime] and their adroit combinations of virtuality and polity present a strong challenge to the regulatory and governance authority of existing states and illuminate the shifting spatiality of power in the digital age" (Zook 2007, 68).

The increasing sophistication of these Internet crimes, and the growth of Internet banking in African counties might create a portentous combination, if these cyber criminals turn their focus on banks and their customers in Africa. If institutions in the advanced countries, with their better resourced and more sophisticated intelligence architecture, cannot effectively address these crimes, chances are banks in Ghana, and Africa in general, are likely to be even more vulnerable with the expansion of networked services. As Blommaert and Omoniyi (2006, 574) reveal, "the largest 419 scam on record is a South-on-South crime that led to the collapse of Banco Noroeste in Sao Paolo, Brazil after Nigerian scam perpetrators siphoned US$242 million from the bank" (see also ThisDayonline 2004).

It is ironic that the abuse of ICTs, the very technologies that have provided opportunities for employment for Ghanaians in the integrated global economy, might lead to the elimination of the country as a credible destination for such opportunities. Some organizations in the United States, for example, have outsourced their data processing operations to companies in Ghana. As noted by the BBC (2005), "Some 1,600 people in Accra work day and night transferring U.S. health insurance information from filled-in forms to computerised databases. New York parking tickets have been coming all the way to Ghana for processing too. This is of course low-grade work. But Ghana's entrepreneurs have their eyes on the sort of call centre work currently being done in India. They can do it, they claim, for half the Indian price, if U.S. and maybe European companies will entrust their business to Africa." With suspicions of Africans mounting as a result of the scams outlined above, and related anxieties about the integrity of data that is processed there, Ghana's credibility as a destination of choice for outsourcing may be eroded, despite the advantage of low labor costs. In an analysis of delegated authority among various entities in other contexts, Marshall and Tompsett (2005, 130) allude to these anxieties by suggesting that while organizations "may use other bodies to provide their e-mail and web presence on the Internet . . . the auditable and trustworthy chain of associations that link the network identity with the bona fide usage may be harder to establish and easier to replicate fraudulently."

The damage done to the reputation and identity of countries and their law abiding citizens, who have to suffer the ignominy brought on by the actions of their compatriots, can be far-reaching. Zook (2007, 80) cites an instance "at an Interpol meeting in 2003 [where] 122 out of 138 countries represented complained about Nigerian involvement in financial fraud in their countries. . . . This makes it exceedingly difficult for those associated with the Nigerian state to act, rather than simply be resented or ridiculed." By fomenting perceptions of guilt-by-association, fraudsters are jeopardizing not just the reputation, but the lives, of their compatriots. This is tragically illustrated by a case in 2003 when "a Czech pensioner—who had apparently been scammed—shot the Nigerian consul and his secretary in Prague" (Edelson 2003, 393).

CHALLENGES IN ADDRESSING THE PROBLEM AND EFFORTS AT GLOBAL COLLABORATION

In the midst of the new challenges posed by transnational cyber fraud, it is clear that law enforcement agencies in Ghana do not have the skills or the resources to deal with the problems enabled by the Internet and other ICTs. Obviously, the police cannot solve cyber crimes if it does not have the basic equipment with which to monitor illegal activity on the Internet. It is also insightful to note that many of the scammers who engage in computer fraud are ahead of the cops in terms of their knowledge of the technology and how to manipulate it. Constraints faced by law enforcement agencies dealing with illegal activities on the Internet are not limited to Africa, even though the situation there is more debilitating; it is a global challenge to law enforcement agencies around the world (see Wolfe 2000; Allison et al. 2005, 21).

The Ghana police service is hampered in other ways. Victims of 419 scams, particularly those who had agreed to be accessories to crime, are reluctant to report their predicament because of their own complicity in what is an illegal activity. In the United Kingdom, for example, Part 7 of the Proceeds of Crime Act 2002 makes it an offence "to conceal, disguise, convert or transfer criminal property or if they enter into an arrangement which they know or suspect facilitate the acquisition or use of criminal property. . . . The penalty for these offences is substantial" (Burden and Palmer 2003, 225). Corporate victims, on their part are reluctant to report because of fears that it might affect the public's perception of their integrity and security and, hence, damage confidence in their operations (Wolfe 2000, 102).

Analysts have highlighted the irony of the catch-22 nature of cyber crime. They point out that while the interconnectedness of the technology allows cyber crimes to take place, the disconnectedness of some states from the global technology nexus hampers efforts at combating such crime (Sofaer and Goodman 2001). This is a critical problem in view of the fact that the world is dealing with a technology that knows no geographical boundaries and with which crimes can be perpetrated from locations other than where their impacts are felt. It is nevertheless heartening that as the incidence of cyber crimes grows, the relevant authorities are beginning to respond desperately, albeit still very slowly given the rate and pace of these activities. There is also an emerging trend of increased collaboration among law enforcement agencies from around the world.

The Criminal Investigations Department (CID) of the Ghana Police is working with other police organizations to curb cyber crime within and outside the West African subregion. The mushrooming of illegal Internet activities has also led to the formation of the African Working Party on Information Technology Crime, of which Ghana is a member. This is a law enforcement organization aimed at exchanging knowledge and experience in IT crime (Interpol n.d.). Efforts are also underway by Interpol to train and equip a number of police forces on the African continent. Another collaborative initiative currently in place is one by the United States Department of Justice. The department is training and equipping law enforcement officials from several countries, including Ghana, Nigeria, and Romania. As a result of this collaboration, the Ghana police service worked with its U.S. counterparts on "Operation Cyber Sweep" that led to the arrest of 125 Internet crime suspects, and the location of 125,000 victims who had lost over $100 million. The Ghanaian authorities were credited with helping to recover millions of dollars (Reuters 2003). These efforts and achievements notwithstanding, the fact remains that "one of the components of fraud committed via the Internet that makes investigation and prosecution difficult is that the offender and victim may be located anywhere in the world. This is a unique characteristic not found with other types of 'traditional crime'"(Computer Fraud and Society 2007, 5).

Legislators are also working frantically to enact laws that deal with cyber crime. This is because, according to a CID official, "you cannot prosecute someone for misusing a computer under current law." Consequently, the government has come out with a draft Computer and Computer Related Crime Bill and a draft Electronic Transactions Bill. The bills were circulated in 2005 but still have not been turned into laws. It is important that action be expedited on them to provide the legal framework that will give some direction to law enforcement officials, even though examples from other jurisdictions in the developing world indicate that even where laws are in place to deal with cyber crimes, the unfamiliarity of law enforcement agents with the complexities of the technologies leave them wanting when it comes to enforcement (see Abhilash 2003, 278). There is the need not only for a sustained law enforcement focus, but the continuing development of expanded industry partnerships as well, which help to build a community of relevant knowledge for tackling the problem.

In this spirit of partnership, some Internet Service Providers and cyber café operators are doing what they can to stem these activities. They are promising to have in place an "authentication system" whereby users present their IDs with their credit cards and have them verified before being allowed access to e-commerce sites. The cost of these efforts is, however, above the means of a lot of small and medium size cafés, which are located in the poorest neighborhoods where most of these crimes are said to take place. These facilities also lack the technical skills for restricting access to sites. Various individuals and organizations have appealed to moral values as a means of curbing the involvement of their compatriots and others in criminal behavior via the Internet. So far, these appeals do not seem to be yielding the expected results. "The clash between the 'feel good' appeal of moral rectitude and the economic expedience of risky cyber activity is a difficult to resolve dilemma for a lot of youth tethering on the brink of economic survival" (Tettey 2006, 50–51).

CONCLUSION

As we explore the phenomenon of cyber crime in Ghana and other African countries, it is important that we do not extricate it from the vicissitudes brought on by neoliberal economic regimes and prescriptions that these countries have had to contend with. Arguably, economic globalization has not produced benefits for many people in these areas. They have, therefore, had to be creative in order to surmount economic deprivation and social marginalization. One of the ways in which these creative abilities have manifested themselves is through innovative adventures into the underworld of cyber fraud, which can be described as part of the process of "globalization from below" (Falk 1993) and the enunciation of "subversive alterity" (Sandywell 2006).

There is no question that these engagements with the global, as a conduit for exploring economic opportunity, have been facilitated by the new information technologies, especially the Internet. As Tettey (2006, 51–52) observes: "In the new transnational social space made possible by these technologies' capacity for time-space compression, one does not have to cross physical boundaries in order to engage directly with the center or periphery of the world capitalist system." The intersection of globalization and Internet-enabled criminal behavior not only transnationalizes the impact of cyber fraud, but also complicates criminal activity in ways that have law enforcement agencies scrambling for solutions. It has also produced significant impacts on societies that are unique to this era of global transformation. Sandywell (2006, 42) captures this complex reality by pointing out that "global communications facilitates *extraterritorial* connectivity where the normative boundaries of body, self and society can be morphed to create new hybridized forms of post-human experience." Evidence from the preceding discussions shows that as the dual processes of globalization and the information technology revolution synthesized into a phenomenon of unprecedented global proportions, some Africans are distilling that synthesis into a crime-enabling mechanism with which to challenge the authority structures and prescriptions of the global capitalist market, a market that simultaneously perpetuates their economic peripheralization and/or exploitation.

These perpetrators of cyber crime have no ethical qualms about their activities, particularly those involving credit cards and solicitations to transfer illegal assets. At a religious forum in Accra, for example, a contributor raised objections to the idea that the credit card scam is a crime and asserted that Europeans and Americans were paying back for the crimes of their forefathers who had plundered Africa's wealth during the colonization of Africa (http://www.accra-mail.com/story.asp?ID=2066). This notion of retributive justice, as well as the moral numbness that is associated with a faceless victim, is shared by Serbian youth, one of whom said: "I think it's a way to get back at America for bombing us last year. Why should I feel guilty? VISA takes the hit, not the cardholder" (Todorovic 2000, 122). Clearly, there is a new moral ethos engulfing the new imaginary constituted by Internet fraudsters, particularly those at the periphery of the global capitalist economy who assuage their consciences by calibrating their activities as a form of postcolonial, subaltern justice meant to rectify inequities wrought by the hegemonic impositions of powerful actors in the colonial and postcolonial political economy. Furthermore, they see these transactions as reflecting a rupturing of extant global power relations and the emergence of a new ecology of power that seeks to invert, disrupt, and, in some way, reverse power relations to the advantage of the subaltern in the periphery of the global political economy. In order to understand the behavior of fraudsters in the fluid and deterritorialized contours of cyberspace, and why they insert themselves into the new imaginaries of opportunity and contorted morality that are being generated in these spaces, we need to acknowledge the importance of "analyzing the changing spatiality of power, and theorizing the ways in which the relational space of cyberspace amends and subverts the political control of states" (Zook 2007, 73).

ACKNOWLEDGEMENT

Research for this chapter was made possible, in part, by a grant from the Social Science and Humanities Research Council of Canada. I am grateful for this support.

REFERENCES

Abhilash, C. M. 2003. E-Commerce law in developing countries: An Indian perspective. *Information and Communication Technology Law* 11 (3): 269–81.

Allison, Stuart F. H., Amie M. Schuck, and Kim M. Lersch. 2005. Exploring the crime of identity theft: Prevalence, clearance rates, and victim/offender characteristics. *Journal of Criminal Justice* 33:19–29.

Antiphishing Working Group. 2007. Substantial spike in phishing campaigns greets the fall. http://www.antiphishing.org/.

BBC. 2005. Talk is profitable in Ghana. http://news.bbc.co.uk/2/hi/programmes/from_our_own_correspondent/4473073.stm.

———. 2007. UK police in Nigerian scam haul. http://newsvote.bbc.co.uk/mpapps/pagetools/print/news.bbc.co.uk/2/hi/uk_news/7027088.stm.

Blommaert, Jan, and Tope Omoniyi. 2006. Email fraud: Language, technology, and the indexicals of globalisation. *Social Semiotics* 6 (4): 573–605

Bluestein. 2003. U.S. targets internet crime, arresting 135 in broad sweep. *The Wall Street Journal*, May 19, B4

Burawoy, Michael, Joseph A. Blum, Sheba George, Zsuzsa Gille, Teresa Gowan, Lynne Hanney, Maren Klawiter, Steven H. Lopez, Sean O. Riain, and Millie Thayer. 2000. *Global ethnography: Forces, connections, and imaginations in a postmodern world.* Berkeley: University of California Press.

Burden, Kit, and Creole Palmer. 2003. Internet crime: Cyber crime—A new breed of criminal? *Computer Law & Security Report* 19 (3): 222–27.

Castells, Mauel. 2001. *Internet galaxy.* Oxford: Oxford University Press.

Chapkis Wendy. 1997. *Live sex acts: Women performing erotic labor.* New York: Routledge.

Chua, Cecil Eng Huang, Jonathan Wareham, and Daniel Robey. 2007. The role of online trading communities in managing Internet auction fraud. *MIS Quarterly* 31 (4): 759–81.

Computer Fraud and Society. 2007. U.S. Fraud victims face Internet auction rip-off. *Computer Fraud and Society*, April, 4–6.

Consumer Reports. 2007. Net threats: Why going online remains risky. *Consumer Reports*, September, 28–34.

Durkin, Keith F. 2007. Show me the money: Cybershrews and on-line money masochists. *Deviant Behavior* 28: 355–78.

Edelson, Eve. 2003. The 419 scam: Information warfare on the spam front and a proposal for local filtering. *Computers and Security* 22 (5): 392–401.

Falk, Richard. 1993. The making of global citizenship. In *Global visions: Beyond the new world order,* ed. J. Brecher, J. Childs, and J. Cutler, 39–50. Boston: South End.

Furnell, Steven. 2007. Identity impairment: The problems facing victims of identity fraud. *Computer Fraud and Security*, December, 6–11.

Ghanaweb. 2007a. Cyber fraud: Two nabbed. September 14. http://www.ghanaweb
.com/GhanaHomePage/NewsArchive/printnews.php?ID=130650.

———. 2007b [September 20] The $75,000 "419" orphanage. http://www
.ghanaweb.com/GhanaHomePage/NewsArchive//artikel.php?ID=130998

———. 2007c [January 8] Police bust Nigerian 419 con. http://www.ghanaweb
.com/GhanaHomePage/NewsArchive/artikel.php?ID=116945.

———. November 5, 2006. Online dating scams from Ghana on the rise. http://
www.ghanaweb.com/GhanaHomePage/NewsArchive/artikel.php?ID=113372.

———. January 13, 2004. Two Nigerians attempt to dupe the bank of Ghana. http://
www.ghanaweb.com/GhanaHomePage/NewsArchive/artikel.php?ID=49779.

———. July 1, 2003. Fraud gang busted. http://www.ghanaweb.com/GhanaHomePage/
NewsArchive/printnews.php?ID=38456.

———. December 20, 2001. Nigeria mail scam—Turn $5,000 into $10 million, honest.
http://www.ghanaweb.com/GhanaHomePage/NewsArchive/artikel.php?ID
=20373.

Giddens, Anthony. 1991. *Modernity and self-identity: Self and society in the late modern
age*. Stanford, CA: Stanford University Press.

Goldsborough, Reid. 2007. Beware e-Mail scams seeking your financial information.
Community College Week, November 5, 21.

Granova, Anna, and J. H. Eloff. 2004. Online banking and identity theft: Who carries
the risk? *Computer Fraud and Society* 11:7–11.

Hall, Mark. 2007. Criminal negligence. *Computerworld*, August 13, 4.

Hinde, Stephen. 2005. Identity theft: Theft, loss, and giveaways. *Computer Fraud and
Security*, May, 18–20.

Huey, Laura, and Richard S. Rosenberg. 2004. Watching the Web: Thoughts on
expanding police surveillance opportunities under the cyber-crime convention.
Canadian Journal of Criminology and Criminal Justice, October, 597–606.

Internet Crime Complaint Center. 2007. *2006 Internet crime report—January 1, 2006–
December 31, 2006*. http://www.ic3.gov/media/annualreport/2006_IC3Report
.pdf.

Internet Fraud Complaint Center of the Federal Bureau of Investigation (IFCCFBI).
2003. Internet Fraud Complaint Center referred more than 48,000 fraud complaints to law enforcement in 2002. http://www.ifccfbi.gov/strategy/wn030409
.asp.

Interpol. n.d. African regional working party on information technology crime.
http://www.interpol.int/Public/TechnologyCrime/WorkingParties/default
.asp#africa.

Irish Times. 2007. Irish hostage rescued in Ghana. http://www.ireland.com/
newspaper/breaking/2007/1031/breaking90.html.

ITNews. 2006. US$2m 419 spam scammer in the slammer. http://www.itnews.com
.au/News/35668,us2m-419-spam-scammer-in-the-slammer.aspx.

———. 2007. Aussies still being slammed. http://www.itnews.com.au/News/
52685,aussies-still-being-scammed.aspx.

Kaplan, David E. 2001. A land where con is king. *US News and World Report* 130 (18):
28–29.

Korsell, Emanuelsson L., and Krister Söderman. 2001. IT-related crime—Old crimes
in a new guise, but new directions too! *Journal of Scandinavian Studies in Criminology & Crime Prevention* 2 (1): 5–14.

Kuisma, Tuire, Tommi Laukkanen, and Mika Hiltunen. 2006. Mapping the reasons for resistance to Internet banking: A means-end approach. *International Journal of Information Management* 27:75–85.

Lake Sun Leader. 2002. Secret service joins Morgan probe. http://lakesunleader.com/articles/2002/07/15/news/export11999.txt.

Marshall, Angus M., and Brian C. Tompsett. 2005. Identity theft in an online world. *Computer Law and Security Report* 21:128–37.

McGrew, Anthony. 2000. Sustainable globalization? The global politics of development and exclusion in the New World order. In *Poverty and development into the 21st century*, ed. T. Allen and A. Thomas, 345–64. Oxford: Oxford University Press.

Myfoxtampabay. 2007. Internet scam snares Sarasota woman. http://www.myfoxtampabay.com/myfox/pages/ContentDetail?contentId=4402946.

Myjoyonline. 2007. 419 gang busted. http://www.myjoyonline.com/news/200710/9378.asp.

National White Collar Crime Center and the Federal Bureau of Investigation. 2003. *IFCC 2002 Internet fraud report: January 1, 2002—December 31, 2002.* The National White Collar Crime Center.

New York Times. Russian used list of richest Americans to find targets for theft. Late Edition, East Coast, August 17, 2007, B3.

Ojedokun, Ayoku A. 2005. The evolving sophistication of Internet abuses in Africa. *The International Information and Library Review* 37:11–17.

Petras, James, and Henry Veltmeyer. 2001. *Globalization unmasked: Imperialism in the 21st century.* Halifax: Fernwood Publishing; London: Zed Books.

Reuters. 2003. Cybercrime sweep nets 125 arrests, November 21. http://www.ghanaweb.com/GhanaHomePage/NewsArchive/artikel.php?ID=47020.

Sandywell, Barry. 2006. Monsters in cyberspace: Cyberphobia and cultural panic in the information age. *Information, communication, and society* 9 (1): 39–61.

Schneider, Jacqueline. 2003. Hiding in plain sight: An exploration of the illegal? Activities of a drugs newsgroup. *The Howard Journal* 42:374–89.

Shelley, Louise. 2003. Combating transnational crime and corruption in Europe. Hearing before the U.S. Senate Committee on Foreign Relations, Subcommittee on European Affairs. Testimony presented October 30, 2003. http://www.american.edu/traccc/Publications/Shelley%20Pubs/Testimony/Testimony_Oct_03.pdf.

Sofaer, Abraham D., and Seymor E. Goodman, eds. 2001. *The transnational dimension of cyber crime and terrorism.* Stanford, CA: Hoover Institution Press.

Tettey, Wisdom J. 2006. Globalization, the economy of desire, and cybersexual activity among Ghanaian youth. *Studies in Political Economy* 77: 33–55.

Thisdayonline. 2004. The 242m scam. http://www.thisdayonline.com/archive/2004/02/07/20040207cov01.html.

Thompson, James. 2004. Cyber crime crackdown. http://www.crime-research.org/library/Thompson.html.

Thompson, Nicholas. 2003. You've got fraud. *Foreign Policy*, May–June, 93

Times Online. 2007. How online fraudsters helped themselves on Christmas day. http://business.timesonline.co.uk/tol/business/money/consumer_affairs/article3095537.ece.

Todorovic, Alex. 2000. Hot outlet for Belgrade youth: Internet crime. *Christian Science Monitor* 92:122.

Ultrascan. 2007. *419 advance fee fraud: The world's most successful scam.* http://www
.ultrascan.nl/assets/applets/2006_Stats_on_419_AFF_jan_23_2007_1.pdf.

United Nations. 2000. Tenth congress tackles cyber-sabotage. *UN Chronicle* 2:21.

———. 1996. Safe enough to rest upon? *UN Chronicle* 33 (3): 32–33.

Vijayan, Jaikumar. 2007. Phishers nearly puff off $10M scam of grocer. *Computer-world*, October 29, 14.

Wolfe, Jonathan B. 2000. War games meets the Internet: Chasing 21st century cyber-criminals with old laws and little money. *American Journal of Criminal Law* 28 (95): 95–117.

Zook, Matthew. 2007. Your urgent assistance is requested: The intersection of 419 spam and new networks of imagination. *Ethics, Place, and Environment* 10 (1): 65–88.

Neoliberal Globalization and Africa

Recurrent Themes and a Way Forward

Joseph Mensah and Roger Oppong-Koranteng

So far we have examined the ways in which Africa and its people interlace with the phenomena of neoliberalism and globalization and their associated discursive practices. As with other regions of the world, internal and external forces are exacting considerable pressure on the economies, societies, and cultures of Africa. The recurrent narratives from the preceding chapters suggest that African countries were relatively better-off in the immediate post-independence period up until the early 1970s, after which many of them went into economic tailspin. The decade of the 1980s was particularly horrendous in the continent's modern development history, with some calling it "the lost decade" (Ngagwa and Green 1994; Chazan et al. 1992). To the extent that the rise of contemporary globalization is often tied to the 1980s and beyond, one can argue that the emerging world order, couched in neoliberalism, is not beneficial to Africa and its people. Castells makes a similar point in his *End of millennium* when he notes that "the rise of informational/global capitalism in the last quarter of the twentieth century coincided with the collapse of Africa's economies" (2000, 82). Obviously, Castells is not asserting that Africa's poor performance under contemporary global capitalism is a mere coincidence, given some of the structural causalities he documents in his book.

The chapters in this volume have dealt with a wide range of processes that serve to at once delink and link Africa with the incipient network society. The major issues covered are so intricately interwoven that it is hard to pinpoint a clear-cut entry point for a coherent summary, let alone a way forward for Africa. Still, Patrick Bond's idea of *false diagnoses* is intuitively appealing as a point of departure. With it, one can understand why the various policy prescriptions for Africa have so far failed. And flowing from this line of thinking, it becomes even easier to appreciate the upsurge of social resistance across Africa, as documented by the late Ed Prempeh and Carolyn Bassett in this volume. To eschew massive recycling of the arguments so powerfully articulated by the various authors in the volume, we draw on just a handful of them to seek a feasible way forward for Africa, in what follows.

With the chapter by Francis Adu-Febiri, for instance, we get to know of the "false diagnosis" pertaining to Africa's underperformance in the tourism industry. What we have, Adu-Febiri argues, is a situation where analysts have overlooked the historical and structural factors that seek to subjugate local African cultures to the workings of the neoliberal tourism industry. Similarly, in the chapter by Julius Kiiza, we read of the false diagnosis that generally ties Africa underdevelopment to protectionism, and consequently, advocates for unbridled free trade, or a hands-off approach by African governments, vis-à-vis their economies. As Kiiza convincingly demonstrates, economic nationalism is nothing new: Japan, United States, Britain, France, and Taiwan have all resorted to mercantilism—or the use of state power to solidify their domestic markets and to enhance their influence in overseas markets as well. Thus, only a false diagnosis would lead one to call for unbridled, neoliberal free trade when it comes to Africa's move toward industrialization and economic development. Indeed, it is even clear from Patrick Bond's chapter that poverty in Africa is hardly the result of the continent's lack of exposure to the world market. It just so happened that Africa's connections with the world market over the years have mostly yielded detrimental consequences. Ed Prempeh echoes this point in Chapter 4 with his pithy observation that "accumulation by dispossession has been the definite hallmark of the continent's incorporation into the capitalist system."

Unsurprisingly, given these false diagnoses, the list of poor, or inapposite, prescriptions for Africa's development continues to grow—from Structural Adjustment Programs and their attended Washington and Post-Washington Consensuses, through the apparently disinguous Heavily Indebted Poor Countries initiatives (HIPCs), to the New Partnership for Africa's Development (NEPAD). A close reading of most of the chapters in this volume—notably those by Patrick Bond on accumulation by dispossession; by Wisdom J. Tettey on cybersexuality and Internet fraud; by Eunice Sahle on NEPAD, and on Structural Adjustment Programs and their gender biases; and by Joseph Mensah on time-space compression—points to a systemic link between Africa's underdevelopment and Western imperialism, especially as enacted through contemporary neoliberal globalization. The capitalist world order is inherently uneven, and unless this basic fact is duly acknowledged, it is hard to envisage how any prescription could ever redress Africa's socioeconomic malaise. The looting of Africa; the capital flight from Africa; the predatory lending to Africa; the unfair terms of trade for Africa; the global division of labor that relegates Africa to the production of primary commodities, for which the more Africa produces, the poorer it becomes; and the protectionist tariffs of the West against African commodities, while the former continues to compel the latter to open its borders, are among the key issues to be tackled in any candid endeavor to redress Africa's development problems.

Frustrated by the half-hearted, and arguably hypocritical, attempts at finding solutions within the neoliberal framework, Africans continue to mount various forms of resistance (see Chapter 4). With slogans such as "Africa is not for sale," African social resistance groups, such as the Southern African People's Solidarity Network and the African Jubilee South, have used the African Social Forum, and even the World Social Forum, to voice their vehement opposition to the various neoliberalism-laced initiatives for Africa's development, including those espoused by NEPAD and the Blair-sponsored "Our Common Interest." In Carolyn Basset's chapter, we learn of how social activists, working through the People's Budget Campaign in South Africa, have sought to influence national budgets to make them more socially responsible. And, with Wisdom J. Tettey's chapters on Internet fraud and cybersexuality, we read of how some Africans are even resorting to criminal activities not only to survive the forces of neoliberal globalization, but also to resist them; needless to declare, such criminogenic modes of resistance could only undermine progressive efforts to redress the continent's development problems.

What, then, is the best way forward for Africa? With the conviction that one cannot solve a problem which is not well-defined, we avoid the common practice of development analysts attributing the Africa situation to a long list of what they see as lacking on the continent in terms of human capabilities or goodwill and physical infrastructure (e.g., the lack telecommunication facilities, road networks, schools, hospitals, etc.). For us, the crux of the African problem lies in the *structural power imbalance* between Africa and the *Rest* in the international political economy. Consequently, we argue that prescriptions such as the infamous Structural Adjustment Programs (SAPs) or NEPAD can hardly improve the human condition in Africa, unless they are properly, and quite consciously, retooled to address the structural undercurrents of the African situation, as presented in this book.

We do not place the onus on the West or the so-called world leaders, *per se*; Africans—their technocrats, politicians, intellectuals, and the masses— have to take the lead, by painstakingly increasing their knowledge base on the intricate workings of neoliberal globalization, to better arm themselves with progressive ideas for moving the continent forward. The problems of Africa in the neoliberal world order go far beyond the economic manipulations of the West. As Mensah (2004, 51) once noted "arguably, more than the production and consumption of material goods, it is in the creation of knowledge that the West seeks to sustain its hegemonic grip on the 'Third World' under a purportedly value-neutral development discourse." Pushed to a higher level of abstraction, one can argue that the solution to the African problem could only emanate from inside Africa—it is essentially an internal problem of leadership. To put it more simplistically, the West, or any external neoliberal force/institution—be it the World Bank or the IMF—can only operate on the continent with the tacit agreement, or even the invitation, of (internal) African leaders.

To deal with the leadership problems of Ancient Greece, Plato, in *The republic*, theorized about the ideal ruler, or the philosopher-king, in his ideal city-state—the *Utopian Kallipolis*. Perhaps what Africans need, in this postmodern era, are visionary, morally conscientious, techno-savvy-philosopher-kings, who are sufficiently motivated and well-informed about the "power geometries" of the contemporary world order, from which they are prepared to delink the continent in the event that the powers that be refuse to address the systemic socioeconomic and political imbalances facing the long-embattled continent—Africa.

REFERENCES

Castells, Manuel 2000. *The end of millennium*. Oxford: Blackwell.

Chazan, Naomi et al. 1992. *Politics and society in contemporary Africa*. Boulder: Lynne Rienner.

Mensah, Joseph. 2004. Integrating culture into globalization and development theory: Towards a human factor approach. In *Globalization and the human factor: Critical insights*, ed. E. O. K Prempeh, J. Mensah, and S. Adjibolosoo, 51–66. Aldershot, Hampshire, UK: Ashgate.

Ngagwa, P., and Green, R. H. 1994. *Africa to 2000 and beyond: Imperative political and economic agenda*. Nairobi, Kenya: East African Educational Publishers.

CONTRIBUTORS

Francis Adu-Febiri is a Sociology Professor and former Chair of the Social Sciences Department at Camosun College, Victoria, Canada; he is also an Adjunct Professor in the Faculty of Graduate Studies, University of Victoria, BC. His publications have appeared in the *Berkeley Journal of Sociology, Tourism Recreation Research, International Journal of the Humanities*, and more. Professor Adu-Febiri is a recipient of the 2007/2008 National Institute for Staff and Organizational Development (NISOD) Excellence Award, College of Education, University of Texas at Austin.

Carolyn Bassett is an Assistant Professor in the Department of Political Science, University of New Brunswick, Fredericton, Canada. Her research has been on South Africa's post-apartheid economic restructuring program with a focus on the interventions of organized labor. She has published articles in *Canadian Journal of African Studies; Studies in Political Economy; Review of African Political Economy; Third World Quarterly;* and *World, Organization, Labour, and Globalization.*

Patrick Bond is Professor of Development Studies and Director of the Centre for Civil Society at the University of KwaZulu-Natal in South Africa. His recent books address climate change, South African and Zimbabwe political economy, and African underdevelopment. He is the author of *Looting Africa: The economics of exploitation* (London: Zed Books, 2006); *Talk left walk right* (University of KwaZulu-Natal Press, 2007); *Against global apartheid* (London: Zed Books, 2001); and many other books and journal articles.

Julius Kiiza teaches *Political Economy* and *Development Studies* in the Department of Political Science and Public Administration at Makerere University. He holds a First Class Master of Public Policy from the University of Sydney (Australia), and a PhD from the same University. Dr. Kiiza did his postdoctoral studies at Cambridge University and was a Visiting Professor at Dickinson College in the United States in 2006. He has a growing list of publications in the areas of economic governance, institutional reform, and political economy of development.

Joseph Mensah is an Associate Professor of Geography and Coordinator of International Development Studies at York University in Toronto, Canada. His research interests are in critical development theory, socio-spatial dialectics, transnationalism, and globalization. He is the author of *Black Canadians: History, experiences, social conditions* (Fernwood, 2002); the co-editor of *Globalization and the human factor* (Ashgate, 2004); and the editor of *Understanding economic reforms in Africa* (Palgrave, 2006).

Roger Oppong-Koranteng is a Senior Lecturer at the Ghana Institute of Management and Public Administration (GIMPA). He holds a PhD (Public Policy) from the University of Birmingham, UK; an MA (Policy & Administration) from the Institute of Social Studies, the Hague, Netherlands; and a BA (Hons.) from the University of Ghana.

Edward Osei Kwadwo Prempeh was an Associate Professor of Political Sciences, Sociology, and Anthropology at Carleton University in Ottawa, Canada. He published several articles and books chapters on globalization and the politics of resistance to globalization. He is the author of *Against global capitalism: African social movements confront neoliberal globalization* (Ashgate, 2006). Ed passed away on March 3, 2007, in the middle of this book project, and it is with a deep sense of loss that we dedicate this book, which contains his last intellectual work, to his memory.

Blair Rutherford is an Associate Professor in the Department of Sociology & Anthropology and the Institute of Political Economy at Carleton University in Ottawa, Canada. Since 1992, he has carried out research on the politics of land and labor in Zimbabwe and in South Africa. He is the author of *Working on the margins* (Zed Books, 2001).

Eunice N Sahle is an Assistant Professor in the Department of African and Afro-American Studies at the University of North Carolina, Chapel Hill. Her research interests are in feminist political economy; critical development studies; African diasporic formations in Canada and Europe; and social movement, democracy, and human rights. She is the author of *World orders, politics of development, and transformation* (forthcoming, Palgrave), and co-editor, with Patrick Bond (and a foreword by Samir Amin), of *Social movements and collective action in Africa* (Lexington, 2008).

Wisdom J. Tettey is a Professor in the Faculty of Communications and Culture, University of Calgary, Canada. His research focuses on how information technologies intersect with processes of globalization to shape cyber-sex and cyber-fraud in Africa, and their attendant moral panics. His work also addresses the relationships among ITCs, the African Diaspora, capacity building within African tertiary institutions, and the politics of deterritorialized citizenship.

ABOUT THE EDITOR

Joseph Mensah is an Associate Professor of Geography and Coordinator of the International Development Studies Program at York University, Toronto, Canada. He has written several articles in top journals (including the *Canadian Geographer, SPE, Regional Development Studies, Canadian Journal of Urban Research, TESG*, and *International Journal of Environmental Studies*) and contributed chapters to a number of books. He is the author of *Black Canadians: History, experience, and social conditions* (Fernwood, 2002); co-editor of *Globalization and the human factor: Critical insights* (Ashgate, 2004); and the editor of *Understanding economic reforms in Africa: A tale of seven nations* (Palgrave, 2006).

INDEX